Strategic Management of Information Services: A Planning Handbook

Sheila Corrall

Published by Aslib/IMI

ISBN 0 85142 346 9

Information Management International (IMI) is a trading name of Aslib.

Aslib/IMI provides consultancy and information services, professional development training, conferences, specialist recruitment, Internet products, and publishes primary and secondary journals, conference proceedings, directories and monographs.

Aslib, The Association for Information Management, founded in 1924, is a world class corporate membership organisation with over 2000 members in some 70 countries. Aslib actively promotes best practice in the management of information resources. It lobbies on all aspects of the management of, and legislation concerning, information at local, national and international levels.

Further information is available from:

Aslib/IMI

Staple Hall

Stone House Court

London EC3A 7PB

Tel: +44 (0) 20 7903 0000

Fax: +44 (0) 20 7903 0011

Email: *aslib@aslib.com*

Preface

This book was originally conceived as an expanded version of my Know How Guide on *Strategic planning for library and information services* published by Aslib in 1994. Shortly after its publication several readers suggested the need for a fuller treatment of the subject with more examples and broader coverage to deal with implementing strategy as well as strategic planning. This need to give more attention to implementation is a recurring theme in the strategy literature as plans often fail to fulfil their promises.

The term 'strategic management' not only signals a wider interpretation of the topic but also helps to convey the ongoing nature of the strategy task in times of rapid change. No matter whether strategy-making is formally or casually construed, managers need the ability to think, plan and act strategically on a continuing basis. Moreover strategic capability is not just required at the top of organisations: the contemporary environment demands the full engagement of middle managers, team leaders and specialist staff. Writers on strategy increasingly stress the benefits of involving a wider constituency (including business partners) in planning and managing service developments and improvements.

The shortcomings of traditional strategic planning have been extensively debated in print and elsewhere over the past decade. The result is a much better understanding of how strategy is developed in practice and of what managers can do to facilitate the process and generate useful ideas. Planning needs to be seen in its proper context, not pursued as an end in itself, but used to stimulate thinking and capture insights; writing things down remains one of the best ways to test an embryonic strategy. Strategic management is essentially about planning and leading change, but ensuring also that the organisation then has the capacity to move rapidly in the chosen direction. This means that contemporary approaches to strategy are significantly different from the elaborate exercises of twenty years ago, with streamlined processes in far shorter timeframes, more emphasis given to strategic visioning, and renewed interest in scenario development.

There are numerous publications on business planning and corporate strategy, but relatively few titles on these topics written specifically for information professionals. While much of the general strategy literature is relevant to information service management, it is difficult for busy

practitioners to know where to start. This handbook aims to meet their
needs in several ways—by explaining concepts and terminology, relating
theory to practice, and selecting models and tools that work. It provides
a comprehensive guide to strategic management and also offers a path
through the literature for those who want to pursue the subject further,
drawing on general management and library sources, with examples
from different sectors. The chapters and sections are all relatively self-
contained, with extensive lists of references and annotated suggestions
for further reading, enabling the book to be used as a reference source
as well as a narrative text.

This guide is intended for people involved in information services of
all sizes and types, from traditional libraries through hybrid units to
knowledge centres. Examples in the text are drawn from business, industry, academia and the public sector, and the approaches represented are
applicable to a variety of settings, including converged operations
incorporating IT and/or media services. The messages are also relevant
to managers of other content-based services (such as archives and
records centres) and those concerned with planning local or regional
information provision. In this work I have tried to remedy a perceived
gap in our professional literature, but my particular purpose has been
to make strategy and planning more accessible and attractive to those
whose main interest lies in effective delivery of information services.

Sheila Corrall
February 2000

Acknowledgements

I am indebted to many colleagues who have stimulated and informed my thinking. Some are explicitly acknowledged through their works cited in this text; others have assisted more informally by sharing experiences and ideas over the years. At a practical level I am grateful to the Inter Library Loans team at Reading University Library for their efficiency and speed in supplying me with journal articles. Finally, as this turned out to be a lengthier project than originally planned, I owe special thanks to my publisher, my friends and my family for their understanding and patience—and particularly to my husband, Ray Lester, whose support, encouragement and advice during the last five years has undoubtedly made it a better book.

About the Author

Sheila Corrall MA DipLib MBA FLA MIMgt FRSA

Sheila Corrall is the University Librarian at the University of Reading. She has worked as an information specialist, manager and consultant in public, national and academic libraries. At the British Library, her roles included policy and planning support to top management and responsibility for a portfolio of revenue-earning services in science, technology, patents and business information. She has served on committees and working groups of professional and government bodies and currently chairs the Information Services National Training Organisation, an employer-led body concerned with the education, training and development of information workers in libraries, archives and record centres. She has authored two books and many other publications, specialising in strategic planning, staff development and managing change.

Contents

List of figures

Chapter 1

Planning paradigms

Managers need to know about strategy and planning. The huge volume of published literature on strategic management indicates the significance attached to the subject not only by the academics and consultants who write this material but also by the students and practitioners who buy it. Surveys of senior managers and analyses of job advertisements invariably identify strategy or planning among their most important responsibilities, yet there are still those who are not convinced that the topic deserves their time and attention, particularly in a situation where the pace of change threatens to overtake plans before they are fully formulated (never mind implemented). It is worth exploring further the purposes and benefits of adopting a formalised or organised method of planning as an understanding of the fundamental issues surrounding the strategic planning process enables a more informed view of how to go about it. This chapter also relates the history and concepts of strategic management to contemporary thinking on information strategy and knowledge management.

Planning benefits

Why plan? The short answer is that planning helps us to prepare for a better future; it is good management practice, and is often an organisational requirement. A good case can be made for devoting time and effort to strategic planning, even in periods of uncertainty. Indeed, many proponents argue that it is during turbulent times that organisations derive most benefits from having a shared view of their overall aims and constraints. If strategic objectives and priorities are understood by all concerned, day-to-day planning and decision-making becomes easier and more responsibility can be delegated to people at the front line, who can then respond more quickly and flexibly to customers.

Criticisms of strategic planning are often based on an outdated notion of what is meant by the term and confuse the concepts of strategy and planning with the products of traditional long-range planning exercises designed for a different era. It is best to see planning as a way of *thinking* rather than a set of procedures. This book takes the view that services which are planned and managed strategically will be more effective and successful than those that are not. It places particular emphasis on think-ing (and rethinking) before doing, but also stresses the necessity of *invol-ving stakeholders* in the process and following through properly from thoughts to decisions and actions. In addition it advocates writing things down, on the basis that the process of writing often helps to clarify thoughts and a written product is a useful aid to communication, which is a critical factor in the successful management of change. However it does not prescribe specific methods, but outlines general approaches for managers to consider as planning processes – like other organisational processes – must be customised to suit the organisation, subject matter, management styles and interests of those involved.

Commentators cite numerous purposes of strategic planning and man-agement which can be summarised as follows:

- to clarify purpose and objectives
- to determine directions and priorities
- to encourage a broader-based longer-term view
- to identify critical issues and constraints
- to provide a framework for policy and decisions
- to inform resource allocation and utilisation.

In addition to these general purposes there are often specific motives for initiating a strategic planning exercise. American planning expert George A. Steiner gives twenty examples, including the following:

- to change the direction of an organisation
- to shift resources to important areas
- to get better information for decisions
- to develop better internal co-ordination of activities
- to improve awareness of the changing environment
- to set more realistic, attainable or demanding objectives
- to pick up the pace of a 'tired' organisation.[1]

The potential **benefits** of conducting such an exercise include a general improvement in managerial effectiveness through consistent and stream-lined decision-making as a result of articulating objectives and priorities; enhanced standing for the information service with its parent body, having demonstrated its grasp of strategic issues and stated its plans in relation to perceived organisational needs; new perspectives and insights on services, as a result of posing unusual questions and forcing consid-eration of options; and stronger commitment of staff to service develop-ments, through fuller understanding of the issues, involvement in strategy development and appreciation of the wider context of their work.

These general benefits can be translated into a long list of positive out-comes offering significant incentives for engaging in strategic planning:

- more relevant and effective services, through consultation with customer groups and investigation of service trends and developments and competitive offerings;
- improved customer satisfaction, as staff can respond more quickly, flexibly and consistently to special requests, within a clearer policy and decision-making framework;
- better public/customer relations, through encouraging participation in the planning process, raising awareness of the information service's role and improving communication and feedback;
- improved working relations and team spirit, a sense of community and corporate identity, through building consensus and shared understanding of the information service's purpose and objectives;
- more job satisfaction, as a proper strategic framework enables operational decisions to be delegated to a lower level and forward plans to be developed for individuals;
- improved morale and motivation of staff, through feeling they can actively shape their future and have more control over change, rather than just reacting to external forces;
- more confidence in the information service throughout the organisation from showing that it knows where it is going and how it will get there;
- better financial prospects for the service, as annual budget bids and cases for special funding can be presented with a strategic perspective;
- higher profile for the service and its staff, and opportunity to influence key opinion formers by publicising/publishing its plan;
- development of skills and abilities in data collection and analysis, critical and creative thinking, oral and written communication.

The benefits of involving information service staff at all levels in the planning process are considerable. Involvement helps people to understand why change is needed. They are also more likely to feel they have a personal stake in and some commitment to decisions made if they have contributed to the development of a plan or policy, and discussing possible changes in policies or services in advance with those affected will help to identify potential problems in implementation. In addition, staff involved in frontline services are best placed to observe customer reactions to services, and often have valuable suggestions for service improvements. Finally, using cross-functional teams to focus on the future of the service as a whole can help to break down barriers between different parts of the service.

Defining concepts

Strategy has become one of the most overworked words in the vocabulary of management. People use the same terms in different ways and this makes discussion of strategy prone to contradiction and confusion. Some writers separate the *purpose* of an organisation and the *actions* carried out to achieve it, others include the purpose of an organisation as part of its overall strategy. Some distinguish between *strategy* and *tactics* as being about *what* organisations do and *how* they do it; others see strategies as the patterns of actions that move business units towards organisational goals and objectives, and thus being more about the 'how' than the 'what'. This 'ends versus means' argument overlooks the point that strategy exists at several *levels* in organisations – at the top or *corporate* level, at divisional or *business unit* level, and at *operational* level – and therefore one person's strategy can be another's tactics. Strategy can also focus on a particular function (such as marketing or information technology) or a specific problem or issue (for example a strategy for dealing with the 'Year 2000' problem). People also often confuse strategy and its manifestation as a policy or *plan*.

Despite all this, there is some consistency and consensus in the management literature as to the meaning of 'strategy', although this does not prevent ambiguous usage at times. (Perhaps writers should adopt the convention in quality management, where people distinguish external and internal customers as 'big C' and 'little C' and use 'Strategy' for the meaning below, and 'strategy' for lower-level sets of actions to achieve the corporate strategy.) An early interpretation was provided by the American business historian, Alfred D Chandler in 1962, who defined **strategy** as "the determination of the basic long-term goals and objectives of an enterprise, and the adoption of courses of action and the allocation of resources necessary for carrying out those goals".[2] A much later definition from Kenneth Andrews reflects more concern with the external environment and presents strategy as 'a pattern of decisions' which represent "the unity, coherence and internal consistency of a company's strategic decisions that position a company in its environment and give the firm its identity, its power to mobilise its strengths, and its likelihood of success in the marketplace".[3]

Gerry Johnson and Kevan Scholes, authors of one of the most widely-used textbooks on the subject, define strategy as 'the long-term direction of an organisation' and then elaborate this basic definition into a more complete description,

> "Strategy is the *direction* and *scope* of an organisation over the *long term*: which achieves *advantage* for the organisation through its configuration of *resources* within a changing *environment*, to meet the needs of *markets* and to fulfil *stakeholder* expectations."[4]

Richard Lynch, author of another recently-published textbook, equates corporate strategy with an organisation's *sense of purpose* and its associated plans or *actions*. Lynch also sees strategy as the *linking process* between the management of an organisation's internal resources and external *relationships* with its environment, but states that ultimately "corporate strategy is concerned with delivering long-term *added value* to the organisation".[5] This added value is *created* through an organisation's resources and processes, which transform inputs of raw materials or other supplies into outputs of products or services, and then *distributed* to customers, employees, shareholders, etc in the form of benefits, pay, profits, etc. The notion of strategy as the means or art of *creating value* is further elaborated by Richard Normann and Rafael Ramirez in their frequently-cited article for the *Harvard Business Review*,

> "Strategy is the art of creating value. It provides the intellectual frameworks, conceptual models, and governing ideas that allow a company's managers to identify opportunities for bringing value to customers and for delivering that value at a profit. In this respect, strategy is the way a company defines its business and links together the only two resources that really matter in today's economy: knowledge and relationships or an organisation's competencies and customers."[6]

David Hussey sees strategy as "the means by which an organisation moves to attain its long-term aims" and goes on to define *strategic planning* as "the detailed specification of both the long-term aims and the strategy for achieving them" and *strategic management* as "the process by which the long-term aims, the strategy, and its implementation are managed" and adds that "it is thus as much concerned with human aspects of management as it is with markets, factories and finance".[7] These three concepts are inextricably linked, with strategic management encompassing both strategy and (strategic) planning: strategy cannot sensibly be considered without thought to its implementation; strategic planning is not just about documentation, but requires people to think through the implications of the strategy for all aspects and every element of the organisation; and strategic management means managing the business with the overall strategy in mind when gathering information, making decisions and taking actions.

The term **strategic management** was invented by Igor Ansoff in the mid 1970s, but others were quick to develop and elaborate the concept.[8] In 1980, Frederick Gluck and his colleagues at McKinsey defined it as "a system of corporate values, planning capabilities, or organizational responsibilities that couple strategic thinking with operational decision making at all levels and across all functional lines of authority in a corporation".[9]

Strategic planning tends to be interpreted more narrowly today than it was in the past, when the term was often used to embrace the entire strategy process. Thus in 1974 Peter Drucker defined **strategic planning** as "the continuous process of making present risk-taking *decisions* systematically and with the greatest knowledge of their futurity; organizing systematically the *efforts* needed to carry out these decisions; and measuring the results of these decisions against the expectations through organized, *systematic feedback"* and "the planning for a company's long-term future that includes the setting of major overall objectives, the determination of the basic approaches to be used in pursuing these objectives, and the means to be used in obtaining the necessary resources to be employed" with 'strategy' defined in a more limited way as "a company's basic approach to achieving its overall objectives".[10] Similarly, in 1983, Peter Vaill described strategic planning as "planning for the fulfillment of the organization's fundamental purposes. It includes establishing and clarifying purposes, deciding on the objectives whose attainment will help fulfill purposes, and determining the major means and 'pathways', i.e. strategies, to pursuing these objectives."[11] In the same decade John Bryson's classic text on strategic planning for the non-profit sector expressed the same concept more succinctly, defining it as "a disciplined effort to produce fundamental decisions and actions that shape and guide what an organization (or other entity) is, what it does, and why it does it".[12]

The view often advanced today is that strategic planning takes place at the strategy implementation stage; it is more about making the strategy process operational, after the basic *strategic thinking* has been undertaken. Strategic thinking is another key concept that underpins strategic management – managing strategically begins with thinking strategically. At the simplest level **strategic thinking** is about exploring systematically and creatively, discriminating between significant and unimportant events, identifying key inter-relationships and seeing the 'big picture'. Strategic thinking is also flexible thinking: it involves understanding the full range of alternatives and constantly weighing the costs and benefits of each as circumstances change (by asking 'what if?') It includes challenging assumptions and suspending judgement, liberation from old views and stimulation of new ideas. In one of the few books devoted specifically to the subject, Bob Garratt defines it thus,

> " 'Strategic thinking' is the process by which an organization's direction-givers can rise above the daily managerial processes and crises to gain different perspectives of the internal and external dynamics causing change in their environment and thereby give more effective direction to their organization. Such perspectives should be both future-orientated *and* historically understood. Strategic thinkers must have the skills of looking both forwards and backwards while knowing where their organization is now, so that wise risks can be taken by the direction-givers to achieve their organization's purpose, or political will, while avoiding having to repeat the mistakes of the past."[13]

In the same volume, Phil Hanford distinguishes strategic and operational thinking as follows:

Strategic thinking	Operational thinking
• Longer term	• Immediate term
• Conceptual	• Concrete
• Reflective/learning	• Action/doing
• Identification of key issues/ opportunities	• Resolution of existing performance problems
• Breaking new ground	• Routine/on-going
• Effectiveness	• Efficiency
• 'Hands-off' approach	• 'Hands-on' approach
• 'Helicopter' perspective	• 'On-the-ground' perspective

While criticising the 'tyranny of short-termism' Hanford makes the key point that the short term and long term must be kept in balance and managed together. Managers need to put effort into both solving problems and identifying opportunities, but responses to short-term problems should be *purposeful reactions* – informed by (and moving the organisation closer to) longer-term objectives, and people need to keep details in perspective and never lose sight of what is most important.[14]

Commentators offer different views on the respective roles of *analysis* and *intuition* in strategic decisions. Kenichi Ohmae, author of one of the classic texts in this area, is quite clear in his view that strategic thinking requires both analytical method and 'intellectual elasticity'. He argues that analysis is the critical starting point of strategic thinking, but draws a distinction between the fundamental probing he has in mind and the mechanical step-by-step approach of systems analysis, which may lead to a rearrangement of elements but not a transformation or changed configuration. He also argues that decisions based on intuition or 'gut-feel' alone can result in local optimisation or "seeing the tree not the forest". "In strategic thinking, one first seeks a clear understanding of the particular character of each element of a situation and then makes the fullest possible use of human brainpower to restructure the elements in the most advantageous way". The sort of breakthrough thinking that characterises the true strategist can therefore come only from "a combination of rational analysis, based on the real nature of things, and imaginative reintegration of all the different items into a new pattern, using nonlinear brainpower".

Ohmae also argues that there is a discernible sequential pattern in successful foresighted management decision-making which invariably involves the following **five steps**:

1. clear definition of the *business domain,* in terms of the objective function – what the user/consumer actually wants;

2. cause-and-effect extrapolation of *environmental forces,* as a simple succinct statement of the most likely strategic scenario;
3. limited selection of *strategic options,* enabling economic distribution and bold deployment of resources – more resources on fewer options;
4. realistic pacing of *strategy implementation* in accordance with available resources, so as not to overreach the business;
5. consistent adherence to the *basic assumptions* underlying the original choice, but rapidly changing direction if environmental conditions change.[15]

At a more personal level, Vaill provides a list of attitudes and skills that distinguish people who are effective strategic thinkers and planners:

1. Effective thinkers are eclectic in their interests and are not bound by stereotypes and categorical assumptions.
2. They are good at holistic thinking, in addition to having good analytical skills; they can both break down and build up issues and interpretations.
3. They are future-oriented and, in particular, they realise the reality of the future – it is more 'present' for them than for others. They realise what needs to be done now to accrue benefits in the future.
4. They are both whole-headed and whole-hearted. They use both sides of the brain, and they bring a certain passion and intensity to the task of strategic thinking and decision making.
5. They think big; their vision reflects ambition for the organisation. They are not interested in the status quo or in short-range, expedient strategies.
6. They realise that strategic thinking can no longer be the solitary enterprise of one wise person, that it cannot be made in a closet or on a mountaintop, but rather it is a social, interactive process in which the task is to learn to use the diverse talents and experiences available in the organisation.
7. For all their vision and ambition, effective strategic thinkers have their projects grounded in the operational problems and opportunities of some particular organisation. In this sense they are practical as well as visionary.
8. Finally, effective strategic thinkers have combined the relatively passive, contemplative modes of thinking with active 'can-do' modes. They accept responsibility for shaping the organisation and the world around it, but they know also that with shaping goes understanding and insight.[11]

Hanford offers practical advice on how such qualities and abilities can be developed (*see* suggestions for further reading).

Historical trends

The differing views of strategic planning and management need to be seen in their historical context. We can trace the development of strategic management back over the past half-century from early examples of long-range planning in the 1950s to contemporary concerns with strategic change as the predominant theme of management in the 1990s. While it is misleading to suggest that strategic thinking has evolved in an orderly manner, or that each of the phases identified below is clearly distinguishable from what came before and after, we can nevertheless identify some general trends and point to a few salient characteristics signalling changes in approach and shifts in focus over the last five decades. In every period, there are examples of leading-edge thinkers already anticipating the next phase as well as organisations that have not progressed beyond the previous level of maturity.

The evolution of strategic management can be summarised thus:

- *long-range planning (1950s)* – even though Drucker was already urging people to think about more fundamental issues, the focus at this time was mainly financial and the planning being undertaken was in effect *extended budgeting* on a functional basis, extrapolating past figures as forward projections as a means to *operational control*;
- *corporate planning (1960s)* – the focus here moved forwards beyond financial projections to *technological forecasting* in an effort to predict the future for the organisation as a whole and also included techniques such as portfolio analysis, but generally assumed *incremental growth* from the present in preparing a blueprint for the future;
- *strategic planning (1970s)* – the focus then moved outwards to the *external environment* of customers and markets, and there was also a shift to thinking more about the strategic direction of the organisation in the context of *discontinuous change,* with short-term plans driven by longer-term perspectives, but more concerned with *portfolio planning* than with strategic visioning;
- *strategic management (1980s)* – the focus next shifted to industry analysis in the context of *global competition* (using models such as Michael Porter's 'five forces') but also turned inwards to take account of the *soft issues* (represented in the McKinsey 'seven S' framework) and moved beyond strategic planning to *strategy implementation* and dynamic allocation of resources;
- *strategic change (1990s)* – the focus on *internal resources* continued with the identification of *core competences* (and other intangible assets) as a basis for both competitive advantage and *strategic alliances* with partners, and the overall emphasis shifted away from formulating strategy to leading change and managing transformation via creative, flexible planning processes.

Forward planning has matured from a quantitative exercise, based on calculation and extrapolation of raw and processed data, to a qualitative process, informed by explicit and tacit *knowledge*. Thinking about the future has moved from a past-to-present and present-to-future mentality to a future-to-present mindset, and information is more likely to be presented in words and pictures than in numbers. Ownership of the strategy process has passed from planners to managers, who are expected not only to have foresight, but also to bring *insight* to the never-ending search for advantage through differentiation and innovation. Edward Cornish, editor of *The Futurist,* argues that we need a future orientation not just to plan ahead but actually to understand the present, warning that "if we don't know where we are going, we don't know where we are". Cornish challenges the notion of the present world as 'known' and the future as 'unknown', pointing out that if people do not watch trends and think about what they mean, their interpretation of the current situation will be based on past experience and therefore somewhat out of date.[16]

Contemporary lenses

In addition to chronological accounts, various authors have labelled different approaches to strategy according to the perspectives taken on the origins of strategic decisions (the *process* of strategy) and the sources of competitive advantage (the *content* of strategy) while others have looked specifically at the changes in environmental conditions (the *context* of strategy).

Process views can be broadly categorised into the formal/rational model (the 'planning' school, exemplified by Igor Ansoff and others in the 1960s and 1970s) and the cultural/incremental model (the 'learning' school, associated with Henry Mintzberg and colleagues in the 1970s and 1980s) which disputes the separation of strategy formulation (thinking) from implementation (doing). **Content** theories tend to focus either on external market forces/industry structures (the 'positioning' school or 'outside-in' view, typified by Michael Porter in the 1980s) or on internal firm resources/core competencies (the 'inside-out' view, championed by Gary Hamel in the 1980s and 1990s). In the 1990s the resource-based view of the firm has shifted from tangible to intangible assets to become a 'knowledge-based view' evident in organisations looking beyond technology and information systems to a broader (more strategic) concept of knowledge management.

Context issues relating to the external business environment and the internal organisational environment can affect both the content and process of strategy. Many commentators have identified the dynamics or *turbulence* of the business environment as a key issue affecting the processes of strategic thinking, planning, managing and decision-making, notably Igor Ansoff whose research concluded that organisations which failed to match their approach to strategic management with the level of turbulence in the environment suffered business failure in proportion to the mismatch. The concept of **environmental turbulence** is frequently mentioned but not always properly defined; it deserves further attention here as it has a bearing on the overall approach to strategic planning and management adopted and also on the particular tools for strategic analysis and appraisal selected to support the strategy-making process.

Ansoff suggests that the two key issues determining the turbulence of environmental forces surrounding an organisation are their *changeability,* which is a measure of the likelihood that change will take place, and their *predictability,* which is a measure of our ability to anticipate what the change will be. These measures can each be further subdivided into different aspects to provide a four-fold framework for assessing the environment as follows:

Changeability

- *Complexity* of the environment – a measure of the range of environmental factors affecting the organisation (social, economic, political, technological, etc) and the sphere of influence (local, regional, national, international, global)
- *Novelty* of events – a measure of the degree to which environmental conditions represent new (rather than familiar) situations and extent to which the change is radical/discontinuous (rather than incremental/continuous)

Predictability

- *Rapidity* of change – a measure of the rate of environmental change, assessed with reference to the organisation's capacity to respond appropriately (as *faster than, comparable to* or *slower than* organisational response)
- *Obscurity* of the future – a measure of the extent to which changes are unpredictable surprises, rather than recurring or forecastable events, reflecting the availability and usefulness of organisational information about the future.

Ansoff's model (which uses slightly different terminology) identifies five degrees or levels of turbulence, based on the above measures, and specifies the type of strategic response, characterised as **strategic aggress-**

iveness, appropriate for each level of turbulence. The table draws on Ansoff's work and other writers' interpretation of his thinking.

Ansoff's key message is that despite the claims of the strategy gurus there is no strategic management formula with universal validity. He offers his model as a *contingent strategic success formula*, which identifies the conditions under which particular approaches to strategy are more likely to be effective.[17] This model can be used to assess the appropriateness of your organisation's current approach to strategy. It is unlikely that there are many organisations operating under the first two states today, although there may be some who have not adjusted their strategy process to match their current situation. Most organisations will be operating at levels three, four or five, depending on the extent of competitive rivalry, degree of technological change, etc. An important point to note is that different parts of an organisation may be subject to different environmental forces, so a process which requires all business units to plan in the same way will not necessarily produce the best results. This obviously applies particularly to divisions of large multinational corporations operating in several global markets, but the same principle can be applied to information services in all sectors, whose heavy dependence on information technology coupled with the unpredictable costs of information artefacts often means being subject to a much higher level of turbulence than other parts of the same organisation.

While proponents of particular views tend to market their own brand of strategy to the exclusion of others, there are often more similarities than differences in the basic messages, which represent a convergence of current and previous thinking rather than anything-novel. **Knowledge management** typifies this trend, bringing together a range of ideas and initiatives promulgated over the last two decades, including total quality management,[18] the resource-based view,[19] info-mapping,[20] benchmarking,[21] the learning organisation,[22] core competence,[23] communities-of-practice,[24] the balanced scorecard,[25] business re-engineering[26] and intellectual capital[27]. Many managers understandably have difficulty keeping up with the latest strategy models and choosing between the array of tools on offer, but they can take comfort from the fact that there are few genuinely new approaches each year – most are variations on tried and tested methods, and the best ones always find their way into the current editions of management textbooks on strategy and marketing.

Information strategies

During the last two decades the importance of information as a corporate resource and a strategic asset has been more widely acknowledged

Figure 1.1 Environmental turbulence levels and strategic management styles (adapted from Ansoff and others)

Environmental turbulence	Repetitive No change	Expanding Slow change Incremental	Changing Fast change Incremental	Transforming Discontinuous Predictable	Surpriseful Discontinuous Unpredictable
Strategic aggressiveness	Stable	Reactive	Anticipatory	Entrepreneurial	Creative
Decision base	Historical precedent	Recent experience	Extrapolated trends	Strategic vision	Management insight
Organisational values	Stability Longevity	Economy Efficiency	Profit now Growth	Profit later Opportunity	Creativity Risk
Management response	Control – rejects change	Diagnose – adapts to change	Optimise – seeks familiar change	Explore – seeks related change	Innovate – seeks novel change
Process features	Top-down policies Bottom-up budgets	Financial control Extended budgeting	Environmental scan Competitor analysis	Scenario analysis Contingency plans	Early warning signs Ongoing analysis
Control systems	Periodic/operating			Real-time/strategic	

as developments in information and communication technologies have transformed the business landscape. In 1985, strategy guru Michael Porter (Harvard Business School) used his 'value chain' and 'five forces' models to show how information technology was changing the way companies operated in terms of their products and processes, influencing industry structures, and even altering the nature of competition itself. Porter warned that organisations which failed to recognise the strategic significance of the 'information revolution' would find themselves at a serious competitive disadvantage.[28]

Much of the literature on 'information strategy' has developed from this basis, with a disproportionate emphasis on the technology or *conduit,* at the expense of the information *content.* Michael Earl (London Business School) has tried to redress the balance by differentiating three components of information strategy as follows:

- *IT strategy* – supply-led and functionally-driven, owned by IT professionals and concerned with technology and infrastructure, or the 'how' question;
- *IS strategy* – demand-led and business-driven, owned by general managers and concerned with systems and applications, or the 'what' question;
- *IM strategy* – relationship-led and organisation-driven, owned by top management and concerned with management and responsibilities, or the 'who' question.[29]

In the UK (in 1996) the Hawley Committee gave further impetus to information strategy development by proposing that "all significant information in an organisation, regardless of its purpose, should be properly identified, even if not in an accounting sense, for consideration as an asset of the business". Its report provided a structure for information management policy, by producing a booklet with an 'agenda' of ten items for managers and directors to consider, which acknowledges that not all information systems use computers and electronic communications and highlights the link between information strategy and business strategy.[30] Nigel Horne, director of the IMPACT programme under whose auspices this work was done, notes that the need to align IT strategy with business strategy is generally accepted, but "most businesses miss the point that the *information* strategy is not only the link between the two but forms a critical part of the business strategy in the information age". The IMPACT programme has subsequently developed an Information Health Index (IHI) or tool to measure the 'health' (status and progress) of an organisation's information management, which is based on the Hawley Agenda and intended to be "a bedrock upon which to build knowledge management".[31]

The examples of information assets given in the Hawley documentation are largely internally generated (rather than externally published) information – for example, market and customer information, product information, specialist knowledge, business process information, management information and plans, human resource information, supplier information, accountable information. However, the concept of information strategy has been interpreted more broadly in the higher education sector, both in the UK and the US. In 1993, the Follett report introduced the concept of an 'integrated information strategy' specifically to foster *integration* of the library with other aspects of an institution's work and in particular the planning of other resources.[32] In 1997, the Dearing report reinforced this notion, recommending that institutions should have in place 'overarching communications and information strategies' by 1999/2000.[33]

Guidelines for developing an information strategy were issued by the Joint Information Systems Committee (JISC) of the Higher Education Funding Councils in 1995 and revised in 1998. They focus more on the *process* of developing a strategy than on a document or its content, but are distinctive in several respects:

- promoting the need to cover all types of information – not only management-related information, but also the academic information that supports teaching and research;
- presenting the information strategy as not simply derived from the vision for the institution, but forming part of that vision, and substantially influencing it;
- positioning the information strategy at the centre of the institution's strategy process, and making other strategies (such as research, teaching and learning, information services and information technology) subsidiary to it in a hierarchy of strategies.[34,35]

The JISC model has been criticised for apparently elevating information management above the core businesses of universities (namely research and teaching/learning) and not differentiating properly between these strategies and those of support functions (such as human resources and information technology). Yet this model is in line with contemporary management writing on the impact of information and communication technology on 'information-intensive organisations'. Universities are surely in the information business (broadly interpreted) but can also genuinely claim to be in the *knowledge business*. On that basis, a **knowledge strategy** is central to the university mission, with research and teaching as two means of creating and delivering value for stakeholders.

Examples of strategy documents developed by six designated 'pilot sites' can be accessed via the JISC information strategies web site, together with details of another nine institutions later selected as 'exemplar sites' to disseminate experience and expertise to the wider higher education community.[36] The pilot sites have also participated in a parallel initiative on Institution-Wide Information Strategies (IWIS) in the US, sponsored by the Coalition for Networked Information.[37] IWIS project director, Gerald Bernbom, sees two powerful forces driving information strategy development:

- the rapidly changing *network platform*, enabling communication and information sharing among people and places that are geographically, organisationally and socially distant;
- the emerging *network organisation,* providing a flexible and responsive alternative to hierarchies and bureaucracies, and potentially relocating decision-making.

Bernbom lists 13 'enterprise issues' identified by institutions in this context, including centre/periphery relationships, cross-domain information flows, converging information professions and culture shifts.[38]

A key issue for information service managers is how their strategies and plans relate to the strategies and plans of their parent body and other parts of the organisation. As indicated above, library/information and computing/IT services cannot sensibly be viewed now as unimportant support functions, and there is a trend evident in all sectors for information services to be reconfigured or *converged* into different or larger units combining previously separate activities. The term 'information services' is thus open to many different interpretations and the nature and nomenclature of the strategy process will vary accordingly. In some organisations a separate plan may be required for the library/ information centre, along with similar plans for other departments, to inform and/or be informed by the overall plan for the organisation. In others, a library/information component or dimension may form part of a more wide-ranging strategic plan for information covering both content and conduit-related operations.

Irrespective of their sector and situation, wherever they are in the organisational network or hierarchy, information service managers need to think about the relationship of their planning and strategy development to the rest of the organisation. The relationship will at least be one of *interdependence,* ideally one of *integration* (both vertical and horizontal). Managers need to consider whether their service strategy is more about reacting to or initiating change – should the information service follow or lead corporate/business strategy? Some academic libraries have significantly influenced teaching/learning processes within their institutions through changes in information resource provision, and the acquisition (or loss) of special collections might have an important impact on research activities. Information service managers must ensure that information service plans reflect current organisational concerns and *vice versa.*

Marketing strategies

The relationship between marketing, strategy and business planning is also confused. Some people consider marketing as just another function (like personnel or finance) whereas others, notably Peter Drucker, see it as inextricably linked with the fundamental purpose of the business,

> "Marketing is so basic that it cannot be considered a separate skill or work within the business. Marketing requires separate work, and a distinct group of activities. But it is a central dimension of the entire business. It is the whole business seen from the point of view of its final result, that is, from the customer's point of view. Concern and responsibility for marketing must permeate all areas of the enterprise."[10]

Formal definitions of marketing are not very helpful in elucidating this issue, for example the Chartered Institute of Marketing defines it as "the management process that identifies, anticipates and supplies customer requirements efficiently and profitably". Michael Baker offers more clarity in stating that marketing is both a *management orientation* and a *business function*. A marketing orientation requires customer focus, a long-term perspective, innovation and full use of organisation-wide resources. The marketing function involves managing the 'marketing mix' (product/customer value; place/convenient access; price/cost to the customer; and promotion/communication) but does not necessarily require a specialist marketing unit.[39]

In practice, strategic marketing planning is often subsumed in corporate strategy/strategic planning, while tactical and operational marketing planning is either treated as a specialist responsibility of a designated department, team or individual or combined with the strategic planning of business units or service departments. The inextricable links between strategy and marketing are evident at several levels. Many of the analytical tools and concepts associated with strategic planning and management are actually marketing tools and concepts (notably SWOT analysis, portfolio matrices and market segmentation). Similarly, much of the statistical data and information used in strategic thinking and decisions comes from marketing specialists and market research (such as briefings and reports on products, customers and competitors).

The challenge, especially in large organisations, is to ensure that inputs from relevant departments or business units are effectively managed, irrespective of whether marketing is regarded as a specialist activity. Dedicated marketing units can usefully contribute to strategic management throughout the planning process, by undertaking information gathering and processing in environmental appraisal; by identifying strategic options and choices for strategy formulation; and by translating broad goals and strategies into action plans in strategy development and implementation. This process will not work as an independent sequence of actions, but must be managed as an iterative and interactive series of activities, with marketing information and ideas informing strategic decisions, which in turn inform marketing targets and tactics. This topic is explored in more depth from both theoretical and practical perspectives by Kenneth Peattie and David Notley in the *Journal of Marketing Management*.[40] The respective *content* of strategic plans and marketing plans is covered in Chapter 4.

Conceptual models

Despite differences in terminology and presentation, published literature suggests a general consensus as to what strategic planning and management actually involves. There is agreement about the elements, but not the sequence. However, as most commentators stress the cyclical iterative nature of the process, the latter is not a significant issue. In general terms, strategic management is about having a vision, knowing your resources, understanding the business arena and asking the right questions. Strategy is basically about shaping the future for an organisation (or other entity) and one way of approaching strategic management is to pose **a series of fundamental questions:**

- Why are we here? What business are we in? (mission)
- Where are we now? How did we get here (situation audit)
- What factors will impact our future? (environmental appraisal)
- What do we want to be? Where do we want to go? (vision and goals)
- How can we get there? What are the implications? (strategic options)
- What needs to be done? Who will do it? When? (action plans)
- How will we track progress? (performance indicators)

The following paragraphs set out a more detailed conceptual model of the iterative and interactive process of strategic management as presented in this book, which can be likened to **a set of interlocking components**. As indicated below, the details of the parts vary in different models, but they all add up to much the same thing.

Environmental appraisal
This involves researching and analysing the forces of the external world, including your own industry/sector and its marketplace, as well as reviewing and auditing the internal situation, especially your performance and resources. It is essentially about *gathering and processing information* to find out and assess the views of customers and others about what is happening within and outside the organisation; it requires both analysis and synthesis, by individuals and groups, with 'one-off' and ongoing elements. The *tools and techniques* commonly used include

environmental scanning, PEST analysis, stakeholder mapping, competitive benchmarking and SWOT analysis; typical outputs include a set of planning assumptions, to serve as a basis for other aspects of the planning process. This component is sub-divided by some commentators into external and internal appraisals; other terms used for these activities include current/corporate appraisal, planning premises, situation/position/market/business audit and strategic analysis. **Chapter 2**, *Environmental issues,* deals with this area.

Strategic profiling
This involves discussing and agreeing fundamental issues, such as the scope, purpose and functions of your organisation, its guiding principles and philosophies, your desired future situation and the direction required to get there. It is essentially about *making and communicating decisions* which in effect set the overall objectives for the organisation; it requires both divergent and convergent thinking, asking questions, challenging assumptions and reviewing articulated statements throughout the strategy process. The *tools and concepts* commonly employed include mission, positioning, vision and values statements, critical success factors and key result areas; typical outputs include a series of related statements of objectives and goals, to serve as a basis for further strategy development and communication with stakeholders. This component is grouped by some commentators with environmental analysis, combined by others with strategy formation; other terms used for these activities include master strategies, posture plans and strategic choice/direction/intent. **Chapter 3**, *Strategic focus,* covers these topics.

Strategy development
This involves forming and determining strategies, action programmes and resource plans, by identifying and evaluating options and sensitivities, considering supporting strategies and contingency plans, and specifying performance indicators. It is essentially about *generating and selecting options,* checking identified strategies for coherence, resources, risk, etc and translating them into a workable programme; it requires creative thinking, rational analysis and managerial judgement, and benefits from significant input from operations staff. The *tools and models* commonly used here include generic strategies and portfolio matrices, break-even and cost-benefit analysis, and the seven S framework; typical outputs include a formal strategic plan incorporating a budget summary, sometimes with additional divisional and/or functional plans. This component is grouped by some commentators with strategic profiling, but this aspect is more about finding the route forward than choosing the destination; other terms used for these activities include portfolio plans and programme strategies. **Chapter 4**, *Strategy formation,* explores this

area, with more detailed coverage of cost analysis and financial planning in **Chapter 5**, *Money matters.*

Programme management
This involves taking actions and monitoring progress, reviewing object-ives and refining plans, elaborating tasks and incorporating targets into annual budgets and operational plans, managing strategic projects and day-to-day operations. It is essentially about *leading and supporting people* through change, balancing development and innovation with 'business-as-usual' and tracking internal and external events; it requires careful communication with targeted information and continuous assess-ment of progress and priorities. The *tools and techniques* commonly used include force field analysis, gantt charts and network analysis, mile-stone planning, responsibility charts and performance measurement; typ-ical outputs include project plans, progress reports, budget statements and other performance indicators. This component is sub-divided by some commentators into implementation and evaluation/control; other terms used for these activities include change management, medium/short-range planning, strategic implementation, strategy execution and controls. **Chapter 6**, *Achieving change,* explores these topics, with addi-tional comment on infrastructure issues and resource management in **Chapter 7**, *Securing capability.*

A key point to note is that the model is a hybrid of 'left brain' (logical) and 'right brain' (creative) thinking. While some aspects seem more dependent on analytical abilities and others more associated with intuit-ive approaches, in practice almost every element requires both types of input. Managers need to strive for balanced decision-making, giving due attention to both hard data and softer issues, aiming to see the situation 'in the round'. There are many different ways of translating the concep-tual model into an operational process. Planning processes vary in terms of their ambition, complexity, formality and timeframes. Among the key factors influencing the process adopted are organisational scale and scope, management structure and style, business composition and com-petition, and environmental turbulence. Generally, more formal and detailed systems are associated with large organisations, authoritarian styles, little competition and stable environments. **Chapter 8**, *Managing flexibility,* covers operational models of the planning process in more detail, and suggests issues which require further thought in the future as strategic concerns for information service managers.

References

1. Steiner, G. A. *Strategic planning: what every manager* must *know*. New York; London: Free Press, 1997
2. Chandler, A. D. *Strategy and structure*. Cambridge, Ma.: MIT Press, 1962
3. Andrews, K. *The concept of corporate strategy*. 3rd ed. Homewood, Ill: Richard D. Irwin, 1987
4. Johnson, G. and Scholes, K. *Exploring corporate strategy*. 5th ed. London: Prentice Hall, 1999
5. Lynch, R. *Corporate strategy*. 2nd ed. London: Financial Times/ Prentice Hall, 2000
6. Normann, R. and Ramirez, R. From value chain to value constellation: designing interactive strategy. *Harvard Business Review*, 71 (4) 1993, pp. 65–77
7. Hussey, D. *Strategy and planning: a manager's guide*. Chichester: John Wiley, 1999
8. Ansoff, H. I., Declerch, R. P. and Hayes, R. L., ed. *From strategic planning to strategic management*. New York: John Wiley, 1976
9. Gluck, F. W., Kaufman, S. P. and Walleck, A. S. Strategic management for competitive advantage. *Harvard Business Review*, 58 (5) 1980, pp. 154–161
10. Drucker, P. F. *Management*, an abridged and revised version of *Management: tasks, responsibilities and practices*. Oxford: Butterworth-Heinemann, 1974 (1988)
11. Vaill, P. B. Strategic planning for managers. In: *The NTL managers' handbook*. Arlington, Va: NTL Institute, 1983, pp. 186–200.
12. Bryson, J. *Strategic planning for public and nonprofit organizations: a guide to strengthening and sustaining organizational achievement*. San Francisco, Ca: Jossey-Bass, 1988
13. Garratt, B., ed., *Developing strategic thought: rediscovering the art of direction-giving*. London: HarperCollins, 1996 (pp. 2–3)
14. Hanford, P. Developing director and executive competencies in strategic thinking. In: Garratt, B., ed. *Developing strategic thought: rediscovering the art of direction-giving*. London: HarperCollins, 1996, p. 190
15. Ohmae, K. *The mind of the strategist*. London: Penguin, 1983 (pp.13–15, pp. 242–268)
16. Cornish, E. Using the future to see the present. *The Futurist*, 31 (4) 1997, p. 4.
17. Ansoff, H. I. and Sullivan, P. A. Optimizing profitability in turbulent environments: a formula for strategic success. *Long Range Planning*, 26 (5) 1993, pp. 11–23
18. Deming, W. E. *Out of the crisis*. Cambridge, Ma: MIT Press, 1982

19. Wernerfelt, B. A resource based view of the firm. *Strategic Management Journal*, 5 (12) 1984, pp. 171–180
20. Burk, C. F. and Horton, F. W. *InfoMap: a complete guide to discovering corporate information resources*. Englewood Cliffs, NJ: Prentice-Hall, 1988
21. Camp, R. C. *Benchmarking: the search for best practices that lead to superior performance*. Milwaukee, Wi: American Society for Quality Control, 1989
22. Senge, P. *The fifth discipline: the art and practice of the learning organization*. New York: Doubleday, 1990
23. Prahalad, C. K. and Hamel, G. The core competence of the corporation. *Harvard Business Review*, 68 (3) 1990, pp. 79–91
24. Brown, J. S. and Deguid, P. Organizational learning and communities-of-practice. *Organizational Science*, 2 (1) 1991, pp. 40–57
25. Kaplan, R. S. and Norton, D. P. The balanced scorecard: measures that drive performance. *Harvard Business Review*, 70 (1) 1992, pp. 71–79
26. Hammer, M. and Champy, J. *Reengineering the corporation: a manifesto for the business revolution*. London: Nicholas Brealey, 1995
27. Brooking, A. *Intellectual capital: core assets for the third millennium enterprise*. London: International Thomson Business Press, 1996
28. Porter, M. E. and Millar, V. E. How information gives you competitive advantage. *Harvard Business Review*, 63 (4) 1985, pp. 149–160
29. Earl, M. J. Integrating IS and the organization: a framework of organizational fit. In: Earl, M. J., ed., *Information management: the organizational dimension*. Oxford: Oxford University Press, 1996, pp. 485–502
30. *Information as an asset: the board agenda*. London: KPMG IMPACT Programme, 1995 (Chairman: Dr Robert Hawley)
31. Thorne, N. W. Putting information assets on the board agenda. *Long Range Planning*, 31 (1) 1998, pp. 10–17
32. Joint Funding Councils' Libraries Review Group. *Report*. Bristol: The Councils, 1993 (Chairman: Professor Sir Brian Follett)
33. National Committee of Inquiry into Higher Education. *Higher education in the learning society: report of the National Committee*. London: HMSO, 1997 (Chairman: Sir Ron Dearing)
34. *Guidelines for developing an information strategy – the sequel: practitioners' guide*. Nottingham: Joint Information Systems Committee, 1998.
    Available online at: http://www.jisc.ac.uk/pub98/guide_seq/
35. *Information strategies: an executive briefing*. Nottingham: Joint Information Systems Committee, 1998.

36. Information Strategies Initiative. See http://www.jisc.ac.uk/info strat/
37. Institution-Wide Information Strategies. See http://www.cni.org/ projects/iwis/
38. Bernbom, G. Institution-wide information strategies. *CAUSE/ EFFECT*, **20** (1) 1997, pp. 8–11. Available at http://www.educause.edu/ir/library/html/cem9713.html
39. Baker, M. J. One more time – what is marketing? In: Baker, M. J., ed. *The marketing book*. 4th ed. Oxford: Butterworth-Heinemann, 1999, pp. 3–15
40. Peattie, K. J. and Notley, D. S. The marketing and strategic planning interface. *Journal of Marketing Management*, **4** (3) 1989, pp. 330–349

Further reading

Strategic thinking

Hanford, P. Developing director and executive competencies in strategic thinking. In: Garratt, B., ed. *Developing strategic thought: rediscovering the art of direction-giving*. London: HarperCollins, 1996, pp. 188–222
Explains the nature and purpose of strategic thinking and its importance in direction-setting and change management. Argues the need for managers to spend time on development and describes a selection of strategic thinking tools covering reframing, questioning to explore and empower, holistic thinking, deep thinking/paradigm shifts and different thinking styles.

van Maurik, J. *The effective strategist: key skills for all managers*. Aldershot: Gower, 1999
Accessible and interesting guide (c150p) which shows how managers can learn to think and act more strategically by developing and applying key skills and techniques. Separate chapters cover creative thinking, analytical tools, strategic vision, being innovative, managing change and leadership qualities. Draws on wide variety of sources and relates tools to a five-stage strategy process, offering an 'organisational fear scan' to assist with change management.

Corporate strategy

Johnson, G. and Scholes, K. *Exploring corporate strategy*. 5th ed. London: Prentice Hall, 1999

Comprehensive widely-used textbook (560p), also available with appended case studies (972p). Contains 11 chapters arranged in four parts covering general concepts, strategic analysis, strategic choice and strategy implementation in both private and public sectors. Includes mini cases and examples interspersed in text, as well as numerous references, recommended readings and five-page glossary of key terms.

Lynch, R. *Corporate strategy*, 2nd ed. London: Financial Times/Prentice Hall, 2000
Comprehensive textbook (1014p) containing 22 chapters organised in six parts, with short and longer case studies in each chapter. Similar coverage and features to Johnson and Scholes (see above) but distinctive in offering both rational/prescriptive and creative/emergent perspectives on topics throughout the book. Includes 10-page glossary.

Hussey, D. *Strategy and planning: a manager's guide.* Chichester: John Wiley, 1999
Accessible and concise introduction (c. 290p) offered as an alternative to the substantial volumes on the subject. Covers the key concepts and core components of strategic management, including the planning process and plan contents. Also provides separate chapters on marketing, financial and human resource planning.

Drew, S. Building knowledge management into strategy: making sense of a new perspective. *Long Range Planning*, **32** (1) 1999, pp. 130–136
Identifies academic and practical origins of knowledge management, noting cultural and human dimensions (as well as economic and technological aspects) and considers how SWOT analyses, portfolio matrices and other strategy tools can be given a knowledge perspective.

Information strategies

Butler, M. and Davis, H. Strategic planning as a catalyst for change in the 1990s. *College & Research Libraries*, **53** (5) 1992, pp. 393–403
Surveys the literature of library planning and then considers at length the importance and benefits of strategic management for academic libraries, drawing on recent experiences at the libraries of the Michigan State University and the University at Albany, State University of New York.

Favret, L. Local government change and strategic management: an historical perspective and a case study. **Public Library Journal, 10** (4) 1995, pp. 95–101

Relates UK government policies to changes in public services in respect of financial restraint, structural change, market testing, the Citizen's Charter and corporate planning. Considers alternative models of strategy-making and outlines the style adopted at the London Borough of Bromley, featuring a bias for action ('back of envelope planning'), delegated management, and customer focus. Concludes with examples of corresponding library developments (bookshop-style stock arrangements, targeted specialist services, a matrix structure and a development team) and relates Bromley's experience to theories of strategy as an incremental, cultural and political process requiring librarians to develop new business competencies.

Allen, D. K. **Information strategies.** London: Library Information Technology Centre, 1996 (Library & Information Briefings Issue 64)
Ten-page briefing on the background to the JISC information strategies initiative and its significance for university libraries. Notes a policy shift from product to process, and relates this to various theories of strategy and current practice in higher education institutions, with reference to institutional politics, stakeholder involvement and resource allocation. Considers methodologies and tools for analysing 'information topologies' and suggests further reading.

Chapter 2

Environmental issues

Planning and management cannot take place in a vacuum. Understanding the environment in which the service operates and confronting the issues likely to affect its progress is a vital aspect of the strategic management process. The contemporary environment is vast and diverse, and also dynamic and complex. It must be monitored and charted carefully to identify the strategies that will enable our services to survive and thrive. We need to gather and collate information, and then analyse and assess the findings to identify the driving forces and other factors that will have an impact on our service now and in the future. Our appraisal needs to cover external forces, sectoral trends and internal issues. Some people prefer to begin with self-analysis of the business unit and work outwards, others start with global influences to provide the context for a situation audit of both the unit and its parent body. In practice, these strands are often pursued simultaneously, by distributing the work among individuals or groups.

Scanning

The environment is hard to define precisely; it comprises facts, events and issues that might have a large impact on an organisation's performance, but over which it may have little influence – though in turn its actions may affect other organisations and individuals. It is easier to think of the environment as a complex set of variables posing opportunities and threats for organisations in pursuit of their objectives, and to use a model or framework to focus appraisal and assessment.

We can approach our analysis in various ways. A common first step is to separate out the **macro-environment**, also known as the *societal* environment, representing the outside world in general or those conditions that have a broad – and therefore indirect – impact upon the organisation. In contrast, factors and forces in the **micro-environment** have a direct effect on the organisation and its services: we can sub-divide this into the *task* environment – the industry sector or business world in which the organisation operates – and the *corporate* or *internal* environment, to include consideration of the organisation itself (its structure, culture, resources, competencies, etc.).

The conventional way of viewing the macro-environment is to consider issues and influences under four headings: Political, Economic, Social and Technological. This is generally referred to as **PEST** factors or a **STEP** analysis, depending on the order in which the headings are taken. The **SEPTember** formula is an alternative mnemonic, based on the 'meso paradigm', which brings together macro and micro variables, and is a useful framework for situations where both types of variables are needed to explain and account for events and their relationships. The full list then extends from the wider macro-environment into the narrower task/operational environment for the organisation/service. This is a potentially more useful tool as it can be expanded to cover a longer list of key variables that need to be taken into account, individually and collectively. Using the SEPTEMBER formula to focus on the meso-environment provides a richer, more comprehensive and realistic picture, and facilitates inter-dependent levels of analysis.

Figure 2.1 The SEPTEMBER formula for environmental analysis

The SEPTEMBER formula				
Society	Economics	Politics	Technology	Education
Marketplace	Business	Ethics	Regulations	

Here are some examples of the variables to consider under each heading.

- *Society* – includes socio-cultural issues and demographic trends, such as life-style changes, social mobility, birth rates, population distribution and life expectancies;
- *Economics* – issues such as national productivity, interest rates, inflation, currency fluctuations, price controls, employment patterns, wage settlements and globalisation;
- *Politics* – including factors like government stability, public expenditure, industrial policy (e.g. privatisation, deregulation), taxation (e.g. VAT) and special incentives;
- *Technology* – hardware and software developments, relating to both business and consumer markets, including issues such as interoperability, standards and security;
- *Education* – all aspects of learning and skills development (at home, school or in the workplace) including literacy levels, skills gaps, professional and vocational qualifications;
- *Marketplace* – the nature and number of products, services, customers, competitors, and related factors such as growth, maturity, pricing and substitutability;

- *Business* – general trends and specific developments in relevant sectors, including the information and service industries, and the particular industrial/business sector served;
- *Ethics* – organisational policies on corporate/social responsibility, codes of professional conduct, statements of service values and ethical dilemmas in the workplace;
- *Regulations* – health and safety, employment, data protection and copyright legislation; trends in contracts and licensing arrangements (e.g. for information services/software).

A tool commonly used to analyse the marketplace in this context is Michael Porter's **five forces** model, which identifies five basic forces that can impact on an organisation:

- the bargaining power of *suppliers*
- the bargaining power of *buyers*
- the threat of potential new *entrants*
- the threat of *substitutes* for products or services
- the extent of competitive *rivalry* among existing firms.[1]

For example, the power of periodical publishers is a particular issue for information services, as there are no exact substitutes for their offerings and their prices often form a large part of the total costs of the service.

The process of looking at – or looking for – information related to the environment is known as **environmental scanning**. A frequently cited definition is that of Francis Aguilar, credited as the originator of the term,

> ". . . the process that seeks information about events and relationships in a company's outside environment, the knowledge of which would assist top management in its task of charting the company's future course of action."[2]

In an article reporting their survey of scanning activity in the Canadian publishing and telecommunications industries, Ethel Auster and Chun Wei Choo elaborate this description as follows:

> "Scanning not only concerns seeking information to address a specific question (for example, 'How big is this market?'), but also includes doing a broad sweep of the horizon to look for signs of change and opportunities ('Where are the new markets?'). Scanning activities could range from gathering data deliberately such as by doing market research, to informal conversations with other executives, or reading the newspaper."[3]

The term 'scanning' is often used not just to cover the viewing or seeking of information but also to include the subsequent processing of the information obtained, typically involving some form of analysis and assessment, and frequently then extending to forecasts and predictions. While the prime focus of such activity tends to be on the external or macro-environment, commentators also stress the need to search an organisation's internal environment to identify important elements that might affect future performance. The term has gone in and out of fashion over the years, but the concept remains valid, even though covered by other names (such as strategic information systems, corporate intelligence, and – most recently – knowledge management).

Environmental scanning is an idea that looks good on paper, but often proves intractable in practice. The aim is to make informal/inexpensive methods more deliberate and systematic without being overambitious. The **purpose** of scanning is not so much to predict the future accurately, but to identify issues likely to have an impact and prepare for them. Its value feeds in both at the stage of clarifying/formulating *planning assumptions,* and later (with more detailed information) when *strategies* are being developed. In addition, the volatility and complexity of the operating environment of most information services means that managers increasingly need wide-angle scanning to inform the *operational planning* of frontline services.

There are several **benefits** to be derived from putting more effort into environmental appraisal. It raises awareness and deepens understanding of the primary influences on strategic change, and it enriches thinking about the future. In addition, the better informed people are, the more they feel in control and confident about fitting the organisation to its environment. Also, early detection of trends can prevent their perception as a threat – and provide time to anticipate opportunities and develop responses carefully.

While scanning needs to examine recent events and current conditions, it is important to bear in mind the main purpose in documenting developments is to spot *trends* – general directions, continuing tendencies – and assess their future implications for the service in its organisational context. We need to focus on aspects of the environment relevant to our organisations to avoid information overload, so we must guard against unrestrained and indiscriminate data gathering. The amount of information required will depend on several factors, including the scope or magnitude of the issues; the urgency and timing of decisions; the familiarity and complexity of the problems; and the expertise or interests of the people concerned.

In many organisations, scanning tends to be informal, intermittent, irregular, individual, unsophisticated, *ad hoc* and partial, typically triggered by events instead of anticipating them. To cope with the current scale and pace of change, it is desirable to establish a process that is continuous – or at least regular – systematic, proactive, objective, diverse and wide-ranging in the views covered. The challenge then is to move:

- from chance acquisition to *deliberate search*

- from periodic ritual to *ongoing monitoring*
- from description to *interpretation*
- from forecasting to *opportunity-spotting*

In his groundbreaking article on top management information needs, Ronald Daniel argues the need to formalise and regularise the collection, transmission, processing and presentation of information for planning – just as for control – but draws attention to the significant differences between the information required for these two distinct purposes.[4]

Figure 2.2 Information requirements for control and for planning

	Control	Planning
Coverage	Compartmentalised – follows organisational lines	Integrated – transcends the organisational chart
Frequency	Daily / Weekly	Monthly / Annual
Degree of detail	Precise, Detailed	Trends, Patterns
Orientation	Past	Future

If unsure about emphasising or formalising the scanning process, the following checklist will help to determine the need for an environmental audit – the more questions to which you answer 'yes', the greater the need.

- Have previous long-term plans been overtaken by events?
- Is competition growing in your industry/sector?
- Does your service need to become more market/customer-oriented?
- Do more/different kinds of external forces seem to be influencing decisions?
- Is management unhappy with the results of past planning efforts?

Process guidelines

In large organisations scanning has often been carried out by corporate planning offices and product/market specialists, or sometimes by public relations/external affairs departments (but less frequently by information service units). Information services are unlikely to be able to dedicate staff permanently to this activity for their own purposes, but in any case current thinking is generally inclining towards a more participative collaborative approach, on the basis that the process should be multi-level, multi-phased and multi-unit.

A sensible first step is to select some categories or themes to focus research, which can then enable responsibility for fact-finding and analysis to be shared among staff. Possible headings for an information services sectoral analysis include scholarly communication/publishing; information and communication technologies; human resource management; customer services; co-operation and resource-sharing. Additional categories can be added to reflect the particular sector served – for example, academic libraries need to assess developments in further/ higher education; public libraries must take account of local government developments; and special libraries have to track developments in the industries which they serve.

Suggested steps for structuring scanning

1. *Select and structure* themes of interest and people to research them
2. *Collect and collate* data, information and opinions from target sources
3. *Sort and sift* information into relevant variables, with significant influence
4. *Analyse and assess* variables, identifying critical factors with substantial impact
5. *Interpret and integrate* information into planning assumptions
6. *Project and picture* the future operating environment

Sources of information
There is a vast array of sources potentially available to help people find out what is happening in the wider world, and even more possibilities since the phenomenal growth of information available electronically via the Internet and the World Wide Web. Sources can be broadly categorised as documentary (impersonal) and human (personal) on the one hand, external/publicly available or internal/organisationally generated on the other. Commonly used sources include:

- *published documents* – particularly material outside your immediate speciality and on interdisciplinary subjects (for example, a popular general science magazine, a weekly digest of news stories)
- *organisational contacts* – especially people with formal planning or research roles, senior managers and experts in their field;
- *professional meetings* – from conferences to informal gatherings, especially events with exhibitions, demonstrations and cross-sectoral participation;
- *electronic newsgroups* – offering similar opportunities to meetings, but on a global scale.

The table gives further examples of sources.

Figure 2.3 Sources of information for environmental appraisal

	Internal Organisationally restricted	External Publicly available
Personal – Human	Subordinates Peers Superiors Functional specialists Planners/researchers	Customers Suppliers Competitors Consultants Professional contacts Business associates Government officials
Impersonal & Documentary	Scheduled meetings Memos/circulars In-house studies Regular reports Internal databases Company library	Lectures/speeches Newspapers/ periodicals Trade magazines Commercial databases Conferences/trips Fairs and exhibitions Professional bodies Trade associations Government agencies Statistical series Press releases Broadcast media Research reports Review articles External libraries

Tips
- Choose a *time horizon* that is twice that of your strategic planning period – short horizons tend to limit thinking, and lead to more threats than opportunities being identified.
- Brainstorm first to map the territory, and identify *key factors* – then follow up with specific (quantifiable) research to check out gut feelings.
- Ensure your *scanning process* is integrated with other processes, and sequenced with your planning and budgeting cycles.
- Aim for stability and continuity with the *people* involved.
- *Share* information periodically to derive maximum benefit.

Stakeholders

Organisations in general, and services in particular, are composed of people – individuals and groups – and their day-to-day operation and longer-term development depends on how these people interact with each other, and with the outside world. A convenient way of identifying people whose opinions and activities affect the organisation is to draw a **stakeholder map** and/or to conduct a **stakeholder analysis.** Definitions of the term 'stakeholder' vary from the frequently-cited but quite narrow interpretation of the Stanford Research Institute, "those groups without whose support the organisation would cease to exist", to the broader ones currently in use. A **stakeholder** can be seen as any individual or group with an involvement or interest in the organisation, actual or potential – in the past, present or future. John Bryson provides the following definition,

> "A stakeholder is any person, group or organization that can place a claim on an organization's resources, attention or output, or is affected by its output."[5]

The concept of stakeholding has attracted a lot of attention in both business and political circles within the last decade. The term 'stakeholder theory' dates back to the 1960s, and the concept has experienced cycles of interest for much of this century, but has resurfaced recently in both the UK and US. It is a concept that can be applied at both the (micro) level of the organisation or firm and at the (macro) level of society, and interpreted differently in different contexts, resulting in the use of phrases such as a 'stakeholder company', a 'stakeholder economy' and a 'stakeholder society'. Today's business leaders fall broadly into two groups: those who argue that business success depends on an exclusive focus on maximising *shareholder* value, and those who claim that in the long run sustained success depends on a business meeting the expectations of all its *stakeholders* – employees, customers, suppliers and the community (as well as shareholders). The latter point out that long-term shareholder value is the result of giving due weight to the concerns of customers, employees, suppliers and the community – companies derive value from relationships with these groups (as they do from those with their investors).

The stakeholder theory is exemplified in the UK by the 'Tomorrow's Company' initiative of the Royal Society for the encouragement of Arts, Manufactures & Commerce (RSA), which now favours the term 'inclusive approach' on the basis that the stakeholder concept has acquired political connotations.[6] This inclusive approach acknowledges the wide range of possible relationships that an organisation can have with individuals and entities in its environment, but advocates concentration on five 'key relationships':

- with those who invest in it, its *shareholders;*
- with those who buy its goods and services, its *customers;*
- with those who work for it, its *employees;*
- with those who supply it with goods and services, its *suppliers;*
- with those among whom it operates, the *community,* locally, nationally or internationally.

A service's stakeholders include not only its clients or customers (subdivided into various categories), but also top management in the host organisation, service staff, funding authorities and other regulators, suppliers, partners, competitors, trade bodies and 'the local community'. These groups can be divided into *internal* and *external* stakeholders, and also into those *directly* and *indirectly* affected by the service. The groups are not mutually exclusive, but often overlap, with some people featuring under several headings. There are also other ways of categorising individuals – for example, as spokespersons, or 'key opinion formers', which cut across the above classifications. In addition, groups can be successively divided into further sub-groups almost indefinitely, but a balance must be struck to ensure that the resulting categories are sufficient to represent the main viewpoints without making the ensuing analysis too complicated and unmanageable. Bryson explains the **purpose** of stakeholder analysis thus,

> "A stakeholder analysis is the means for identifying who the organization's internal and external stakeholders are, how they evaluate the organization, how they influence the organization, what the organization needs from them, and how important they are."[5]

After initial identification, the analysis can be pursued at various levels. Common approaches include rating and ranking stakeholders according to their interest and power or influence; the latter can cover the nature and extent of the group's influence on the service, as well as the service manager's capacity to influence the group. For example, groups (such as committee members) can be categorised as advisers, decision-makers or monitors in relation to policy, resources, etc. A more penetrating analysis will look at what *criteria* the different stakeholder groups use to judge the organisation or service, and then try to assess performance from these stakeholder perspectives. Evaluations can be based on a range of 'hard' and 'soft' inputs, from explicit statements through observed behaviour to informed guesswork.

Peter Block identifies four generic categories of stakeholders in a matrix model positioning them according to perceived levels of *agreement* about where the organisation is heading, and *trust* concerning the way it operates in pursuit of that future.[7]

Block suggests different approaches for these groups, assigning them time and energy in the following order of priority:

1. *Allies* (high agreement, high trust) – typical examples include customers who are successful users of products or services; embrace them as members of the organisation, and ask them for advice and support.
2. *Opponents* (high trust, low agreement) – includes trusted but dissatisfied customers who test your thinking in a positive way; regard

Figure 2.4 Stakeholder influence model (adapted from Block)

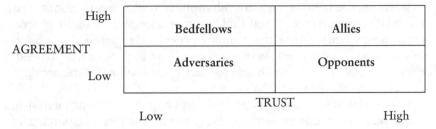

them as great assets, and engage them in conversation and problem-solving.

3. *Bedfellows* (high agreement, low trust) – accept some responsibility for having contributed to the difficulty in the relationship; resist the temptation to be manipulative, and try to agree how you can work together.

4. *Adversaries* (low agreement, low trust) – stop trying to persuade them, avoid doing anything to undermine or destroy them; reduce tension and threat, and either break off contact or help them feel understood.

A common method of mapping or representing stakeholders diagramatically is to position them to reflect their perceived *importance* to the organisation, either grouped in concentric circles showing how direct the influence is, or in a series of boxes linked by lines to the central box representing the organisation, where the length of line indicates the level of influence.

A stakeholder analysis is likely to reveal conflicts or at least tensions between the interests and expectations of different groups (for example, where employees desire higher salaries, but customers require low prices). Organisations have to balance these competing interests and this can sometimes be achieved by looking for trade-offs between stakeholders' primary and secondary expectations (for example, employees may accept low salaries in return for good training or job security; customers may accept higher prices in return for superior quality or personalised service). A reasonably thorough analysis which identifies a range of criteria, expectations or objectives for each stakeholder group is thus likely to reduce the difficulties in reconciling such conflicts.

Stakeholder analysis can be used initially to identify people who could or should be involved in the strategic planning process, but may need to be reviewed as strategy development proceeds. Often the differences in stakeholder views only emerge in relation to specific strategies, so it is during the strategy evaluation process that stakeholder mapping can be especially valuable, and sometimes an initial map may have to be redrawn in the light of such consultation. It is also worth noting that the relative importance of stakeholders may change as a result of strategic choices made during the planning process; for example, a decision to outsource a particular function will create an important new dependency relationship with the chosen partner organisation. (Outsourcing is covered in more detail in Chapter 4.)

Jeffrey Harrison and Caron St John explicitly link current interest in stakeholder management with business trends such as outsourcing of operations, delayering of management and the notion of the 'boundaryless organisation'. They argue that organisations need to move beyond *managing* stakeholders through 'buffering' techniques as a defence against environmental uncertainty, to proactive *partnering* through boundary-spanning or 'bridging' techniques, which will create organisational flexibility. Examples of customer partnering tactics cited include their active involvement in planning sessions, design teams and product testing, rather than more traditional arms-length involvement in market research activities. Supplier partnering similarly includes involvement in design teams, as well as shared information systems and co-ordinated quality control. Harrison and St John also provide examples of management and partnership tactics for several other stakeholder groups (including competitors, government agencies, local communities and activist groups). They offer the following **guidelines** for forming strategic **stakeholder partnerships**, which are based on various publications on joint ventures and strategic alliances:

1. Communicate frequently and openly to foster the development of a shared interpretation of the situation.
2. Avoid formalisation and monitoring of contractual agreements, which lead to conflict and distrust. Informal psychological contracts provide better safeguards over time.
3. Strive for long-term agreements in which partners are more likely to be willing to work out difficulties and devote adequate resources to the partnership.
4. Make a commitment. Large investments of non-recoverable assets to a partnership are critical to success.
5. Avoid excessive trust, which leads to its violation (e.g. embezzlement, fraud).
6. Retain some control over outcomes from the partnership, regardless of the amount of resources committed to the venture.
7. Share information during the agreement stage and during the implementation of the partnership.
8. Clearly delineate what is expected from the partnership and develop a strategy for achieving it through partnership activities.

9. Resolve conflicts through joint problem-solving techniques.[8]

Examples of information service stakeholders

Peter Brophy and Kate Coulling suggest ten stakeholder groups for an *academic* library:

- students
- academic staff
- university support staff
- library managers
- library support staff
- university managers
- the government
- society: internationally, nationally, regionally and locally
- international research communities
- posterity.[9]

Other groups that could be added to the above list include:

- trade unions
- employees' families
- co-operating libraries
- the library's suppliers
- professional associations

Thomas Childers and Nancy Van House chose seven key 'constituent groups' to test the hypothesis that different groups would view the effectiveness of *public* libraries in different ways. The groups chosen were considered by the researchers and their advisers "to be influential, directly or indirectly, in organization-level decisions".

1. *Library managers* at the highest level of the library.
2. *Library service staff* who serve the public directly, in a professional capacity with or without formal professional status.
3. *Trustees* of the library, elected or appointed.
4. *Users* chosen as they come through the library's doors.
5. *Friends* of the Library group members, or equivalent, currently active.
6. *Local officials* from the library's funding or jurisdiction, with an official role related to the library, elected or appointed.
7. *Community leaders* who have some influence, direct or indirect, on library decisions.

This study broke new ground in organisational effectiveness research in using both preference and performance questions – asking respondents directly about the usefulness of various criteria – and covering several key constituencies, rather than only one or two. There were six items that fell in the top ten for all the groups: convenience of hours; range of materials; range of services; staff helpfulness; services suited to community; and materials quality.[10]

Nick Moore encourages information service managers to take a broader view of their potential partners. In addition to the library and information sector, he list thirteen stakeholders in an information society:

- text-based information producers and providers
- audio-visual producers and broadcasters
- education providers
- museums, galleries and archives
- community-based information and advice services
- government information
- research and management consultancy
- cable and telecoms providers
- Internet service providers
- hardware providers
- software houses
- computer service providers
- information-intensive organisations

Moore points out that with technological convergence boundaries have become blurred and many stakeholders are playing multiple roles, and he urges the information services sector to find ways of working in partnership with these other players.[11]

Auditing

Any form of strategic review of an information service requires an assessment of the situation of both the information service and its parent body. If preparing a strategic plan for the first time, then a more thorough review of the organisation's history and traditions, as well as its current resources and services, is desirable to enable proper understanding of how it arrived at its present position.

Much of this information will be readily available via institutional/company planning documents, annual reports and promotional literature, but it is also worth seeking out other internal reports, statistics and committee/discussion papers as additional background; meetings with key people in the organisation will help to identify useful sources, as well as being sources in themselves. Important issues to address are the organisation's financial health, technological base and competitive position, as well as paying special attention to the ambitions and prospects of other units involved in information provision and use, such as IT/

computing centres and PR/press offices. A useful way of spreading awareness and stimulating discussion is to invite senior staff from key functions in the organisation (for example, finance, marketing, personnel) to speak to information service staff and give their assessment of the current situation and predictions for the future.

Scrutiny of the library or information unit's own past and present is also essential, and can similarly begin with a review of relevant documentation. An audit of human, physical and financial resources is required to complement consideration of how effective the service is in meeting the needs of its customers. If a previous strategic or other plan exists, an assessment of progress against objectives and analysis of the causes of any shortfalls or slippage should be carried out, but with the emphasis on understanding what went wrong rather than on apportioning blame, so that lessons can be learned for the future. While 'hard' data in the form of statistics and other performance measures will provide valuable input, the key source here is people – to obtain their perceptions and judgements of the quality of current service provision.

Managers need to pose a range of questions covering both the delivery of services offered and the supporting activities and resources underpinning day-to-day operations, bearing in mind that the **purpose** in doing this is to identify the gaps between the current situation and anticipated future needs. The box shows some examples of the sort of questions to ask.

In addition, professional bodies have produced guidelines and standards for service provision in specific sectors which contain checklists that can be used for internal appraisal purposes. For example, the (UK) Library Association has issued guidelines covering children and young people[12], college libraries[13], housebound people[14] and prison libraries[15], and has also produced a model statement of standards for public libraries[16].

This initial investigation will probably identify areas for further scrutiny, where a more rigorous approach may be required, using a sequence of testing questions, sometimes known as six-word diagrams.

- *Why* are we doing this?
- *Who* benefits from or values it?
- *Where* is the evidence of success?
- *Which* strategic objective does it meet?
- *What* would/could happen if we stopped it?
- *How* should it be improved?

Value-for-money audit

A fundamental requirement for information service managers today is to ensure that their services are not only effective in the sense of

Figure 2.5 Sample questions for an internal service review

People

What knowledge, skills and attitudes do staff have now?
Is the balance of staffing right across different areas?
What is the staff turnover rate?
What are our levels of attendance/absenteeism?
How does all this match anticipated needs?

Facilities

Do we have the buildings, furniture and equipment we need?
How does our accommodation compare with peers?
Will our space need to be extended and/or remodelled?
When do we expect to replace existing equipment?
What will we need for the future?

Funding

What are our main sources of income?
Does current provision meet identified needs?
Do we have enough flexibility in the allocation of resources?
Is there scope for savings, eg via purchasing consortia?
Are our current suppliers reliable and cost-effective?

Services

What are the areas of high/low demand?
Is the pattern of use changing?
What is the competition?
Are new offerings emerging?
Is there scope for partnerships?

Customers

Who are the current users?
Who are the potential users?
What are their needs?
Are we meeting them?
Will their needs change?

delivering benefits to customers but also *perceived* as such, especially by those who provide their resources – their parent bodies/funders. The need to demonstrate 'value for money' is often stated, but rather less easy to achieve. Managers of special libraries or information services in the industrial and corporate sectors face real threats of being downsized or run down if their contribution to the organisation is not properly understood at the highest level. It is not enough to be appreciated by users on the ground, nor to rely on senior management intuition about the importance of information services; information service managers need to be confident that they add value to their organisation's activities, and they need to be able to demonstrate this *in business and management terms*.

As a result of research into evaluation techniques for library-based information services, Marianne Broadbent developed ten questions which provide "an agenda for demonstrating information service value to the organisation". These questions are applicable to information services in all sectors, and serve as a useful checklist underlining the importance of ensuring that information services are strategically aligned with their host organisations. This list reinforces the message that internal appraisal must consider the library or information service unit (ISU) in the specific context of the current business situation of its parent body. The first five questions are prerequisites for answering the last five, and provide a convenient framework for checking out the organisation's strategic parameters.[17] (The specific techniques of *cost-benefit analysis* are dealt with in Chapter 4.)

An agenda for demonstrating information service value

1. What are the *mission*, the *values* and the *critical success factors* for my organisation?
2. What is the *business* of this organisation and what is its *strategic orientation* in that business?
3. What is the nature of the *strategy formation process* in this organisation; who participates in it and where is it documented?
4. Who are the *key decision makers* in this organisation and how often do they receive an ISU product?
5. What are the *core business drivers* of this firm/government agency?
6. How do the *services and products of the ISU* relate to each of these business drivers?
7. What are the information service and product *priorities of the key stakeholders* in this organisation?
8. What is the *perception of the key stakeholders* in this organisation of performance and benefit for high priority information services and products?
9. What are the real *costs* to the organisation of each of the ISU products we provide?
10. What are the quantitative and qualitative *benefits* to the organisation of each of the ISU products we provide?

Two areas often omitted from internal reviews, but critical to success, are *communication* and *information*. (For *ethical* and *social* auditing, see the discussion of Values in Chapter 3.)

Communication audit

Communication is often acknowledged as the key to success in strategic planning, organisational change and service delivery, but there is an apparent reluctance to take a strategic approach to its management – even though there is an obvious need to assess effectiveness of both internal and external communication. The 'communication audit' is a management tool – a set of techniques – designed for this purpose. The term dates back to the 1950s, but became more popular in the 1970s and 1980s. Like other types of audit, it is a fact-finding, analysis, interpreting and reporting process, and it should cover both the practice (for example, structure and style) and the principles/philosophy of organisational communication, and consider economy, efficiency and credibility.

An audit can extend to the whole organisation or concentrate on a particular department or location, and focus on internal and/or external communication, according to needs and resources. It should be repeated (fully or partially) at regular intervals. A key issue is the choice of **auditor** – an internal one has the advantage of lower costs and organisational familiarity, but may lack expertise, objectivity and the time to focus on the exercise; a combination of internal and external inputs is often most successful, with the external person acting as a process consultant. A typical **process** will involve an *inventory* of communication items, *interviews* of selected staff and a *questionnaire* to all staff; other techniques commonly used include communication *diaries* and *network analysis*.

The audit should aim to examine every aspect of communication, and the techniques indicated all have a potential part to play. Both formal and informal channels need to be explored to build up a comprehensive picture of accessibility, adequacy, clarity, timeliness and utility of communication, and participants should be asked to provide examples of critical communication episodes, successful and unsuccessful experiences, etc.

- **Interviews** with selected staff from top management to the front line can provide useful initial input to survey design, with a later round being used to clarify and explore survey findings; middle managers, supervisors and secretaries are particularly important groups.
- **Questionnaires** allow people to comment anonymously on strengths and weaknesses of existing arrangements, and offer suggestions for improvements, as well as identifying issues to pursue further in individual or group interviews.
- **Network analysis** helps to map communication flows and to reveal discrepancies between the formal organisation chart and the informal communication structure, as well as identifying strong and weak links, gatekeepers and gateways, bottlenecks and isolation zones.
- **Diaries** enable staff to provide a comprehensive record of the variety and frequency of communication occurrences over a particular period, including details of sources, channels, duration and quality.

- **Inventory** work generally covers predictable items – such as internal memoranda, minutes of meetings, notice boards, staff newsletters, and e-mail lists – but can be expanded as the audit progresses.

Management commitment is another key issue: an audit will raise questions and expectations, so it is important to provide feedback to staff throughout the process, clear and candid reporting of the findings, and a positive statement of intended actions.

Information audit

An 'information audit' is a related but different exercise, which is similarly worth considering in this context. Information plays a crucial role in the planning process, yet it is frequently an under-developed resource within organisations – and library and information services (ironically) often neglect their own internal information needs, while attending to those of their customers. Information audits vary significantly in scale and scope. At the simplest level, it can be equated with an information needs analysis conducted within an organisational context. A useful working definition is the following promoted by the Aslib Information Resources Management Network,

> "An information audit is a systematic examination of information use, resources and flows, with verification by reference to both people and existing documents, in order to establish and monitor the extent to which they are contributing to an organisation's objectives."[18]

Within this overall aim, there might be several more specific **objectives**, for example:

- to relate information management to business objectives;
- to clarify responsibilities for specific information functions (for example, current awareness, information technology, records management)
- to develop a framework for common standards and procedures;
- to identify duplication and gaps;
- to identify expertise and training needs.

Information service managers need to consider an information audit at two distinct *levels:* on the one hand, to examine their own internal needs for information to support planning and decisions about information services; and on the other, to investigate their customers' needs for information to support planning and decisions about their business operations or other activities. The two levels are related and overlap, but it is worth considering using an (internal) information audit of the library or information services unit as a preliminary to a larger-scale exercise, particularly to familiarise staff with the methodology and procedures if embarking on such an exercise for the first time. Audits can be defined in other ways, for example by concentrating on a known problem area, a particular functional unit or a specific type of information (such as internally-generated information). In all cases, managers need to define the *scope* of the exercise, and in particular to clarify how 'information' is being interpreted. For example, Graham Robertson defines information broadly as:

> "Any piece of text or data, document, report, book, collection, knowledge, market intelligence, link, association, perception, rumour, hunch or simple idea held in any medium".[18]

This definition will suit information service managers eager to move into knowledge management, but many information professionals currently conceive their roles more narrowly, concentrating on published or publicly available information, and leaving other categories to records managers, planning offices, marketing departments, etc. Managers also need to consider the *depth* of the exercise. Robertson suggests seven levels of information auditing, based on a financial auditing model:

- information processing
- information control and security
- information cost, price and value
- information presentation, usage and circulation
- information storage, maintenance and destruction
- information ownership, responsibility and accountability
- other general operating issues

The audit **process** typically has similarities and some elements in common with a communication audit, notably a *physical stocktake* (or inventory) of information resources and the *needs analysis* (usually via interviews). The output from the stocktake may take the form of a directory, listing or register (in print or electronic format) and may be supplemented by *information mapping* to provide a diagrammatic representation of the location of information resources, by departmental, functional or geographical area. The output from the information needs analysis will probably be a report and/or tabular summary, and this may be complemented by *process flowcharting* (the equivalent of network analysis) to provide a graphic presentation of the way information moves around the organisation through the various acquisition/production cycles.

If individual and group **interviews** are to be the main method of enquiry, they will require careful planning, with regard to the selection of interviewees and focus of questions. The audit will raise questions which have both technical and cultural implications (for example, about standardisation and resource sharing) so top management involvement or endorsement (via a launch event or announcement) is advisable. Interviewees should be selected on the basis of the perceived *information intensity* of their roles, likely target groups including managers, planners, researchers and secretaries.

Information audit interviews typically begin with questions about the role and tasks of the people being interviewed, including details of products or services provided, and reports produced by them. While the object of the exercise is to find out how, when and why individuals or groups seek, obtain and use information, this will not necessarily be accomplished by asking directly 'What information do you need?' as few decision-makers have a clear view of their information needs. Questions about activities undertaken, decisions made regularly and obstacles or challenges faced in meeting strategic objectives and goals may encourage people to 'open up' about their use of information, and provide greater insights than direct questions. However, it is useful to have a list of the questions to which you want answers, even if you decide not to put these directly to the interviewees. Such questions will vary according to the nature of the audience, the purpose of the audit, the procedures already in place, and the information resources and services currently on offer. Some examples are shown in the box.

Figure 2.6 Sample questions for an information audit interview

What kinds of information do you use regularly?
    Where do you get it?
    How often do you seek it?
    How rapidly do you need it?
    What do you reach for every day?

What information resources do you have in your area?
    What do you create or produce?
    What do you collect/maintain?
    What do you disseminate?
    What do you control?

What do you value most in information products/services?
    How critical is cost?
    How significant is speed?
    Do you have a preferred supplier?
    Do you have a predominant format?

Do you have any kind of ideal scenario for information provision?
    What have you not even looked for because you knew you
        wouldn't find it?
    What information would help you overcome the challenges faced?
    What kind of information tool or service do you wish existed?
    What would be your ideal in-house database?

Benchmarking

To complete the process of appraising, assessing and auditing organisational performance, managers need to compare the overall performance of their unit and the operation of its key processes with practice elsewhere to identify areas for improvement. In recent years, increasing interest in quality assurance, performance measurement and 'league tables' has led to more formal approaches to interfirm comparisons, and in particular the adoption of *benchmarking* as a source of information for setting best practice standards. Benchmarking can be summarised as "the continuous, systematic search for and implementation of best practices which lead to superior performances".[19] The working definition most often cited comes from Robert Camp's landmark text on the subject, "the search for industry best practices that lead to superior performance", which he elaborates more formally as "the continuous process of measuring products, services, and practices against the toughest competitors or those companies recognized as industry leaders".[20]

Benchmarking is thus about seeking out and examining superior processes in other organisations with a view to improving your own processes. In its most rigorous form it involves a formal, *continuous* system of measuring and comparing an existing process, product or service against that of recognised top performers ('best-in-class') both within and outside your organisation, in order to identify best practices that lead to *sustained* superior performance. The concept was originally developed by Rank Xerox in 1979, but is now widely used in both private and public sectors, and is particularly popular as a tool for strategic management and organisational learning. Benchmarking can cover big or small operations, and it can – and should – be undertaken by staff at all levels.

The concept is built around the free exchange of information to mutual benefit of all parties – it is not supposed to be about stealing ideas or industrial espionage. There are accordingly important ethical issues surrounding benchmarking that have been usefully captured in an International Benchmarking Code of Conduct, which defines principles of legality, information exchange, confidentiality, use of information and preparation.[21] (This Code offers a helpful checklist for those embarking on benchmarking exercises for the first time, and is summarised at the end of this section.)

Among the benefits generally cited, benchmarking:

- raises awareness of *good practice;*
- encourages *demanding targets,* and ones that are more sensitive to environmental changes;
- facilitates *cultural change,* helping people to shift from conservatism or complacency to creative problem-solving;

- promotes *devolved management,* as well as supplementing and complementing centralised research and data gathering;
- enables *staff involvement* at all levels in the search for quality, helping to build commitment to and ownership of continuous improvement.

Benchmarking can be categorised according to (a) the subject of the benchmarking exercise, and (b) the partners with whom comparisons are being made:
Potential **subjects** include:

- *process benchmarking* – comparison of operations, work practices and business processes;
- *product/service benchmarking* – comparison of product and/or service offerings;
- *strategic benchmarking* comparison of organisational structures, management practices and business strategies.

Typical **partners** are:

- *internal* – comparison with other units (departments/branches/sites) within the same organisation, or measuring productivity or quality gains from one year to the next;
- *external/competitor* – comparison with competitors in the same or different geographical markets, often conducted through means of a consortium and/or a third party;
- *external/functional* – comparison with organisations in the same or related industrial/business sectors, or with national or *international* industry leaders;
- *external/generic* – comparison of 'generic' processes (such as invoicing or recruitment) with organisations, regardless of industry or sector.

Two other variations of benchmarking are *customer* benchmarking – the comparison of actual/perceived performance with customer expectations – and the comparison of organisational practices and policies against formal performance *standards* (such as the Charter Mark Award scheme, the Investors in People standard or those of professional bodies).

Information service benchmarking

Many library and information services have found it useful to carry out 'peer comparisons' with competing/leading institutions, and have been doing this informally over the years by means of exchanging information, visits, etc. In the last decade there has been considerable impetus to formalise this with institutional and professional interest in quality management and performance indicators, and more information service managers are pursuing this in a systematic and structured manner. Managers can draw on comparative data produced by various bodies (for example, in the UK, the statistical series collated by the Library and Information Statistics Unit at Loughborough University) but benchmarking can be quite simple and does not necessarily have to involve complex procedures for statistical analysis.

In its Strategic Plan for the period 1991-1995, Aston University LIS included *quantitative* data in the form of graphs comparing its expenditure with other UK technological university libraries, and also noted that its outputs approximated to the average for the peer group in several other areas, including loans and consultations of library material, inter-library loan requests, reader visits and occupancy of study places. In contrast, the Massachusetts Instititute of Technology (MIT) Libraries decided to base their comparative analysis on *qualitative* rather than quantitative data. In preparing a strategic plan for the period 1989-1994, MIT identified fourteen institutions which met one or more of the following criteria:

- leading the field in using technology to provide innovative services;
- competing with MIT for students and academic staff;
- supporting a similar mix of academic disciplines;
- beginning to redefine the role of librarians.

MIT staff held interviews with library managers and other staff, and used this information both to validate their own emerging strategies and to clarify their own standing in relation to their peers. A summary of the key findings was included in the final plan. Also, when the plan was reviewed a year later, an update on the comparison with other research libraries was produced as an appendix, confirming that environmental trends and developments were being monitored as part of the ongoing planning process.[22]

More recently, in 1993 the Royal Military College of Science at Cranfield University initiated a pioneering benchmarking project involving twenty academic libraries around the UK.[23] This eventually led to the establishment of a series of benchmarking pilot projects under the auspices of the Standing Conference of National and University Libraries (SCONUL) with different groups covering Counter Services, Advice (Enquiry) Desks, Library/Information Skills, Interlibrary Loans, and the Library Environment.[24] In the public library sector, the 1997 government review of public libraries in England introduced a requirement for all library authorities to produce an annual plan and stated that three types of benchmarking would be used to evaluate the plans: comparison of own performance over time; comparison with similar authorities; and comparison with national sector averages.[25]

Process guidelines

The benchmarking process requires staff to define, measure, understand, change and manage in a cyclical process. There are numerous models for managing a benchmarking project, which vary in the detail and number of steps prescribed, but generally conform to five basic phases:

1. *Select and scope:* determine what to benchmark and how – define the metrics, establish partner(s) and form the team, involving people who carry out the process;
2. *Compare and collate:* investigate how and why the partner is better – conduct benchmarking visits, gather background information, obtain quantifiable data;
3. *Analyse and assess:* decide what is required to close the gap – identify critical differences, and consider whether the practice might be adopted or adapted at home;
4. *Design and develop:* present findings and recommendations – prepare improvement plan, submit to management, and secure approval with commitment to action;
5. *Implement and integrate:* follow through the agreed actions – introduce new practices, measure the results and monitor performance continuously.

There are certain **pitfalls** that can undermine benchmarking efforts. A key point to note is the need to allow plenty of *time* in order to gain *insights* into the real reasons for apparent differences in performance. This requires collection of both quantitative and qualitative data: aim to identify several metrics (perhaps five to seven) for each process; take care to understand the particular contexts (including physical and psychological) that support different approaches; and beware of different costing conventions (notably treatment of overheads) which can produce misleading results.

It follows on from this that the benchmarking team must have key technical and (inter)personal **competences**. In addition to full understanding of the process being benchmarked and the ability to collate and analyse relevant data (using IT), team members must have the objectivity to take a detached view of the process; the creativity to work around practical constraints; the representation skills to present their own organisation/project in a positive way and build rapport with benchmarking partners; and the presentation skills to report their findings and sell their recommendations. Finally, managers should also bear in mind that the 'perfect process' will not work properly in an unsuitable *structure* or without adequate support *systems*.

As indicated above, benchmarking itself requires good practice in terms of ethical conduct. The following checklist is a shortened version of the International Benchmarking Code of Conduct and is offered as a good practice guideline.

The Ten Commandments of Benchmarking

1 Do not extend one benchmarking study's findings to another organisation without first obtaining the permission of the relevant parties to the first study.

2 Be willing to provide the same type and level of information that you request from your benchmarking partner to your benchmarking partner in return.

3 Communicate fully and early in the relationship to clarify expectations, avoid misunderstandings and establish mutual interest in the benchmarking exchange.

4 Treat all benchmarking communications as confidential to the individuals and organisations concerned, and do not pass on without prior consent.

5 Use information obtained through benchmarking only for the purposes of improving organisational performances.

6 Respect the culture and ways of working of your benchmarking partner's organisation, and work within mutually agreed procedures.

7 Obtain an individual's permission before providing his or her name in response to a contact request.

8 Make the most of your benchmarking partner's time by preparing properly for each exchange, and providing a questionnaire and agenda prior to benchmarking visits.

9 Follow through with each commitment made to your benchmarking partner in a timely manner, and complete each study to the satisfaction of all partners.

10 Understand how your benchmarking partner would like to have the information he or she has provided handled and used, and handle and use it in that manner.

Tips

- Begin gradually with basic fact-finding, through a search for simple improvements to the relentless/persistent quest for the best.
- Start with internal benchmarking to ensure all parts of the organis-

ation are brought up to the same standard, and to give people experience of the methodology before involving third parties.

- Make your first external benchmarking partner a similar type of organisation.
- Discuss their willingness and ability to exchange information with your targets in principle before embarking on the exercise in detail.

Surveys

Market research should be an integral part of a service's ongoing management processes. However, as well as drawing on the results of past surveys, it is desirable to consult customers (and other stakeholders) as an explicit part of any strategic planning process. This provides an opportunity to confirm and update previous findings, and to focus research on emerging issues of strategic significance. (It also offers the chance to raise awareness of the service's planning activities through involvement at an early stage which will help to secure eventual acceptance of the final plan.) Surveys also have a potential role in establishing customer priorities for planning emergency alternative services in the event of a disaster (see Chapter 7). Various methods can be used to identify perceptions and preferences of individuals and groups, most of which will generate both qualitative and quantitative data. Whatever combination of questionnaire, observation, interview and discussion is chosen, careful thought must be given to design and structure, and adequate time set aside for pre-testing; this will determine the usefulness of the data collected and the ease of subsequent analysis.

Quantitative usage data can be derived from library management systems which now offer quite sophisticated report generation facilities. Qualitative data can be gathered from customer comments, simple quality check forms distributed with products/documents supplied, suggestion schemes, and *ad hoc* or regular user satisfaction surveys (typically involving focus group discussions and questionnaires, and sometimes individual interviews, in person or by telephone). Among other issues, managers need to decide whether to opt for continuous monitoring or 'snapshot' surveys – for example, sampling enquiry activity at fixed times during the year, rather than keeping records of every query handled. It is also important to ensure that well-intentioned efforts to obtain customer feedback do not result in survey fatigue for the user population – and staff – of the information service. In addition, it is essential as part of the process to feed back to customers the findings of surveys and your plans for action, for example via display boards, regular newsletters, special leaflets or your web site. Rewards and incentives for participating in focus groups or completing questionnaires are also worth considering (for example, book tokens or prize draws).

The following are some examples of **survey methods** used in information services and reported in the literature:

- *Diaries* – useful for documenting the actual behaviour patterns of library/information users, as represented by their recorded use of particular services, facilities and materials, ideally including comments on events at the time of occurrence; dependent on the motivation of individuals, and therefore subject to unpredictable response rates. Diaries should be provided for participants, as data will be difficult to digest and analyse without a standard format for recording activities and experiences; the design must incorporate helpful prompts, but not be over-prescriptive.
- *Questionnaires* – useful for dealing with large populations, especially over a wide geographical base, and for contacting those reluctant to be interviewed; a relatively low-cost method, in terms of cost per respondent, particularly if administered electronically. However, response rates are often disappointing, findings are not necessarily representative, and the information gathered tends to be quite superficial. Questions should always be pre-tested (by pilot or through interviews) and customised to the target population, to avoid alien or ambiguous language; the survey instrument must therefore be developed from close contact with the survey population in order to establish a rapport with respondents and collect useful data.
- *Focus group interviews* – a qualitative method useful for obtaining in-depth responses, for investigating the reasons for people's views, and as input to questionnaire or interview design; more efficient and economical than one-to-one interviews, but a relatively high-cost method, in terms of participant and administrative time, requiring a skilful trained moderator. Interviews typically involve six to twelve people, for 90 to 120 minutes, in a structured discussion on a particular topic. Focus groups have been widely used in academic, national, public and special libraries, generally as 'one-off' exercises; the use of ongoing user panels is less common, but enables more longitudinal and comprehensive data collection.
- *Nominal group technique* – another structured group discussion process, which in theory combines the benefits of individual consultation and group discussion; particularly useful for identifying issues and priorities for planning, and also as input to survey design. The technique involves a five-step process: facilitator puts a question to the group; individuals write down ideas in silence; facilitator records ideas via round-robin reporting; participants clarify and evaluate ideas through discussion; individuals vote on ideas, from which a group ranking can then be derived.
- *Critical incident technique* – a structured individual interview tech-

nique, useful for in-depth exploration of experiences and problems; a time-intensive method, which requires a lot of time for transcription and analysis of interview data. Interviews are guided by a series of prompts (e.g. "Can you remember a time when. . .?"). This technique is often used in the business world, but has not been widely reported in library and information services; it is in theory well-suited for investigating problems experienced by individual library users, particularly those belonging to minority groups.

Many information service managers are now turning to 'off-the-shelf' solutions for their survey methodology. In the UK, following pioneering work by the University of London Library, involving development of entry-gate and survey software for both quantitative and qualitative measurement, academic libraries are increasingly adopting the methodology and software developed by the company Priority Search – anapproach which offers various levels of consultancy support, as well as a user group facilitating exchange of experience among practitioners. [26,27]

In North America and Australia, academic, public and special libraries have adapted the PZB 'SERVQUAL' model, based on extensive research in the United States across five different service industries.[28,29,30,31] Parasuraman, Zeithaml and Berry identified ten dimensions (represented by 97 individual issues) that consumers use in forming expectations and perceptions of services, which transcend different types of services – reliability, responsiveness, competence, access, courtesy, communication, credibility, security, understanding and tangibles.[32] They subsequently reduced and refined the original multiple-item scale to 22 items spread among five dimensions, known as the RATER criteria:

- *Reliability* – ability to perform the promised service dependably and accurately;
- *Assurance* – knowledge and courtesy of employees and their ability to inspire trust and confidence;
- *Tangibles* – physical facilities, equipment and appearance of personnel;
- *Empathy* – caring, individualised attention the firm provides its customers;
- *Responsiveness* – willingness to help customers and provide prompt service.[33]

The SERVQUAL model provides a basic skeleton that can be adapted or supplemented to fit the needs of particular organisations. The authors argue that it is most valuable when used periodically to track service quality trends in conjunction with other measurements. The actual survey instrument is in two sections, with 22 separate questions for customer expectations (what they feel the service *should* provide) and their perceptions (what they feel it *does* provide). A version adapted for use in information services is given in Appendix 1.

Such surveys are time-consuming and sample selection can be difficult, particularly for public libraries which have very diverse customer bases, so it is worth considering alternative lower-cost methods of obtaining useful feedback and pointers for planning the future. Here are a few **tips** for quick and simple methods of canvassing opinions, by announcing the strategic review and inviting people to tell the library what it does well and not so well, and what new or improved services/facilities they would like to see in the future:

- use existing channels of communication – for example, newsletters, bulletin boards, online catalogue;
- take advantage of both formal and informal meetings – within the organisation and outside;
- place special notices on issue counters, enquiry desks and other points around the library.

Irrespective of whether you issue such an invitation to comment, do not overlook the potential value of *anecdotal evidence* which accumulates on a daily basis at public service points, but often is not captured simply because there is no formal procedure encouraging frontline staff to do so. Staff at issue desks and enquiry points (and in other parts of the library) are in an excellent position to pick up signals – verbal and non-verbal – about what customers like and dislike, and while it would probably not be practicable to document this on a continuing basis, it is worth trying over a limited period, and is also a way of involving all levels of staff in the market research process.

Analysis

Collecting data is only the first part of the process and the next critical task is to extract from all the evidence the key messages which will influence decisions about the future. It is easy to spend a lot of time assembling facts, opinions and ideas, and then find it quite difficult to make sense of the results, so it is important to give proper thought at the outset to the organisation and management of all the hard and soft data accumulated during the process. As indicated above, the key purpose of the exercise is to document the current position, identify trends and major forces impacting the information service from within the organisation and outside, and pinpoint discrepancies or gaps between present provision and the desired future. It is essential to specify at the start what is expected from the exercise so that the individuals and groups concerned will have a clear idea of the form of output required. Analysis of the data must be followed by synthesis to bring together the findings from the different strands. It is therefore helpful where possible to use standard checklists or models to focus information processing.

One way of identifying key strategic issues is to construct an **issues priorities matrix,** scoring each issue as High, Medium or Low in relation to its potential *impact* and its perceived *uncertainty*.

Figure 2.7 Issues priorities matrix showing importance and criticality

Degree of uncertainty

		Low	Medium	High
	High	*Critical planning issues*	*Important scenario drivers*	*Critical scenario drivers*
Level of impact	Medium	*Important planning issues*	*Important planning issues*	*Important scenario drivers*
	Low	*Monitor*	*Monitor*	*Reassess impact periodically*

Any issues identified as Medium or High impact require further attention. Issues in the top left box are relative certainties (known forces) for which you *must* plan. Issues in the top right corner are critical uncertainties for which you should prepare, by identifying strategic *options* or developing alternative *scenarios* (see next section).

Another method commonly employed is **cross-impact analysis,** which uses a matrix to explore how seemingly separate events might have impacts on each other, by asking the question if event A occurs, what effect will it have on events B, C, D, etc. (for example, positive/negative impact, more/less likely to occur).

SWOT analysis

A tool commonly used to bring together the findings of the investigation of external forces and internal capabilities is the SWOT analysis, which involves identifying the organisation's Strengths and Weaknesses in relation to the marketplace, and the Opportunities and Threats presented by predicted environmental trends. (In strategic planning, the alternative acronym **WOTS UP** is sometimes used, to stand for **W**eaknesses, **O**pportunities, **T**hreats and **S**trengths **U**nderlying **P**lanning. Another name sometimes used for this is a **SOFT** analysis, standing for Strengths, Opportunities, Faults and Threats.)

SWOT is the most widely used of practical analytical tools for strategic planning, but it is often used in a sloppy and ineffectual manner, through lack of thought and focus. There is frequently little evidence of *analysis* with the work failing to move beyond description in the most general terms. Often the exercise involves comparing and combining the work of different groups – and sometimes also the findings from previous exercises – and if not properly managed it can result in overlong unstructured lists, with no prioritisation or weighting of factors, unclear and ambiguous words and phrases, and apparently conflicting statements (for example, the same point listed as a strength and a weakness).

The key point here is to focus on the likely future situation to highlight areas requiring attention; many current strengths may seem less strong when judged against expected competition or standards of the future, and conversely some weaknesses may be less important if they relate to services no longer considered to be a high priority. For this reason it is important not to accept as given the results from previous SWOT exercises – even if the strengths and weaknesses previously identified still exist, they will not necessarily have the same significance as before. Two other points worth remembering are first, that long lists will not assist the creation of a clear strategic picture, so it is essential to concentrate on significant issues and synthesise as appropriate; and secondly, that business experience suggests that technical and managerial competence tend to be the most critical factors, and the absence of the latter substantially undermines the effectiveness of the former. Some people suggest using standard categories (such as People, Place, Plant, Process and Product) to categorise strengths and weaknesses; others argue that prompts inhibit critical thinking.

The following are some **tips** to improve effectiveness:

- test each alleged strength and weakness by asking whether there is any evidence that *customers* see these features as strengths and weaknesses in the same way as staff;
- deal with statements about things alleged to be both a strength *and* a weakness by asking what *particular aspects* of these characteristics are a strength or a weakness;
- limit opportunities and threats to conditions identified in the *external* environment, to avoid 'jumping the gun' by listing *internal* strategies and tactics to deal with the situation, before proper analysis has taken place.

When the initial listing is complete, assess each threat according to its potential severity – High, Medium or Low, depending on the likely loss of money or prestige if it materialised – and the probability of its occurrence; and similarly, assess each opportunity for its attractiveness – measured by potential revenue or other benefits – and probability of success in realising these benefits.

Equilibrium analysis

Another tool that can help to identify the most critical strengths and weaknesses is equilibrium analysis, which is also known as *force field analysis* (particularly when used in the context of managing organisational change). This simple device involves drawing a horizontal line to represent the current state of some things (such as staff turnover, service throughput, market share, customer satisfaction) and a vertical line with a scale to rate the relative significance of factors influencing the situation in a positive or negative way. The various factors are represented by arrows drawn above or below the line, whose length reflects their perceived importance. The exercise is initiated by asking a question, such as 'what is holding up/holding down our customer satisfaction rating?' When a sufficient number of factors has been identified, further questions should be asked along these lines:

- can we achieve more by strengthening a positive factor or removing a negative one?
- are there any factors not worth considering because they cannot be altered?
- what can we do about the really important factors?

Figure 2.8 Example of equilibrium analysis for customer satisfaction

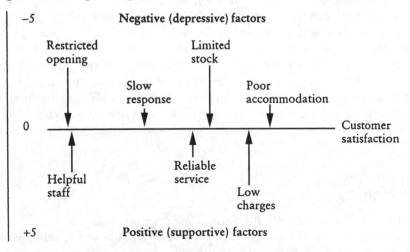

Planning assumptions

The final outcome of this part of the planning process ought to be a set of planning assumptions that can inform and guide the development of strategies to meet the information service's objectives. It is important to remember that an assumption is not a fact, but an *opinion* about the occurrence of an event (outside the control of the planner) which is treated as a fact for the purposes of planning. Such assumptions have a significant role, not only in providing a **foundation** for planning, but also in assisting with **co-ordination** of planning throughout an organisation, which should be based on *common assumptions*. It is therefore sensible to include a statement of assumptions in all planning documents, but restricting this list to factors that are relevant to understanding and using the plan or achieving its objectives, thus creating a checklist for ongoing environmental monitoring. Some commentators suggest labelling assumptions to signal their different status at various stages of the planning process:

- *initial assumptions* are often just educated guesses, which must be researched further if confirmed as essential to the strategy;
- *working assumptions* are generally more confident forecasts, but will probably be re-examined for their validity and relevance;
- *final assumptions* are those eventually agreed for incorporation in the formal written plan.

Assumptions about the external environment (for example, trends in literature costs, pervasiveness of IT, growth in electronic publishing) need to be translated into statements directly related to the future character and operation of the service. Such statements might thus include predictions about the balance between meeting information needs from a library's own holdings and from external sources; levels of computer literacy among customers; the transition from print to electronic information resources; passing on more costs to customers; and the mix between information staff undertaking research on behalf of customers and on helping customers to do their own research. For an example of a formal set of planning assumptions, *see* the SCONUL Vision statement, which records the collective view of national and university library directors in the UK.[34]

Scenarios

Rather than concluding with a list of assumptions, some libraries have preferred to take this exercise one stage further and put the statements together in a more coherent and dramatic form to create a picture of what the library will look like in five or ten years time, often reproducing this as a vision of the future which forms the introductory part of the formal strategic plan. If there is concern about the predictability of a number of critical assumptions, then it may be advisable to create more than one image of the future organisation, by deciding a range of possible outcomes for several key environmental influences and then identifying possible combinations of these alternative states to develop several plausible visions or **scenarios**.

The pace and scale of change in the world today has put a premium on managerial ability to think ahead and to anticipate events, rather than just letting things happen. 'Futuring', 'futurism' and 'futurology' are terms commonly used for an expanding trans-disciplinary set of methods used to study the future. Though often referred to as a science, the nature of its subject makes futuring both an art and a science, drawing from disciplines such as history, sociology, psychology, ecology and urban planning. The aim of such studies is not so much to produce an accurate picture of the future, but to provide a basis for purposeful action in the present. Indeed, it is the depiction of *multiple* futures – alternative images, projections or visions – that is particularly beneficial in improving the quality of decisions about an organisation's strategic plans. Studying the future thus assumes that planning (for) the future is better than awaiting it passively, and implies that anticipating and participating can help to shape events.

A wide range of formal **methods** can be used for researching the future, individually or in combination. These methods generally take the present (or past) as the point of departure – usually concentrating on what are considered enduring, modern and progressive elements. As Peter Schwartz points out, "Hindsight is useful for sharpening your foresight".[35] 'Foresight' in this context can be contrasted with the *technology forecasting* which was popular in the 1970s. The task of the latter was to predict the future of technology using modelling techniques and econometrics, whereas *technology foresight* is about *shaping* the future and requires sustained discussion between technology researchers and technology 'users'.[36] Most futuring methods combine logic or mathematical calculation with subjective judgement; some take account of interdependencies and attempt to assess their causes and effects. Examples include:

- *relevance trees* – using a pictorial representation to plot and compare alternative goals as options branching out at each decision point;
- *trend extrapolation* – projecting past and present patterns of behaviour into the future with the use of statistical techniques;
- *Delphi studies* – bringing together the individual opinions of recognised experts through a process of informative feedback;

- *simulation / gaming* – simplifying and approximating some aspects of reality to produce dynamic models of ongoing activities or situations;
- *cross-impact analysis* – looking at both the probabilities and interrelationships of events, by considering their causes and effects;
- *scenario development* – devising hypothetical but plausible descriptions of future situations, usually in a vivid narrative form.

The latter, sometimes known as *multiple scenario analysis,* has become an increasingly popular management technique within the last few years, with a surge of new publications on the subject and evidence of widespread interest and use in all sorts of organisations. Scenario writing combines *environmental scanning* with *strategic visioning* to articulate different – often surprising – views of the future. The scenario approach acknowledges that the future is uncertain but economic, political, social and technological assumptions have to be made, and constructing alternative scenarios on the basis of different assumptions reduces organisational vulnerability to unforeseen events.

The RAND Corporation developed this technique (and the Delphi method) in the 1950s and 1960s, but the Royal Dutch/Shell Group is generally regarded as the model for its widespread application. Shell planners pioneered the scenario approach to market analysis in the early 1970s as a result of dissatisfaction with traditional long-term planning techniques and realisation that creating a single plan to be followed with military precision did not work in the real world of business. When the dramatic oil price rise happened in 1973, they were better prepared than their rivals as they had thought about how to react and already had a plan, even though they did not think it a likely occurrence – but it was one of the possibilities considered. Many of the leading writers on scenario planning today – notably Peter Schwartz and Kees van der Heijden – learned their art through working at Shell, before moving on to apply their thinking with other organisations. The view of scenario planning as a form of organisational learning is also an important aspect of the Shell approach.[37]

Characteristics of scenarios

Commentators stress the fact that the scenario approach is best characterised as a disciplined way of thinking, rather than a formal methodology; scenarios are about *preparation* rather than *prediction*. Schwartz defines the technique as "a tool for ordering one's perceptions about alternative future environments in which one's decisions might be played out".[35] Van der Heijden similarly sees scenarios as "perception devices" –

"a set of reasonably plausible, but structurally different futures ... conceived through a process of causal, rather than probabilistic thinking, reflecting different interpretations of the phenomena that drive the underlying structure of the business environment".[38]

Cliff Bowman and David Faulkner define a scenario as "a self-contained envelope of consistent possibilities which describe the future".[39] Scenarios are often described as conceptual *stories* which are composed around carefully constructed *plots* that make significant elements of the business scene stand out boldly. Each story is developed logically from a different set of assumptions to describe a range of possible future operating environments.

A key point is that scenarios combine facts and perceptions; they can deal with both 'hard' and 'soft' inputs. They also change several variables at a time and try to capture the different states that will develop as a result of such changes. In this way they have a richness that distinguishes them from *contingency planning* and *sensitivity analysis,* which generally focus on only one uncertainty while keeping all other variables constant. Their composite nature also forces people to consider the dynamics and details of situations, and to explore a range of probable and possible outcomes. Another important point is that scenarios are not just reactive tools, enabling people to adapt to what is happening around them; they are also *generative* tools, helping people to shape and influence the future – to create both plausible and *preferable* futures.

Paul Schoemaker distinguishes 'scenario planning' thus,

"In short, scenario planning attempts to capture the richness and range of possibilities, stimulating decision makers to consider changes they would otherwise ignore. At the same time, it organizes those possibilities into narratives that are easier to grasp and use than great volumes of data. Above all, however, scenarios are aimed at challenging the prevailing mind-set."[40]

Scenarios can be used for a variety of **purposes**. In addition to strategic planning and vision building at the corporate level, they can be used to anticipate changes in roles or to take specific decisions about future service development. Scenarios are especially valuable where there is a high degree of uncertainty and/or strong differences of opinion surrounding a number of critical assumptions – they can help to create a common language and framework without stifling diversity. Scenarios are also useful in situations where strategic thinking has become bureaucratic or routinised, as they open people up to new perspectives and more options with different interpretations of events.

The technique can be used to complete an environmental appraisal process, pulling together the results of a situation audit, SWOT analysis, etc. Alternatively, the concept of scenario development can be interpreted broadly to embrace the whole environmental appraisal process, and thus act as a focus for data gathering and discussion groups. Ian

Wilson identifies different ways that scenario planning can be used in strategic management, for example in planning assumptions, strategic visioning, strategy development, contingency planning, sensitivity/risk assessment and strategy evaluation.[41]

The following are some of the main **benefits** claimed for scenario planning:

- it helps people to cope with complexity and to have a more positive view of uncertainty;
- it enhances awareness of the impact of environmental changes on plans and operations;
- it provides a new focus and structure for seemingly unrelated environmental insights;
- it indicates the relative scale and significance of different factors or sets of circumstances;
- it improves understanding of interdependencies and cause-and-effect relationships;
- it enables fresher and sharper perceptions of external events, threats and opportunities;
- it highlights criticalities in planning assumptions and identifies warning signs of change;
- it offers a coherent framework for reallocation of resources if conditions alter rapidly.

Information service scenarios

Scenarios are frequently used to convey the impact and implications of information technology on organisations and their products, services and facilities, and many of the best known examples from the library and information services sector have concentrated on this aspect. An early example in the LIS field was the four scenarios designed by the (US) Association of Research Libraries in 1984 to use in strategic planning of library staff needs for the next decade.[42] In 1989, Bruce Shuman published nine "alternative scenarios for the information profession", which included 'utopian', 'dystopian' and 'incrementalist' depictions of the public library in the year 2015.[43] In 1996, in an effort to aid thinking about a future network-based scholarly communication system, Paul Evans Peters formulated four scenarios depicting a wide range of outcomes, written from the perspective of higher education institutions and their libraries: *Another marketplace for global enterprises; Mass customisation for and by individuals; Knowledge guilds reign supreme*; and Ivory towers in cyberspace.[44]

In the UK, the Library and Information Commission report, *New library: the people's network,* presented six scenarios to illustrate the potential of a networked public library system to meet people's needs in the digital age, depicting people of all ages using electronic resources to pursue their educational, business and personal interests.[45] Recently, the Science Policy Research Unit (SPRU) at the University of Sussex published a report which offers five scenarios illustrating "alternative pathways towards a distributed library future" for the years 2000 and 2005. While most of the published library examples take the form of 'word pictures' – narratives of one or two pages in length – the SPRU scenarios combine a pictorial presentation with a descriptive title, a single-sentence caption and a short explanation of around a dozen lines of text. The scenarios are prefaced by comments on two sets of major environmental factors affecting the service path – the development of the telecommunications infrastructure, and innovation in the application of information technologies (labelled *Connect* and *Tech* respectively); and action-oriented transformational policies and strategies, and the awareness and abilities of service users (labelled *Action* and *Awareness*). Each scenario is then headed with a shorthand summary of the assumptions made about the environment, indicating the level of network connectivity, technological innovation, transformative activity and user awareness assumed (high/low, even/uneven or mixed).[46]

Scenarios can be used at various levels – for example, the organisation as a whole, a particular department, or a specific project – and for a variety of purposes. At Reading University Library, this technique was used to make the case for a new building and proved to be a much more effective communication device than a more conventional paper. Two scenarios of approximately 900 words each were produced to illustrate the difference a new building could make to the local learning environment. The second scenario represented a genuine attempt to remodel current accommodation to meet future needs; it was not intended to be a 'doomsday' vision, although it was obviously a less attractive picture than the first one, and showed resources spiralling downwards as a knock-on effect of space constraints.[47] The following year, a more structured approach to scenario development was used at the University's Bulmershe Library serving the Faculty of Education and Community Studies, in an exercise involving a wide range of stakeholders, which surpassed the expectations of library staff in terms of both the level of engagement of participants and the radical nature of the vision of reconfigured accommodation for collaborative provision which emerged as the preferred future.[48]

Process guidelines – how to build scenarios

1. *Establish the scope and scale of the exercise – in terms of the focus,*

timeframe, stakeholders and participants. Potential contributors include customers and suppliers, and external experts, as well as representatives of a broad range of internal functions; the core team needs imaginative, receptive team-players who are able and keen to contribute.

2. *Identify the key environmental influences – in terms of the known features, significant factors and critical uncertainties.* As part of this process, consider which organisational strengths are distinctive, which weaknesses are structural or fundamental and which are operational/practical.

3. *Select the initial scenario logics or themes – in terms of possible combinations and 'cross-impacts' of the key drivers.* The drivers can be depicted graphically (for example, using a 'rich picture' or a matrix) to aid visualisation of 'plots' which capture the dynamics of the situation and communicate the key points.

4. *Turn the embryonic plots into narratives – including checks for consistency and plausibility and selection of titles.* Titles need to be informative, memorable, short and vivid to reinforce key messages, but can be supported by longer sub-titles – novel/film titles may provide useful sources of inspiration (for example, *Great expectations, Hard times*).

5. *Feed through to planning and decisions – including study of comparative impacts and choice of distinguishing indicators.* The implications of each scenario need to be considered and compared so that sensitive areas where characteristics are particularly affected by changing assumptions can be identified and then monitored by establishing early warning checkpoints or milestones that indicate which of the scenarios is unfolding (typically three or four 'events' for each scenario).

Tips

- Involve a wide range of well-informed and free-thinking stakeholders in identifying the key issues and influences.
- Take care in selecting the scenario team as the exercise requires capable conceptual thinkers with multi-disciplinary abilities.
- Allow time for people's latent understanding to surface, using workshops with an overnight stay or spread over several days.
- Try to balance the known and the novel so that the scenarios are anchored in the past but stretch forward to the future.
- Beware of putting everything that is desirable into one scenario, and all the undesirable things into another.
- Aim for two or four scenarios not three, as the latter often results in best and worst cases and a middle road.

- Allocate resources for communicating the scenarios and their operational implications, effectively and imaginatively.

Summary checklist

Do you understand your service environment?

Scanning
Have you identified themes or topics to focus environmental monitoring?
Have you assigned responsibilities for information gathering and processing?

Stakeholders
Have you identified key stakeholder groups for your service?
Have you considered their different interests and expectations?

Benchmarking
Have you identified examples of best practice in your field?
Have you considered adopting their ways of working?

Customers
Have you established methods for identifying customer perceptions and preferences?
Do you report back to customers on your response to survey findings?

Issues
Have you identified the key issues for management attention?
Have you considered how the issues relate to each other?

Assumptions
Are all your plans based on common assumptions?
Are your assumptions monitored by regular environmental scanning?

References

1. Porter, M. E. *Competitive strategy: techniques for analyzing industries and competitors.* New York: Free Press, 1980
2. Aguilar, F. J. *Scanning the business environment.* New York: Macmillan, 1967
3. Auster, E. and Choo, C. W. Environmental scanning by CEOs in two Canadian industries. *Journal of the American Society for Information Science*, 44 (4) 1993, pp. 194–203

4. Daniel, R. D. Management information crisis. *Harvard Business Review*, **39** (5) 1961, pp. 111–121

5. Bryson, J. M. and Alston, F. K. *Creating and implementing your strategic plan: a workbook for public and non-profit organizations.* San Francisco, Ca.: Jossey-Bass, 1996. (p. 43)

6. Royal Society for the encouragement of Arts, Manufactures and Commerce. *Tomorrow's company: the role of business in a changing world.* London: RSA, 1995 (RSA Inquiry) [final report]

7. Block, P. *The empowered manager: positive political skills at work.* San Francisco, Ca.:Jossey-Bass, 1987 (1990), pp. 130–151

8. Harrison, J. S. and St John, C. H. Managing and partnering with external stakeholders. *Academy of Management Executive*, **10** (2) 1996, pp. 46–60

9. Brophy, P. and Coulling, K. *Quality management for information and library managers.* London: Aslib Gower, 1996 (p. 41)

10. Childers, T. and Van House, N. A. The grail of goodness: the effective public library. *Library Journal*, **114** (16) 1989, pp. 44–49

11. Moore, N. Partners in the information society. *Library Association Record*, **101** (12) 1999, pp. 702–703

12. Blanshard, C. (ed.). *Children and young people: Library Association guidelines for public library services.* 2nd ed. London: Library Association Publishing, 1997

13. Ennis, K. (ed.). *Guidelines for learning resource services in further and higher education: performance and resourcing.* 6th ed. London: Library Association Publishing, 2000

14. *Guidelines for library services to people who are housebound.* London: Library Association Publishing, 1991

15. *Prison libraries: Library Association guidelines for library provision in prison department establishments.* London: Library Association Publishing, 1988

16. *Model statement of standards for public library services.* London: Library Association, 1995

17. Broadbent, M. A management perspective on information service value. *The Electronic Library*, **10** (6) 1992, pp. 323–4

18. Robertson, G. Information auditing: the information professional as information accountant. *Managing Information*, **97** (4) 1997, pp. 30–35

19. Definition used by The Benchmarking Centre Limited, Truscon House, Station Road, Gerrards Cross, Bucks SL9 8ES

20. Camp, R. C. *Benchmarking: the search for best practices that lead to superior performance.* Milwaukee, Wi: American Society for Quality Control Quality Press, 1989

21. Coopers & Lybrand. *Benchmarking human resource activities: main*

report. Cabinet Office, Office of Public Service, Development and Equal Opportunities Division, 1997 (Appendix D, p. 33)

22. Baker, S. A. Strategic planning for libraries in the electronic age. *Iatul Quarterly*, **3** (4) 1989, pp. 200–206

23. Town, J. S. Benchmarking as an approach to quality. In: Knowles, B. (ed.) *Routes to quality: proceedings of the Conference held at Bournemouth University, 29–31 August 1995*. Bournemouth University Library & Information Services, 1996, pp. 71–79

24. Martindale, C. SCONUL Benchmarking Study Group Seminar. *SCONUL Newsletter*, **12**, Winter 1997, pp. 31–32

25. Department of National Heritage. *Reading the future: a review of public libraries in England*. London: The Department, 1997

26. Robinson, E. Studying user satisfaction: why do it? how to do it? where next? One library's experience. *The New Review of Academic Librarianship*, **1**, 1995, pp. 179–185

27. Bell, A. User satisfaction surveys: experience at Leicester. *The New Review of Academic Librarianship*, **1**, 1995, pp. 175–178

28. Coleman, V., Xiao, Y., Bair, L. and Chollett, B. Toward a TQM paradigm: using SERVQUAL to measure library service quality. *College & Research Libraries*, **58** (3) 1997, pp. 237–251

29. Hebert, F. Service quality: an unobtrusive investigation of interlibrary loan in large public libraries in Canada. *LISR*, **16**, 1994, pp. 3–21

30. White, M. D. and Abels, E. G. Measuring service quality in special libraries: lessons from service marketing. *Special Libraries*, **86** (4) 1995, pp. 36–45

31. Armstrong, B. Customer focus: obtaining customer input. *Australian Library Journal*, **43** (2) 1994, pp. 108–117

32. Parasuraman, A., Zeithaml, V. A. and Berry, L. L. A conceptual model of service quality and its implications for future research. *Journal of Marketing*, **49**, Fall 1985, pp. 41–50

33. Parasuraman, A., Zeithaml, V. A. and Berry, L. L. SERVQUAL: a multiple-item scale for measuring consumer perceptions of service quality. *Journal of Retailing*, **64** (1) 1988, pp. 12–40

34. *The SCONUL Vision: the academic library in the year 2002* / prepared by . . . a task force convened by SCONUL's Advisory Committee on Information Systems and Services. London: Standing Conference of National and University Libraries, 1998 (SCONUL Briefing Paper) Available at: http://www.sconul.ac.uk/vision.htm

35. Schwartz, P. *The art of the long view*. New York; London: Doubleday, 1991

36. Anderson, J. Technology foresight for competitive advantage. *Long Range Planning*, **30** (5) 1997, pp. 665–77

37. de Geus, A. P. Planning as learning. *Harvard Business Review,* **66** (2) 1988, pp. 70–74

38. van der Heijden, K. *Scenarios: the art of strategic conversation.* Chichester: John Wiley, 1996

39. Bowman, C. and Faulkner, D. *Competitive and corporate strategy.* London: Irwin, 1997

40. Schoemaker, P. J. H. Scenario planning: a tool for strategic thinking. *Sloan Management Review,* **36** (2) 1995, pp. 25–40 (p. 27)

41. Wilson, I. The effective implementation of scenario planning: changing the corporate culture. In: Fahey, L. and Randall, R. M., eds. *Learning from the future: competitive foresight scenarios.* New York; Chichester: John Wiley, 1998, pp. 352–368

42. Jurow, S. and Webster, D. Building new futures for research libraries. *Journal of Library Administration,* **14** (2) 1991, pp. 5–19

43. Shuman, B. A. *The library of the future: alternative scenarios for the information profession.* Englewood, Co: Libraries Unlimited, 1989 (*See also* Shuman, B. A. The public library: some alternative futures. *Public Library Quarterly,* **11** (4) 1991, pp. 13–23)

44. Peters, P. E. From serial publications to document delivery to knowledge management: our fascinating journey, just begun. *Serials Librarian,* **28** (1/2) 1996, pp. 37–55

45. Library and Information Commission. *New library: the people's network.* London: The Commission, 1997. Available online at http://www.ukoln.ac.uk/services/lic/newlibrary/

46. Gristock, J. J. and Mansell, R. *Distributed library futures: IT applications for 2000 and beyond.* Brighton: University of Sussex Science Policy Research Unit, 1997 (1998) (SPRU Report No 19)

47. Corrall, S. University library: visions of the future. The University of Reading Bulletin, **313,** 1997, pp. 6–7. Available at: http://www.rdg.ac.uk/libweb/Lib/Report/scenarios.html.

48. Brewerton, A. First, find some visionaries. Library Association Record, **101** (6) 1999, pp. 354–6. *See also*: http://www.rdg.ac.uk/libweb/Lib/Report/bulm2002.html.

Further reading

Scanning

Bates, C. S. Mapping the environment: an operational environmental analysis model. *Long Range Planning,* **18** (5) 1985, pp. 97–107
Presents three-stage MAP model, and describes the steps involved in Monitoring, Analysing and Predicting the operating environment. Includes checklist to aid scanning and sorting, and provides worked examples of trend-impact and cross-impact analysis.

Lester, R. and Waters, J. *Environmental scanning and business strategy.* London: British Library, 1989 (Library and Information Research Report 75)
Summarises findings of empirical study of seven UK companies, and provides synthesis of 15 published studies of scanning, with detailed comments on processes and methods used, information sources and problem areas. Also reviews literature on information use by decision-makers and considers roles in scanning for information professionals.

Ginter, P. M. and Duncan, W. J. Macroenvironmental analysis for strategic management. *Long Range Planning,* **23** (6) 1990, pp. 91–100
Uses a series of questions to focus on needs and areas for analysis, amounts and sources of information, techniques and procedures. Draws on published and practical experience, concluding with one-page profile of approach taken by a telecommunications firm.

Stakeholders

Goyder, M. *Living tomorrow's company.* Aldershot: Gower, 1998
Sets out the case for the 'inclusive approach' advocated by the RSA Tomorrow's Company Inquiry and offers guidance for directors, managers and others, based on the five essential stages: define purpose and values; review key relationships; define success; measure and communicate performance; reward and reinforce. Appendix includes four action checklists.

Scholes, E and Clutterbuck, D. Communication with stakeholders: an integrated approach. *Long Range Planning,* **31** (2) 1998, pp. 227–238
Explains reasons for the growth of stakeholder power and considers how organisations relate to stakeholders regarding strategy and values. Criticises typical compartmentalised approaches to communication and suggests ways of improving listening and involvement. (Contribution to a special issue devoted to stakeholding as a modern business philosophy.)

Auditing

Cortez, E. M. and Bunge, C. A. The communication audit as a management tool. *Journal of Library Administration,* **8** (2) 1987, pp. 41–64
Explains the concept, describes typical components of an internal communications audit, and discusses management and methodolo-

gical issues. Provides sample survey questions, diary forms and network instrument, with suggestions for further reading.

Burk, C. F. and Horton, F. W. *Infomap: a complete guide to discovering corporate information resources.* Englewood Cliffs, NJ: Prentice Hall, 1988
Detailed step-by-step guide (c. 250pp.) to identifying and evaluating information resources, with chapters on the concept and context of information resources management; the conduct of surveys; costing and valuing; mapping and analysis; and pinpointing significant resources. Includes a case example, annotated bibliography and comprehensive glossary.

Griffiths, J-M. and King, D. W. *Special libraries: increasing the information edge.* Washington, DC: Special Libraries Association, 1993
Based on 27 studies of special libraries' contributions to their organisations over 10 years; covers 16 companies, 7 government agencies and 4 national surveys. Combines details of evaluation methods with research results, showing costs of library provision and users' time generally recouped through other savings and quality gains.

Ellis, D., Barker, R., Potter, S. and Pridgeon, C. Information audits, communication audits and information mapping: a review and survey. *International Journal of Information Management,* **13,** 1993, pp. 134–51
Based on extensive literature review, identifies several distinct approaches to information and communication audits, and describes the different steps involved in the processes covered.

Booth, A. and Haines, M. Information audit: whose line is it anyway? *Health Libraries Review,* **10,** 1993, pp. 224–232.
Describes audit of a regional health authority, covering management and methodological issues. Discusses conference to launch process, questionnaire design, interview training, data analysis and report structure (drawing on Soft Systems Methodology).

Benchmarking

Buchanan, H. S. and Marshall, J. G. Benchmarking reference services: step-by-step. *Medical Reference Services Quarterly,* **15** (1) 1996, pp. 1–13
Draws on management textbooks and personal experience to provide practical guidance on conducting a benchmarking study. Covers what to benchmark, forming the team, identifying partners,

collecting and analysing information, and taking action. Gives advice on preliminary reading and stresses focus on customer requirements and service CSFs.

Drew, S. A. W. From knowledge to action: the impact of benchmarking on organizational performance. *Long Range Planning,* **30** (3) 1997, pp. 427–441
Traces development of benchmarking as formal approach to adopting best practice: describes different types of benchmarking; explains their benefits, drawbacks and circumstances for use; and discusses barriers to success. Concludes effectiveness depends on situation, but can have strategic impact and act as catalyst for change.

Town, J. S. Benchmarking as an approach to quality. In: Knowles, B (ed.) *Routes to quality: proceedings of the Conference held at Bournemouth University, 29–31 August 1995.* Bournemouth: Bournemouth University Library & Information Services, 1996, pp. 71–79 (BUOPOLIS 1)
Defines and explains different types and methods of benchmarking, with reference to quality management literature. Describes project undertaken by Royal Military College of Science Library with 20 academic libraries, using a questionnaire and visits to conduct three user-related measurement studies related to identified CSFs.

Surveys

Clayton, P. Nominal group technique and library management. *Library Administration and Management,* **4** (1) 1989, pp. 24–26
Describes steps involved in Nominal Group Technique (as a variant of brainstorming) and discusses its strengths and weaknesses as a research methodology, suggesting use in library planning to identify strategic issues, solve problems and design surveys.

Andrews, J. The use of critical incident technique in an academic library. *Library and Information Research News,* **14** (50) 1991, pp. 22–27
Describes the use of Critical Incident Technique to discover problems encountered by library users at Manchester Polytechnic Library, and discusses its limitations and viability as a research method, drawing on practical experience and published literature.

Armstrong, B. Customer focus: obtaining customer input. *Australian Library Journal,* **43** (2) 1994, pp. 108–117
Describes methods used by Telecom Australia's National Informa-

tion Resource Centre to obtain feedback on the timeliness, relevance, presentation and overall ratings of its products and services – quality check cards, product questionnaires and a service quality survey (based on SERVQUAL). Includes examples of rating scales and questions used.

Russell, A. and Shoolbred, M. Developing an effective questionnaire. *Library and Information Research News*, **19** (63) 1995, pp. 28–33
Describes the successful development of a survey instrument to investigate public library use by students with literacy problems. Discusses design aims, language, pre-testing, special features and reciprocity, with references to relevant articles and books.

Connaway, L. S. Focus group interviews: a data collection methodology for decision making. *Library Administration and Management*, **10** (4) 1996, pp. 231–238
Draws on published literature to explain the techniques and procedures of focus group interviews. Covers data analysis and reporting and value as a research methodology, with references to LIS applications and comments on advantages and disadvantages.

Goodall, D. Using diaries to collect data. *Library and Information Research News*, **20** (66) 1996, pp. 39–45
Describes the format and content of diaries used to document student experience of library use and their added value as an aide-memoire in focus group discussions, arguing that this combination provided better data than either method on its own.

Line, M. B. What do people need of libraries, and how can we find out? *Australian Academic and Research Libraries*, **27** (2) 1996, pp. 77–86
Distinguishes 'needs' from 'wants', 'demands' and 'uses', and discusses the strengths and weaknesses of both common and less conventional methods of market research. Also comments on what is already known about people's likes and dislikes in relation to library services and facilities, and suggests some fundamental rethinking is required for the future.

Scenarios

Schwartz, P. *The art of the long view*. New York; London: Doubleday, 1991
A discursive account (c. 250p) of the purpose and process of scen-

ario building, illustrated with business examples and personal anecdotes. Discusses targets and tactics for information gathering; driving forces, predetermined elements and uncertainties; and common plots. Finishes with three views of the future and eight steps to developing scenarios.
See also Schwartz, P. Using scenarios to navigate the future. Available at: http://www.gbn.org/Scenarios/Usingsp.html

Schoemaker, P. J. H. Scenario planning: a tool for strategic thinking. *Sloan Management Review*, **36** (2) 1995, pp. 25–40
Combines theory and practice by explaining rationale and process of scenario development. Describes ten-step methodology, using two case studies to illustrate techniques for addressing interrelations among uncertainties. Includes examples of trends and uncertainties identified, scenarios developed and extensive bibliography.

van der Heijden, K. *Scenarios: the art of strategic conversation.* Chichester: John Wiley, 1996
Comprehensive guide (c. 300pp.) to theory and practice, presenting scenario planning as an approach to strategic management. Introduces the concept of the 'business idea' and includes detailed guidance on SWOT analysis, competitive positioning, scenario development, option evaluation and the planning process.

Mercer, D. *Future revolutions: unravelling the uncertainties of life and work in the 21ˢᵗ century.* London: Orion, 1998
Reports the results of a joint project of the Open University Business School and Strategic Planning Society incorporating predictions of change from experts around the world. Organised in 12 chapters of which four collect together all the key developments ('incremental technology', 'society's winners', 'a shared world' and 'dark fears'). Project web site offers additional material including 'six drivers of the future'. Available at: http://www.oubs.open.ac.uk/future

Information service scenarios

Shuman, B. A. *The library of the future: alternative scenarios for the information profession.* Englewood, Co: Libraries Unlimited, 1989
Introduces techniques of futuring and discusses their application to libraries. Outlines eight common methods before concentrating on scenarios; presents nine futures for the public library in the year 2015, with utopian, dystopian and incrementalist examples. Concludes with criteria and guidelines for futures work and sources for further reading.

Brewis, W. L. Futures studies and the future of the library. *Mousaion* **10** (1) 1992, pp. 28–51
Discusses purpose, nature and value of futures studies and outlines different methods. Summarises forecast changes in society and comments on implications for special, academic and public libraries and for professional education, concluding that future librarians will be subject specialists and experts in the business side of information.

Shuman, B. A. *Beyond the library of the future: more alternative futures for the public library.* Englewood, Co: Libraries Unlimited, 1997
Reproduces some parts from his previous work and then offers eight more radical – and somewhat farfetched – scenarios set in the period 2019–2029. Includes 16 pages of Future Quotes, and an updated Bibliography of more than 100 books and articles from The Futurist and other sources on the future of libraries, information institutions and learning.

Giesecke, J., ed. *Scenario planning for libraries.* Chicago; London: American Library Association, 1998
Explains the purpose and nature of scenarios, describes an eight-step process, and provides guidance on writing plots with examples of common story lines. Includes three extensive case studies of scenario planning in libraries, and concludes with suggested readings and web sites.

Chapter 3

Strategic focus

Having established planning assumptions and envisaged what the information service of the future will look like in fairly general terms, the next stage is to develop (or confirm) your *strategic focus* and clarify a path towards the desired future state. Essential to this process is a clear statement of the service's purpose and objectives, which may be expressed in various ways but most frequently now takes the form of a written mission and/or vision statement, supported by objectives/goals at successive levels of specificity. This process of *strategic profiling* involves discussing and agreeing fundamental issues, such as the purpose and function of your unit, its guiding principles, your view of the future and the direction in which you want to go, and then articulating the outcomes in a series of succinct statements.

Objectives

Objectives can take many forms, operate at different hierarchical levels, and serve various functions. The main differences between different types of objectives are those of scale and time. Various other words can also be used almost interchangeably for the term 'objective' – common examples include 'aim', 'goal', 'purpose', 'strategy', and 'target'. The terms used are not significant in themselves, but it is important to agree standardised terminology within your organisation in the interests of consistency and to avoid confusion and misunderstanding. Objectives provide clarity and focus to an undertaking, team or project, and that focus can be expressed in a variety of ways and at different levels, both strategic and tactical.

Viewed corporately, the process involves setting objectives for the organisation as a whole and then interpreting and elaborating these strategic objectives in relation to departments/business units/functions (including specific services or products) to produce complementary tactical and operational objectives. Ideally the process should combine top-down and bottom-up inputs. Objective-setting needs to take account of the resources required to achieve them; it should precede financial planning (budgeting) but specific objectives may need to be revisited when detailed financial projections have been produced. Setting objectives is thus an iterative process whereby strategic/corporate objectives are complemented by operational objectives that are made more specific as they are 'rolled down' the organisation to departments, teams and individuals.

The **benefits** of objective-setting include some of those generally claimed for strategic management and planning. Objectives have a particular contribution to make in:

- confirming or communicating purpose, direction, etc
- helping people to make plans and set priorities
- guiding and informing decisions or actions
- determining progress and success
- mobilising and motivating staff

Without objectives, people don't know where they are heading, whether they are on the right track, or when/if they have achieved their goal. There are specific issues to consider in relation to particular types of objectives, but some points are of general applicability. A commonly used mnemonic for checking the efficacy of objectives statements is **SMART** – on this basis, objectives should be:

- **Specific,** in terms of desired results and responsibility for delivery
- **Measurable,** either quantitatively or by demonstrating achievement
- **Acceptable** to – ideally agreed with and owned by – stakeholders
- **Realistic** in relation to environmental factors and resources available
- **Timebound** (in years, months, weeks or days, according to context).

There are some additional criteria to bear in mind. Objectives should also be:

- **Consistent** with your overall philosophy (and compatible with other objectives)
- **Unambiguous** in wording (and understandable to the whole community)
- **Testing** and thrusting, as an expression of organisational ambition and aspiration
- **Empowering** and encouraging, particularly to the individuals directly involved.

The hierarchy of objectives

Before considering the typology of objectives that represents the strategic framework described in this book, we can categorise objectives broadly into a hierarchy of five types:

1. *Purpose objectives* – answer the questions, Why are we here? What is our business? They are usually broad, philosophical statements,

and their achievement is hard to prove; for example, "to support research" or "to meet information needs". Purpose objectives are commonly known as aims, missions or statements of intent.

2. *Function objectives* – answer the questions, What do we do? What needs do we meet? They are also broad, but more practical statements; such activities can be quantified, but success is difficult to measure, for example, "build collections", "provide information", "supply documents". Functional objectives are also known as aims, key activities or role statements.

3. *Direction objectives* – answer the questions, Where are we going? What sort of change are we seeking? They generally indicate movement, improvement or development, and are hard to measure quantitatively; for example, "from ownership to access", "towards the virtual library", "focus on self-service provision". Direction objectives are also known as goals, key result areas or strategic thrusts.

4. *Result objectives* – answer the questions, What (exactly) do we want to achieve? They are much more specific, and will often incorporate at least two forms of measurement (expressed in terms of quantity, quality, time or money) and may also include a priority rating; for example, "to train X people in the new system within the next 6 months", "to generate £/$ from the publication programme over the next three years". Result objectives are also known as targets, programme goals or tactical objectives.

5. *Task objectives* – answer the questions, How will we do this? and Who will do it? They define specific activities and the date by which they must be completed, and they should also specify the person responsible for achieving them; for example, "to deliver revised text to publisher by 25 September", "to install software before the beginning of term". Task objectives are also known as deliverables, individual targets or operational objectives.

A typology of objectives

Mission and vision statements are often derided as empty platitudes, but some sort of statement of an organisation's terms of reference is needed to inform stakeholders. This can take a variety of forms, and – as already indicated – the formal terminology of planning is confused and inconsistent with various terms used to describe how organisations wish to position themselves. The number of levels in the hierarchy of objectives will depend on the size and complexity of the information service unit and the timescale of the plan. The term 'hierarchy of objectives' can cause confusion as people often equate types of objectives with levels of management as represented in a hierarchical organisational structure, when in practice the different types of objective can operate at every level. George Steiner uses the term **network of aims** as an alternative, which is helpful both in liberating us from this vertical perspective and in reminding us that objectives should also have *horizontal linkage*. As previously noted, objectives (and sub-objectives) should be linked to basic purposes/overall philosophies, but they should also be consistent with objectives in other parts of the organisation or business unit.[1]

The type of statements, labels given to them and their contents will also be determined by organisational context and culture. Such statements are commonly publicised in strategic plans, promotional literature and annual reports. Few organisations have a complete set as suggested below, and some of these concepts can be combined into one statement; managers need to select a mix to fit their particular circumstances. Mission, vision and values in whatever combination provide long-term perspective and inform strategy development. Goals, strategies and targets give purpose and direction to people's work and help to focus effort in the short to medium term. The approach adopted here is only one of several possible interpretations; it does not matter which terms are used – they are all 'objectives' in the generic sense – but it makes sense, as suggested above, to standardise on terminology within organisations to avoid misunderstandings.

A *framework for strategic objectives*

- *Values* – a statement of the beliefs and/or guiding principles that underpin organisational, professional and personal philosophies, and influence staff behaviour and attitudes; typically stated as four to eight headings elaborated by two to three phrases or sentences; assumed to be enduring and for the long term.
- *Mission* – a concise summary in a few sentences or paragraphs of the organisation's purpose or reason for existence, indicating its business area, customer base and distinctive contribution; sometimes incorporates values and/or objectives; expected to be medium- to long-term, although the wording may need to be updated periodically.
- *Objectives* – a short list of five to eight broad, general points indicating the continuing functions, main programmes or areas of activity of an organisation, elaborating the mission statement (and often combined with it); again assumed to be relatively stable, but subject to regular reviews with relatively minor changes in the short to medium term.
- *Vision* – a coherent description in narrative form depicting a preferred scenario or desired future state for the organisation fulfilling its potential, frequently using powerful or dramatic imagery; typically embracing a long timeframe (5/10/20 years) but requiring more frequent revision than the mission.

- *Positioning statement* – a pithy slogan or catchy 'soundbite' expressing the organisation's strategic intent (aspiration) and/or summarising its role, often in idealistic or challenging terms; requires regular refreshment to remain current, and typically reviewed every two to three years.
- *Strategic thrusts* – the major directions in which the organisation must move to make the vision become a reality; can be equated with priorities and expressed as Critical Success Factors (CSFs) or Key Result Areas (KRAs) where success is essential, improvement is necessary or concerted effort will bring most benefit; usually formulated for each strategic review or development plan, typically every three to five years.
- *Goals* – a list of new developments or improvements representing the directions in which the organisation wants to move within a set timespan, grouped under broad headings, capable of translation into precise targets; usually reformulated for each new or revised plan and incorporated in both strategic and operational planning documents.
- *Targets* – sets of qualified/quantified statements of the results expected in relation to each goal; formulated as part of the planning cycle indicated above, but subject to review and refinement as necessary during the planning period.
- *Tasks* – lists of specific targets representing the actions and actual deliverables required (of individuals) within specified timescales to achieve the goals; incorporated in project schedules and/or work plans/objectives of individuals; reviewed and updated regularly, with new objectives formulated at least annually.

Missions

A mission is essentially a clear description of what you do for whom and why you do it. Peter Drucker is generally regarded as the person who first put business purpose and business mission on the management agenda when he suggested (in the 1970s) that inadequate thought given to purpose and mission was perhaps the single most important cause of business frustration and failure. He sees mission and purpose as the essential foundation for managers' strategies, plans and designs,

"Only a clear definition of the mission and purpose of the business makes possible clear and realistic business objectives. It is the foundation for priorities, strategies, plans, and work assignments. It is the starting point for the design of managerial jobs, and above all, for the design of managerial structures. Structure follows strategy. Strategy determines what the key activities are in a given business. And strategy requires knowing 'what our business is and what it should be'."[2]

Drucker goes on to argue that the answer to this fundamental question is always a *choice* between alternatives resting on different assumptions, but this must be a *conscious* decision – not just the suppression of dissenting opinions and points of view – and that conscious choice must be based on the *customer,* as the customer defines the business. He also provides a series of questions about customers to focus managers' thinking, which are listed below as a checklist for mission formulation.

A **mission statement** defines in broad terms the enduring fundamental and distinctive purpose of an organisation and its role in the community – what it is trying to accomplish. It must be broad enough to allow changes in the product/service portfolio as long as the core business remains the same, but sufficiently specific to distinguish the organisation from others of its type. While the statement ought to be reviewed regularly, the message should be expected to have a lifespan of at least three to five years to build constancy of purpose, although the actual wording may need to be reviewed and refined more frequently to maintain vitality and currency.

If properly constructed, mission statements can bring significant **benefits** to organisations. They have particular value in providing:

- direction and *definition* – setting parameters for planning (strategic and operational) and resource allocation;
- focus and *distinction* – identifying the special and unique characteristics of the organisation or business unit;
- meaning and *purposefulness* – creating a shared understanding and a sense of capabilities among employees and other stakeholders.

Mission statements are also credited with improving decision-making, raising the energy levels of staff, reducing the need for supervision, promoting constructive behaviour and stimulating passion.

Published writings on missions, visions and values interpret these concepts in lots of different ways, indicating that there is no one agreed approach to their definition and presentation. Some distinguish a formal mission statement from a 'sense of mission' or more enduring purpose, arguing that 'purpose' has a stronger *motivational* dimension, while 'mission' has an important *differentiating* aspect. The two main approaches can be broadly categorised as the business/strategy school and the philosophy/ethics school. The former sees mission formulation as an intellectual exercise, advocating a precise description of what business the organisation/company/unit is going to focus on and where the boundary lines are; the latter views mission as a communication task, conveying a cultural message about the organisation's purpose as a succinct encapsulation of its core values and beliefs. (Other terms used for this second type of statement include 'creed', 'company credo', 'company philosophy' and 'statement of general principles'.) It is of course possible – and indeed quite common – to combine 'hearts and minds' in statements which reflect both commercial (left-brain) and emotional (right-brain) logic. Managers may opt for a comprehensive statement covering all aspects, or a series of related but separate ones. The suggested approach is to work through the key questions and to decide on the nature and format of your statements on the basis of what emerges from discussions.

The Ashridge Mission Model (developed by the Ashridge Strategic Management Centre) is an example of the broad interpretation and has four components:

- *Purpose (the ultimate rationale)* – why the company exists
- *Strategy (the commercial rationale)* – its competitive position/advantage and distinctive competence
- *Values (the emotional rationale)* – what the company/senior management believes in, underpinning its style, relationships and ethics
- *Standards and Behaviours* – the policies and behaviour patterns that guide how it operates, and underpin the distinctive competence and the value system.[3]

The framework presented in this book considers the second two elements under the heading of Values (below). James Stoner's definition illustrates the approach taken here:

> ". . . a broad goal based on managers' assumptions about the organization's purpose, competencies, and place in the world. A mission statement is a relatively permanent part of an organization's identity and can do much to unify and motivate members of the organization."[4]

The business/strategy school stresses the need to specify the business domain quite precisely, going beyond the general sector which represents the organisation's area of activity to the specific part in which it operates, and also indicating its strategic position – the latter can also be covered by a separate statement. It is not advisable to mention current product lines or customer segments in a mission, unless you are very clear that you are only going to participate in certain lines of business.

The following **examples** of company missions illustrate some of these points.

> "To make a contribution to the world by making tools for the mind that advance humankind."
> Apple (IT company – not limiting itelf to specific products)

> "The purpose of McKinsey & Company is to help leading corporations and government be more successful."
> (management consultancy firm – very clear about its market segments)

Based on his review of the literature, Graham Peeke identified seven **criteria** for an effective mission statement:

1. It should specify clearly the nature of the enterprise in terms of its products or services.
2. It should reflect the concerns of organisation members.
3. It should specify the enterprise's markets and customers.
4. It should specify the beliefs and values prized by organisation members that it wishes to communicate.
5. It should specify the technology in use.
6. It should specify the growth policy of the organisation.
7. It should be general enough to be flexible, but specific enough to enable priorities to be established.[5]

Others have questioned the extent to which growth – or profitability – properly belongs in a statement intended to have relatively permanent value; beliefs and values may be implicit (rather than explicit) if a separate statement of organisational values is produced.

Additional qualities to aim for when drafting statements include brevity, clarity, feasibility and vitality. The statement must be based on an objective assessment of both strengths and weaknesses, and take full account of the latter, as well as reflecting the distinctive advantages of the organisation. A mission statement should therefore also be:

- concise, yet complete – memorable, but full enough to identify the organisation;
- comprehensible to stakeholders in the concepts and terminology used;
- credible and measurable – expressed in concrete terms, not remote from reality;
- alive, relevant and open to suggestions for improvement – not seen as sacrosanct.

Information service missions

What business are we in? – document supply? information provision? knowledge management? learning support? network literacy?
What are our core competencies? – information selection? information retrieval? metadata management? information design? information analysis?

The questions 'what is our business' and 'what should it be?' are not straightforward. In recent decades there has been considerable debate as to the nature of the core business of library and information services. It is easy to define this in broad terms, as the 'information business' or the 'knowledge business' (or the 'learning business') and it can be tempting to settle for neat phrases, such as 'education, enlightenment and entertainment' or 'information, imagination and innovation', but in today's competitive environment where 'information' and 'knowledge' are being viewed as corporate resources and strategic assets, it is crucial for information services to distinguish their role from that of other agencies. This requires a fundamental re-examination of the nature of the products, services and facilities that libraries and information units – or, more pertinently, information professionals – provide. Otherwise, there is a real danger of formulating a mission statement which could equally apply to a bookstore or an IT unit, or a cybercafe. Publicly available documents indicate that many services are rethinking their missions and objectives in the context of economic constraints, technological advances and socio-demographic changes. The following patterns are evident:

- *a progressive shift of emphasis,* from providing information to facilitating access and transferring skills to end-users – in all sectors, including public libraries assuming an active role in network literacy, moving from the 'corner shop' style of mediated provision to the self-service model of the 'virtual superstore';
- *a substantial expansion of functions,* resulting from the convergence or merger of library/information services with other information-related functions – such as computing/IT services, audiovisual media, educational technology and photographic/reprographic units, particularly in higher education;
- *a significant change in role,* arising from new activities or functions introduced by the parent organisation – for example, extending a library's remit to cover internal information resources in addition to publicly available sources and/or reinventing it as a 'knowledge centre', notably in the corporate sector.

A key point here is that information service staff are more than a passive link in the information chain; even where services are highly automated and offered to a large extent on a self-service basis, there is a significant professional contribution, which involves using particular expertise to facilitate access to information. Defining – and demonstrating – the *value* which the staff and service *add* to the community, and distinguishing their contributions from other professionals is a key task for information service managers. Several commentators have argued that information specialists need to promote their *analytical abilities,* for example, the Information Resource Center Manager of GE Capital Services Structured Finance Group, "As information finds its way directly to the desktops of more and more end-users, simply retrieving information is not a marketable skill". She identifies a range of activities that add value to information retrieval, and represent more than just *delivering information* – from sifting, monitoring and customising at the lower end of the scale, to statistical analysis, in-depth conclusions and data presentation at the higher end.[6]

At DuPont Research and Development, realignment of corporate information provision groups (libraries, languages services, patent information and proprietary resources) prompted information professionals to articulate their *core competencies* and to relate these to the seven *core functions* of DuPont Corporate Information Science – patent information, published information, proprietary information, library, database access, publication procurement and language services. They first developed a working definition of a library/information science professional,

> "An information professional is one who solves information problems using analysis, creativity, education and experience. This includes, but is not limited to, actually providing the data, information, knowledge or resource needed; providing guidance in the design, development and content of information products and systems; anticipating and implementing cost-effective solutions to unperceived information needs that will significantly improve the organization's ability to do business; and educating individuals to solve many of their own information problems."

Du Pont Corporate Information Science Core Competencies

- Ability to conceptualize information
- Knowledge of internal and external information resources
- Understanding of information resource management
- Ability to synthesize and tailor information

> "In the library and information science profession, understanding our core competencies and our customers' needs allows us to focus on those value-adding services that require our special expertise and allows us to eliminate redundant and extraneous activities. It enables us to better recognize how we might leverage our knowledge to assist in the resolution of information needs. It also positions us to communicate with corporate management about our accomplishments, requirements and potential value."[7]

What is our reason for existence?

> "The role of the librarian is to teach the concept that having information is having power."[8]

What is our role?

> "A library is an organization which facilitates the interaction between people and the information they need."[9]

What will it be?

> "To provide technical, business and marketplace information to individuals and groups throughout [the enterprise] at a competitive cost".

David Penniman quotes the above corporate library mission statement as an example of a broadening of scope (from technical information to other types) and a broadening of audience/market (from the R&D function to the whole enterprise). He also offers a generic mission for libraries and librarians in the future, which moves beyond document access to signal the profession's potential contribution to social and educational change,

> "to help current and future generations of citizens become independent problem solvers – who have available, and know how to use, information tools to address the challenges that face them, whether they are scholars, technicians, professionals, students, parents or lifelong learners of all ages."[10]

Formulating a mission statement can be quite a difficult task in practice, especially if a short, memorable statement is wanted. However, it is worth spending some time brainstorming a long list of key words and phrases in order to define the essence of the service properly. An *extended statement* can then be developed, and the key points picked out for summarising into a *condensed version*. The following example (taken from the Mapping Project Report by EDMC Management Consultants) demonstrates the transition from an elaborate statement to a more succinct summary, and as the "key purpose statement" of the Information and Library Services Lead Body (the UK development body for occupational standards and vocational qualifications in information and library services) it can also be viewed as a generic mission statement for libraries.

Information and Library Services Key Purpose Statement
– Early Draft

"To determine/anticipate, stimulate and satisfy the information needs of existing and potential users/clients through the design and operation of systems for creating, synthesising, gathering, categorising, storing, providing access to, retrieving, interpreting, and presenting information from all media and personal sources, in a cost effective manner, and by so doing, speeding the free flow of information to improve the business and social environment of an open society.

Information is defined in its broadest sense as meaning data, facts, imaginative materials, ideas, opinions, and cultural values, in a variety of media ranging from the printed form, through audio and visual media to electronic processes, and including in-house personal knowledge and external sources and referrals."

– Later Version

"To anticipate, determine, stimulate and satisfy the needs of existing and potential users for access to information in an ethical manner."

If a brainstorm fails to generate sufficient breadth and depth of ideas, then examination of other services' mission or purpose statements may stimulate thinking; similarly, e-mail discussions and published comments on changing service roles can help to challenge assumptions. Published examples of mission statements vary considerably in their format, length and specificity, ranging from single sentences to several paragraphs or pages. The former have the advantage of being easily memorised, but it can be quite difficult to convey a service's distinctive style of provision in one sentence. Another common approach is to begin with a sentence or paragraph summarising the overall role, and then supplement this with four to five bullet points or sentences, highlighting key functions and activities. This model works better if the opening statement is short enough to be memorised, and headings are added to the supporting points. The temptation to express the totality of the library's operations in the mission statement should be avoided as it suggests a lack of focus (and there are other ways of conveying this information).

In addition to examples from specific services, generic statements which offer definitions of the aims, activities, missions, roles or scope of information services in particular sectors can be another source of inspiration. The definition of Information Resources Management proposed by the Aslib IRM Network could be the starting-point for a mission discussion in an industrial or commercial information unit.

Information Resources Management

"Information Resources Management seeks to make individual information resources manageable, efficient and effective so that their provision and upkeep may be consistent with organizational policies and strategies for information generation, maintenance and development.

To improve manageability, IRM applies the general principles of resource management to identify discrete information resources, establish ownership and responsibility, determine cost and value, and to promote development and exploitation where appropriate. To improve efficiency and effectiveness, IRM seeks to promote communication, understanding and co-operation among information practitioners, information systems and IT staff, and among them, their managers and information users.

By improving the manageability of information resources and encouraging a co-operative culture, IRM transcends the traditional barriers between paper-based and electronic media, and among their respective practitioners, managers and users, and enables information from all sources, of all types, and in all forms, to meet the requirements of the organization."

The article from which this was taken elaborates the resource management principles encapsulated in the above statement, and in addition provides clarification of the *scope* of the information resources covered by the definition,

"Business information is used here in the broadest sense to mean all recorded information that is produced or acquired by an organization in the conduct of its business. It applies to all forms of organization across all industry sectors. It also applies to all forms of information whether derived from data processing systems, office systems, the library or pen and paper, provided it is recorded on some physical medium."[11]

For public libraries, the UNESCO Public Library Manifesto (revised in 1994, in collaboration with the International Federation of Library Associations and Institutions) is intended to "inspire sustainable library development worldwide and to meet new trends in global change".[12] It lists twelve 'key missions'.

Missions of the Public Library

The following key missions, which relate to information, literacy, education, and culture, should be at the core of public library services:

1. creating and strengthening reading habits in children from an early age;
2. supporting both individual and self conducted education as well as formal education at all levels;
3. providing opportunities for personal creative development;
4. stimulating the imagination and creativity of children and young people;
5. promoting awareness of cultural heritage, appreciation of the arts, scientific achievements and innovations;
6. providing access to cultural expressions of all performing arts;
7. fostering inter-cultural dialogue and favouring cultural diversity;
8. supporting the oral tradition;
9. ensuring access for citizens to all sorts of community information;
10. providing adequate information services to local enterprises, associations and interest groups;
11. facilitating the development of information and computer literacy skills;
12. supporting and participating in literacy activities and programmes for all age groups, and initiating such activities if necessary.

Other sources for public libraries include the National Mission Statement for the Public Library Service and fourteen 'key activities' produced by the (UK) Library and Information Services Council (LISC) Working Group on Public Library Objectives[13] and the thirteen 'service responses' set out in the American Library Association's Public Library Development Program manual, *Planning for results*. The latter suggests that libraries should choose a *limited* number of (three to five) responses, on the basis that even relatively large libraries cannot fulfil all roles with excellence, but must focus their resources on the roles most appropriate to their circumstances. Each service response is elaborated in terms of the community needs addressed, what the library provides, some possible service components, target audiences and service aspects, resource allocation issues and possible performance measures.[14] For academic libraries, the (British) Library Association Colleges of Further and Higher Education Group has provided a sample mission and aims[9] and the (American) Association of Research Libraries has gathered together examples of missions and plans of its members.[15] Additional examples of information service missions can be found on many web sites.[16]

Process guidelines

Given the difficulty in distinguishing between the concerns and issues underpinning mission, vision and values, the recommended approach is to brainstorm key words for the different statements together, and then group them according to where they fit in the framework. The most common method used is for an individual or group (for example, the chief executive, the top team, a special task force, a team of specialists from different areas) to draft an outline of the contents, then collect and interpret information from a wider constituency, and then draft an initial statement and test it on key opinion formers, before more general consultation. Alternative methods include the use of questionnaire surveys of stakeholders to clarify their views of goals or activities, and inference from practice – basing a draft on messages from interviews, published documents and resource allocation decisions.

As already indicated, the mission should provide a basis for evaluating both current and prospective activities, but it also needs to be sensitive to changes in technology, political, social and economic conditions to allow for creative growth. It should be market-oriented, addressing the questions of who the customers are and what needs will be met, thus defining the nature of the business.

Thirty questions to establish your strategic focus

Values

- What do we value?
- What do we believe in?
- What are our guiding principles?
- What do we stand for?
- How do we want to do things?
- What standards of behaviour are expected?
- What do we celebrate?

Mission

- What is our reason for existence?
- What business are we in?
- What are we trying to accomplish?
- What are our core competencies?
- What is our role?
- What is the scope of our service?
- What is special about it?

- What value does the service add to its community?
- What would the community lose if the service ceased to exist?

Focus on the customer – Drucker's questions

- Who are our customers?
- Who should our customers be?
- Where are they?
- What do the customers buy?
- What do they consider value?
- What are the customers' unsatisfied wants?
- Which of our products, services and activities no longer serve our customers and should be abandoned?

Vision

- What or where do we want the service to be?
- What is our desired position in the marketplace?
- What is this organisation going to look like five years from now?
- What are going to be the driving forces in technology?
- How are people going to be seeking information?
- What are they going to be looking for?
- How would our 'library' function if we were optimally meeting their needs?

While it is important to involve people in the process, ultimately one person will have to draft each statement and then revise it in the light of comments from others. It will probably not take long to agree the basic content, but the actual wording may require several iterations to find a formulation that is acceptable to the majority of staff. It is unrealistic to expect everyone to agree on every detail, but every effort should be made to obtain a broad consensus. The actual wording is less important than agreement about the concepts represented.

Pitfalls

- A poorly formulated statement can become a straitjacket.
- An intellectual approach may be perceived as irrelevant to operational reality.
- A badly managed exercise can irritate and alienate people.

Tips

- Don't work to a tight deadline – develop the statement as a continuous or phased process over a period which enables the involvement of staff/stakeholders.
- Don't define the business too narrowly – aim for a statement with a 5–10 year lifespan.

- Don't over-promote the statement – seek gradual adoption and assimilation.

The mission statement defines the fundamental purpose and context for the service's operations. If a short statement is used, this needs to be supplemented with some broad, general statements indicating the main programmes or areas of activity, which ought to be seen as relatively long-term in nature. Often referred to as aims or goals as well as **objectives statements**, these can be conveniently described as *functional* objectives which reflect the type of service the information unit is or wishes to become. The statement of objectives provides further definition of the broad aims expressed in the mission – answering the question *why are we here?* – but they will not usually be measurable in precise terms. Such objectives should be limited in number (preferably no more than five to eight in total) to guard against a dilution of focus. The public library roles and 'key activities' referred to above indicate the level of generality/specificity suggested. Examples of functions that typically form the basis of such statements include:

- to organise collections of information resources;
- to supply documents/other information products;
- to provide personal assistance to users;
- to develop skills in information handling;
- to collaborate with other information providers;
- to contribute to the wider community.

While the basic functions of many information and library services may remain broadly unchanged over several years, managers generally need to review such statements periodically to consider whether new wording and/or a change of emphasis is required, particularly in the light of advancing technology and organisational developments. Redefined functional objectives reflecting such changes might include:

- to negotiate rights of access to information;
- to solve problems of information overload;
- to provide gateways/links to networked resources;
- to create learning environments for individuals and groups.

Values

Vision and values are increasingly being seen as the foundations of business success, and formal statements are becoming a lot more common. Values are essential and enduring tenets, defined earlier as the beliefs and/or guiding principles that represent organisational, professional and personal philosophies, and influence attitudes and behaviour. They can be seen as relatively permanent desires that seem to be good in themselves, and they answer the question, 'What do you stand for?' The 'value set' of an organisation may only be acknowledged by the leader or top team, but if it is shared throughout the organisation it can be described as *value-driven*. Values do not have to be formally articulated to affect behaviour, but many organisations are now choosing to do so, by developing a *statement of values and principles* to answer the question above. Such statements are also referred to as a 'creed', 'company credo', 'company philosophy' or alternatively as an *enterprise strategy* (sometimes abbreviated to *E-Strategy* for short).

Values in business are being considered more important in the context of a post-industrial society where people have many more choices than before. Recent research commissioned by consultants Blessing/White suggests that values-driven businesses with explicitly stated sets of values have experienced significant benefits in several areas, for example:

- staff recruitment, development and retention – the loyalty effect;
- staff motivation, commitment and empowerment – a framework for discretionary decision-making;
- change management – providing fixed points and creating shared aspirations;
- crisis management – acting as a guide and offering a touchstone.

However, the report warns that values are not a quick fix or a magic charm, and it requires time and effort to identify common ground between organisational and individual values to secure alignment of organisational and individual goals.[17]

The fundamental human values of *honesty, justice, respect* and *stewardship* tend to feature prominently in most statements – although the actual wording used varies considerably, with integrity, openness, equity, evenhandedness, courtesy, love, accountability and responsibility being common variants. References to 'open doors', 'putting people first' and 'working as a team' are widespread. The challenge for organisations is to move beyond banalities and cliches, and to find a form of expression which is fresh and meaningful to its individual members. This is often approached by translating general statements into actions, elaborating the summary values with descriptive phrases outlining the standards of behaviour or styles of management expected.

Defining and managing values is not easy: there are tensions between *espoused* and *practised* values, between *corporate* values and *individual* values, and between *new* values and *old* values, as organisations develop and change – particularly as a result of mergers and acquisitions. Asking people what they see as the three most important behaviour standards in an organisation can be a useful way of identifying differences in perceptions, especially between managers and frontline staff. Mark Goyder, Director of The Centre for Tomorrow's Company, predicts that,

"Tomorrow's Company ... will have clearly stated the values that it stands for. It will make such values a part of its appraisal processes."[18] He cites the example of Hewlett Packard, whose organisational values are summarised below.

HP's values

We have trust and respect for individuals
We focus on a high level of achievement and contribution
We conduct our business with uncompromising integrity
We achieve our common objectives through teamwork
We encourage flexibility and innovation

The HP statement elaborates each of these values with a few sentences, explaining how they should be interpreted in their particular context, thus differentiating the HP way of doing things. For example,

We have trust and respect for individuals. We approach each situation with the belief that people want to do a good job and will do so, given the proper tools and support. We attract highly capable, diverse, innovative people and recognize their efforts and contributions to the company. HP people contribute enthusiastically and share in the success that they make possible.

Ethics is a related concept, which can be viewed as the *expression of values in action,* represented by people's behaviour; as such, ethics can be observed, assessed, checked and evaluated. Business or workplace ethics is the set of values practised by an organisation; it is concerned with the way people behave in the grey area where 'right' and 'wrong' are debatable, and can be formally expressed in the form of an ethical code or 'code of conduct' (such as those produced by professional bodies).

Ethical auditing is a relatively new concept, representing an attempt to measure the ethical performance of an organisation (for example, whether people are abiding by a company code of conduct). It is a diagnostic process which evaluates the soundness – internal and external consistency – of an organisation's values, in order to inform senior management about ethical vulnerabilities, by identifying pitfalls and problems. It is based on listening to stakeholders (especially employees) and finding out what is really going on, to uncover problem areas – gaps between expressed and practised values, culture clashes, potential conflicts of interest, and structures and processes which prevent staff from doing the right thing. It typically uses interviews, group discussions and workshops (often supported by questionnaires). *Social auditing* is a related concept but somewhat broader, which attempts to measure an organisation's social performance in terms of its effects on society.[19]

The following checklist summarises key points to consider in assessing the state of your organisational values.

- Are we clear and consistent about our values?
- Do we have an explicit statement of our values and principles?
- Does it indicate how we will conduct our business and key relationships?
- Can we show that we really practise what we publicise?
- Is this reflected in staff recruitment and rewards?
- What do we celebrate on the ground?

Information service values

As indicated above, mission statements vary enormously in length from a few words to several pages, and there has been considerable debate as to whether they should go beyond the reason for the organisation's existence to cover its beliefs and aspirations, its competitive position and distinctive competencies, or even the underpinning policies and behaviours. If the mission is seen as an all-embracing statement, then there is an argument for including these different elements; but if it is supported by further statements of objectives, strategies and policies, then the case for a short, memorable statement is a strong one, bearing in mind the desirability of having a statement capable of motivating and uniting staff towards a common purpose. The question of including values is more difficult, as evidenced by the wide variation in practice of existing UK library examples. One solution offered by US library practice is to produce a separate statement of organisational values, and this is recommended as a way of ensuring that this dimension is not overlooked but at the same time does not divert or dilute the focus of the mission.

A key issue to be addressed here is whether people are concerned to express universal timeless *human values,* to focus on those that sum up our *professional philosophy,* or to concentrate on the values judged to be critical to achieving *cultural change* associated with building a particular kind of organisation for the future. For example, as part of its strategic planning process, Harvard College Library produced a complementary statement of organisational values, which deliberately emphasised values critical to its new vision/culture – unity with diversity; open communications and trust; collaboration; innovation and initiative.[20] Often, values emerging from a strategic planning process will represent a mix of established tenets and desired new behaviours. In its 1990 strategic plan, the State University of New York included a statement of 'Organizational Values and a Philosophy of Service' for the University Libraries at Albany, presenting the professional and organizational values identified by staff. It comprises four paragraphs of six to nine lines each under the headings: Focus on the user; Library as place/ library as gateway; Librarians as educators and collaborators; Organisational diversity and flexibility.[21]

Values statements can be particularly useful during periods of substantial organisational change: they can be used to reassure people that even though everything around them seems to be changing, enduring values remain; alternatively, as indicated above, they can be used to assert and promote values implicit in a new vision requiring a change of attitude or behaviour (for example, diversity, innovation, risk-taking). When a new organisation is created out of the merger or combination of previously separate organisations or departments (for example, the convergence of a library and computing/IT service) the opportunity can be taken to involve people from both sides to build a new culture, starting with a participative exercise to generate a new statement of service values, which all staff of the combined units can own. Early attention to such issues can help to reduce inherent difficulties in bringing together professional groups with different service traditions and outlooks. This approach was also used successfully to bring people together for a collaborative project at the Massachusetts Institute of Technology (MIT) where a statement of values and beliefs was created for the Distributed Library Initiative, a five-year programme involving MIT Libraries and MIT Information Systems.[22]

The core professional values of information services which emerge from scrutiny of published writings on values and ethics have remained constant over many years, and can be summarised as follows:

- *service* to the individual and the community, including the concept of *social responsibility;*
- the pursuit of *truth* and the advancement of *knowledge;*
- universal *access* to information and ideas, with respect for *privacy;*
- *impartiality* in the acquisition and presentation of material;
- the *preservation* of our cultural heritage;
- *competence* and continuing professional development.

American and British statements are remarkably similar, with only minor differences in terminology and emphasis – for example, US statements tend to refer more explicitly to *intellectual freedom, diversity* of opinion, information *literacy* and *equity* of access. The codes of ethics and professional conduct produced by the various professional associations provide further evidence of generally accepted core values and expected standards of behaviour. The (UK) Institute of Information Scientists published its draft guidelines for professional ethics in 1998, which included an explicit statement of seven core values similar to those outlined above, but in addition asserted that "Information professionals should seek, in the course of their professional work, to ... develop their *knowledge of the organisation* in which they work." A set of real-life case studies of ethical dilemmas was subsequently added to the guidelines to demonstrate their practical application.[23]

A common concern (also mentioned in the Institute's Guidelines) is the potential impact of developments in electronic information provision. Many information professionals feel that traditional professional values are threatened in the networked environment, for example

- the shift from holdings to access undermines the preservation of the cultural record;
- the publication of information in electronic form introduces technical and/or financial barriers to access;
- the availability of sexually explicit materials on the Internet represents a conflict between intellectual freedom and social responsibility.

The values of information professionals can thus be summed up as the desire to promote and protect access to information for diverse client groups. Formal statements of organisational values for library and information services tend to include fundamental human values along-side core professional values, as shown by the statements collected by the Association of Research Libraries.[15]

Vision

Strategic visioning ability is now widely cited as the most important leadership skill sought in senior managers. Visioning has become a more common activity in all types of organisations, as an integral part of strategic planning and management, particularly associated with rapid and radical organisational change, and as a means of supplying a unifying coherence to decentralised flattened organisations. Visioning exercises and vision statements are seen as an effective way to capture information and ideas about the future and to convey to people the scope and scale of the transformation envisaged.

Visioning can bring significant **benefits**. Vision statements have particular value in providing:

- a direction and a *destination* – serving as a 'routemap' through uncharted territory and helping people to deal with uncertainty;
- focus and *integration* – acting as a 'capstone' document and over-arching articulation of the mission, values, goals and other elements of strategic planning;
- meaning and *inspiration* – promoting change as a positive and attractive phenomenon, empowering people and energising them to implement plans.

As with mission statements, while there is general agreement about the concept, there are differing views about the content and length of vision statements. Those who favour a comprehensive interpretation have in effect reinvented strategic planning as strategic visioning; they see vision as an over-arching concept, and thus include in the vision document full and detailed statements of organisational values, mission, goals and strategies. Others distinguish between these elements, and see them as complementary to the vision. James Collins takes a broad view and sees 'vision' comprising two major components, a deep element in the background – the 'guiding philosophy' of an organisation (incorporating both the fundamental purpose and the core values and beliefs) and a surface element in the foreground – its 'tangible image' (represented by its mission and a 'vivid description') which is directly related to its future environment. Collins uses 'mission' here in the narrow sense often equated with positioning or 'strategic intent' (see below) and he uses the term *vivid description* to denote what many other writers see as 'vision'

> "Vivid description . . . represents a vibrant, engaging, and specific description of what it will be like when the mission is achieved. It provokes emotion and generates excitement. It transforms the mission from words into pictures – it's a way of conveying the mission so that people carry around a clear, compelling image in their heads."

He sees passion, emotion and conviction as essential parts of it, which should help to generate the commitment needed to achieve high performance. Collins also advocates vision-setting at all levels of the organisation, arguing that middle management visioning initiatives often usefully encourage peers, subordinates and upper management to think about such things.[24]

The style and tone of the document is critical to its success in achieving these outcomes. Most commentators emphasise the need for visions to be both aspirational and inspirational, to present a dramatic description – a dramatised depiction – of the organisation successfully accomplishing its mission in the future, showing how people are behaving as well as what they are doing, in a manner that is impressive and attractive. There is also consensus about the notion of a vision embodying the tension between ambition and capability, and striking the right balance between idealism and realism, to avoid criticisms of leaders being out of touch with the realities of the marketplace or the values of their staff. Mark Lipton captures this challenge effectively,

> "A challenge in defining vision is to acknowledge adversity but to develop a perspective of success. . . Visions require a dose of idealism and the ability to imagine what an organization will be like when it has solved all its nagging problems.
> Although it must be challenging, a vision cannot be the equivalent of an unrealistic New Year's resolution – exciting, ambitious, and worthwhile at

the time, but not grounded in what is even remotely achievable. The problem with finding idealistic missions, strategies, and values broad enough to inspire is that they can be too idealistic and abstract. The process therefore requires managing the inherent paradox of creating a vision that is sufficiently idealistic yet realistic and tangible enough so that people can believe it is achievable in some respects."[25]

While still retaining connotations of a 'best', 'desirable' or 'ideal' future state, visions have shifted noticeably from 'soft' statements to harder, more *realistic* and *specific* descriptions, with *actionable* concepts or components. Ian Wilson defines visioning in these terms, "A coherent and powerful statement of what the business can and should be (ten) years hence … dramatically contrasting the company of the future with the present, strategic vision helps convey the totality of internal changes the organization must make and the reasons for them." Wilson identifies six key elements to be covered:

- *scope* – the range and mix of businesses for the organisation to pursue;
- *scale* – the desired future size of the organisation (e.g. steady-state/ growth)
- *focus* – the specific product lines, service programmes, market niches;
- *competition* – the basis of its competitive edge (e.g. technological leadership)
- *relationships* – its alliances, image and presentation (e.g. empowering employees)
- *organisation* – its culture, structure, management systems, etc.[26]

Gary Hamel and C K Prahalad have suggested five **criteria** for judging an effective vision statement, namely

- *foresight* – how imaginative and far-reaching is it?
- *breadth* – how extensive and wide-ranging are the changes anticipated?
- *uniqueness* – will it surprise your competitors?
- *consensus* – do you have a shared view of the future?
- *actionability* – have you considered the immediate steps and core competencies required?[27]

The qualities of a good vision share some similarities with other types of strategic statement. Additional characteristics include:

- *clarity* – relatively simple in its key messages, emphasising basic principles and driving forces, and painting a picture with words;
- *consistency* – within the organisation, consistency between the words and images of the vision and the actions and behaviours of decision-makers; and externally consistent with market and competitive conditions;

- *flexibility* – open to new signals of change, with managers alert to the need for frequent rethinking;
- *power* – communicating enthusiasm and excitement, with the force-fulness to infuse action throughout the organisation.

Information service visions

Irrespective of whether they produce formal vision statements, there is evidence of many more library and information services engaging in visioning exercises in recent years. In most cases, visioning is part of a larger strategic planning process and represents an effort to extend environmental scanning into the future. Library vision statements are typically one to two pages in length, but published examples range from a few paragraphs to several pages. For example, in the (American) Association of Research Libraries collection of excerpts from the strategic plans of ten members, seven contain vision statements, of which two are lengthy examples – of four and eight pages respectively.[15] Other libraries are using visioning exercises to plan shorter-term changes and for team-building at branch or department level.[28] There are also examples of generic vision statements for specific sectors. In the UK, the British Library-sponsored Libraries of the Future project set out to develop an achievable vision of libraries in education (schools and colleges) and in 1996 produced 'A glimpse of the future' as part of a staff development pack for librarians, teachers and others.[29] In summer 1997, the Standing Conference of National and University Libraries (SCONUL), which represents 135 library and information services in the UK and Ireland, initiated a collaborative exercise to articulate a vision of the networked information world, in order to stimulate thinking and assist corporate planning. The resulting statement presents a collective view of academic information services in universities, national libraries and museums, and of the primary roles of library staff in the year 2002.[30]

Corporate libraries have also been actively involved in visioning: Eugenie Prime, Manager of the Corporate Libraries at Hewlett-Packard Laboratories, sees visioning as a useful technique to make the necessary quantum leap – rather than an incremental step – towards the virtual information centre and the "ubiquitous portable desktop". She describes her experience of visioning thus,

> "Visioning, in a sense, is dreaming – it's imaging. It's taking a look into the future and seeing pictures. . . . It's like looking through a kaleidoscope. Each new concept changes the total world and you find yourself asking questions that you would never have asked before."

Prime emphasises the iterative nature of the visioning process, which allows the vision to keep changing as technology changes. She also points to the benefits of stakeholder involvement and exposure to new thinking, referring to her task force as

". . . an eclectic group of people. There were physicists, a linguist, engineers, a software specialist, several library staff members, and myself. Just the juxtaposition of these people, bringing their own different perspectives, their own vision of what they felt this organization should look like was very exciting."

But she stresses the need for leadership, the need for someone to have – and to believe in – the initial vision that is the springboard for collaborative thinking, and to sell it to others.[31]

While an extended vision enables a more vivid picture to be built up, a lot can be captured in a few sentences, as this example for an imaginary company library demonstrates.

"The leading researchers in the company count on us for authoritative and timely information. If they can't find what they want from the Intranet (via our 'research pathfinders') within a few minutes, they call us for help. They rely on us for information that is hard to track down or cannot be conveniently retrieved from one source. They appreciate the coaching we give them on available sources and search techniques, but they know we can save them time and money by expert sourcing and sifting. Our team members feel highly valued as a vital part of the organisation. When you ask people to name the business unit that adds most value to the research process – and to the organisation – the vast majority say "IRC – the Information Resource Centre"."

Process guidelines

A key question to consider is who should be involved in the visioning process, and at what stage. Participation of a broad range of stakeholders from the beginning is desirable, and this will make it more likely that the vision relates to the outside world and motivates people at all levels. In practice, it often proves difficult to involve all relevant stakeholder groups, and a suggested alternative is to identify the 'major players' and ask staff to impersonate them – to speculate and imagine what their concerns and desires would be. It is essential for the top team to be *deeply* involved and to lead the process; other key opinion formers must be *directly* involved, and 'diagonal slice' groups representing people from different areas, functions and levels will enable all staff in large organisations to be *selectively* involved.

Various different approaches to developing the vision can be adopted, notably the use of questions or checklists to stimulate thinking, and just asking people to describe (in writing or in conversation) what the organisation will be like in three, five, seven or ten years time. Peter Block offers the following prompt,

"... we are in a time capsule, visiting our unit three years from now, hovering above like a helicopter. Describe what we would see happening. How would we be working with customers and each other? What would meetings look like, what would be the nature of our projects, how would people be spending their time, what would the product or service look like as it came out the door?"[32]

Twenty-four hour residential workshops away from the day-to-day working environment can enable people to become more creative, and in large organisations a series of events (with some overlaps in participants for continuity) can be used to create the initial vision, and then work through subsequent iterations to test and refine it. In small organisations (where it can be difficult to involve everyone because of the logistical difficulties in maintaining service) an alternative is to organise 'drop-in' workshops where different members of staff can contribute to discussions at various times in smaller groups and record their contributions and comments on flip-charts. Drafts can also be circulated electronically for comment, but face-to-face interactions and discussions are generally seen as more effective for at least the initial stages of this type of exercise.

Vision statements come in various shapes and sizes to suit the purposes of their organisations – ranging from a few lines to several pages, embracing bullet-points, numbered paragraphs, unstructured narrative, or a mix of styles and formats including diagrams and pictures. Many commentators emphasise the need to allow the statement to find its own form. Some organisations have produced several versions of their vision; for example, the University of Surrey's Vision Statement exists in four different forms. There are versions of different lengths for use in different situations: the *full strategic version* of three A4 pages; the *summary version* of half a page; the *short version* of five lines; and the *strapline* of four words – *Understanding the real world*.[33] The vision was developed over a period of two years by a broad cross-section of staff led by the Vice-Chancellor, and the text publicised in a special issue of the University's Newsletter, *Surrey Matters*. In the introductory paragraphs, the vision is referred to as "the key reference point for the strategic decisions which will be taken throughout the University for many years to come". The document also indicates some of the different ways in which the Vision will be used:

- as a key part of the University's annual planning processes;
- making decisions about the allocation of resources;
- staff training and development courses;
- presentations to external audiences;
- communications with agencies, institutions, companies and other bodies;
- identifying and making links with potential collaborators.[34]

Pitfalls

Executive impatience, tunnel vision and a failure to trust intuition are common problems, especially where visioning is being attempted for the first time: people may feel discomfort with the apparent 'softness' of the exercise, they may also disparage the lack of analytical rigour, or just have difficulty in seeing things differently from 'the way they are'. A vision which is not sufficiently far-reaching will rapidly become obsolescent; similarly, a vision that is full of detail is likely to provoke disagreement and require early revision. Finally, it is worth noting that vision exercises can sometimes be hijacked by stakeholders' short-termism, represented by their pet problems or current concerns; in such situations, even though the issues may be outside the scope of the exercise, it is advisable to acknowledge and record them, so that the visioning process is not undermined by continuing dissent.

Tips

- Get depth and breadth from the interplay of different perspectives
- Base your description in the future, but write it in the present tense
- Test your near-final draft on a sample of people before going 'public'
- Accept that total consensus is unlikely – aim for incremental negotiation

Positioning

Many organisations find it useful to have a statement in the form of a memorable phrase or 'strapline' that can be used frequently to reinforce a message contained in their vision. A statement of this type often has some of the abstract, idealistic and qualitative attributes of a vision statement, but its brevity makes the content more accessible and memorable. Such a statement is sometimes simply referred to as a 'vision' (or a 'mission') but is more usually described as a *positioning statement* or a statement of *strategic intent*. It normally takes the form of a few words or a short phrase, and once adopted will generally appear on most of the organisation's publications, and usually also on letter-heads, compliments slips, etc. (Positioning is also a key concept in *marketing*, where it is most often applied at the service or product level, and is particularly concerned with the position of organisational offerings in relation to identified market segments. This involves considering where to place a product or service in terms of dimensions such as grade/level and price/value.)

A **positioning statement** of this strategic type can provide the organisation and its staff with a shared sense of opportunity, pride and significance, but a key point here is that the statement must be supported by a mission, vision and goals, which provide the context and confidence for aspiration and achievement. Positioning statements vary significantly in the extent to which they convey any sense of ambition; many seem more intent on capturing the essence of the organisation in terms of its purpose or 'standing objectives', rather than its thrusts or 'change objectives'. James Collins (who uses the term 'mission' here) describes this latter concept as follows,

> "a clear and compelling goal that serves to unify an organization's efforts. [It] must stretch and challenge the organization, yet be achievable. It translates the abstractness of the philosophy into a tangible, energizing, *highly focused goal* that draws the organization forward. [It] has a finish line and a specific time frame for its achievement."[24]

Several commentators cite the NASA moon mission, as articulated by President Kennedy in 1961, as a good example of this concept,

> "Achieving the goal, before this decade is out, of landing a man on the moon and returning him safely to earth."

Collins distinguishes four basic approaches to such statements:

- *targeting* – which can include non-quantitative targets (for example, to become the dominant player in a market, or to reach a pre-eminent position in an industry)
- *competitive* – which are also referred to as *common enemy* missions (exemplified by explicit intentions to surpass or eclipse particular rivals)
- *emulative* – which are also referred to as *role model* missions (explicit intentions to match the performance of a particular firm)
- *internal transformation* – which focus on internal changes needed to remain healthy or to regain a competitive position.

Statements of the first three types described above are most often associated with large organisations which aspire to a leading position in their field. A notable example in the library world is the British Library, which formulated such a statement a few years ago, and actually described it as a positioning statement,

> "The world's leading resource for scholarship, research and innovation"

This phrase now appears on the vast majority of British Library literature, and also then provided the title for the published version of its strategic objectives, *For scholarship research and innovation*. Information and library services generally seem to have been slow to publicise their strategic intentions or summary visions in this form, but some examples have begun to emerge in recent years:

> "At the forefront of information service development"
> (Aston University Library & Information Services)

"Organising, preserving and communicating knowledge of the natural world"
(The Natural History Museum, Department of Library & Information Services)

Priorities

The mission and objectives define the service's broad areas of activities and general approach, but these in turn need to be supplemented with more specific statements indicating what it wants to achieve in the medium-term future and how it intends to achieve it. As already noted, the literature of planning is characterised by inconsistency and confusion in its use of a proliferation of terms to describe how organisations should set about accomplishing their missions, with 'aims', 'objectives', 'goals', 'strategies' and 'targets' used almost interchangeably to denote various levels in a hierarchy of statements about the directions in which an organisation intends to go and the methods by which it will get there. The terminology adopted here uses the term **goals** for the medium-term objectives that represent the developments, initiatives or improvements required to move the organisation forward. These goals can also be described as *strategic* objectives or statements of *direction*, which reflect *movement*. They help to chart the major paths to accomplish the mission and achieve the desired future state – answering the question *where are we going?* – and will normally be expressed in action-oriented terms, capable of conversion into precise targets. Such goals form the heart of a strategic plan and need to be carefully defined to ensure a coherent framework for the formulation of strategies, action plans and performance indicators.

Peter Drucker argues that objectives of this type are needed in every area where performance and results directly affect the survival and prosperity of the business, and specifies eight areas applicable to all businesses (though not necessarily to all information services) –

- marketing
- innovation
- human organisation
- financial resources
- physical resources
- productivity
- social responsibility
- profit requirements.[35]

Work done in analysing the environment will inform this process, in particular the results of SWOT exercises, which should have identified gaps between the current situation and the desired future. For larger units, before starting to set a long list of specific goals, it is best to prioritise in more general terms and to determine the *strategic thrusts* or *major directions* in which the service must move to make the vision become a reality. There are various ways of approaching this, with a confusing range of terminology used in the literature. The different methodologies are all basically concerned with identifying **priorities** for management attention – the things people must get right if the organisation is to succeed. The most widely used terms are Critical Success Factors and Key Result Areas. Alternative terms, used almost interchangeably, include *strategic success factors, strategic factors, success factors, key success factors* and *key performance areas*.

Critical success factors

Critical success factor (CSF) research – the study of factors of particular importance to the success of individuals, departments, organisations, business units, corporate enterprises, industry sectors, even whole economies – has evolved from a concept developed in the 1960s and 1970s in the specific context of **management information systems** to an area of inter-disciplinary interest and broader conceptual relevance to management and planning in different arenas. CSFs have gained prominence recently in the context of total quality management (TQM). Ronald Daniel, who is generally credited with introducing the concept, argued that senior managers required management information systems tailored to their particular needs, with a focus on the **success factors** of their industry, suggesting that, "In most industries there are usually three to six factors that determine success; these key jobs must be done exceedingly well for a company to be successful".[36] These areas then become the focus for *performance monitoring*.

John Rockart, introduced the term **critical success factors** in an article generally regarded as the first systematic presentation of the CSF approach, again in relation to the information needs of top management. In this article he defined CSFs thus,

> "Critical success factors thus are, for any business, the limited number of areas in which results, if they are satisfactory, will ensure successful competitive performance for the organization. They are the few key areas where 'things must go right' for the business to flourish. If results in these areas are not adequate, the organization's efforts for the period will be less than desired.
>
> As a result, the critical success factors are areas of activity that should receive constant and careful attention from management. The current status of performance in each area should be continually measured, and that information should be made available."[37]

CSFs can be considered and investigated at various levels, but the most

common approach is based on an aggregation of management perspectives, usually reached through structured discussions, including brainstorming. As CSFs are by definition small in number and high level,
they are often expressed in rather abstract terms. They then need to be
translated into some form of performance indicator to enable systematic
monitoring and measurement; but the indicators may combine 'hard'
(quantitative) and 'soft' (qualitative) data. Manageability, clarity and
credibility are more important than comprehensiveness and methodological rigour, as the aim is to produce managerially useful information.
In his classic text on TQM, John Oakland defines CSFs as "the most
important subgoals of a business or organization ... what must be
accomplished for the mission to be achieved" (identification of which
should be followed by then identifying the key, critical or business processes of the organisation – representing the activities that must be done
particularly well for the CSFs to be achieved). Later he refers to development of the mission into its CSFs "to coerce and move it forward" arguing that failure to translate the mission through its CSFs into the critical
processes results in "goals without methods".[38]

In this context CSFs are defined as a list of distinct and specific issues
which taken together are *necessary* and *sufficient* to accomplish the mission. The recommended technique involves brainstorming a long list of
issues – often as many as 30-50 diverse items – and then grouping and
combining these into a shorter list. The aim is to end up with no more
than eight in total – Oakland suggests no more than four if the mission
is survival. CSFs are normally expressed in the form, 'We must have . . .'
or 'We need . . .'. They can include both strategic and tactical issues –
and indeed usually do contain a mix of both – but each CSF must
identify a specific concept or factor. The use of 'and' is not permitted in
the statement itself, although it can be included in a phrase or sentence
to elaborate the main statement.

Oakland offers the following **examples** of typical CSF statements,

- We must have right-first-time suppliers.
- We must have motivated, skilled people.
- We need new products that satisfy market needs.
- We need new business opportunities.
- We must have best-in-the-field product quality.[38]

This exercise can then be followed through by scoring the CSFs in a
matrix against the organisation's main *processes* to find those which
have both a primary impact on the mission and perceived need for
improvement – the *most critical processes*. A **process** in the organis-
ational/business context can be defined simply as the transformation of
inputs into outputs to meet customer needs. The inputs can include materials, procedures, equipment, people, information, etc, and outputs can

be in the form of a finished product or service (e.g. a publication or seminar) or an intermediate output (e.g. a catalogue record or a search result as an intermediate stage in answering an enquiry). A process should be formally expressed in the form of verb+object (e.g. catalogue information items) though it is often shortened for day-to-day use (e.g. cataloguing). Most organisations will have sets of smaller processes that can be grouped into larger processes, which comprise the organisation's *key, critical* or *business* processes, but each process at each level needs a formal owner.

Key result areas

The term key result area (KRA) is less well defined in the literature, but more commonly used in the published plans of library and information services. It can be used in a similar way to CSFs to mean those aspects of a unit or organisation that must function effectively for the entire unit or organisation to succeed, which are usually identified as areas involving major organisational activities or groups of related activities that occur throughout the organisation or unit. Identification of these **key performance areas** – an alternative term often used in this context – can then be followed by definition of the control systems (and standards) needed, including decisions about what needs to be controlled and how often progress needs to be measured. KRAs can also be interpreted more generally as areas where *success* is essential, *improvement* is necessary or concerted effort will bring most *benefit* – in other words, areas which represent *strategic priorities.*

A recommended method of identifying KRAs (which is similar to, but simpler than, the formal CSF methodology) is to involve staff in small groups, each taking part of the SWOT data – and vision of the future, if developed – and then combining and refining the results to produce a set of five to ten major direction statements.

Suggested steps for formulating KRAs

1. Small groups identify gaps between the current situation and desired future state.
2. They discuss what is needed to close the gaps, by articulating statements in the form 'In order to. . . , the service/unit needs to become more (or less) . . .'
3. The groups come together to cumulate their results, and clarify the statements to eliminate any overlaps, before proceeding to rate and rank the statements.
4. For each issue, people first assess how important it is to make the change (on a five-point scale, where 5 is most important).

5. For each issue, they then assess how practical it is to make the change (again on a five-point scale, where 5 is most practicable).
6. Finally, they multiply the two scores together to provide a ranked list of strategic priorities or Key Result Areas.

Information service priorities

Research studies have investigated CSFs common to particular industries or functional areas, but there is relatively little published work on CSFs for library and information services. A relatively smallscale study conducted in 1991 of Australian library and information unit (LIU) managers produced a ranked list of 43 result areas. The responses covered both public and private sectors, and while the majority came from special libraries with a small number of staff, the ranking is interesting as an indication of information professionals' perceptions of importance. The top ten items were:

1. Competence and qualifications of LIU staff
2. Availability and accessibility of LIU staff
3. Image of LIU and its staff within the organisation
4. Top management support
5. A clear role and purpose for the LIU
6. Quality of information services and products (reliability, currency, etc)
7. Quality of LIU staff assistance and support to users
8. Timely delivery of LIU products and services
9. People and service orientation of LIU staff
10. Responsiveness of LIU staff to user requests[39]

Research in other sectors suggests that there are some *generic* factors relevant to any company in a particular industry, but that CSFs are also dictated by issues such as geographical location, competitive strategy, environmental changes and internal organisational considerations – so that similar organisations (for example, information services) will have differing CSFs, especially at particular periods. Rockart also points out that CSFs can be useful at each management level, not just at the top of an organisation, and he specifically advocates their use in the planning process – either as an informal planning aid, or as a part of the formal planning process.

As part of an institutional TQM initiative at Aston University, the Library & Information Services formulated a list of CSFs for the service as a whole, which echo several of the priority areas identified in the Australian study.[40]

Aston University Library & Information Services

Critical Success Factors

We must have:

- **a strategic framework** – an articulated strategy, represented by a shared vision and mission, agreed strategic and operational plans and priorities;
- **staff of the right calibre** – at all levels, trained and developed through continuing programmes, to enable them to achieve their full potential;
- **focus on the customer** – an open and inviting physical environment, with quick flexible responses and services targeted to meet the needs of all user groups;
- **a supportive culture** – encouraging innovation and ownership, allowing devolved responsibility, identified as an 'achievement/people(support)' model;
- **effective communication** – internally and externally, at all levels;
- **a robust IT infrastructure** – with adequate technical support;
- **a secure resource base** – to match customer demands;
- **comprehensive management information systems.**

The strategic plan for the **Purdue University Libraries**, entitled *A shared commitment to excellence: a plan for the future,* lists "five **key strategic directions** . . . expressed in the form of results" all of which are described as "critical to the fulfilment of the Libraries mission":

- user access increased
- collection quality enhanced
- library instruction redefined
- information delivery expanded
- internal resources optimised

Each key direction is then elaborated in a single sentence, supported by a rationale, with specific strategies, programmes and actions, and a table of implementation milestones.[41]

Goals

Having determined the major directions, the next stage is to define goals under the broad headings identified. The number of goals set will depend on several factors, including the timespan of the plan, the scale and scope of the service, and the degree of specificity of the goals themselves. However, the focus at this level should be on major goals, typically for the information service as a whole, aiming to set around four to six for each broad area. In keeping with the general criteria for objectives set out above, these are the main characteristics or criteria for **well-formed goals:**

- compatible with the vision and mission;

- clear, concise and unambiguous in wording;
- realistic and attainable within the lifespan of the plan;
- stated as desired ends, rather than activities leading to ends;
- acceptable to those likely to be involved in their achievement;
- capable of translation into precise (quantifiable, measurable) targets.

The **goal-translation process** is the key to successful strategy implementation: each goal in due course needs to be converted from a general statement of what you want to achieve to a more specific description of how it will be done, and this what→how translation needs to take place right down the hierarchy of people and processes. Communication is a crucial part of this process, and the guiding principles of *simplify* and *shorten* must be applied to all objective-setting activities. Care taken in the initial formulation and later refinement of goal statements will be rewarded further down the line.

Strategies

The goals specify the key directions for the service over the planning period, but they cannot be finally confirmed until strategies have been developed, and the tasks and resources required taken into account. The formulation of strategies involves evaluation of the options open to the service to achieve its goals and selection of the preferred courses of action; this requires more detailed consideration of the targets or *results* wanted and the activities or *tasks* involved, often referred to as *tactical* and *operational* objectives. Strategies specify the action steps along the path to accomplish the mission – answering the questions *what do we want to achieve?* and *how will we do it?* – and they should also cover timescales, responsibilities and performance measures. Dealing with strategy, and following it through to action, forms the next major consideration of the planning process.

Summary checklist

Do you have a strategic profile?

Mission
Do you have a stated purpose that is meaningful to stakeholders?
Does it define your business domain and customer base?

Vision
Do you have an imaginative and inspiring statement about your desired future?
Is it viewed as attractive and actionable by your key stakeholders?

Values
Do you have a statement identifying values that link with your purpose?
Do the values resonate with and reinforce your strategic thrusts?

Positioning
Do you have a statement that captures succinctly your preferred strategic positioning?
Is this statement known, owned and used frequently by you and your colleagues?

Goals
Have you set strategic objectives in the areas that really matter?
Are the objectives expressed in a way that enables success to be measured?

Character
Do your statements provide a portrait that captures your organisational culture?
Are the statements easy to find, read and understand?

References

1. Steiner, G. A. *Strategic planning: what every manager* must *know*. New York; London: Free Press, 1997 (pp. 149, 163)
2. Drucker, P. *Management: an abridged and revised version of Management: tasks, responsibilities, practices*. Oxford: Butterworth-Heinemann, 1974 (1988) (pp. 68–85)
3. Campbell, A., Devine, M. and Young, D. *A sense of mission*. London: Pitman Publishing, 1990 (1993)
4. Stoner, J. A. F., Freeman, R. E., and Gilbert, D. R. *Management*. 6th ed. Englewood Cliffs, NJ: Prentice-Hall International, 1995 (pp. 265–66)
5. Peeke, G. *Mission and change: institutional mission and its application to the management of further and higher education*. Buckingham: The Society for Research into Higher Education & Open University Press, 1994 (p. 42)
6. van der Voort, S. Are you into analysis? *Online*, 22 (1) 1998, pp. 58–60
7. Nichols, M. T., Sikes, J., Isselmann, M. M. and Ayers, R. S. Survival in transition or implementing information science core competencies. *Bulletin of the American Society for Information Science*, 22 (2) 1996, pp. 11–15
8. Sonntag, G. Our raison d'etre: teaching information competencies. *College & Research Libraries News*, 58 (11) 1997, pp. 770–71

9. Library Association. Colleges of Further and Higher Education Group. *Guidelines for college libraries: recommendations for performance and resourcing.* 5th ed. London: Library Association Publishing, 1995 (p. xi)

10. Penniman, W. D. Strategic positioning of information services in a competitive environment. *Bulletin of the American Society for Information Science,* **23** (4) 1997, pp. 11–14

11. Willard, N. Information resources management. *Aslib Information,* **21** (5) 1993, pp. 201–205

12. *UNISIST Newsletter,* 23 (1) 1995, pp. 8–10

13. Library and Information Services Council. Working Group on Public Library Objectives. *Setting objectives for public library services: a manual of public library objectives.* London: HMSO, 1991 (Library Information Series No 19)

14. Himmel, E. and Wilson, W. J. *Planning for results: a public library transformation process: the guidebook.* Chicago; London: American Library Association, 1998

15. Association of Research Libraries. Office of Management Services. Systems and Procedures Exchange Center. *Strategic planning in ARL libraries.* Washington, DC: ARL, 1995 (SPEC Kit 210)

16. For example, *see* http://bubl.ac.uk/docs/missions/ which provides links to mission statements from various types of information services.

17. Dearlove, D. and Coomber, S. J. *Heart and soul: a study of the impact of corporate and individual values on business.* Skillman, NJ; Maidenhead, Berks: Blessing/White, 1999. Available online at: http://www.blessingwhite.com/values.html

18. Goyder, M. *Living tomorrow's company.* Aldershot: Gower, 1998 (p. 48)

19. Ethical auditing: uncovering the shadow side of organisations. *RSA Journal,* **CXLV** (5481) 1997, pp. 24–28

20. Lee, S. Organizational change in the Harvard College Library: a continued struggle for redefinition and renewal. *Journal of Academic Librarianship,* **19** (4) 1993, pp. 225–30

21. *Excerpts from* University Libraries, The University at Albany, Strategic Plan 1990–1995. In: Association of Research Libraries. Office of Management Services. Systems and Procedures Exchange Center. *Strategic planning in ARL libraries.* Washington, DC: ARL, 1995 (SPEC Kit 210) (p. 175)

22. Anderson, G. MIT – the Distributed Library Initiative: collaboration, vision, prototyping. In: Helal, A. H. and Weiss, J. W., eds. *Information superhighway: the role of librarians, information scientists, and intermediaries: 17th International Essen Symposium, 24*

October – 27 October 1994. Essen: Universitatsbibliothek Essen, 1995, pp. 61–89

23. Draft IIS guidelines for professional ethics for information professionals. *Inform*, (201) 1998, pp. 4–5. See also http://www.iis.org.uk/ethics/

24. Collins, J. C. and Porras, J. I. Organizational vision and visionary organizations. *California Management Review*, Fall 1991, pp. 30–52

25. Lipton, M. Demystifying the development of an organizational vision. *Sloan Management Review*, 37 (4) 1996, pp. 83–92

26. Wilson, I. Realizing the power of strategic vision. *Long Range Planning*, 25 (5) 1992, pp. 18–28

27. Hamel, G. and Prahalad, C. K. *Competing for the future*. Boston, MA: Harvard Business School Press, 1994 (p. 122)

28. Hewison, N. S. Achieving change in libraries: vision at the department, branch, and team levels. *Library Administration & Management*, 9 (3) 1995, pp. 153–158

29. *Libraries of the future: a staff development pack*. Coventry: National Council for Educational Technology, 1996

30. *The SCONUL Vision: the academic library in the year 2002* / prepared by . . . a task force convened by SCONUL's Advisory Committee on Information Systems and Services. London: Standing Conference of National and University Libraries, 1998 (SCONUL Briefing Paper) Available at: http://www.sconul.ac.uk/vision.htm

31. Jajko, P. Visualizing the virtual library: an interview with Eugenie Prime, June 1991. *Medical References Services Quarterly*, 13 (1) 1994, pp. 97–109

32. Block, P. *The empowered manager: positive political skills at work*. San Francisco, Ca: Jossey-Bass, 1986 (1990)

33. Available at: http://www.surrey.ac.uk/Corporate/vision.html

34. *Surrey Matters*, 2 (56) 27 May 1998

35. Drucker, P. F. *Management: an abridged and revised version of Management: tasks, responsibilities and practices*. Oxford: Butterworth-Heinemann, 1974 (1988). Note that his list of eight areas varies slightly in his different books.

36. Daniel, R. D. Management information crisis. *Harvard Business Review*, 39 (5) 1961, pp. 111–121 (p. 116)

37. Rockart, J. F. Chief executives define their own data needs. *Harvard Business Review*, 57 (2) 1979, pp. 81–93 (p. 85)

38. Oakland, J. S. *Total quality management: the route to improving performance*. 2nd ed. Oxford: Butterworth-Heinemann, 1993. (pp. 33, 414–416)

39. Broadbent, M. and Lofgren, H. *Priorities, performance and benefits: an exploratory study of library and information units*. Melbourne:

Centre for International Research on Communication and Information Technologies & Australian Council of Libraries and Information Services, 1991
40. Corrall, S. M. The access model: managing the transformation at Aston University. *Interlending and Document Supply*, **21** (4) 1993, pp. 13–23
41. Purdue University. A shared commitment to excellence: a plan for the future. In: Association of Research Libraries. Office of Management Services. Systems and Procedures Exchange Center. *Strategic planning in ARL libraries*. Washington, DC: ARL, 1995 (SPEC Kit 210) pp149–161

Further reading

Raynor, M. E. That vision thing: do we need it? *Long Range Planning*, **31** (3) 1998, pp. 368–376
Discusses confusion in the use of the terms 'vision' and 'mission' with reference to published definitions and statements. Presents a conceptual framework to improve understanding of the different concepts and their relationships, and redefines mission and vision in relation to other terms (values, core competencies, strategy and goals).

Mission

David, F. R. How companies define their mission. *Long Range Planning*, **22** (1) 1989, pp. 90–97
Reviews published literature and survey findings on the contents and functions of mission statements, noting that service firms had shorter and less comprehensive statements than manufacturing firms. Concludes by advocating list of nine basic components as a practical framework for evaluating and writing mission statements.

Campbell, A., Devine, M. and Young, D. *A sense of mission*. London: Pitman Publishing, 1990 (1993)
Defines the concepts of mission and 'sense of mission' and examines the use and misuse of mission statements, drawing on published literature, documentary evidence and case studies. Provides ten questions to test effectiveness of mission statements, and concludes with advice on mission planning and mission thinking for leaders and others.

Hooley, G. J., Cox, A. J. and Adams, A. "Our five year mission – to boldly go where no man has been before. . .." **Journal of Marketing**

Management, 1992, 8, pp. 35–48
*Reviews literature on missions and presents the findings of research
on the content, creation, use and impact of statements in both public
and private sector organisations, drawing attention to a significant
shift in focus away from the long-term strategic intent (or vision) to
the medium/short-term "operationalization of achieving longer term
strategic intent".*

Information service missions

Wilson, P. Mission and information: what business are we in? *Journal
of Academic Librarianship*, 1988, **14**(2), pp. 82–86
*Considers the fundamental question of the business of a university
library, arguing that "the information business" is too broad and
empty a definition, concluding that the most important function of
an academic library is "to facilitate the acquisition and production
of knowledge".*

Brophy, P. The mission of the academic library. *British Journal of Academic Librarianship*, 1991, **6** (3), pp. 135–147
*Explores the concept of mission with reference to both business and
library literature, and reports on study of UK academic libraries;
notes that statements focus on what business we are in (purpose)
and/or how we do things (values), with overall similarity of content
but different emphases (e.g. building collections, providing access,
information skills).*

Values

Forsman, R. Incorporating organizational values into the strategic planning process. *Journal of Academic Librarianship*, **16** (3) 1990, pp.
150–153
*Offers six ideas for drawing values into strategic (and day-to-day)
management, including use of an assessment instrument in the planning process and alerting new employees to the relevance of values
and philosophy to daily decisions, as well as using organisational
values as a 'benchmark' of desired attitudes and beliefs for recruitment.*

Mason, R. O., Mason, F. M. and Culnan, M. J. *Ethics of information
management.* Thousand Oaks, Ca; London: Sage Publications,
1995
*Interprets information management broadly to include accountants,
consultants and journalists, as well as archivists, librarians, software*

engineers, etc. Discusses the unique characteristics of information and the ethical challenges for individuals and organisations in the context of technological and social change. Concludes with six sample codes of ethics.

Symons, A. K. and Stoffle, C. J. When values conflict. *American Libraries*, 29 (5) 1998, pp. 56–58
Asserts that librarianship's core values and how they are implemented are what distinguishes it from other information professions. Identifies nine core values and gives examples of dilemmas arising from conflicting values at both national and local levels, noting further challenges presented by the Internet. Argues the need for an agreed hierarchy of values to guide us in our choices.

Vision

Block, P. *The empowered manager: positive political skills at work.* San Francisco: Jossey-Bass, 1986 (1990)
Concerned particularly with the empowerment of middle managers, through the development of their political skills and creation of an entrepreneurial spirit as an antidote to bureaucracy. Contains two substantial chapters on 'Creating a vision of greatness' (30pp) and 'Building support for your vision' (21pp) and provides practical advice and examples.

Wilson, I. Realizing the power of strategic vision. *Long Range Planning*, 25 (5) 1992, pp. 18–28
Defines the concept of strategic vision, identifies six interlocking elements, and provides guidelines for a visioning process based on eight key steps. Discusses the pros and cons of individual versus collective approaches (preferring the latter) and the benefits of involving informed outsiders. Concludes with five characteristics of successful visions and seven pitfalls to avoid along the way.

Stewart, J. M. Future state visioning – a powerful leadership process. *Long Range Planning*, 26 (6) 1993, pp. 89–98
Presents Future State Visioning as a comprehensive framework or set of processes that can be used for a range of purposes, such as developing a business or team vision, as well as planning the future of particular organisation functions or solving specific problems. Distinctive features include the focus on the future environment, expression of actionable concepts, involvement of stakeholders, broad and early participation, and explicit integration of organis-

ational and personal values (broken down into beliefs, philosophy and principles).

Finlay, J. S. The strategic visioning process. *Public Administration Quarterly,* **18** (1) 1994, pp. 64–74
Provides a step-by-step account of the visioning process advocated by Peter Senge, covering guided imaging, brainstorming, affinity diagrams, cause-and-effect (fishbone) diagrams and interrelationship diagraphs, concluding with the relationship between the organisational vision and statements of mission, and of principles and values.

Lipton, M. Demystifying the development of an organizational vision. *Sloan Management Review,* **37** (4) 1996, pp. 83–92
Discusses the benefits and functions of vision statements, and defines them in relation to mission, strategy and culture. Explains reasons for failure, and offers advice on managing participation, and creating a vision that is sufficiently idealistic yet realistic. (Illustrates points with references to published literature and many practical examples.)

Information service visions

Jajko, P. Visualizing the virtual library: an interview with Eugenie Prime, June 1991. *Medical References Services Quarterly,* **13** (1) 1994, pp. 97–109
The Manager of the Corporate Libraries at Hewlett-Packard Laboratories explains the paradigm shift required to visualise the library of the future, with reference to experience at HP. Discusses the difficulty of proving the value of information in the corporate environment, suggests managing change via pilot projects, and recommends a broadly top-down approach (while emphasising the need to sell the vision to others).

Hewison, N. S. Achieving change in libraries: vision at the department, branch, and team levels. *Library Administration & Management,* **9** (3) 1995, pp. 153–158
Advocates a participative 'upstream' approach to creating vision statements, with reference to experience at Purdue University Libraries of using visioning techniques both for strategic planning and for planning shorter-term changes. Describes the 'focused conversation' technique of using predetermined questions to guide discussion and comments on the skills and attitudes needed by facilitators.

Messenger, M. Visions in the air. *Public Library Journal*, **12** (5) 1997, pp. 97–99
Explains the background to the vision statement produced by a working group of the Advisory Council on Libraries for the Secretary of State in 1996, and reproduces the full text of the statement, in three main sections – Why have a public library service? What should be provided to fulfil these aims? and How is all this to be provided?

Positioning

Hamel, G. and Prahalad, C. K. Strategic intent. *Harvard Business Review*, 1989, 67(3), pp. 63–76
Argues that the hallmark of Japanese strategic management is the 'leveraging' of resources to reach seemingly unattainable goals – rather than fitting/trimming ambitions to match current capabilities – and being clear about the ends, but flexible about the means of achieving them.

Critical success factors

Hardaker, M. and Ward, B. K. How to make a team work. *Harvard Business Review*, 1987, 65(6), pp. 112–117
Covers the development of mission statements and identification of Critical Success Factors (CSFs) – details criteria for CSFs, and then outlines method to identify most critical business processes, decide nature of improvement needed and establish relevant measurements.

Chapter 4

Strategy formation

The vision, mission, objectives and goals are the foundation for the service's development over the period covered by the plan, but the formulation and implementation of strategies and action plans are equally crucial to the service's progress and success. **Strategies** in this context can be defined as major actions or patterns of actions for achieving goals and objectives (and accomplishing the mission). A key point to note here is that there is likely to be more than one way of achieving each goal, so strategy formulation involves identifying *options* and making *choices* before reaching decisions on the action steps required. Among other considerations, strategies need to be assessed in terms of the knock-on effects for other areas and the risks involved; supporting strategies (for example, relating to staff training) and contingency plans follow on from this. Involving a wide range of staff in this process helps to ensure that different paths are explored and improves the chance of finding creative solutions to problems. Individual thinking and group brainstorming sessions can usefully be combined to generate imaginative proposals for scrutiny by the planning team and senior managers.

Generic strategies

The strategy 'gurus' offer a selection of tools and models to help people think about alternative strategies. They are mainly concerned with securing competitive advantage in the business world and therefore most relevant to information professionals offering priced services in a commercial environment. However, the trend towards internal charging, service contracts and similar arrangements means that more non-profit services now find themselves operating in a competitive internal market, and some are also choosing or being encouraged to explore opportunities for income generation with external customers. The literature of strategic management identifies several 'generic' strategies applicable to various business situations which together represent the *key business issues* and can be used to stimulate thinking about the general approach to adopt.

Among the best known are Michael Porter's three generic strategies for 'sustainable competitive advantage' – *cost leadership, differentiation* and *focus* (the application of either cost leadership or differentiation to a *niche* or narrow segment of the market).[1] Another classic theoretical model of strategic choice is Igor Ansoff's portfolio strategy matrix, which suggests four generic strategies based on options related to products/services and missions/markets.[2]

Figure 4.1 Portfolio strategy matrix showing generic strategy options

Products Markets	*Present*	*New*
Present	**Market** **penetration**	**Product** **development**
New	**Market** **development**	Diversification

The four product-market strategies indicated above represent different ways of developing the business. These and other strategies outlined below can be pursued in respect of the whole organisation or specific services, individually or collectively; joint ventures or *strategic alliances* with other service providers represent an alternative method of achieving development or growth while minimising the risk involved in doing new things.

Development

- *Market penetration* involves improving the take-up of products or services within existing markets, referred to as increasing *market share* (e.g. increasing the number of active borrowers in a library population or the number of loans per borrower)
- *Product development* involves introducing new or modified products or services to existing customers (e.g. extending enquiry services to include in-depth research services, producing publications or organising exhibitions based on library collections)
- *Market development* involves finding new customers or outlets for existing services (e.g. a university library offering services to local businesses or the general public, such as fee-based borrowing facilities)
- *Diversification* involves both new products and new markets, and can take several forms, which are elaborated in a separate section below.

Segmentation

Market penetration and product/market development may be pursued by considering the demand for products and services in relation to particular market segments.

- *Unsegmented* strategies – the 'one size fits all' approach – assume that the same product/service will suit everyone, and are often the most practicable approach for high-volume basic services (e.g. library photocopying services)
- *Segmentation* strategies involve dividing the market into segments or groups of segments and developing offerings for them (e.g. libraries providing special services for ethnic groups and people with disabilities)
- *Niche* strategies involve concentrating on a narrow market segment and designing a product or service to meet its needs (e.g. an information service for local councillors)
- *Customisation* involves designing products and services to meet individual needs:
  — *pure customisation* is usually very labour-intensive and associated with highly-priced bespoke products or consultancy (e.g. specialist research services)
  — *tailored customisation* involves modifying a basic existing product or service to meet individual needs on demand (e.g. information skills training)
  — *standardised customisation* involves offering individuals a choice of features or packages from a predetermined range (e.g. company search services)

Differentiation

Market penetration and product/market development may also be pursued by differentiating the supply of products or services in several specific ways.

- *Cost/price leadership* involves reducing unit costs to become *the* low-cost producer and/or charging less than competing services (e.g. library photocopying services often have institutional and commercial competitors)
- *Quality/design differentiation* involves building in unique or special features to the service itself to enhance or change performance (e.g. installing a new automated system to improve the speed or scope of a document supply service)
- *Support differentiation* involves adding value through peripheral aspects – such as delivery arrangements or help desks – to enhance the total service package (e.g. providing a telephone hot-line for users of unstaffed study/computing facilities)
- *Image differentiation* involves presenting the service or product in a manner that sets it apart from the competition, without necessarily

changing its basic performance (e.g. relaunching a journal contents bulletin as a 'personal information service').

Diversification/integration

Business diversification through extending both the service portfolio and the customer base can be sub-divided into four categories:

- *Horizontal integration* involves expanding sideways by establishing, acquiring or forming a joint-venture relationship with a similar business with related technology (e.g. a university library taking over a former college library through the merger of their respective institutions)
- *Vertical integration* involves expanding *'upstream'* by taking over a supplier or setting up a supplier function (e.g. a library acquiring a bindery, or setting up as a 'library supplier' acquiring books direct from publishers) – or *'downstream'* by taking over a distributor or end-user function (e.g. a library operating a transport service to facilitate transfer of goods or people between service points)
- *Concentric diversification* involves taking over or setting up a business of a related type with strong connections to one or other of its features (e.g. a library setting up a publishing company, such as a university press)
- *Conglomerate diversification* involves expanding into a completely new product-market situation, usually by acquisition or joint venture (e.g. a university library with a cafe or restaurant open to the general public).

Divestment/exit

The need to reduce costs or reallocate resources to service development may force consideration of dropping non-core or low-priority services. Divestment strategies include *selling off* non-core businesses units (e.g. a library bindery), *closing down* unprofitable services (e.g. a priced research service) and *withdrawing* from a particular site (e.g. closing a branch library).

Rebirth/reconception

The extent of development or contraction needed may be so significant that business redefinition and reconfiguration is necessary. Reconception strategies often involve service *recombination,* organisational *restructuring* and/or physical *relocation* (e.g. the merger of a library and computing service, the shift from decentralised to centralised information service provision).

No change/consolidation

At the other extreme, the final option is to maintain the *status quo,* concentrating on serving existing customers with established offerings, and limiting changes to small incremental improvements. Consolidation can be a sensible strategy to adopt following a period of intensive development – but it is better to state this as a positive decision, rather than leaving people to deduce it.

Options and choices

The generic strategies outlined above can be used as a framework for thinking about the way forward for services in terms of product or market development, market segmentation, product and service differentiation, business diversification or divestment and other forms of reorganisation, within the overall context of the organisation's vision, mission and objectives. Practical examples of service developments by other libraries and information services can be another useful source of inspiration, though managers must ensure that strategies are developed with the local situation firmly in mind and they cannot assume that what has worked successfully in one organisation will transfer to others – some adaptation may well be needed. However, it makes sense to keep in touch with developments elsewhere, particularly as a guide to general trends and as a means of learning about the benefits and drawbacks of different approaches.

At a general level, two common options considered by libraries and information services in the context of a strategic review are *charging* for services and *outsourcing* of operations. At a more specific level, many managers are rethinking their reference/enquiry services, researching different sources of document supply, and developing offerings for particular user groups – as well as reconsidering the balance between stock held locally and sources accessed remotely, between print and electronic resources, and between mediated and self-service provision.[3,4,5,6,7] Charging and outsourcing are explored in more detail below; other service options are covered in the suggestions for further reading appended. This section also introduces two analytical tools that can be used to narrow the range of options under consideration and assist decision-making on the final choice for strategy development.

Charging – fee or free?

The 'fee or free' debate has been characterised by significant resistance over a long period, but the 1980s represented a turning point in the UK. In 1983, the ITAP report promoted the notion of information as a *tradeable commodity*[8] and then the 'PUPLIS' report suggested public-private sector *joint ventures* in publishing and information services.[9] This was closely followed by the Library Association's *Guidelines* on charging for services[10] and the government's Green Paper on *Financing our public library services.*[11] The Association's guidelines endorsed the view that it is simply not practicable for library and information services to be provided by the public sector free of charge to meet every conceivable demand and suggested a four-fold classification of services to inform charging policies,

> "The task then is to define
> (a) which services should be fully supported from the public purse;
> (b) which services should be partially supported;
> (c) which services should not be supported at all (being charged at cost);
> (d) which services should be provided at profit (either within or outside the public sector)".

The guidelines also made the important point that different types of customers and demands will mean significant local variations according to circumstances and needs. The fee-or-free debate has now moved beyond acceptability of charging to definition of free and fee-based services. Charging has progressed from a control mechanism for limiting use to a means of covering costs and even providing modest profit. A common policy in libraries is to differentiate between the primary clientele whose use of the service has been subsidised (via local taxes, membership subscriptions, tuition fees, etc.) and others.

One option often considered is whether services regarded as peripheral activities or ranked as lower priority could or should continue to be offered on some sort of charged basis. Most libraries charge for some services (notably photocopying) and many have contemplated or experimented with charging over the last two decades as a response to budget constraints and other pressures. There are various reasons why service managers might decide to introduce charges and it is essential to be clear about objectives when considering pricing strategies and to communicate the rationale for charging to both staff and customers. Reasons commonly offered for introducing charges are set out below – note that several may apply at once.

Why charge?

- to compensate for reduced funds;
- to control or constrain demand;

- to comply with organisational policy;
- to ensure services meet real needs;
- to differentiate core/basic and marginal/optional/value-added services;
- to signal the costs and/or benefits of provision;
- to enable new or improved services to be offered;
- to generate income to support core activities;
- to raise your profile, impress your funding body;
- to publicise the existence of services and stimulate use.

The range of products, services and facilities charged for also varies significantly, from those for which charges represent a contractual or legal requirement (such as photocopying, to comply with current copyright regulations) to those for which fees are often seen as highly controversial (for example, loans and enquiries). The 'services' also vary in terms of their identification/integration with what is generally perceived as 'core business' for library and information units, the likely competition, and the degree of risk. Some examples of charged services are given below, in broad categories.

What for?

- photocopying, printing and specialist reprography;
- interlibrary loans and reservations;
- current awareness/SDI services;
- publications, post cards, etc.;
- enquiry and (re)search services;
- hire of lockers, carrels and meeting rooms;
- stationery and computer disks;
- membership schemes – library facilities for 'outside' users;
- special exhibitions of rare books/heritage items;
- binding and conservation work;
- filming and reproduction rights;
- training courses and consultancy work.

Pricing and payment methods adopted show similar variations. Some services (e.g. library memberships, locker hire) are generally offered as annual subscriptions, but most are charged as individual transactions, with a few examples of upfront/bulk purchase options (e.g. photocopying cards, research services). Library managers do not always take into account the amount of time required to administer different income-generating activities (which might involve cheques, cash tills, inter-departmental transfers and credit card payments) when they consider introducing such services; often, when properly costed, these initiatives are shown to cost a lot more money than previously assumed. The significance of this will depend on the objectives identified, but it is important to be aware of the costs involved even if making money (in the sense of generating a surplus) is not the prime objective.

The main approaches to **pricing** evident from information service literature are as follows:

- *token contribution/nominal sum* – typically used to control demand and/or ensure the service is really needed (for example, charging 20% of the cost of an interlibrary loan; setting an annual membership fee at a level' that has no relationship to the costs incurred)
- *cost-related* – often used to differentiate core and non-core services, sometimes conceptualised as different categories of services for which the cost-recovery policy varies depending on where the service category is placed on the core-periphery spectrum (for example, recovering only *marginal costs* for services closely related to core activities, recovering all the *direct costs* for those further removed, *total* costs at the next level and full *costs plus* a surplus for services defined as peripheral)
- *buyer-, demand-* or *market-related* – based on perceived *value* to the customer ('what the market will bear') and used to discriminate among different market segments, including charging different amounts to different customer groups for the same service (for example, charging a nominal sum to a member for an interlibrary loan, total cost to others) and charging different amounts according to the time of day, week or year in order to influence customer behaviour and spread demand more efficiently over the operating hours of the service;
- *competitor-related* – based on assessment of the competition, which can include charging the same amount ('the going rate') as well as undercutting/discounting or differentiating the service in some way in order to charge a higher price.

(*See* Chapter 5 for more detailed discussion of pricing, including *transfer pricing* for internal markets and particular issues related to *pricing information.*)

Charging for library and information services is more complex than many managers realise and is an area where they may encounter unexpected resistance and problems. Service customers may object to paying for a service they see as not only essential but also a right; service staff may oppose proposals to charge on both practical grounds and as a matter of principle; and service funders may argue that past investment was made on the assumption of continuing free access. While legal liability is not necessarily affected by the presence or absence of fees, customers are more likely to be litigious if they are paying for services. The 'fee or free' debate has been complicated by reducing budgets, advancing technology and the development of electronic commerce in a changing global economy.

Peter Young (Executive Director, US National Commission on Libraries and Information Science) argues that changes in the way information is created, shared, controlled, transmitted, valued, protected, distributed and exchanged are changing public- and private-sector roles and organisational relationships, and creating new opportunities for libraries, librarians and information service providers. Young summarises the familiar pro- and anti-fee arguments, listing seventeen and sixteen points respectively, which reflect the two broad views of information as a *public good* on the one hand and an *economic commodity* on the other. He goes on to outline the changes in the economic structure of library and information services – and of publishing and bookselling – that are forcing a re-examination of values and policies, and to assess the impact of network technologies that are fostering a paradigm shift, advocating new roles and cross-sector partnerships to ensure an appropriate balance between social and commercial interests.

> "Amid the confusion of cross-industry alliances, commercial mergers, vertical integration, and investment partnerships involving cable television, entertainment program providers, interactive digital information systems, and the telecommunications industry, discussions need to occur which center on the creative potential, access equity, and balance between social values and economic need inherent in determining appropriate public- and private-sector roles within the emerging network multimedia interactive digital services marketplace.
>
> We need to move beyond the either/or, us/them, public/private dichotomy that has characterized discussion and debate of the fee-or-free issues of the last several decades. The library and commercial communities need to recognize that together they constitute an integrated fabric of knowledge services... Infrastructures of the future are probably going to be hybrid commercial/public ventures where entertainment, information, education, and business applications, free and fee, travel the global glass superhighway together, rather than on separate channels."[12]

Charging is also not a cost-free activity: managers need to consider the accounting and administrative effort required on a continuing basis, as well as the planning and development overhead, and whether they can find 'pump-priming' funds to cover any initial start-up costs. In addition, many public sector services have found that existing staff do not have the necessary competence or confidence to market commercial-style services: some have recruited staff specifically to launch new services; others have entered **joint ventures** with commercial partners, which can not only provide access to needed expertise but also be a means of dealing with procedural and financial constraints. Managers need to decide whether charged services should be organisationally separate from or integrated with free services, and how competition for resources and conflicts of interest will be handled, bearing in mind that paying customers tend to be more assertive than others.

Charging has both **benefits** and **pitfalls**. On the negative side, it can reduce or restrict usage and generate ill will; it can create additional work for staff, harm customer relations, and result in inefficiencies, when users spend time searching to avoid paying fees. On the positive side, charging can actually help to promote services and increase users' valuation of them; it can enable better services to be offered, make the library or information unit appear more professional and businesslike, and improve efficiency and credibility. There can be real 'bottom line' gains both through increased income/turnover (irrespective of profit) and invisible earnings, such as a higher profile and improved status for the service and significant development of knowledge, skills and insights among staff.

Outsourcing – in-house or contracted out?

Outsourcing is an arrangement whereby an organisation – or part of an organisation, such as a library or information unit – purchases goods or services from a vendor rather than producing or providing them itself. It is not a new practice, though the term 'outsourcing' is a relatively recent invention, which is now generally used in place of the expression 'contracting out' (prevalent in a previous era). Other variants in use include *insourcing,* where an internal department wins an open market tender; *intrapreneuring,* where an organisation fosters and 'spins off' business operations to compete both internally and externally; and *smart sourcing,* which involves the use of shorter, less comprehensive contracts for specific purposes. Under the general heading of outsourcing, there are various options, from 'fully managed' to partially outsourced, for example having contractors working on-site while still retaining a few direct employees. Joint ventures or *strategic partnering* and *time-sharing* are further examples of current approaches in business-to-business relationships. (Strategic partnering was mentioned in the context of stakeholder relationships in Chapter 2.)

However, though not new, there has been significant growth in outsourcing over the past decade, both in the volume of activity and in the range of functions involved, which has also been reflected in the phenomenal volume of literature published on the subject during the 1990s. Many commentators link this growth with the concept of 'core competency' and related ideas, including the notion of the 'lean organisation' and *core* and *peripheral* business operations – or value-creating and non- (or lower-) value-adding activities. In the UK public sector, as a result of Conservative government measures in the 1980s, there has been a statutory requirement for both central and local government departments (including library and information services) to use the most cost-effective methods for service and support functions, through *market testing, compulsory competitive tendering* and (more recently) the Labour government's 'Best Value' initiative. The reasons generally cited for outsourcing are:

- to cut costs
- to improve quality
- to obtain specialist expertise
- to gain access to a larger resource pool
- to cope with fluctuations in demand
- to concentrate on core business activities
- to comply with formal requirements
- to follow management 'fashion'

Organisations often have multiple motives for outsourcing, which makes decision-making more complicated. However, Edward Cunningham of the PA Consulting Group, argues that in the current environment, cost reduction and quality improvement are only 'hygiene factors' and organisations should be seeking added value from their outsourcing arrangements,

> "Outsourcing has moved from being a tactical weapon towards being a strategic tool generating more value for organisations. The revolution continues as value maximisation is set as the basis for determining the best sourcing strategy."[13]

Common examples of outsourced activities in the wider environment include: advertising, catering, equipment maintenance, graphic design, IT, legal services, office cleaning, printing, recruitment, security, telephone helplines, training and transport.

Information service outsourcing
Outsourcing in library and information services has a long history, and includes some of the examples quoted above (such as equipment maintenance and IT services) as well as activities more specific to the library environment, for example:

- binding and conservation work
- book processing
- cataloguing (e.g. BNB/LC catalogue cards, retrospective conversion contracts)
- document supply
- serials acquisition and check-in (i.e. 'consolidation' services of subscription agents)

Total service outsourcing is most common in special libraries, and has covered all categories from government agencies to gas and chemical industries – in the US and UK.[14] However new ground was broken in 1997, when Riverside County, California handed over the management and operation of the entire public library service to a private enterprise, Library Systems and Services Inc.[15]

In the US, the most widely discussed instance of outsourcing has been Hawaii State Public Library System, which outsourced materials selection to book wholesaler Baker & Taylor, as well as acquisition, processing, cataloguing and distribution for the system's 49 libraries, as a response to massive budget cuts.[16] The level of professional interest and concern generated by this case is evidenced by the subsequent establishment of an Outsourcing Task Force by the American Library Association, to consider the impact of such practices on library and related services in the context of professional values and the Association's Code of Ethics and other policies.[17] In the UK, more recently, Westminster and Hertfordshire Libraries announced collaborative projects to experiment with 'supplier selection'.[18]

The operations chosen for outsourcing have typically been 'backroom' functions, although some libraries have experimented with outsourcing their public service photocopying operations on a fully managed basis (rather than just using equipment maintenance contracts). As well as releasing staff time from such functions to enable more effort to be put into customisation and personal attention to service users, it can be argued that information services should abandon the kind of functional *vertical* integration represented by these 'upstream' activities as a strategic move towards more *horizontal* integration, as they extend the reach and range of their frontline services to embrace IT help, learning support and other cognate functions alongside traditional library roles. Service managers should therefore consider whether undifferentiated tasks such as serials acquisitions and check-in would not be better performed by a specialist agent, who could achieve economies of scale in comparison with both small and large library operations.

Robert Renaud of the University of Arizona Library makes a convincing case for continuous reassessment and reallocation of resources in this context, pointing out that "as technology changes, libraries may identify new candidates for outsourcing, while in other cases they may decide to reverse the process and insource an activity". Drawing on the thinking of Michael Porter, he concludes

"Competition theory enables the campus library to understand its economic context, or industry structure, the barriers to entering new markets and exiting old ones, the power of partnerships to leverage resources, and the value chain of activities that serves customers. On a local level, the library needs to be able to build a capacity for shared learning, to understand the emerging industry structure, to define and rank services, and to reallocate resources to high value, differentiated activities. In reallocating resources, the library may decide to outsource an activity when it can be performed at a reduced cost and can be linked seamlessly with existing processes."[19]

Among the key issues which service managers need to consider when contemplating outsourcing arrangements are mechanisms for quality control, the technical competence and track record of the proposed partner, and the operational and *cultural* compatibility of the two organisations. Cost data on the activities to be outsourced is obviously a prerequisite, but the costs of managing the outsourcing contract must also be taken into account – managers need to look at both transaction costs and *co-ordination* costs here. The problems and risks most often cited are dependency on external providers and below-contract performance levels, the loss of in-house skills and undermining of internal staff morale, and concerns about confidentiality.

Cliff Bowman and David Faulkner offer a matrix selection tool that emphasises the strategic significance or corporate criticality of activities and relative competence or comparative capability of the actors, in order to determine which things should be done/made in-house, which should be outsourced/bought and which should be achieved through some form of strategic alliance or partnership.

Figure 4.2 Outsourcing strategy matrix (adapted from Bowman and Faulkner)

Competence compared with
the best in the industry

		Low	Medium	High
Strategic importance of activity	High	Partner	Invest & DIY	DIY
	Medium	Partner	Partner	DIY
	Low	Buy-in	Buy-in	Buy-in

Bowman and Faulkner point out that this matrix does not take account of potential economies of scale, scope and learning – the relationship *between* competencies associated with different activities.[20]

The key **criteria** for judging the viability of outsourcing can be summarised as the Six Cs – Capability, Commitment, Compatibility, Control, Cost and Criticality. In its published guide to outsourcing, the Institute of Personnel and Development (IPD) identifies seven factors which constitute a "winning outsourcing methodology". These points are consistent with views expressed elsewhere and are of general applicability.

Critical success factors for outsourcing
- Top level support from both customer and supplier
- Clear understanding of the scope of the agreement
- Firm, binding contracts based on measurable service parameters
- Skilled, experienced contract managers
- An honest approach to problems
- Clear problem solving processes
- Mutually beneficial terms

The IPD also advocates a phased approach, enabling organisations to progress at their own pace through progressive stages of maturity in their adoption of outsourcing practices, noting that few large public or private sector organisations have yet reached the fourth stage:

1. A few simple, short-term 'supply' contracts designed to achieve cost reductions and to facilitate a focus on core business.
2. A mix of supply and partnership contracts, a few of which will be for extended periods, for key products and services (e.g. telecommunications, IT, logistics) these will focus on the supply of required skills and developing new products and ways of doing business.
3. Many and varied partnership contracts, often flexible and for long periods with an emphasis on sharing risk and reward.
4. The 'virtual enterprise', when the organisation does none of its own manufacturing.[21]

Priority-based planning

Questions suggested as part of the environmental appraisal and situation analysis covered in Chapter 2 may already have identified products or services whose continuation ought to be reviewed. In addition to considering dropping things altogether, managers should think about whether services could be managed differently and (especially) more cost-effectively, including options for modifying services by offering different levels of provision. A tool that can help with the task of prioritising services, programmes and activities in this context is the framework developed by Coopers & Lybrand in the 1980s for Priority Base Budgeting (PBB) – a management process for allocating resources cost-effectively. It is a structured approach to planning and budgeting, which helps managers to identify discretionary or optional activities and thus consider different levels of service provision in relation to their costs and benefits. (PBB is also discussed under Budgeting in Chapter 5.)

The PBB process requires managers to establish the purposes of their activities and evaluate alternative means of achieving them, by first defining the absolute minimum level – and the lowest cost – at which service could be provided to satisfy *essential* requirements only; and then identifying successive incremental levels of service, and their costs and benefits, to satisfy the more *discretionary* elements of the function. The resulting priority listing enables top management to determine budgets within resource constraints, but with a clearer understanding of the service implications.

Although designed to assist with the annual budgeting process, the descriptors can also be used just as a planning tool to focus thinking on what constitutes the core business, and to help separate and rank 'essential' and 'desirable' service increments. Several libraries and information units have used the framework in this way, and have found that the ten-point scale has helped them to differentiate core and optional services, to define baseline levels of provision, and to determine relative priorities among the current portfolio. In a conventional PBB exercise, the ratings are normally assigned by service managers, but the framework can also be used as the basis for a consultation exercise among various stakeholder groups.

PBB Rating Scale

[10] **Essential** to the business – unavoidable corporate or legal requirement
 [9] **Critical** – unavoidable without substantial loss or damage
 [8] **Very attractive**, important and productive increments of service
 [7] **Important** – hard to see how they could be dropped
 [6] **Significant benefits** but could conceivably be dropped
 [5] **Desirable** but first to be dropped if funding curtailed
← *Benchmark*
 [4] **Marginal** but first to be supported if funding increased
 [3] **Possible** but only if much increased funding available
 [2] **Doubtful** – not sufficient justification at present
 [1] **Unlikely** ever to be funded

Cost-benefit analysis

Properly interpreted, cost-benefit analysis determines and evaluates the *social* costs and benefits of an investment, aiming to measure the benefit of a particular activity to an individual, agency or society at large and to relate that to the actual cost. The objective of a cost-benefit study is typically to determine the economic feasibility of alternative proposals for achieving defined objectives, by identifying both the monetary/financial and opportunity/social costs and benefits. It attempts to answer the question, 'is the product worth the price?' by looking at both the proposition and the 'price' in the round. Such studies are both *objective* in terms of financial cost data and *subjective* regarding determination of values for non-monetary and intangible costs and benefits. Cost-benefit analysis can be used both prospectively, as a *planning* tool, and retrospectively, as an *auditing* tool for *post hoc* evaluation (or to follow through previous studies). It is regularly used in public service investment decisions or other situations where benefits go beyond sales and profits and the beneficiaries are not directly investing their own funds.

Because non-marketed costs and benefits are difficult to measure and evaluate – particularly in terms of assigning pecuniary values – the results of cost-benefit analysis are often seen as highly controversial, but it can nonetheless be a useful means of forming a rounded view of all the strategic and operational issues, even if quantification is not really practicable. In effect, cost-benefit studies try to justify the existence of a programme or activity by demonstrating that the benefits outweigh the costs. In an organisational context, management judgement of what qualifies as a 'benefit' becomes a critical issue; differing stakeholder perspectives of benefits will affect the way the analysis is viewed, and can pose problems in deciding how much emphasis to give the wider *economic* costs of the undertaking – compared with the *financial* costs to the organisation. Separation of the quantitative and qualitative aspects of the analysis in the final report may improve the general reception and credibility of the findings.

Ideally, all the costs and benefits should be expressed in the same units of measurement (in £, $, or some other currency) but this is very hard to do in a satisfactory and credible manner. Further difficulties arise with the range of data theoretically required, which usually includes estimates of not only service usage but also time spent by both service staff and service users – and possibly other stakeholders – on various activities (for example, staff time spent on trouble-shooting and problem correction; staff *and user* time spent on assisting and instructing users). Estimating costs and benefits properly thus requires significant input from users as well as management approval and support. Another problem is that the costs and benefits of an undertaking often occur in varying timeframes, with benefits typically being more long-term (as well as uncertain and intangible).

F W Lancaster notes that more attempts at cost-benefit analysis have been applied to industrial libraries than to libraries of other kinds. He discusses various approaches to the measurement of benefits, none of which can be regarded as entirely satisfactory, but they are nevertheless worth some consideration by those under pressure to justify their services. Lancaster lists these approaches in order of increasing sophistication:

1. Net value approach;
2. Value of reducing uncertainty;
3. Cost of buying service elsewhere;
4. Librarian time replaces user time;
5. Service improves organisation's performance or saves the organisation money:
   a. duplication avoided;
   b. loss of productivity avoided;
   c. cheaper solution suggested;
   d. invention stimulated.[22]

As indicated earlier, developments in electronic information provision have widened the options for service delivery to the extent that information service managers are very frequently faced with decisions among alternatives, notably the choice between journal subscriptions and inter-library loans as a source for scholarly articles. This version of the 'access-versus-ownership' debate provides a good illustration of the different interpretations of what is 'cost-beneficial' in such circumstances. Bruce Kingma and Suzanne Irving conducted a study at the libraries of the State University of New York, based on an economic model identifying both the financial and opportunity costs of document supply, including commercial and consortial options. Their report provides details of the associated user survey, comments on the cost factors of co-operative resource-sharing, and offers three "decision rules" for determining the most cost-effective method, using break-even analysis (*see* Chapter 5) and based respectively on:

- the *financial* cost of each alternative to the library;
- the *economic* costs to the library and to its customers;
- the *economic* costs to the borrowing library and its customers, and also to the lending library.[23]

The following guidelines and framework for analysis are based on various published accounts of cost-benefit studies of library/information products and services.

Suggested steps towards cost-benefit analysis

1. Identify the stakeholders who benefit and pay for the product or service.
2. Itemise the potential costs and benefits for each stakeholder group.
3. Verify your assumptions with senior management and selected users.
4. Consider how to measure or assess the value of each cost and benefit.

5. Construct a matrix to show the above, marking the relevant boxes as appropriate (£/$ or X, depending on whether a monetary value is readily available for the item).
6. Consult selected users to clarify costs and benefits – via standard methods, such as a questionnaire survey, focus groups, interviews using critical incident technique.
7. Complete the costing and the quantitative/qualitative analysis.
8. Indicate the net values and show whether the total benefits exceed total costs.
9. Prepare a report with your findings and recommendations.
10. Present to key stakeholders and act on decisions.

Figure 4.3 Cost-benefit matrix showing information service components

	STAKEHOLDERS			
	Group A *eg* service staff	Group B *eg* service users	Group C	Group D
COSTS				
Accommodation/storage				
Consumables				
Equipment				
Information resources				
Opportunity cost of time				
Salaries & wages				
BENEFITS				
Alternatives not purchased				
Better informed decisions				
Creativity gains				
More timely information				
Productivity gains				
Psychic value ("Warm glow")				

Strategy development

While it is essential not to constrain thinking, a systematic approach to strategy development is desirable to ensure that emerging plans are realistic. A simple method of achieving this is to focus on a series of key questions. This six-step process is known as a STRIDE exercise – Situation, Target, Restraints, Insights, Delivery, Evaluation:

- **Situation** – what is the current situation? Summarise the salient features, drawing on previous analysis.
- **Target** – what is the target? State the overall goal, and intermediate objective(s) or milestone(s) if applicable.
- **Restraints** – what are the restraints preventing progress? Note any known constraints, such as policy and resourcing issues.
- **Insights** – what information and ideas are needed to arrive at a workable strategy? Seek suggestions for improvement or change, based on understandings about the process. Ask frontline staff about customer needs. Check whether the delivery process is the best way of doing things.
- **Delivery** – what exactly must be done? Develop the insights into practical strategies and set out what is to be delivered, by whom and when.
- **Evaluation** – how will progress be evaluated? Specify how success will be judged and suggest mechanisms for monitoring and measuring.

Supporting strategies

The process of strategy development extends beyond the development and selection of primary strategies designed to achieve identified goals. The strategies selected are likely to have both policy and resource implications which require review and amendment of existing procedures and practice. They may also have wider implications, notably in areas such as staff development and training, service promotion and information technology infrastructure. Some of these issues may already have been identified for attention when considering major directions and goals, but further scrutiny is needed at this stage to ensure that any necessary *supporting strategies* are put in place to provide a total picture of how the library or information unit intends to move forward. Other more far-reaching changes may need to be considered, for example organisational restructuring to enable the service to become more responsive to customer needs. Organisational design has emerged as a critical issue in the literature of business strategy, acknowledging the interdependencies which exist between different aspects of managing an organisation.

Seven S framework

A useful model for thinking about organisations and strategy implementation is the '7-S' framework developed at the McKinsey consulting firm and popularised by ex-McKinsey consultants such as Tom Peters[24] and Richard Pascale[25]. The framework identifies seven interrelated factors that determine the effectiveness of an organisation and its ability to change, and is normally presented as a 'managerial molecule' showing how each element is connected to all the others. Although the choice of seven dimensions or variables is somewhat arbitrary, the essential point is that it is difficult to make significant progress in any one of these critical areas without making progress in the others. The seven factors have been grouped as 'hard' and 'soft' Ss, reflecting the fact that it is the latter that often receive insufficient attention in strategic planning; they are also sometimes referred to as the "cold triangle" and the "warm square".

The Hard Ss	*The Soft Ss*
Strategy	Staff
Structure	Style
Systems	Shared values
	Skills

(This tool can also be used as a checklist for appraising the information service and its parent body during the initial situation analysis.)

The Seven S framework is widely cited as a landmark contribution to strategic management, on the basis of its focus on behavioural/cultural issues and its contribution to thinking on strategic or transformational leadership and the management of change. The model can serve as a valuable reminder to information managers of the interdependencies which characterise and underpin their services. However, it has been criticised for not highlighting other areas now acknowledged as important for business success, such as innovation, quality and customer focus. There are also some distinctive and critical features of information services which are not represented in the standard model but require special attention in strategy development and evaluation. The model below has been developed specifically to assist information service strategists in formulating and testing their strategies for the electronic era.

- **The information Seeker** is the customer or user of our services, products and facilities. S/he will be affected by service developments and changes, and strategists need to consider whether improvements introduced for one group of customers will have adverse implications for others (for example, adjustments to loan periods). Service managers may decide to target new market segments and thus deliberately expand the customer base, and even though the strategy is to offer established services to this new group, there may be knock-on effects (such as pressure on space and equipment). The customer base may also change as a result of external or organisational forces (for

Figure 4.4 Seven S framework for information services

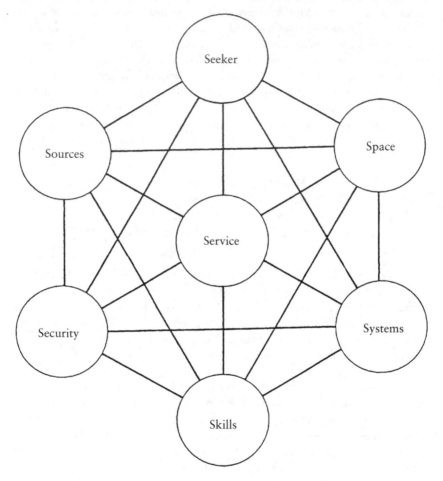

example, a university recruiting more mature, part-time or overseas students) and managers may need to rethink their service strategies in the light of such developments.

- **Information Sources** include the physical stock held in the library or information centre, the electronic media to which the service has established rights of access (for example, via licensing agreements) and other print-based and electronic sources potentially available on demand. The sources required will be affected by the changing needs of information seekers, who will inevitably have different preferences and priorities. If service managers decide to change the balance between local holdings and remote access or between print-on-paper and electronic media, this will probably have knock-on effects on space utilisation and possibly also have implications for systems and skills development among both service staff and service customers.

- **Space** represents the physical environment of the library or information unit, and its significance as a resource and a constraint is sometimes overlooked. Migration from print to electronic media may require extensive re-wiring and larger areas for customer workstations. Networked access to information services from laboratories, offices and other locations may reduce pressure on information service PCs, but for services which still hold large quantities of printed material it is likely that information seekers will still view the library or information centre as a place to do their research, and somewhere they can get help if necessary. The training needs of both service staff and service customers will almost certainly require new or improved physical facilities for hands-on instruction and practice in accessing electronic information systems.

- **The Service** at the centre of the model can refer here either to the service as a whole or to specific offerings (services, products, facilities) depending on the type of strategy under consideration.

- **Systems** here covers the procedures and processes described in the original Seven S framework, but in the Information Services model 'systems' has a particular focus on IT-based systems – the hardware, software and other infrastructure required to support service delivery, communication with customers and suppliers, and other operational and management activities. Information service improvements are often dependent on system developments, which in turn may have skills and training implications. Alternatively, new or upgraded systems often offer opportunities or trigger thoughts for service developments not previously considered. Similarly, system developments can influence choice of supplier (for example, a switch to electronic data interchange) or lead to redesign and reorganisation of operational processes.

- **Security** here includes protection of both physical assets (stock, equipment, etc.) and intellectual/electronic property against accidental or malicious damage or loss. Many information services are having to commit substantial sums annually to various aspects of security (such as alarms, card-entry systems, video cameras) and to invest significant amounts of staff time in preventative activities (back-up routines, passwords, security patrols, etc.). It is easy to overlook the resource implications of securing new equipment and systems, and ensuring that staff and users are aware of copyright and data protection regulations, and licensing restrictions on the use of data sets and software. Extending service opening hours into the evening or at weekends is also likely to have security implications.

- **Skills** in this context refers both to the capabilities of service personnel (as in the original Seven S model) and to the competencies of service customers. Pascale argues that 'skills' is the *dependent* variable, the derivative of the other six – strategy, structure, systems, staff, style and shared values – which must be fine-tuned to support skills development. For information services, skills development is a particularly important issue, first because our services are dependent on professional competence and secondly because our role involves facilitating the development of information skills among our customers/users. Many planned information service developments assume levels of competence among information service users that turn out to be inaccurate or unrealistic. It is therefore essential to think through the skills needs and training implications for both staff and users before finalising timetables for service changes.

Several of the Seven Ss will have already been considered in earlier parts of the planning process, but these lists underline the iterative nature of strategic planning and the importance of repeatedly checking back to ensure congruence between the different components which together form the overall organisational strategy. Another point to bear in mind is that strategies, goals and objectives can apply at different levels of the organisation. Just as the set of strategies embodied in the library or information unit's strategic plan can be viewed as one component in the overall strategy of the parent organisation, in the same way the key strategies identified for the information service as a whole may need to be elaborated for different parts of the service or aspects of its operations (e.g. geographical sites, specialist functions, technical processes) to form separate supplementary planning documents. In formulating strategies for accommodation, equipment, human resources, information systems, promotion/publicity, etc., the essential requirement in the context of strategic planning is to develop plans to the level necessary to identify significant organisational, policy and resource implications.

Sensitivities and contingencies

Managers generally select strategies which reflect their considered judgements or best guesses about what will happen in the future – the most likely occurrences. In some cases it is advisable also to prepare for less likely eventualities by developing *contingency strategies* and *plans*. Information managers will probably not wish to expose their services to a high level of risk, but there may be instances where an element of risk-taking is acceptable. If plans are judged particularly vulnerable to changes in the internal or external environment, the basic options are: to abandon that path altogether; to delay implementation until the situation becomes clearer; to modify plans in order to avoid or reduce the risk; or to go ahead, but manage the risk by defining it and preparing a contingency plan to minimise the threat. (The analysis and management of risk is covered in more detail in Chapter 7.) Where strategies appear to be especially sensitive to factors beyond the library or information unit's control, a series of 'what if' questions can be asked in order to identify possible outcomes, and then position the service so as to be able to offset the effects of such occurrences.

Contingency planning involves identifying and selecting alternative courses of action in anticipation of less likely events; it helps the library or information unit to provide a more flexible response and to avoid the practice of 'crisis management'. The term is also used for situations where an event is quite likely or almost certain to happen, but its *timing* cannot be predicted – for example, a major system failure, interruption of supplies, loss of a key manager, an economic recession or a change of government. The techniques of contingency planning are therefore relevant and applicable to both strategic planning for service development and operational planning of day-to-day business activities. (Back-up arrangements for computer systems and cover rotas for staffing frontline services are common examples of the latter.) Contingency plans vary from plans which enable continued pursuit of a basic strategy with only minor modification to those which involve complete alternative strategies allowing the organisation to follow a new path to its chosen destination without losing significant ground.

The main benefit of contingency planning is that reactions to chance events can be decided in advance in a relatively calm atmosphere based on proper consideration of the consequences, but managers need to weigh up the pros and cons before investing time and effort in plans that may never be put into effect.

Advantages of contingency planning

- Enables rapid but considered response to unexpected events.
- Makes staff aware of how unpredictable the future is.
- Trains people not to think in absolute terms, thus making them better prepared to deal with crises for which no contingency plans have been made.

Disadvantages of contingency planning

- Can take up time and energy that might be better spent on researching assumptions and refining strategies.
- Can generate pessimism, negative thinking and fear among staff.
- Can make people over-optimistic and complacent.

Ideally every strategy would have an alternative in reserve, but in practice most organisations can only afford to concentrate on a few areas where errors in assumptions would have a significant effect – generally areas of high priority or that are highly sensitive to change. Selection of subjects for contingency plans is generally based on *sensitivity analysis* which assesses the impact on a strategy or project of errors in planning assumptions or failures in task execution. Both the *probability* (likelihood of occurrence) and the *criticality* (level of impact) need to be considered. Impact can be expressed or felt either in financial terms or in other ways, such as market share, customer relations or community goodwill. **Sensitivity analysis** involves studying the key assumptions on which plans are based and systematically altering them using 'what if' questions to assess the most optimistic, most pessimistic and most likely occurrences, and the probabilities of each possibility. Analysis is difficult where there are large numbers of variables as this generates numerous permutations when the different possibilities are combined, so it is advisable to be quite selective when choosing variables to analyse.

Key steps for contingency planning

1. Select subjects on the basis of their criticality and probability of occurrence.
2. Develop strategies and tactical plans to deal with the possible occurrence of each selected event.
3. Identify monitoring mechanisms and trigger points or warning signals to initiate planned action.

Tips

- Focus on the really *critical* areas, which are likely to be no more than six in total (i.e. don't attempt to cover all troublesome eventualities).
- For each selected area, explore and evaluate *alternative* strategies before finalising plans (using the evaluation criteria specified below).
- Consider whether some areas warrant action in *advance* as well as action in response to events (e.g. training staff to replace key personnel).
- Develop plans in more detail for areas of most critical impact and/or least reaction time.

Strategy evaluation

When strategies have emerged for consideration by the planning team, they should be assessed against standard criteria for their feasibility, compatibility and attractiveness. Strategic decisions are generally based on a mix of quantitative and non-quantifiable factors. Rational analysis can help to narrow the options, but the final decision is often a matter of intuition and judgement. Broadly speaking, the more important the decision is, the more dominant the non-quantifiable factors are likely to be. Qualitative criteria are generally more important in the not-for-profit sector. Again, the simplest method of evaluation is to pose a set of questions to test the strategies and select the best options. The **CRITERIA** below can be used both to evaluate alternative strategies – different ways of achieving a particular goal – and to prioritise selected strategies for the final plan. This model has eight elements – Coherence, Resources, Impact, Timing, Environment, Risks, Insights, Approval.

- **Coherence** – does the strategy have internal logic and consistency, and is it consistent with organisational objectives, policies and priorities? Review the *typology of objectives* (see Chapter 3) and check the strategy against relevant formal statements, and also consider how it fits with other explicit or implicit organisational plans and operating practices – are there any potential conflicts or knock-on effects on other areas?
- **Resources** – are the required financial, human, information and physical resources available or obtainable when needed? Consider the phasing of capital investment and recurrent funding, the technical and managerial competencies required, information systems needs, and the capacity and demands on your equipment and facilities – does the strategy optimise existing resources and exploit your strengths?
- **Impact** – will the strategy fulfil the stated goal and achieve a measurable result, and how important is it to your mission and primary objectives? Think about the strategy in relation to your *critical success factors* or *key result areas* and also the priorities of major stakeholders – does it make an essential, a desirable or only a marginal contribution?
- **Timing** – is the timescale clear, and realistic in the light of known conditions and constraints? Consider both the amount of time (hours, days or weeks of work required) and the actual scheduling of this initiative in relation to other commitments, and check the criticality of timetables – are deadlines significant?
- **Environment** – does the strategy take account of macro and micro environmental issues – the driving forces, industry developments, consumer trends, etc? Revisit the *SEPTEMBER* model – are there any Social, Economic, Political, Technological, Educational, Market, Business, Ethical or Regulatory factors that have been overlooked?
- **Risks** – does it involve a significant element of financial or other type of risk? Reflect on how vulnerable it is to errors in planning assumptions and consider the need for sensitivity analysis (*see* above) – is the risk of failure commensurate with the potential benefits?
- **Insights** – does the strategy demonstrate understanding about the pro-

duction/delivery process and the needs of customers? Does it incorporate the ideas and know-how of operations staff (about new ways of
doing things, needs of particular groups, relationships with suppliers,
etc.) – have they been involved or consulted about it?

- **Approval** – is it understandable and acceptable to key stakeholders,
  internally and externally? In particular, consider the likely reactions
  of suppliers, funders, customers and the people expected to carry out
  the strategy, whose wholehearted commitment is desired – will they
  be prepared to support it, both in principle and in practice?

Strategic options and evaluation criteria can be set out in a matrix and
scores or comments inserted in the appropriate boxes (High/Medium/
Low, Yes/No/Partially, etc.) – using the model suggested above, adding
other more specific criteria if desired to fit particular circumstances.

Figure 4.5 Strategic options decision matrix showing evaluation criteria

Options _Criteria_	A	B	C	D
Coherence				
Resources				
Impact				
Environment				
Risks				
Insights				
Approval				
Other criteria				
Other criteria				
DECISION				

If you have developed alternative scenarios in the course of thinking
about the future, your proposed strategies should also be assessed for
the breadth of their applicability in different circumstances. Scot Hornick and Joan Giesecke offer the following classification:

- _robust strategies_ are sub-divided into 'no-brainers' which hold under
  all scenarios, and 'no-painers' which hold under some scenarios and
  are essentially indifferent in others;
- _contingent strategies_ are sub-divided into 'big gains' which hold well
  under some scenarios, and 'big pains' which are adverse in others;
- _losing strategies_ are those which are ill-advised in all scenarios.[26]

Formal plans

While 'strategy' and 'strategic' have become two of the most overworked words in the management vocabulary in the 1990s, 'planning' and 'plans' have gone out of fashion. Management gurus (such as Tom Peters) have told us to burn our plans and scrap our strategic planning processes, and similar comments have come from library directors. Others have affirmed the need to think, manage, and plan strategically, but have argued that it is the *process* that really matters – not the *product* as represented by a written document. There is no doubt that it is the quality of thought and insight which is critical here and this is inextricably linked with the organisational process or processes that produce or form the strategy. Henry Mintzberg, another management guru, has long argued that strategies in reality are often not deliberately planned but emerge as *patterns* of consistent behaviour, and thus they can *form* as well as be *formulated.*[27]

The main argument against the production of formal plans is that they become out-of-date almost as soon as they are written and therefore have limited value, particularly as practical working tools. This view is largely based on the assumption that a formal plan is a static document, unalterable and complete in every detail; but this need not be the case, if proper thought is given to the *purpose* of formulating strategies and plans, the *content* of strategic and other types of plans, and the *process* for refining and updating both the plans and the assumptions on which they are based. Many managers are actually required to submit some form of plan to a higher authority, typically to secure recurrent funding and/or win pump-priming investment; to obtain approval of their proposed course of action and use of funds; and to provide a basis for performance evaluation. In some organisations the format for such submissions is quite tightly prescribed, in others there is more flexibility; irrespective of formal requirements, managers need to think about the sort of documentation which will be most useful to themselves, their colleagues and other stakeholders, in helping them to manage effectively and to fulfil their missions.

Three key reasons for documenting the process – in print or electronically

1. Many people find that the *process of writing and editing* a strategy document forces them to think through their goals and objectives carefully, and serves as a double check on overall consistency, organisational capacity and other critical issues – which may have been missed earlier as a result of rushing over strategy evaluation.

2. Written plans also provide a *visual medium of communication* with both internal and external audiences, and form a useful back-up to oral presentations, making it easier to convey a consistent message to different people in different places at different times – particularly in response to requests for further explanation.

3. In addition, as a formal record of intended activity, they are potentially a *vital mechanism for control,* enabling regular and *ad hoc* checks on whether specified actions have been carried out and underlying assumptions have proved correct – but they must incorporate space for annotation and amendment to fulfil this function.

Although more detailed planning can be reflected in supplementary documents relating to particular functions or specific services and covering various timespans, in order to assess resource implications it is advisable to include within the strategic planning process the translation of the chosen strategies into more explicit **action plans**. These plans should set out for each goal the precise results required (targets) and the main action steps (tasks) to be carried out, together with the persons responsible and completion dates. The results should be measurable, and tasks assigned to particular years in the lifetime of the plan; the actions can then be regrouped by year and by section or team, so that resource implications can be properly assessed and the phasing of strategy implementation revised if necessary when the total picture emerges. Financial projections for the years covered by the planning exercise can then be produced, indicating areas where budget adjustments (upwards or downwards) are envisaged. It can be useful as part of this process to construct a **strategy matrix,** in order to show how each function/section/ team will contribute towards achieving the goals, to identify any gaps or mismatches in activities, and to provide a convenient overview.

Planning principles

Several commentators have set out basic principles of planning for managers, that are applicable to any form of plan. The following set of precepts is based on the lists offered by Roger Bennett[28] and David Hussey[29]. It is presented here as a reminder of points covered in previous sections and as an initial checklist for managers preparing written plans.

1. As far as possible, base plans on *facts* rather than opinions.
2. Incorporate some degree of *flexibility* to accommodate unforeseeable events.
3. Do not plan *too far* into the future, so that prediction becomes impossible.
4. Identify and consider all practicable *alternative* courses of action.
5. Examine the side effects and *implications* of the actions envisaged.

Figure 4.6 Overview strategy matrix showing team inputs to goals

	Goal 1	Goal 2	Goal 3	Goal 4		Summary statements of each team's strategy
Team 1						
Team 2						
Team 3						
Team 4						
Summary strategy for each goal						

6. *Define* the chosen course of action properly and explain the reason for the choice.
7. Specify the *results* expected, so that management can follow the logical outcome of accepting the plan and measure progress against it.
8. Set *reasonable* targets – overambitious ones lead to low morale and cynicism.
9. Allocate *responsibilities* clearly to individuals/departments, so that there is no doubt as to who is to do what task.
10. Consider all aspects of the organisation's operations, but place the greatest emphasis on identifying and examining the *key factors* crucial to its success.
11. *Communicate* the reason for and purpose of the plan to all concerned.
12. Keep the written plan *concise,* yet long enough to make it clear what is intended.

Minimum requirements for any planning statement
The document must have a *title* and indicate the *subject* of the plan and its *timespan.* It must state *what* you intend to do and *why, how* it will be done, by *whom* and *when* – with enough information on *background* and *resources* to convince readers.

The level of detail you choose to provide in your plan will determine the length of the document; this decision will be influenced by formal requirements, personal preferences and whether you wish to develop a hierarchy of plans presenting successively more detailed elaborations of strategies, actions and timetables. (For example, if the latter approach is adopted, comments in the top-level document on when and by whom actions are to be taken might be confined to indicating the intended year and the department or team responsible for completing them.) Any document of more than five pages should be prefaced with a *summary* – of one to two pages, depending on the length of the document – giving a brief outline of key points, including the financial implications of the plan and any significant risks involved.

Terminology in this area is – as usual – confused and inconsistent in its application and interpretation in different sectors and organisations. The terms *strategic, corporate, business* and *marketing* plans can all be used in relation to an organisation's general statement of intent over the medium to long term (typically three to five years now, whereas in previous decades the most common timespan was five years, and sometimes ten years). Some organisations and commentators give precise meanings to these different terms, and while there are many variations in practice and in the literature, there is enough common ground on which to base a typology in order to guide information service managers and strategists through this maze. The following sections indicate the focus and scope of the various types of plans which can collectively be described as 'strategic' and also outline the core components and other elements typically contained in such planning statements. (Other types of plan, such as *financial, operational* and *project* plans, are covered in later chapters.)

In England, as a result of a government review that reported in 1997, all public library authorities are required to prepare and submit Annual Library Plans, devised around a three-year structure, with standing information and medium-term strategy reviewed triennially, but performance appraisal, new developments, action plans and performance targets updated annually. The formal guidelines issued in 1998 are highly prescriptive and offer an interesting (if rather elaborate) model for managers in other sectors to consider.[30] A list of the chapters and sections prescribed is given in Appendix 2.

Strategic plans

Examples of published and unpublished strategic planning statements vary enormously in their format and content, but in recent years there has been a discernible trend towards more concise documents, covering shorter timespans, with a sharper focus on the 'bottom line'. Lengthy descriptions and extensive lists of bullet points have given way to concentration on key strategic issues and articulation of performance indicators to enable demonstration of measurable results. Vision statements have become more prevalent than before, often forming the main narrative section of the plan. Many elements previously found among the main sections of strategic plans are now either relegated to appendices or lower-level documents, or excluded altogether. This streamlined approach makes more sense at a time of rapid change and also allows the details of how strategies will be implemented to be worked out by the managers responsible (and recorded in their functional, operational or project plans as appropriate).

Strategic plans – recommended core components

- *Mission* – a statement of your purpose and functions (why your service exists, what it does, whose needs it meets)
- *Context* – a summary of the current business situation and assumptions about the future, covering environmental forces, market trends and your competitive position (strengths and weaknesses) and critical issues identified
- *Vision* – a statement of your desired future state (where you want to be in the long term, which may be quite different from your present position)
- *Strategy* – your top-level 'strategic thrusts' representing the major directions in which you intend to move, reflecting your critical success factors/key result areas, and which determine the prime areas for investment of resource (time, money, effort)
- *Goals* – your key objectives and medium-term targets, with sufficient information on the existing situation and desired position to explain the change required, the proposed approach (strategies) and specific indicators that will enable progress to be monitored and measured
- *Resources* – a commentary on the financial, human, information and physical resource implications of the proposed strategy, indicating the phasing of any capital investment required, and financial or other risks involved, concluding with a budget summary.

Other elements sometimes included in strategic plans (in the main text or as appendices) are a statement of organisational values; a brief description or short history of the organisation; an outline of principal assets – buildings, equipment, materials, staff; product and service specifications; business relationships/partnerships; a review of progress since the last plan; findings of a SWOT analysis and/or other research; supporting strategies, risk assessments and contingency plans; a schedule of projects and action plans, with milestones and responsibilities; statistical data on customers and service usage; income and expenditure projections; an organisation chart.

In addition it is common to include in the preliminary material an *introduction,* preface or foreword, explaining the purpose and scope of the document, its relationship to other plans, and the process and people involved in its production; a *table of contents*; and an *executive summary* (see above). If the document contains a large number of acronyms, a *list of acronyms* should be provided at the beginning; if there are only a few such terms, they can be defined in the main text or listed in an appendix. Substantial documents can also be given a cover and/or *title page,* which is a useful place to put the *date of issue* and a *statement of confidentiality* (if applicable).

Marketing plans

There is considerable overlap between overall organisational strategy and marketing strategy. Marketing is about identifying, anticipating and satisfying customer needs, and is thus a fundamental business function, virtually indistinguishable from its key purpose. Many of the issues addressed and the tools and techniques used in strategic planning are concerned with marketing variables (such as market share, market development and market growth). In the world of business and corporate strategy, marketing is often seen not just as one of several business functions, but as the major or central function – and on that basis the term 'marketing plan' is sometimes used interchangeably with 'strategic plan' or 'business plan', particularly in small or medium-sized enterprises. However, in large organisations, marketing is often – but not exclusively – considered at the level of the strategic business unit rather than at the corporate level; in this model, *strategic planning* defines the business (or businesses) of the organisation, and *marketing plans* elaborate strategies to accomplish the overall business objectives.

The relationship between marketing and strategic planning should be seen as an iterative and interactive one, with marketing providing inputs to environmental analysis, which informs overall business objectives, which in turn determines marketing objectives and plans. Marketing plans can also be subdivided into longer-term *strategic* marketing plans (typically covering three years) and *tactical* or *operational* one-year marketing plans. The focus and scope of strategic marketing plans, and their differences and similarities in relation to strategic plans, are best illustrated by reference to Malcolm McDonald's classic text on marketing planning.[31] He lists the key components for a three-year (or longer) strategic marketing plan as follows:

Strategic marketing plan – core components

- *Mission statement* – covering the role or contribution of the unit, e.g. profit generator, service department, opportunity seeker; definition of the business; distinctive competence; indications of future direction.

- *Market overview* – summary of significant changes covering structure, decline/growth, segments, and trends in each, e.g. changing patterns of demand (presented visually, i.e. bar charts, pie charts, product life cycles, etc.).
- *SWOT and issues analyses* – Strengths and Weaknesses (in relation to identified CSFs) and Opportunities and Threats (from environmental influences) for key segments; brief statement of key issues to be addressed during the planning period.
- *Portfolio summary* – using a 'directional policy matrix' to summarise SWOTs and show for each market its attractiveness, the organisation's relative strengths (competitive position) in it, and its relative importance.
- *Major assumptions* – outside features and anticipated changes related to key issues that would significantly influence achievement of marketing objectives (e.g. assumptions about market growth rate, organisational costs, capital investment).
- *Marketing objectives and strategies* – quantitative objectives expressed in terms of profit values, sales volumes and market shares; strategies indicating positioning and based on the 'marketing mix' of four Ps (or seven Ps for services—see below).
- *Summary of resource requirements* – financial projections for the full planning period under all the main standard revenue and cost headings specified by the organisation.

The distinctive features of marketing plans are their focus on market *segments*, expression of objectives in *quantified* market-related terms, and use in strategy formulation of the *marketing mix* – generally expressed as the **four Ps** of Product, Price, Promotion and Place, but often extended for services to include People, Processes and Physical Evidence.

Marketing strategies indicate the broad approach selected to achieve the marketing objectives, including how the service is to be *positioned* and perceived by customers (for example, as general or specialised, traditional or modern, 'up-market' or value-for-money, etc.). In McDonald's model, a strategic marketing plan costs out these strategies approximately, looking at *alternatives* until a satisfactory solution has been found, which then becomes the *budget*. In a one-year tactical plan, the general marketing strategies are developed into **programmes** – specific *subobjectives* each supported by more detailed strategy and *action statements*. Plans may be devoted to particular functions or specific services: thus, a function-based organisation might have an advertising plan, a pricing plan, a sales promotion plan, etc.; a product- or service-based organisation might have plans for different offerings; or an organisation with a few major customers might have plans organised around them.

Do you need a separate marketing plan?
Strategic plans should cover much of this ground, but at a summary level; production of a separate marketing plan is recommended if an information unit serves diverse customer groups and/or it proposes substantial investment in marketing activities to achieve significant growth in usage or income. Alternatively, the marketing plan (or plans) could form an appendix to the strategic plan.

Business plans

The term 'business planning' is sometimes used synonymously with strategic planning, but in its more specialised sense it tends to refer to a costed business proposal or case for funding. Like marketing plans, business plans overlap in content with strategic plans but are distinguished by their particular emphasis and level of detail. While the focus in the marketing plan is on selecting target markets and matching offerings to customer demand, in a business plan the central concern is with the *financing* of business operations and expected *return on investment*. Business plans need to cover marketing, technical, financial and organisational issues, but the financial section (showing estimated income and expenditure, year-by-year and cumulatively) is the most important part for which the marketing and technical (operations) sections provide the context.

Marketing issues include the current situation, size, state and stability of the market, its profitability and *strategic fit* – how the proposal under consideration fits with the overall strategy and objectives of the enterprise. Technical issues include the chosen strategy – how the product or service will be delivered – and the alternatives considered and rejected, as well as *operational fit* with existing systems and procedures. Financial issues include anticipated costs and benefits, when they are expected to occur, what assumptions have been made, and their sensitivity to error.

Business plans – core components

- *Introduction* – background and purpose, covering history of the business; its past performance; outline of current conditions and the business 'concept' (including scope of operations, nature of product or service, success factors, unique features, etc.).
- *Objectives* – overall and specific targets (quantified) for sales, profits, market share, innovation and efficiency, for medium and longer term (e.g. two years and five years) also indicating strategic direction/aims for the next five to ten years.
- *Marketing plan* – analysis of customers, suppliers, competitors and substitutes (overall market and specific segments) and other influences;

positioning and approach to pricing, channels of distribution, advertising and branding/packaging; sales forecasts.

- *Operations plan* – plans for researching, developing, producing and delivering the product or service (in-house or sub-contracted) and requirements for supplies, labour and equipment; quality, production and inventory control; contingency plans.
- *Financial plan* – summary of past, present and projected performance including assets; start-up costs; profit-and-loss, cash-flow analysis, balance sheet, break-even estimates; capital required and proposed use; projected return for investor; financial controls.
- *Organisation* – organisation chart; management responsibilities and competencies; business partners and relationships; workforce numbers and skills, turnover and availability; legal constitution of organisation/ form of business and ownership.

In addition to an *executive summary,* business plans generally have a summary as a *conclusion,* which highlights: the overall strategic direction and rationale for success; financial assets; expected sales and profits, with timescales; the capital required and projected return; and unique features of the organisation. A chart providing a timetable or *schedule* for starting the business or project showing critical dates is often included. Business plans frequently have many *appendices,* and these should form a concise set of raw data, support analyses and reference material linked to the main sections of the plan. For example, market information might include lists of products and competitors, results of SWOTs and market surveys; technical information typically includes product specifications with illustrations, operations flow charts, sample advertisements and price lists; financial information will include full statements for profit and loss, cash flow, etc. (as summarised in the main text), sensitivity analysis, a table of start-up costs, and calculations for break-even points.

Do you need a business plan?
In the information service context, business plans are typically used to demonstrate viability of revenue-earning activities, to present a case for a new product or service, or to justify funds for existing services whose continuation is in doubt. Such plans are often used to support a case for pump-priming funds, to provide an initial subsidy for a service expected to become self-financing or profit-making over time.

Corporate plans

The term 'corporate plan' is also often used interchangeably with 'strategic plan', but in large organisations it is commonly used to refer to the overall organisational or company plan, which brings together the plans of the various divisions or strategic business units into a coherent whole, within a common strategic framework. Bennett sees the *corporate plan* as this type of umbrella document, and interprets *strategic plan* much more narrowly as one component within the total corporate/company plan – the section which contains details (where appropriate) of how the company will diversify, expand/contract, rationalise its operations, etc. In his model, in addition to sections on assumptions behind the plan; contingency plans for various eventualities; targets, schedules and time horizons; resourcing; and budgets; the corporate plan includes:

- *functional plans* for new product development, marketing and distribution, human resources, research and technical development, operations, etc.;
- *divisional* and *departmental plans*;
- *project plans.*[28]

In this context, an information service might feature as (part of) a functional plan and/or in divisional and departmental plans, depending on the structure of the organisation. A very large library or information service, with many branches and/or different service units, might wish to adopt such a model to provide a comprehensive statement of its objectives, while allowing divisional heads, unit managers, etc. to develop and articulate their individual strategies tailored to their particular situations.

Plan formats

Just as the title, length and content of plans vary significantly, likewise the physical form can range from a substantial bound volume to a series of separate documents covering different subjects or subsets of the whole. Common formats used include:

- Unbound internal report or discussion paper;
- Book form, with all collateral material bound together;
- Ring binder, with clearly delineated sections and appendices;
- Series of reports or papers, produced (and considered) over an extended period;
- Sections bound as separate modules, which can be included/excluded as required;
- Separate summary version, published as a promotional leaflet or newsletter feature.

Factors to take into account in considering the form of the end-product include production and distribution costs, potential readership – it makes sense to think about modified versions for different stakeholder groups – and the purpose of the document:

- Who is it for?
- What do they already know?
- Why do they want/need the plan – for information? for consultation? for decision?

David Freemantle picks out five **target audiences** and reasons for aiming at them:

Yourself

- To clarify your own thinking about the future
- To produce a clear focus for monitoring and controlling future progress

Your team

- To involve your team in determining the future direction of the business and thus to secure their commitment and motivation

External funders
- To put up a convincing case to secure external funding for the future development of the business

Internal funders

- To present a clear 'business case' to persuade senior executives to support your proposal for developing the business unit for which you are responsible

Shareholders/owners/trustees/boards/governors/politicians, etc.

- To reinforce the confidence of shareholders, owners (or politicians, etc., if you are in public services) that you have the capability to manage successfully your business in the future.[32]

The extent to which information is judged politically or commercially sensitive is another important consideration; one possible approach is to produce a full version for restricted circulation within the organisation (e.g. for information service staff and top management) and an edited version for wider distribution. Managers also need to think about the message conveyed by the format selected: investing a significant sum in a prestigious publication with colour illustrations and photographs may help the library to make an impact, but might also raise questions about the use of (scarce) resources for such purposes. Both print-on-paper and electronic publication – on your web site and/or Intranet – will probably be required, and if the plan is to be discussed by a committee or presented to a large group, you may also need to produce visual aids or specially tailored handouts. Special attention needs to be given to the plan as a practical day-to-day working tool for service staff: at the very least, any hard-copy 'staff version' must be bound to lie flat when open, but thought should also be given to mechanisms for updating before the plan format is finally decided.

Production tips

- Don't overload it with detail (such as data gathered in environmental analysis)
- Do include references to the parent body's mission and objectives
- Involve several people in drafting/vetting, but leave the final edit to one person
- Keep the use of technical language, jargon and acronyms to a minimum
- Use diagrammatic summaries to break up text and present the total picture
- Use graphs rather than tables to show trends in usage, expenditure, etc.
- Give the plan a title – perhaps based on a phrase from your mission or vision

Finally, test the finished document – read it and re-read it, and get someone else to check it for:

- *Credibility* – is it sensible and convincing?
- *Accuracy* – is it an honest assessment, do the facts and figures add up?
- *Presentation* – does it look good, and has the <u>entire</u> text (including charts and diagrams) been checked for spelling, punctuation, etc?

Summary checklist

Can you move from strategy to action?

Options
Have you identified alternative ways of achieving your strategic objectives?
Have you considered their relative costs and benefits?

Details
Have you worked out exactly what is to be delivered?
Have you specified how success will be monitored and measured?

Impacts
Have you considered side effects on other areas or activities?
Have you developed supporting strategies to build capability?

Risks
Are any of your strategies particularly vulnerable to environmental changes?
Have you decided how to manage the risks?

Selection
Have you assessed your strategies for their attractiveness, compatibility and feasibility?
Have you recorded your decisions on strategies and reasons for choices?

Plans
Have you determined broad timescales, individual responsibilities and provisional budgets?
Have you considered how to communicate information to different stakeholders?

References

1. Porter, M. E. *Competitive advantage*. New York: Free Press, 1985
2. Ansoff, H. I. *Corporate strategy*. rev ed. London: Penguin, 1987
3. Whitson, W. L. Differentiated service: a new reference model. *Journal of Academic Librarianship*, 21 (2) 1995, pp. 103–110
4. Ward, S. E. Document delivery: the perspective of industrial information services. *Interlending & Document Supply*, 24 (2) 1996, pp. 4–10
5. Green, A. Open and flexible learning opportunities. *Public Library Journal*, 10 (5) 1995, pp. 123–126
6. Brin, B. and Cochran, E. Access and ownership in the academic environment: one library's progress report. *Journal of Academic Librarianship*, 20 (4) 1994, pp. 207–212
7. Morrow, Virginia. To serve or not to serve, that is the issue. *Library Association Record*, 99 (6) 1997, pp. 312–314
8. Cabinet Office. Information Technology Advisory Panel. *Making a business of information: a survey of new opportunities*. London: HMSO, 1983
9. Office of Arts and Libraries. *Joint enterprise: the roles and relation-*

ships of the public and private sectors in the provision of library and information services. London: HMSO, 1987 (Library and Information Series No 16)

10. Public and private sector relationships: LA Guidelines. *Library Association Record*, **89** (3) 1987, pp. 142, 145

11. *Financing our public library services: four subjects for debate.* London: HMSO, 1988 (Cm324)

12. Young, P. R. Changing information access economics: new roles for libraries and librarians. *Information Technology and Libraries*, **13** (2) 1994, pp. 103–114 (pp. 112–3)

13. Cunningham, E. The great outsourcing revolution: no longer a tactical weapon, outsourcing is now a strategic tool. In: Rock, S., ed., *Outsourcing IT: a real business guide.* London: Caspian Publishing/ CBI, 1997, pp. 8–15 (p.15)

14. Agada, J. Outsourcing of corporate information services: implications for redesigning corporate library services. *International Information & Library Review*, **28** (Summer) 1996, pp. 157–176

15. Dubberly, R. A. Why outsourcing is our friend. *American Libraries*, **29** (1) 1998, pp. 72–74

16. Angry Hawaiian librarians denounce B&T outsourcing. *American Libraries*, **28** (1) 1997, p. 12

17. Outsourcing Task Force to meet at Midwinter. *American Libraries*, **29** (1) 1998, p. 9

18. Hall, C., Valentine, S. and Fletcher, S. Into the age of supplier selection. *Library Association Record*, **100** (9) 1998, p. 476

19. Renaud, R. Learning to compete: competition, outsourcing, and academic libraries. *Journal of Academic Librarianship*, **23** (2) 1997, pp. 85–90

20. Bowman, C. and Faulkner, D. *Competitive and corporate strategy.* London: Irwin, 1997 (pp. 211–215)

21. *The IPD guide on outsourcing.* London: Institute of Personnel and Development, 1998 (p. 16)

22. Lancaster, F W. *If you want to evaluate your library ...* 2nd ed. London: Library Association Publishing, 1993 (pp. 294–304)

23. Kingma, B. R. and Irving, S. The economics of access versus ownership: the costs and benefits of access to scholarly articles via interlibrary loan and journal subscriptions. *Journal of Interlibrary Loan, Document Delivery & Information Supply*, **6** (3) 1996, pp. 1–76

24. Peters, T. and Waterman, R. H. *In search of excellence.* New York: Harper & Row, 1982 (p.10)

25. Pascale, R. *Managing on the edge.* London: Penguin, 1990 (pp. 40–43)

26. Hornick, S. and Giesecke, J. Radar versus road map: developing strategies through scenario planning in an uncertain world. In: Gie-

secke, J., ed. *Scenario planning for libraries.* Chicago; London: American Library Association, 1998, pp. 18–25

27. Mintzberg, H. Crafting strategy. *Harvard Business Review,* **65** (4) 1987, pp. 66–75

28. Bennett, R. *Corporate strategy and business planning.* London: Pitman, 1996

29. Hussey, D. *Strategic management: from theory to implementation.* 4th ed. Oxford: Butterworth-Heinemann, 1998 (p. 491)

30. Institute of Public Finance. *Appraisal of annual library plans 1998: final report.* Croydon: IPF, 1999

31. McDonald, M. *Marketing plans: how to prepare them, how to use them.* 4th ed. Oxford: Butterworth-Heinemann, 1999. Alternatively, *see* McDonald, M. and Payne, A. *Marketing planning for services.* Oxford: Butterworth-Heinemann, 1996 and/or McDonald, M. Strategic marketing planning: theory and practice. In: Baker, M. J., ed. *The marketing book.* 4th. ed. Oxford: Butterworth-Heinemann, 1999, pp. 50–77

32. Freemantle, D. *The successful manager's guide to business planning: seven practical steps to producing your best ever business plan.* Maidenhead: McGraw-Hill, 1994 (p. 52)

Further reading

Options

Charging

Nicholson, H. Uncomfortable bedfellows: enterprise and academic libraries. *Journal of Librarianship and Information Science,* **24** (1) 1992, pp. 9–13
Discusses motives, benefits and pitfalls of introducing income-generating activities in public-sector institutions. Includes guiding principles, comments on staffing and a matrix of examples of revenue-earning services categorised by type, size and risk.

Yates-Mercer, P. A. and Pearson, D. Charging policies and practice in corporate information units in the UK 1: to charge or not to charge? and 2: how to charge. *Journal of Information Science,* **18** (1) 1992, pp. 11–25 and **18** (2) 1992, pp. 127–137
Discusses results of survey of UK product-based industries and London service-based companies, covering arguments for and against charging, opinions of service managers and organisational factors. Second article discusses methods of charging and pricing,

*including services charged for and the elements taken into account
in cost calculation.*

Smith, W. Fee-based services: are they worth it? *Library Journal,* **118**
(11), pp. 40–43.
*Surveys the rising number of charged services offered by US public
and academic libraries, and explores some of the ethical and practical issues raised.*

Mowat, M. *Legal liability for information provision.* London: Aslib,
1998 (Aslib Know How Series)
*Compact guide (c.60 pp) to the legal status of information, the con-
cepts of negligence and reasonableness, and the laws of torts and
contracts, with advice on minimising the risk of litigation and four-
page bibliography. Notes differences in UK and US law, and
between the print and electronic environment; also covers problems
associated with fee-based services.*

Outsourcing

Eddison, B. Our profession is changing: whether we like it or not. *Online
Magazine,* January-February 1997, pp. 72–81
*Traces the development of outsourcing practices in US information
services and elsewhere, covering private and public sectors, including both full and partial contracting-out to librarians and others.
Provides references to many relevant articles and reports, some with
annotations. Concludes with discussion of outsourcing online
searching and advice for people concerned.*

David, A. Consolidation services: the British Library experience. *Serials,*
10 (1) 1997, pp. 45–47
*Discusses benefits of using US subscription agent for consolidated
supply of c.3500 (later c.5500) American STM journals to BL Document Supply Centre, including earlier arrival, lower costs, automatic
claiming, and availability of services tailored to needs.*

Libby, K. A. and Caudle, D. M. A survey on the outsourcing of catalog-
ing in academic libraries. *College & Research Libraries,* **58** (6) 1997,
pp. 550–560
*Based on literature review and questionnaire survey of 187 Amer-
ican libraries: 28% of respondents had outsourced and 14% were
considering doing so. Comments on factors influencing decisions,
choice of vendors, range of coverage and the success of projects.*

Marcum, J. W. Outsourcing in libraries: tactic, strategy, or "meta-

strategy"? *Library Administration & Management,* **12** (1) 1998, pp. 15–25
Explains the background and development of outsourcing in its various forms, with reference to general management literature and placing it within the context of other organisational trends. Discusses its application in libraries, drawing on recent practical accounts, and offers a rationale and advice for deciding which activities to outsource.

Outsourcing. *American Libraries,* **29** (1) 1998, pp. 66–82
Four articles offer different perspectives on outsourcing, drawing on personal experience and practical examples from different types of libraries, and all pointing up the crucial need for the profession to articulate and assert its core competency and its ability to add value.

Service options

Day, D., McKim, G., Orchard, D., Purcell, A., Wachsmann, D., and Davenport, E. Agents for document supply: who are the likely players? *Aslib Proceedings,* **45** (7/8) 1993, pp. 189–199.
Considers five potential providers (Dow Jones, Geac, OCLC, Faxon, RLG) of electronic information/document supply services to information centres and consumers in the future. Included both for its speculative view of particular players in relation to their competitors, and its application of strategic analysis tools (Porter's five forces and value chain).

Ferguson, C. D. and Bunge, C. A. The shape of services to come: values-based reference services for the largely digital library. *College & Research Libraries,* **58** (3) 1997, pp. 252–265
Argues the need to develop and deliver high quality reference service and instructional support through the network and in person, at remote locations and around the clock. Discusses different service elements and staffing configurations, and concludes that collaborative working and integrating technologies will maintain values and aid success.

Winzenried, Arthur. Information providers: a growth area. *The Electronic Library,* **15** (6) 1997, pp. 469–471
Argues that end-user searching of the Internet is unlikely to be efficient or cost-effective without expert help from intermediaries and suggests key future role for information specialists in provision of gateways fulfilling three inter-related functions – a point of access

to resources, a place for user instruction, and a source for services and support.

Analytical tools

Broadbent, M and Lofgren, H. *Priorities, performance and benefits: an exploratory study of library and information units.* Melbourne: Centre for International Research on Communication and Information Technologies & Australian Council of Libraries and Information Services, 1991
Part B (c.40p) includes discussion of various approaches to cost-benefit analysis (CBA) of information services, and provides two detailed worked examples of CBA for current awareness products. The authors advocate a combination of cost-effectiveness and cost displacement/avoidance methods and provide a 14-step guide to conducting such studies.

McDonald, M. H. B. and Leppard, J. W. *Marketing by matrix: 100 practical ways to improve your strategic and tactical marketing.* Oxford: Butterworth-Heinemann, 1992
Argues that matrices (bi-polar diagrams) help to clarify relationships, to simplify complex situations and prevent application of one-dimensional thinking to multi-faceted problems. Organised under nine headings: general strategic issues; organisational issues; products and services; customers; sales; pricing; advertising and promotion; distribution and customer service; and exporting. Concludes with index and glossary of 33 marketing planning terms.

Broadbent, M and Lofgren, H. Information delivery: identifying priorities, performance, and value. *Information Processing & Management,* **29** (6) 1993, pp. 683–701
Based on the authors' project report cited above, the second half of this article outlines an approach to cost-benefit analysis and discusses its application to a current awareness product.

Meyer, R. W. Locally mounted databases ... making information as close to free as possible. **Online, 16** (1) 1992, pp. 15, 17–24
Explains the formula developed at Clemson University to determine which databases to mount locally, based on an assessment of marginal costs and marginal benefits to three user groups. Concludes that a mix of local mounting with mediated and end-user searching of remote databases ensures that each user segment has optimal access to online information.

Hawbaker, A. C. and Wagner, C. K. Periodical ownership versus fulltext online access: a cost-benefit analysis. *Journal of Academic Librarianship*, **22** (2) 1996, pp. 105–109
Compares the costs of providing access to business periodicals via subscriptions to print products with the costs of access via a fulltext database (Business ASAP) and then identifies other factors influencing purchase decisions – such as user preferences, operating costs, multiple access, vendor reliability, equipment requirements and browsing capability.

Harris, G. and Marshall, J. G. Building a model business case: current awareness service in a special library. *Special Libraries*, **87** (3) 1996, pp. 181–194
Describes the techniques used by a Canadian government library to assess value for money of in-house current awareness bulletin, which included a questionnaire survey, focus groups, and cost-benefit analysis comparing existing service with outsourcing or withdrawal. Refers to other published studies and reproduces the survey instrument in full.

White, G. W. and Crawford, G. A. Cost-benefit analysis of electronic information: a case study. *College & Research Libraries*, **59** (6) 1998, pp. 503–510
Discusses the nature of CBA with reference to published library studies. Describes a project at Penn State University to compare the costs and benefits of Business Periodicals Ondisc with traditional interlibrary loans and also comments on benefits not examined in the study; argues that CBA can be used as a marketing tool for new products and services.

Formal plans

Schilit, W. K. How to write a winning business plan. *Business Horizons*, **30** (September/October) 1987, pp. 13–22
Offers guidelines for developing convincing plans to obtain business investment followed by detailed guidance on contents: lists sections and sub-sections to include and points to cover in both the main body and appendices; suggests including contingency plans for production aspects, marketing effort, and also for company organisation and management.

McDonald, M. H. B. Ten barriers to marketing planning. *Journal of Marketing Management*, **5** (1) 1989, pp. 1–18
Sets out ten fundamental principles (the 'Ten S' approach) to over-

come identified problems in marketing planning, including the need to develop strategy *before tactics; to* structure *activities around customer groups, rather than functions; to* scan *the environment thoroughly; to* summarise *information in SWOT analyses; and to* systematise *the process.*

de Saez, E. E. *Marketing concepts for libraries and information services.* London: Library Association, 1993
Concise textbook (c.150pp) introducing basic marketing concepts and techniques in relation to information services, with references to standard texts and seminal works of marketing gurus. Chapters include the corporate mission; the marketing mix; market segmentation and targeting; marketing research; corporate identity and corporate image; the marketing plan.

Baker, W.H., Addams, H.L. and Davis, B. Business planning in small firms. *Long Range Planning,* 26 (6) 1993, pp. 82–88
Drawing on the findings of a survey on the use of business plans in small US firms, discusses contents of plans, their stated purposes and perceived benefits, frequency and methods of communication and evaluation, and advocates at least quarterly formal reviews.

Freemantle, D. *The successful manager's guide to business planning: seven practical steps to producing your best ever business plan.* London: McGraw-Hill, 1994 (1996)
Practical primer (174p) aimed particularly at managers of business units within larger organisations; covers vision and values as well as business basics, and includes numerous checklists, worked examples and concise advice presented in non-technical terms.

Chapter 5

Money matters

The future success of every information service is directly dependent on managerial ability to plan, direct, organise and control financial resources. Managers cannot afford to neglect financial matters, as failure here can undermine or even undo good efforts in other areas. Financial resource issues have been touched on in previous chapters but not pursued in detail. The decision to devote a separate chapter to 'money matters' reflects both the critical importance of financial management to strategic planning and the perceived weakness of this area in information services. It is essential to note here that although financial plans will probably only emerge as formal budgets at a relatively late point in the planning process, financial issues need proper consideration throughout the strategy process, and any major strategic decisions must include consideration of financial implications at an early stage. A common problem with strategic plans is the failure to follow through from strategy to action and to secure the resource base for implementation. Information service planning frequently suffers from the absence of a practical, *operational* dimension, and this problem is often compounded by budgeting *only* at the operational level, without establishing a strategic framework for financial management – or even adopting a strategic perspective. Financial strategies in information services are too often predominantly operational, and at best tactical – how to deal with this year's crisis.

It is beyond the scope of this volume to cover financial management in depth, for which purpose readers are referred to the books and articles suggested for further reading. This chapter offers a selective treatment of the subject, with the main aim of delineating key issues and demystifying the concepts and techniques that underpin effectiveness in this arena.

Accountability

Competence in financial management and management accounting has never been more important. The networked information environment poses complex questions about financial, managerial and technical responsibilities for connectivity, equipment and support, often split among libraries, computer centres and other departments in an uneasy mix. Managers have to consider how to deal with issues such as corporate purchasing and site licensing for software and datasets, and monitoring and auditing the usage and costs of Internet services at organisational, departmental and individual level. Libraries and information services are characterised by a high degree of interdependencies among activities, and the situation is exacerbated by the difficulty of separating system costs from service costs. More than ever before, managers today are being required, explicitly or implicitly, to justify expenditure on particular items – or for the whole service.

This is an area that in the past has arguably been given insufficient attention by many information service managers, but in the future will undoubtedly be a critical factor in determining organisational success. As Stephen Roberts rightly points out, "Improving budgetary practice should be affirmed as a strategic goal of all information and library service managers".[1] Likewise, service managers must invest more effort in co-ordination and communication on financial matters, with financial controllers, other specialist staff and key stakeholders. In addition to the obvious functions, such as finance/accounting, purchasing and audit, managers may need to build relationships with fund-raisers and legal departments (for advice on licences for electronic information).

Roberts also advocates progression from discrete one-off problem-centred cost studies to a regular continuous comprehensive management accounting system. Information professionals of the future will require a deeper understanding of costs and pricing, and the ability to handle financial data and accounting concepts. People need to know the difference between cash flow/movement (receipts and payments) and revenue activity/performance (income and expenditure). They need to be able to speak the professional language of accountants to finance people and to present such issues in non-technical terms to their colleagues and customers. Participative management, devolved budgeting, the rapid pace of change and the imperative for service responsiveness all reinforce this need. If service managers do not give due thought to the alignment and attunement of strategic plans, management structures and budgetary models, they may have problems in resourcing their programmes, they will find it harder to track progress, and they are more likely to fail to meet their objectives.

The pressure on budgets over the last several decades has affected information services more than others because of the particular factors affecting information provision. In addition to spiralling prices for printed materials – well above the level of general inflation – and unpredictable costs for electronic media, there are the additional complications of copyright clearance, consortial purchasing, and multi-year subscriptions. Most information service managers are faced with decreasing financial and human resources, but increasing customer demands and wider delivery options, requiring complex decision-making, which in turn requires effective management information systems – particularly information on costs.

As indicated in the last chapter, there are usually several ways of meeting goals, and strategic planning generally requires preparation of costed options to inform decision-making; such exercises are much easier if relevant data are collected routinely and a comprehensive management information system is already in place. The use of formal cost-benefit analysis techniques can help to clarify issues and inform decisions when faced with alternative strategies to achieve objectives (for example, choosing between journal subscriptions or individual article supply via a remote document delivery service). In the past, people have often taken such decisions on an informal and subjective basis; a more objective approach requires an understanding of the difference between economic/opportunity and accounting/financial/monetary costs, and knowledge of the circumstances, needs and priorities of users (and other stakeholders). For example, multi-year subscription offers for journals may look attractive to the library manager, but will not necessarily be the best option, especially in the corporate environment where the 'churn rate' for journals is high.

Information service managers also need to be able to contribute to the debate and influence the development of pricing models for electronic information to replace the current 'bridging' strategies, and to reduce the unit cost per use, as provision expands but funding remains stable. Within their own organisations, a key issue is *virement* – the authority to determine the balance among different types of expenditure. In the context of building a flexible organisation for information services at the University of Birmingham, Clive Field points to the need for sensible and effective deployment of all the resources available to service providers,

> "With regard to financial resources, the maximum possible amount of virement authority for service providers is desirable, subject to appropriate checks and balances on them, the agreement of a rolling service plan, and suitable audit trails. This applies, for example, to the balance between capital and recurrent expenditure, between staff and non-staff expenditure, between expenditure on libraries and other services, and between expenditure on different information formats. In an ideal world, service providers should have the ability to manage the totality of the direct and indirect costs for their service, within a prescribed budget, and to vire between the different budget heads."[2]

Accountability in this context requires a lot more of managers than was assumed in the past. It is not enough to ensure that expenditure is kept within budget; managers are generally expected to provide the best level of performance possible for the funds available, and may be set both cost targets and income targets as part of the process. Managers therefore need to take responsibility for developing their own knowledge and skills in financial management, and also for providing the necessary training for staff in their unit. All staff need to be aware of the financial context in which they operate and any financial *performance indicators* by which the service is judged. Most staff should also understand the basis for *funding* the service, and the processes for planning and *budgeting*. Many staff also need to know about *costing* services (for planning and decision-making purposes) and should have some knowledge of *pricing* (not only in the context of *charging* for information services, but also in the context of *purchasing* information from suppliers). Procedures for *accounting* and administrative *control* complete the financial management agenda.

Funding

Most library and information services are dependent on a parent organisation, and their main source of income has traditionally been a *grant* (allocation, subsidy or 'vote') with some additional funds coming from *income-generating* or *revenue-earning* activities. Various economic and political factors have combined to change this situation so that library and information services are increasingly characterised by multiple sourcing – often reflecting diversification of income streams flowing into the parent organisation – and a shift in the balance between grants and earnings (or other supplements to their income). In many higher education institutions in the UK, the government grant now accounts for a much lower proportion of total income than before (in some cases less than 50%) but their annual allocations to their libraries are still based on this 'block grant'.

In both universities and companies, the trend towards *devolved budgeting* has created *internal markets* which have changed the way funds are allocated and managed internally, through business units, cost centres and other arrangements, sometimes leaving the information service entirely dependent – at least on paper – on payment for services rendered. General cutbacks in public expenditure have also prompted library directors to put more effort into *fund-raising*, in the hope of supplementing their basic grant with donations, sponsorship or grants from other sources (notably charitable foundations) – although this type of income is normally not intended for general operating expenditure. The growth in fund-raising activity is shown by the number of publications and seminars on the subject, and the range of methods and techniques used. For example, the Library Fundraising Resource Center developed under the auspices of the American Library Association has gathered fund-raising literature from libraries throughout the country, and holds campaign materials, articles, bibliographies and other information on around 50 different topics.[3] Among novel examples is the affinity card introduced by the Libraries at the University of New Mexico (UNM) as a joint venture with UNM Athletics.[4]

The range of revenue-earning services offered has also expanded and diversified. For example, the British Library has expanded its income generating activities so that in 1997/98 30 per cent (£36.2 million) of its total expenditure came from that source, compared with 11 per cent (£1.5 million) in 1974/75, its first full year of operation.[5] In addition, some academic and special libraries have extended their clientele beyond their primary constituency – by selling their services to other libraries, other organisations and individuals, and also through 'franchising' and other contractual arrangements – and thus begun to operate in more competitive mode, albeit with mixed success.

This shift from grant to earnings has several implications. It represents a significant change in the predictability of income, and it puts more pressure on the library to attend to the needs of multiple constituencies – both funders and users – to ensure an adequate resource base. When non-grant income moves beyond ten to twenty per cent of the total, it becomes a strategic issue, as the loss of such budgeted income would lead to a weakening of organisational capacity. With internal charging systems, even if the sums available for library and information services are in theory unchanged, the introduction of *transfer pricing* (sometimes known as 'shadow pricing') creates a different psychological climate which makes service consumers/customers more sensitive to costs and value, and more likely to consider alternative sources of supply – or indeed alternative resources (other than information) that could be purchased. There will also almost certainly be an additional cost to the library in terms of the staff time required to administer any form of priced service.

Commentators on library finance view these developments in different ways. Ann Prentice follows the traditional line,

> "The funding for an information service comes primarily from the parent funding agency, be it local government, academic budget, association resources or other source... Fees for service are directed toward special services and are therefore not an integral part of general operating revenue. The health of the organization is determined by the primary funding agent. Other resources enrich a program but do not maintain its viability."[6]

Stephen Roberts, argues for a pragmatic and positive response to market realities,

> "Rather than seeing revenue problems as a source of restriction and inconvenience, the opposite view can be taken: growth in the information economy is associated with opportunity to develop new products and services

and open up new markets. . . The maxim must be that desired and essential growth is funded out of income, generated by revenue-earning activities, where direct public funding falls short. The changes are as much psychological as economic. In this context, diversity of funding should be a longer term professional aim. . ."

" . . . information managers must therefore consider financial growth as a corollary of developing a business strategy while maintaining their traditional competence at managing collection growth and its physical and spatial consequences."[1]

Internal markets

The introduction of an internal market can take many different forms. Many academic libraries have traditionally allocated budgets to academic departments for the purchase of books (and other information resources) but in most cases although academic staff played a major role in purchase decisions, the funds were only notionally allocated to departments, they represented only a proportion of the library's total acquisitions budget, and the library had ultimate control over their use. In recent years institutions have experimented with different models: it is now quite common for user departments to have virement between expense heads, so that they (rather than library staff) decide how to distribute the budget among books, periodicals, interlibrary loans, etc; in other institutions, departmental allocations are not confined to information resources, as the entire library budget is allocated/apportioned to departments, often to support the introduction of *service level agreements,* some form of 'trading company' model, or to improve *transparency* in resource management; in a few universities, *devolved budgeting* has meant the direct allocation to departments of some or all of the funds assumed to be required for library support, in an arrangement similar in effect to the charging-back system operating in many companies.

Various factors have influenced such developments, including changes in the methods used by the UK Higher Education Funding Councils to determine the block grants awarded to institutions and the general organisational trend towards decentralisation/devolution. Irrespective of the models adopted and the reasons for doing so, the implications are clear: accountability has moved to a different level, and service managers will require effective systems and structures for management accounting and customer liaison. Both areas are crucial, especially liaison arrangements, as continuing dialogue will be necessary to deal with both operational and strategic issues. Devolved models often make it harder for service managers to obtain funding for strategic initiatives or developments planned to benefit the whole community, as customers frequently focus on their own shorter-term needs. Other problems encountered include difficulties in funding multidisciplinary information resources and general reference works. New financial management models therefore often require not only a review of individual roles and responsibilities (within the service and the client department) but also new channels of communication, committees or working groups to handle liaison, negotiation and decisions on purchasing and investment.

In the corporate sector, the internal market is often seen as a first step towards other developments. On the one hand, the status of the information service might shift from being a service unit or part of the 'central overhead' to becoming a (commercial) business unit in its own right, trading initially just within the company, but then offering its services to other external clients; an alternative model is for the information service to operate as a totally independent organisation, and sell its services back to the company (and to others) on a contracting out or outsourcing arrangement. The management arrangements and terminology adopted by organisations in this more market-oriented environment have become more complicated, and this situation is further confused by considerable variations in practice both between and within sectors.

Cost centres

The term *cost centre* is used in various ways in different organisations/ sectors. Basically it denotes anywhere that costs are ascertained and collected or grouped together for the purposes of cost control, which can be defined in terms of one or more departments or other operational units, functions or processes, items of equipment, or people. A cost centre represents an aggregate of lower order functions, known as *cost units* (typically, a job, batch, (sub)process/step, individual item/element (of product, service, etc) or a period of time). Cost centres can be responsibility (line) oriented or programme/function oriented. The term 'cost centre' can also be used more specifically to distinguish departments (or other units) that have discretion over costs only, with no specific revenue targets.

The term **responsibility centre** is sometimes used instead of cost centre to signal the fact that a manager is *responsible* for the cost performance of a particular unit, and that his or her personal performance will thus be judged on some measure of cost control – typically a comparison between the amount of (direct) cost budgeted and the amount actually incurred. The term *responsibility accounting* is associated with a system of decentralisation and delegated responsibility for day-to-day operating decisions, including authorisation of expenditure. The term 'responsibility centre' can be used in a more general sense to mean any organisational function or unit whose manager is responsible for all its activit-

ies, and also as an umbrella term for more specific types of responsibility/
cost centre as listed below:

- **managed cost centre** (sometimes known as an *expense centre*, or *discretionary expense centre*) – the manager is responsible for giving the best level of performance while keeping within his or her budget, typically used for administrative, maintenance, research and service units;
- **standard cost centre** – the manager is responsible for achieving the standard *controllable* costs (also known as *engineered* costs) for which an input/output relationship can be defined, such as direct labour, direct material and variable overheads; typically used for operations and production units;
- **revenue centre** – the manager is responsible for achieving a revenue target ('sales quota') or maximising sales revenue while keeping within his or her budget and selling at pre-set prices, thus having little or no discretion over costs; typically used for sales units or small branch outlets of large retail chains;
- **profit centre** (sometimes also known as a *contribution centre*) – the manager is responsible for maximising profit, with complete discretion over both the costs incurred and prices charged (and any trade-offs between them) typically used for large retail branches or retail service outlets;
- **investment centre** – the manager is responsible for achieving a percentage 'rate of return' on capital or maximising *residual* profit (or 'residual income') which takes account of the resources or assets used in making it (the amount of 'capital employed') typically used for relatively autonomous divisions of large organisations.

The term **budget centre** is also used as a slightly different concept to the framework of responsibility centres outlined above, where the focus is specifically on comparing actual performances with the budget for the same thing, and analysing resulting variances, in order to identify corrective actions required and to emphasise the need for control and accountability with the budgeted parameters.

Budgeting

The budget is in effect a statement of organisational intent expressed in financial/monetary terms – a series of conscious or implied goals with price tags. Budgeting involves the allocation of (scarce) resources among competing activities, programmes or services; this implies a knowledge of the costs of the activities and an understanding of the objectives of the organisation. Ideally, the budgeting process is integrated with a planning process, which determines objectives and priorities for various timespans, and supported by data collection and analysis to inform decision-making. Thus five-year service strategies will be accompanied by five-year financial projections, and the annual budget submission will be considered in this context, as part of a review or 'rolling forward' of longer-term plans. (An annual budget cycle is the accepted practice, but budgets for special undertakings, such as research projects, may have timespans of more or less than twelve months.)

Budgets often fulfil several **purposes** and functions simultaneously, and managers need to be alert to this. A budget is both a plan for the distribution of resources and a tool for the prediction of costs. It covers a defined period, is approved in advance, and can be either directive or participatory in nature. At one level the budget can be seen as an action plan expressed in monetary terms, which in turn acts as a control mechanism and as an evaluation tool; it thus has a crucial integrative role in translating strategic plans into current actions. However, it can also serve as a communication aid and a co-ordinating device, or it may be viewed as a service contract. In addition, the budget can be used to highlight – or hide – strategic issues, and to set precedents. It is vital to be aware of these different dimensions: budgeting requires both technical and behavioural skills, it is a social process, which can be approached reactively or proactively, and it also has motivational and political aspects. Budgeting systems (like planning systems) must be compatible with the culture and characteristics of an organisation.

Budgets – like plans – can be defined in terms of their timescale, scope and focus. The main types of budget are:

- **capital budgets**, which are usually multi-year budgets, to fund things of enduring worth that are not consumed quickly (typically high-cost changes or improvements, such as a new building or a computer network, and possibly also major purchases for special collections)
- **operating** or **revenue budgets**, which are year-by-year budgets, generally drawn up on an annual basis, for the organisation as a whole and for its constituent parts, to fund current operations;
- **special budgets**, which have varying time periods and may include both capital and operating funds, to fund smaller-scale projects (typically single-purpose grants from government agencies or charitable foundations, which need to be treated separately for accounting and reporting).

Traditionally different arrangements have applied to recurrent, operating income and expenditure and large 'one-off' capital expenditures, but a five-year financial plan may bring these two types of expenditure together (and sometimes these large purchases have to be depreciated year-by-year during their useful life). Moreover, with budget reductions and diversity of income streams, the traditional division of budgets into capital and recurring is disappearing. Many service managers are now expected to find the funds for major purchases such as library management systems or CD-ROM networks from their operating budgets by achieving savings in salaries or other areas of the budget, either making provisions over several years or taking out a loan (with interest) from the parent organisation. The assumptions of funders that information technology will reduce staff costs and replace – rather than enhance – traditional activities poses particular challenges in this respect.

The different **methods** of preparing and presenting budgets vary in complexity and level of detail. The main approaches used are the following:

- **line-item** – the simplest, most common form, where each category of expenditure is represented by a line. Lists components of expenditure and amounts projected for each (for example, salaries, equipment, supplies, library materials, which might be further sub-divided into categories of staff, types of materials, etc). Usually based on past year's budget with amounts adjusted marginally to reflect inflation, and often shows actual spend for previous year and budgeted spend for the current year alongside the proposed budget. This has limited value as a planning tool, with its focus on *inputs* (rather than outputs) and inability to relate spend to services or objectives; it makes services especially vulnerable to cuts as it is difficult to identify implications of cuts on particular services or users. (Also known as *object-of-expenditure* or *incremental* budgeting.)

- **programme** – the next stage, more prevalent now, especially with the development of devolved provision and service level agreements. Designs budget around service areas, typically reflecting organisational structure (for example, bibliographic services, lending services) and then develops detailed line-item budget for each. This supplements rather than substitutes for the line-item method and is time-consuming as it requires staff and other costs to be calculated for activities, but is useful as a planning tool with its focus on *services*. It is also known as *functional* budgeting, but can be applied to different groupings (e.g. client- or geographically-based units, such as faculty teams in academic libraries, community services in public libraries). Provides linkages between inputs and outputs, but can make services vulnerable to cuts by drawing attention to their costs.

- **performance** – takes programme budgeting a stage further. In addition to providing basic data, identifies measures of performance to enable evaluation of programme *effectiveness*. A variant of this is the *Planning Programming Budgeting System* (PPBS) which stresses – as the name suggests – the planning aspects of budgeting at the level of the organisation as a whole. This requires identification of goals and sub-goals for an organisation's main spending programmes over time, consideration of alternative ways of achieving them and selection of output indicators according to set criteria. It encourages focus on the long term, but is not widely used now because of the complexity in relating departmental activities and costs to programme areas, although some elements such as measurable targets and performance indicators have survived. Alternatively, the term *performance* or *activity* budgeting can be used to mean a more specific level of budgeting, so that expenditure is presented not only for a service area (such as bibliographic services) but for specific activities (such as cataloguing) which enables isolation of unit costs, and provides a focus on *efficiency*.

- **zero-base** – the most complex and least used method. Zero Base Budgeting (ZBB) goes further than PPBS as it requires full justification of all programmes at all levels, and is a decentralised method, also known as *bottom-up* budgeting. Departments are required to identify component programmes or 'decision units' and then build up a budget representing different levels of activity, from the minimal (zero cost) to ideal funding situation; each unit must specify objectives, operational details, consequences of discontinuation, and costs and benefits of different methods and levels. The programmes are then evaluated, ranked and acceptable/possible funding levels decided. Although effective in prioritising, ZBB is extremely time-consuming and more likely to be used for a 'one-off' review or in relation to business development or expansion.

- **priority base** – a variant of ZBB, designed to resolve the conflicting demands of improving or maintaining services and minimising costs. Developed by Coopers & Lybrand in the 1980s and pioneered by Texas Instruments in the US, Priority Base Budgeting (PBB) requires managers to establish the purposes of their activities and evaluate alternative means of achieving them, by defining the absolute minimum level (and cost) of the service to satisfy essential requirements, and then identifying successive increments with costs and benefits, representing optional activities to satisfy discretionary requirements of the function within the framework of a ten-point rating scale. The resulting priority listing enables top management to determine budgets within resource constraints, but with a much better understanding of the service implications. The *PBB rating scale* is a useful tool for prioritisation and service level definition, irrespective of whether the framework is used for budgeting. (See discussion of priority-based planning in Chapter 4.)

- **formula-based** – generally associated with publicly-funded services. In formula-based funding, factors such as the size of population served and levels of usage are used to determine either all or part of the allocation to the library, or the percentage share of the budget to be allocated to each sub-division or client group – in effect, a different type of *incrementalism*. This method is most commonly used in academic libraries for allocating acquisition funds, where the different variables often include weighted numbers of faculty and students, average literature costs, levels of demand, patterns of use, any special needs and institutional priorities. It has the advantages of transparency, objectivity, flexibility and equity, but also disadvantages in its complexity and subjectivity (in determining the relative weightings of the various factors).

Other methods sometimes used include **option budgets** (embodying some ZBB principles) where budget holders are required to respond to various percentage reductions/increases in budget provision, and **lump-sum budgets**, where a service gets a *one-line* budget (usually based on incrementalism) with no explicit link to a plan – although a plan is generally required.

The common incremental approach to budgeting, which takes the previous year as the starting point and adds – or subtracts – a percentage amount, is the method typically favoured by organisations which do not plan strategically or holistically, and tends also to be associated with unsophisticated evaluation of financial performance. Output-/performance-oriented methods represent an attempt to avoid routine requests for more of the same and force managers to plan before they budget. Service managers have to shift their thinking from 'how shall we spend our money?' to 'what will it cost to achieve our goals?' (and 'how will we fund it?') Over the last few decades, the focus in many organisations has moved from executive control (associated with line-item budgets) to planning (programme budgets) and accountability (performance budgets). The wider range of options for service delivery in the networked environment also means that information service managers need more sophisticated systems to enable proper assessment of costs and benefits when planning and evaluating their services.

Budget cycles

Planning and budgeting are iterative and interactive processes that should take place as a systematic and cyclical activity. The financial or fiscal year varies from sector to sector and country to country. In addition to the calendar year (January to December), common variants include April to March (UK central and local government) and August to July (UK higher education). To complicate matters, some institutions use different periods for financial and non-financial reporting. During any one year there will be tasks associated with the budget for the current year, the previous year and forthcoming year(s). The box summarises the key stages and steps in creating, executing and documenting the budget.

Figure 5.1 Key stages in the annual budget cycle

PREPARE	Plan	Strategic objectives reviewed and confirmed by senior management/strategy group. Operational plans drafted by middle managers/team leaders.
&	Collate	External data gathered from colleagues, publications, suppliers, etc. Internal cost data collected from colleagues/management information system.
ESITIMATE	Moderate	Institutional guidelines notified (e.g inflation allowance, savings target). Financial planning assumptions confirmed by senior management.
SUMBIT	Propose	Bids invited from service managers/budget holders (supported by operational plans, commenting on changes and items related to strategic initiatives).
&	Decide	Options appraised, priorities assigned and draft budget agreed by resource co-ordinator and senior management (and communicated to colleagues).
APPROVE	Inform	Provisional allocations confirmed or revised, and notified to budget holders and other service staff, local accounts team and organisation's finance office.
CONTROL	Monitor	Monthly system reports from accounts team to budget holders (showing spend to date against benchmark targets) with summary reports to senior managers.
&	Analyse	Monthly/quarterly management reports from budget holders to senior managers (commenting on variances and indicating whether corrective action is required).
MONITOR	Review	Quarterly and year-end evaluations by resource co-ordinator and senior management, leading to corrective actions and/or prospective decisions.

This is a simplified representation, based on a budget process for a medium-sized information unit; these steps then have to be related to the planning and budgeting cycle of the parent organisation, as there will be further iterations 'up the line'. For larger service units, the internal process may similarly have several iterations as section heads invite bids from team leaders, etc.

Process guidelines

Data gathered for budget estimates can come from a variety of internal and external sources. Both the Library Association and the American Library Association regularly publish information showing trends in periodical prices, giving average prices by subject categories and percentage increases over previous years.[7,8] In the US, Marcia Tuttle circulates a *Newsletter on Serials Pricing Issues* by electronic mail.[9] In the UK, the Library and Information Statistics Unit at Loughborough University regularly publishes reports on the average prices of British and USA academic books[10,11] and also surveys of public library budgets and materials funds.[12] Subscription agents and other suppliers also provide forecasts for customers, and will often provide figures tailored to reflect the customer's particular subscription profile, and also guidance on currency fluctuations.

Internal cost data may be based on existing management information systems or compiled specifically for the bidding exercise – on the basis of sample measurements, formal estimation or informed guesswork. Many organisations maintain 'ready reckoners' to aid the calculation of average staffing costs by category, and also have conventions for the notional number of 'effective hours' worked in a year, which can be used in conjunction with diary-based recording methods. Some managers use 'rule-of-thumb' standards, drawing on received wisdom or best practice to determine allocations for particular expense heads (for example, allocating the equivalent of two per cent of payroll costs for staff training, or assuming that the cost of purchasing equals the cost of processing). Alice Sizer Warner lists 18 such 'standards' covering academic, school, public, special and law libraries, but such an approach is questionable in the current budget environment.[13]

Ann Prentice is critical of library managers as information users in this context,

> "Although library personnel are information specialists, they tend to short-change their own information gathering needs. They often do not place the organization and management of information needed to operate their service at a particularly high priority level. Either they work with relatively little management data, or large amounts of information are collected, the purpose of which may be vague. . . Until recently, too few library managers and planners were comfortable with basic statistical techniques or understood the value of such analysis to the improvement of their operations. Because of the amount of data libraries collect but often do not analyze for use, they are among those organizations called 'data rich but information poor'."[6]

Formal budget submissions or presentations should include sufficient background information on the service and its plans for the period, showing how these relate to the parent body's goals, with comments on alternatives considered, significant changes from the previous year, and any special factors (for example, impact of inflation or currency fluctuations) indicating phasing of expenditure if appropriate. On this basis, the full budget statement combines qualitative, quantitative and fiscal information. In practice, annual budget submissions are quite often treated just as number-crunching exercises, with minimal commentary requested or provided, largely confined to explanation of tactics to achieve savings targets ('efficiency gains') and/or changes from previous allocations.

Regular budget reports need to be accurate, timely, clear, auditable, tailored to management requirements (bearing in mind that senior management and operational managers require different levels of detail) and consistent in their content and format (to enable comparisons). Such reports are typically set up to include the budget allocation for each item for the year, the expenditure to date (sometimes also expressed as a percentage) and the amount remaining. Budgetary control and expenditure analysis can be improved by setting month-by-month targets; in some cases managers will expect an even pattern of expenditure throughout the year (8.3% per month) but in many cases there will be predictable seasonal variations, which should be reflected in the benchmarks used.

Tips

- For estimating and monitoring purposes, break down **equipment** expenditure into separate categories for maintenance contracts and other ongoing commitments; a rolling programme of upgrading and replacement for standard items; and 'one-off' larger purchases or capital items.
- To support strategic developments and quality improvements, and to enable quick flexible responses to good proposals emerging during the budget period, create a separate expense head for **projects** (with no limitations on the type of expenditure, so that it can be used for staffing, equipment, consultancy, etc).
- Keep special records for multi-year and 'packaged' **subscriptions**, to avoid over-estimating and over-payment – but also ensure that you do not forget to make proper provision for them in the right years.

Costing

The ability to cost activities has become more important with diminishing resources, increased accountability, more choice in methods of delivery, and continuing interest in benchmarking, charging and out-sourcing. An inherent problem for information service managers is that information work is labour-intensive, with staff costs typically account-ing for 35%–55% of the department's costs (depending on whether accommodation costs are charged to the service). This reduces the scope for short-term budget adjustment (unless many staff are employed on fixed-term contracts) and puts a premium on accounting for staff time, which runs counter to tradition (especially in public-sector organisations). Various methods of data collection can be used, includ-ing work sampling and selective or continuous time-logging/diary-keeping, but there are real dangers here in introducing systems which are themselves labour-intensive, demotivating and ultimately counter-productive; attempts to control staff time too rigidly may inhibit initiat-ive, reduce responsiveness and damage service quality and customer rela-tions. A further problem for information service staff is the amount of time likely to be required for professional updating and skills refresh-ment, which may be difficult to attribute to specific services.

Costing **information** is complex and different from costing other types of goods and services; unlike other commodities, information can be shared without diminution, it can be jointly consumed, and it can also generate benefits and costs for those who are not direct users or produ-cers. In addition, costing information is complicated by the range of different elements that must be included to arrive at the total cost of a product or service, which has been exacerbated by information techno-logy developments (bringing in the challenge of apportioning the capital and recurrent costs of, for example, hardware, software, technical sup-port and user documentation). Confusion often arises over the identi-fication of *fixed* and *variable* costs, the difference between *marginal* and *unit* costs, definition of *direct* and *indirect* costs, treatment of organ-isational *overheads* (including utilities and other accommodation-related costs) and policy for *depreciation* of capital purchases, such as work stations and furniture. As always, internal consistency and institutional compliance are important considerations. A glossary of common cost concepts is provided in Appendix 3.

Costs are resources expressed in monetary/cash values that have been exchanged for goods or services. The term is often used synonymously with *expense,* but more properly it means the *value* of resources exchanged for past, present or future benefits, represented by the *outflow* of resources in return for assets. Traditionally **cost accounting** has been about accumulating and assigning costs to departments, products and services, etc for *inventory* and *budget* purposes, but it is currently more concerned with costing for *decision-making,* both for regular evaluation and non-routine decisions (for example, about introducing or with-drawing services). With the prospect of a continuing requirement for efficiency savings in both the public and private sectors, costing becomes a more important activity for managers generally – but especially for information professionals, as savings on salaries and running costs are often sought to pay for investment in equipment or to compensate for above-average price rises in information resources.

Costing methods and techniques

There are various approaches to costing. The following are the main types of cost study.

- **Cost analysis** can be used as a generic term for cost study or more specifically to describe the primary stage of assessing the basic costs of a cost element, task, cost centre, or other appropriate unit. It involves converting labour and/or machine hours to monetary values, and adding other expense elements (such as materials and overheads). This requires identification of all the expense categories for a given function or task, and calculating their costs either by measurement or estimation, which then provides information for other types of study (and for accounting, estimating, budgeting and performance measurement).
- **Cost allocation** is a term often used for the process of assigning costs from one cost objective to others, particularly the assignment of overhead or indirect costs of administration, building and other organisation-wide functions to particular departments, services or products. Alternatively, *cost allocation* is used specifically to describe the allotment of whole items of *direct* cost to cost centres/cost units, and can thus be distinguished from *cost apportionment*, which is the preferred term for the process of assigning proportions of *indirect* costs to services etc.
- **Unit costing** is another level of study, which combines information from cost analysis with measures of output to give cost-per-unit data, used for performance measurement and benchmarking (including comparisons year-on-year, from library to library, and of alternative methods of performing a task). Unit cost data must be used with discretion, particularly for comparative purposes, as the definitions of tasks and treatment of overheads may vary significantly among different organisations and services.
- **Absorption costing** assumes that all costs (direct/indirect, fixed/variable) must not only be apportioned to cost centres, but actually charged to or *absorbed* by particular cost units, and thus takes into account the fixed costs of production that are not affected by changes in the volume of activity. Absorption costing is particularly used for long-term decision-making, including pricing decisions.
- **Marginal costing** or *contribution costing* deliberately separates costs

into fixed and variable categories, and does not apportion the fixed costs to individual products or services, thus avoiding the problem of arbitrary and unsatisfactory assignment of overheads. *Marginal costing* is particularly concerned with the *behaviour* of costs (rather than their function) and it is used to analyse cost/volume/profit relationships, and to set prices for products and services – particularly in the not-for-profit sector. The difference between sales revenue and variable costs is known as the *contribution,* on the basis that it contributes towards covering the fixed costs.

- **Cost-efficiency** studies focus on inputs, aiming to minimise costs at a given level of output – not necessarily the most effective solution in relation to service objectives (that is, the aim is to maximise effectiveness of *spending,* not effectiveness of *performance*).
- **Cost-effectiveness** studies focus on outputs, aiming to maximise performance output at a given level of input cost – keeping costs to a minimum, but not necessarily favouring the least-cost solution – or to find the cheapest means to achieve a defined objective. Cost-effectiveness thus requires information on the costs of existing processes, and also model cost data for alternative options, to determine which method performs best according to the effectiveness criteria specified.
- **Cost-benefit analysis** determines and evaluates the *social* costs and benefits of an investment, aiming to measure the benefit of a particular activity to an individual, agency or society at large and to relate that to the actual cost. It draws on data from other types of cost study, but considers wider impacts, is more subjective and takes a longer-term view than cost-effectiveness (but is often confused with the latter). This can be used to decide whether a product or service is worth the price, to identify economic levels of service or to determine the feasibility of alternatives to current arrangements. (See Chapter 4 for further details and suggested steps towards cost-benefit analysis.)
- **Cost-value analysis** is a less common, less formal and less precise type of analysis than cost-benefit, with the measurement of value being more subjective and qualitative, but the term is included here to complete the picture.

F. W. Lancaster argues that a defect of many library and information service cost studies is that they view user time – the time spent by customers using the service – as free, but for many types of evaluation (notably cost-effectiveness and cost-benefit analysis) a realistic analysis of the cost of using the service is an important factor.[14]

Beyond these basic approaches to costing there are various tools and techniques that can be used in the course of such studies. Managers need to be aware of the different methods commonly employed and to understand the differences between them as this can have a significant impact on their financial situation. These techniques underpin managerial effectiveness in critically important areas such as *cost apportionment, cost control, cost recovery* and *investment appraisal*. Service managers need to take an active interest and become more involved in discussions and decisions on costing methodology within their organisations. This is particularly crucial in the context of devolved budgeting and internal charging arrangements. A brief explanation of techniques to consider and explore is given below. For further details, readers are referred to management accounting textbooks (*see* suggestions for further reading).

Cost apportionment is necessary to build understanding of the 'true' costs of activities, and to encourage optimal use of organisational resources. Several techniques can be used for this purpose, both at the initial stage of transferring costs from one department to another, and then to distribute costs to final products and services. Traditional methods (often based on headcount or machine time) do not always produce sensible results. **Activity-based costing** is a relatively recent technique which acknowledges that many indirect costs are variable, and uses the concept of *cost drivers* to determine cause-and-effect relationships as the basis for apportioning overhead. Managers also need to decide whether to use the *direct* method for distributing costs among final products and services, or to choose a more complex method (such as *step-down, reciprocal* or *double distribution*).

Monitoring of costs as they are incurred at the transactional level enables better budgetary control for the service as a whole. *Standard costing* combined with *flexible budget variance analysis* helps managers to identify how much of the variance can be attributed to economy, efficiency, etc. **Standard cost analysis** in effect sets budgets at the *unit cost* level (for example, the cost of processing a book) and facilitates delegation of budgetary control and generation of meaningful performance measures. **Break-even analysis** is the classic method used for determining the point at which a priced service or product covers its costs. This tool also helps managers to understand volume and cost relationships as reflected in changes in variable, stepped and fixed costs.

In both strategic and operational planning, managers often have to compare the costs of different options for service delivery (for example, access versus holdings, charging for services, leasing or purchasing equipment, in-house activity versus outsourcing) and the distribution of those costs as future annual cash flows. **Life-cycle costing** is a technique which acknowledges that similar assets may have proportionately different initial and ongoing costs, and offers a framework for identifying costs in three broad categories – planning and design; purchase and installation; and operation and maintenance. Its use in libraries dates back to the British Library Review of Acquisition and Retention Policies, which developed models showing the hidden downstream costs of library acquisitions.[15] It is especially useful for appraising the costs of IT-based systems and services. Life-cycle costing is often used in conjunction with *net present value analysis* – a technique which acknowledges that the value of money changes over time, and uses *discount rates* to express this as net cash inflows and outflows over the life of the investment. **Payback analysis** is a quicker investment appraisal tool, which simply measures the time required to repay the initial investment on the basis of anticipated annual earnings or savings, but completely ignores the 'time value' of money.

A basic model for costing

1. Decide the focus and level of the costing exercise – the product, service, process or system which will be the subject of study or *cost objective*.
2. Determine a sensible activity or period base – unit measures of output, or time units (such as an hour, day, week, month, year).
3. Identify all the relevant cost components, gather available data, and plan how to collect data not readily available (such as staff time spent on various tasks).
4. Classify the costs according to their type – direct/indirect, fixed/variable – and establish behaviour patterns of variable and any stepped costs.
5. Calculate (via measurement or estimation) and allocate the *direct* costs.
6. Group or aggregate the indirect costs, on the basis of their homogeneity or similar causal relationships with the cost objective, to form *cost pools*.
7. Identify *cost drivers* as the basis for relating costs to objectives, select a method for (re)distributing overheads and apportion the indirect costs.
8. Consolidate the data and choose a suitable form of presentation.

Tips

- Consider the degree of local management control in assessing whether costs should be regarded as fixed or variable for practical purposes;
- Take advice from staff in choosing a method for gathering data on the use of their time, and bear in mind the time required for both recording and analysis;
- Keep the number of different allocation bases to a manageable level by pooling overhead costs that exhibit similar trends or tendencies in behaviour.

Pricing

All profit-making organisations and many non-profit ones have to set *prices* for their products or services (which is used here as a generic term for charges, fees, subscriptions, etc). Poor pricing can suppress or over-stimulate demand, and thus affect an organisation's ability to provide products or services which the community wants or needs. The same principles apply to both external and internal markets, but unfortunately many managers give insufficient thought to *transfer pricing*, viewing this as mainly an *administrative* matter.

Price can be defined in several ways – as the amount of money charged for a product or service or, more broadly, as the values consumers exchange for the benefits of having or using the product or service. In general terms, it represents an *exchange value* from both the producer/supplier and the consumer/buyer viewpoint. Pricing can also be seen as a rationing device – a mechanism for allocating scarce resources – and/or a means of recovering costs or generating additional income. **Pricing objectives** can be divided into short-term tactical manoeuvres and longer-term strategic moves. Typical examples of the former include: attracting new customers; matching existing competition; using spare capacity; or trimming off overfull demand. Examples of the latter include: achieving return on assets; realising target market share; keeping competitors out of key markets; and strategic pricing in different markets.

Factors influencing pricing include internal issues (such as service objectives, production/process costs and income targets) and the external environment (nature of the market, level of demand, existing competition, regulation, etc). The overall strategy and marketing objectives for the product or service will determine the pricing strategy. These might be ambitious (market domination, profit maximisation, quality leadership) or more cautious (market stabilisation, customer retention, organisational survival). There will often be multiple – and sometimes conflicting – goals that need to be prioritised. It is generally unrealistic to try to maximise market share and profits in a competitive market; managers have to balance short-term and longer-term obectives, which might involve cross-subsidisation of products or services. (A classic example here is the decision by Microsoft to give away its Internet Explorer web browser, in order to take market share from Netscape.) Public sector and non-profit organisations are often concerned to maximise use and optimise resources, which can be expressed in marketing terms as increasing market share and/or volume of sales (although this begs more fundamental questions about the best use of resources).

Prices will thus be affected by:

- *organisational objectives* – strategic, marketing, and financial;
- *product/service costs* – especially cost behaviour in relation to volume;
- *market interactions* – of buyers and sellers, activities of competing suppliers;
- *consumer behaviour* – their need for the goods, their ability and willingness to pay
- *economic conditions* – inflation, interest and exchange rates, government policy.

The term 'price elasticity of demand' is used to denote how responsive or sensitive demand is to changing price. Price tends to be more *elastic* (responsive) for non-essential items, especially if close substitutes are available; thus goods and services that have many alternatives tend to have elastic demand curves (for example, library photocopying facilities). Price tends to be less elastic when goods/services are essential and there are few or no substitutes or competitors, and when buyers are slow to change their habits, do not readily notice the higher price or think they are justified by quality improvements, normal inflation, and so on; thus things that are considered extremely valuable, important or necessary have *inelastic* demand curves (for example, academic journal subscriptions).

Pricing decisions are often arbitrary, hurried and ill-informed. There are three general approaches, which are respectively *cost-based, buyer-oriented* and *competitor-related*. However, reliable information on service/product costs and an understanding of cost behaviour is essential for effective price-setting, irrespective of the system or method adopted; most firms will calculate their costs and use this as their 'floor price' – consumer perceptions set the ceiling, and competitor offerings must also be taken into account. There are many variants within each category; the box summarises the main approaches described in the marketing literature. Buyer-oriented approaches are also referred to as *demand-oriented, market-related* and *value-based* systems; the term 'market-related' can also be applied to competitor-related approaches.

Transfer pricing

Putting a price on the internal transfer of good and services is a practice particularly associated with *vertically integrated* organisations (for example, where materials are passed to another business unit for further processing or manufacture) but it has become more widespread with the development of devolved budgeting arrangements, service level agreements and various forms of internal trading in both the private and public sectors. Arrangements of this type apply not just to production and sales operations, but also to centralised services, such as computing,

Figure 5.2 Main approaches to pricing products and services

Cost-based	Buyer-oriented	Competitor-related
o Full cost or absorption cost	o Moral pricing	o Going-rate pricing
o Standard / average cost	o Pricing points	o Price leadership
o Mark-up / cost-plus	o Price discrimination	o Premium pricing
o Target profit / rate-of-return	o Promotional pricing	o Market-share pricing
o Marginal cost / break-even	o Price skimming	o Discount pricing
o Cost-minus pricing	o Prestige/psychological	o Negotiated pricing
o Product analysis pricing	o Penetration pricing	o Sealed-bid pricing

finance, personnel, training, estates, administration – and library/ information services. Transfer pricing is necessary for proper financial evaluation in a decentralised environment because however self-contained in theory, departments/business units have dependencies on other parts of the organisation, including pseudo-trading relationships and shared processing operations, making managers responsible for costs over which they have little or no control. There is also a belief that if managers do not have to pay for goods and services received they will use them uneconomically (by demanding larger quantities or higher quality than they need, or by being wasteful).

Prices are thus needed to evaluate the inputs and outputs from departments/business units and to encourage efficiency and economy. The basis on which transfer prices are set becomes a critical issue for performance evaluation when departments/units are treated as revenue, profit or investment centres. If the transfer price is set too low, the 'selling' unit's profitability is reduced and the 'buying' unit's profitability is overstated, which in turn may result in misallocation of resources and demotivation of managers; if set too high, an autonomous buying unit may shop elsewhere to the overall detriment of the organisation – the introduction of internal trading often leads to reductions in usage/consumption that are not desirable. Pricing decisions therefore need to be based on an overall organisational policy rather than taken in an *ad hoc* fashion. The basic principle is that all prices set and costs apportioned should reflect an accurate measure of efficiency.

An effective transfer pricing regime will meet the following **criteria:**

1. Enable local autonomy and motivate business unit/cost centre managers;
2. Provide a basis for financial control and performance evaluation of cost centres;
3. Generate data that informs and supports sound business decisions;

4. Encourage managers to be economical and efficient in their use of resources;
5. Ensure goal congruence between business unit targets and organisational objectives;
6. Incorporate a negotiating procedure and an arbitration mechanism;
7. Achieve a sensible balance between the interests of competing cost centres;
8. Reflect the competitive market by basing prices on similar products and services.

The main **options** relate to the cost/market/competitor-based approaches outlined above:

- *cost-based* methods use marginal/variable costs or full/standard costs, with or without a profit allowance – *standard costs* (especially ideal/benchmark rates) are preferable to actual costs as this stops the selling unit passing on its inefficiencies to the buying unit, however *cost-plus* can result in prices that are too high when fixed costs are apportioned to low levels of activity;
- *cost plus profit-share* is an alternative method, which can involve transfers made at either total or marginal cost, with margins on the ultimate sale *shared* among the business units concerned according to an agreed formula;
- *market-oriented* methods include open market prices (the 'going rate') and the market price less savings associated with internal trading, or prices *negotiated* by the managers concerned, with or without assistance of a group/divisional manager;
- *dual prices* require a unit to act as intermediary between buying and selling departments, which enables the organisation to achieve different pricing objectives for the two departments – but at the cost of additional administration (and the need to 'net off' the difference in financial reports)
- *surrogate outputs* are sometimes used for service (as opposed to production) units, with charges based on numbers of transactions processed, hours worked, enquiries answered, etc, or they may be based not on consumption but on apportionment if there is concern that charging will result in sub-optimal utilisation – but this gives no measure of whether the service is 'paying its way', with only user satisfaction as a control.

The choice of system will depend on various factors, but particularly on how close the internal trading operations are to external market conditions. Thus a cost-based approach is most appropriate for goods or services that are never likely to be sourced outside the organisation, and market-based or actual competitive prices more appropriate for goods/

services sold to both internal and external customers or produced by both internal and external suppliers. In practice, it can be very difficult to determine 'fair' prices. An imposed settlement by a group/divisional manager may be necessary if either buyer or seller is effectively in a monopoly situation. A device sometimes used to deal with this issue is to allow divisional purchasing officers to purchase a proportion (say 10 to 20 per cent) of supplies from outside, which gives them more leverage with internal suppliers. Internal audit can provide an important check on the application of the organisation's internal trading policy.

The key **factors** affecting systems adopted are:

- the proportion of activity that the transfer-priced element represents;
- the freedom given to managers to trade outside the organisation;
- the existence of alternative external suppliers and/or customers;
- the availability of market price information and the time to research it.

Information pricing

Prices for information services need to take account of the peculiar characteristics of information resources, including their 'public good' and 'merit good' attributes. The characteristics that distinguish information from other economic resources are as follows:

- **non-depletable** – information is sharable and *non-subtractive,* in that it can be used without being consumed, which makes it a *public good* in economic terms;
- **transportable** – information is hard to control and *diffusive,* in that production capacity is virtually unconstrained (for example, via photocopying or downloading) and production cost is disproportionately low for second and subsequent copies;
- **expandable** – information is *structurally abundant* and tends to generate more information (for example, via technology transfer or research reports) often gaining value when shared or re-used, but at the same time it is *compressible* and value may be added by subtracting information (for example, via filtering or editing)
- **non-substitutable** – the content of information products (for example, a journal article or a database record) is frequently unique, although there may be several sources of supply and alternative arrangements for access;
- **unpredictable** – the value of information is often hard to forecast or quantify, and is not necessarily related to production cost.

For information products, the normal laws of *supply and demand* and of *diminishing returns* are upset by the fact that production capacity is often controlled by consumers and production costs are front-loaded, with significant discrepancies between sunk and marginal costs, so that economies of scale become overwhelming. Cost-related pricing is often considered to be 'fairer' by information professionals because they feel there is more certainty about costs than demand or value. Public-sector services often adopt marginal cost recovery or marginal cost pricing as an approach on the basis of trying to keep charges to the consumer as low as possible at the point of use (although this raises the question of inappropriate use of public funds or unfair competition when the service is competing directly with a private-sector provider).

In addition to the above, information is often considered to be something with inherent value and social benefits extending beyond those derived by the individual consumer, which makes it a **merit good** with *positive externalities* in economic terms. Merit goods are often subsidised by governments (and sometimes provided by charities) and this aspect strengthens the argument for marginal cost pricing. Another key point here is that pricing decisions for information services are often taken in the context of existing service capacity (equipment, permanent staff and basic operating conditions). In such circumstances it makes more sense to treat fixed costs as a lump sum (and subtract them from the total) than to allocate them on a unit basis.

Accounting

In general terms, accounting covers the processes involved in categorising, recording and summarising the monetary flows associated with an organisation's activities, and its subsequent communication and interpretation. It is the technical aspect of financial reporting and uses standardised methods, which enable comparisons of performance over time and among organisations. There are three main types of accounting:

Financial accounting is the public reporting and disclosure of financial information according to various professional and legal practices and standards, exemplified in the UK by the accounts deposited by companies at Companies House or the accounts published by universities with their annual reports. Such statements are at a global level, referring either to the whole organisation or semi-autonomous units within it, in a prescribed format, and are intended for use externally by shareholders, government and other outside parties, for purposes such as tax collection, investment decisions and general elucidation and evaluation of an organisation's performance and status. For commercial organisations, the financial accounts are made up as a profit-and-loss account and a balance sheet; for a university, the income and expenditure account replaces the profit and loss account.

Cost accounting is the operational recording and reporting of the cost

in monetary terms of an activity, product or service, based on the identification and calculation of the resources associated with it, using techniques which originated in manufacturing industry but are now commonplace. Such accounts are at a much more detailed level of analysis,
usually relating to sub-units, departments, cost centres, products, services or activities, and are intended for use internally (by managers and
other staff) for purposes such as planning and controlling routine operations, comparison with standard or historical costs, and costing specific
projects or activities prior to decision-making. This type of accounting
is also sometimes referred to as *decision* accounting. It can be further
subdivided into *historic* cost accounting, which ignores inflation and
provides statements based solely on the original value of transactions;
and *current* cost accounting, which produces supplementary statements
clarifying the effects of inflation on both the profit earned and the value
of assets held at the year end. (Information service managers need to
consider the treatment of inflation in their accounts in view of its significant effect on the purchasing power of their budgets.)

Management accounting is the preparation and presentation of finan-
cial/accounting information to assist management with policy-making
and decision-taking, tailored to need in the detail, format and timing of
reports, rather than conforming to any prescribed or standard practice.
The term is often used interchangeably with cost accounting; the functions are similar, but management accounting (which is also referred to
as *managerial* accounting) can also be seen as operating at a higher level
of generality, and embracing *both* financial and cost accounts, to provide a complete picture of the financial state of an organisation for directors, divisional heads, etc. This information is used for various purposes such as strategic and operational planning, evaluating services,
taking decisions on alternative courses of action, decisions about adding
or deleting services, and communicating information to staff and other
stakeholders. Management accounting is thus concerned with producing
information to influence behaviour, and best exemplifies a point true of
accounting in general – that it is a *behavioural* rather than a *mathematical* science.

Accounting methods and techniques

Within this overall framework, all organisations thus have some formal
requirements (both externally-driven and internally-determined) but
they also adopt different methods for recording and reporting financial
transactions. Managers need to be aware of the conventions followed in
their own organisation as practices vary between and within sectors,
and failure to understand what figures actually represent can result in

misinterpretation and lead to ill-informed decisions. At a fundamental level, people need to know at what point an item of expenditure is recorded in the accounts – when the order is placed? when the item is received? when the bill is paid? The three main **methods** used are as follows.

- The **cash accounting** method records a transaction in the accounting system when cash flows in or out of the organisation. This is a simple method, typically used in small organisations or those with unsophisticated systems. It is obviously important to keep track of cash flows for the organisation as a whole, but for subsidiary units (such as libraries) this form of accounting is not very helpful unless there are rigid rules about not carrying over unspent funds from one year to the next – when the cash accounts become more critical. Invoicing and payment delays can obscure the true cost of operations during the accounting period, and give managers an inaccurate or distorted picture of performance against budget targets.
- The **commitment accounting** method records a transaction when a purchase order is raised (or a client is billed for a service). This enables managers to track activity against plans, irrespective of the vagaries of cash flows. Services with more sophisticated systems often combine the cash and commitment methods, and produce statements for managers showing both commitments and payments made to date. If there is a requirement to spend up the budget within the current year, managers will often set commitment targets well above the expenditure targets for areas such as book acquisitions, where a proportion of orders may be unfulfilled (because of delays in publishing or reprinting) and actual costs may vary (with discounts). A commitment can also be referred to as an *encumbrance* in this context.
- The **accruals accounting** method records expenses when they are incurred in providing services, regardless of when they are paid (or ordered) and similarly records revenue when it is earned, rather than when payments are received. This is the most complicated method, practised more in the US than in the UK. It makes a distinction between *expense* (a measure of the materials or services used in a particular period) and *expenditure* (a liability not limited to a particular period). Examples of expenses include salary costs, books and periodicals actually added to stock, staff travel and training. Expenditures include materials to be used over a longer period – for example, supplies purchased in bulk, where a proportion might be recorded as an expense for the current year and the rest held in reserve for later use. In an accrual system, outstanding encumbrances (unfulfilled orders) may be added to accrued (incurred) expenses at the year end to give managers a more complete picture of performance against budget targets.

Irrespective of whether a formal accrual system is in place, the principles are important and a reminder of the need not to take figures at their face value. For example, it is common practice for libraries to bulk-purchase vouchers for inter-library loans (ILLs) – especially if a price rise is in the offing. Under an accrual system, ILL vouchers only become an expense when used; under other systems, managers might have a distorted view of ILL activity for the year. The *modified accrual* method adopts a combination of cash and accrual, for example by allowing supplies and other inventory assets to be treated as either expensed-when-purchased (cash) or expensed-when-used (accrual).

Terminology for recording transactions using the accruals method
Purchase order is
   raised   Recorded as a *commitment* or *encumbrance*
Supplies are
   received   Recorded as an *accrued expenditure*
Supplies are used   Recorded as an *accrued expense* or *applied cost*
Cheque is raised   Recorded as a *cash expenditure* or *disbursement*

Other issues that managers need to consider in the preparation and presentation of accounts include the fact that buildings, equipment and other assets wear out and thus reduce in value or *depreciate* over time, and this situation will be exacerbated if prices rise or *inflate* at a significant rate so that the purchasing power of currency is reduced. Special techniques are often used to adjust figures to provide more 'accurate' statements. These issues are particularly important when preparing financial reports covering three to five years or longer, which is the sort of timespan that might be required to track progress in implementing a strategic plan.

   Depreciation accounting reports the worth of buildings, furniture, etc in relation to their decreasing value. It is based on the assumption that all equipment, from calculators and personal computers to chairs, desks and filing cabinets, has an average usable lifespan. For accounting purposes, a percentage of the replacement cost of each item should in theory be part of the cost of performing tasks associated with it. The two most common methods for calculating depreciation are the *straight line* method, which assumes that equipment will decline in value by an equal amount each year; and the *declining* or *reducing balance* method, which uses a formula and assumes that the depreciation cost is initially high, but then declines slowly and levels off when the item is towards the end of its useful life. The latter is more complicated but has an advantage in that higher annual maintenance costs in later years can be offset by lower depreciation charges. (Other less common techniques include the *annuity* and *sinking fund* methods.)

   Calculating depreciation costs for books and other information materials is more difficult: some reference materials lose value quite rapidly
and must be replaced frequently; other materials provide retrospective
information or are primarily literary in nature so their contents do not
become outdated, and indeed may appreciate in value – but their con-
tainers may become worn out, necessitating replacement or repair. The
relative value of container and content also varies significantly for materials acquired for their cultural, aesthetic or historical value (such as
materials acquired as examples of binding or typographic styles). Depreciation is a tax-deductible expense and therefore of financial importance
in company accounts; in the public sector, in some countries it has not
been a formal requirement, but it has managerial importance in helping
to assess actual programme costs and provide a better basis for business
planning, by raising awareness of the value and life of assets – especially
in the context of longer-term financial plans and where cost-recovery is
required. The critical dependence of information services on information
technology and the shortening replacement cycle for hardware means
that depreciation is not something many managers can afford to ignore.
   Inflation accounting makes adjustments to historic figures to enable
meaningful comparisons with current data. Even a relatively modest rate
of inflation (for example, 5% *per annum*) can have a dramatic effect on
the value of an organisation's assets and its purchasing power, including
its ability to meet the cost of replacement when assets wear out. There
are various methods for adjusting historical figures to reflect changes in
price levels and provide figures as a basis for comparison with current
costs, but difficulties arise as inflation affects services differently,
depending on market conditions, etc. Standard indices can be used, such
as the Retail Prices Index (RPI) or specific indices, such as those regularly
produced for books (by the Library and Information Statistics Unit) and
periodicals (by Blackwells). Sometimes organisations construct their own
in-house indices, or use indexation for selected items only; the latter risks
skewing results and not providing an accurate overall view. For example,
while book and periodical prices have risen at a rate well above general
price inflation in recent years, some items of computer equipment have
actually reduced in cost during this period. The key point is that managers need to be aware of the potential effects of inflation, they need to
find out what conventions are followed in their own organisation, and
to make it clear whether their figures take inflation into account (and if
so, on what basis).

Coding systems

Underpinning the recording and reporting of financial information, there
will normally be some form of *coding system*. Just as the collection,

processing and retrieval of library/information materials is generally supported by a classification scheme, the collection, processing and retrieval of cost data for costing and accounting purposes is usually supported by a system for coding items of expenditure (and income). Likewise, the quality of a coding system can have a similar impact on financial management processes as a classification system has on information management processes: a good coding system is the prerequisite for getting useful output from a finance system. Stephen Roberts emphasises the key role played by coding in management accounting and performance measurement,

> "The categorization and coding of tasks and expenditures occupies a central place in any costing and accounting system, and is the link between the structure of programmes and functions, the extraction and isolation of costs and the ultimate relation of output and performance to all that has gone before to achieve it." [1]

Coding is both a conventional and an essential method of organising cost data so that accountants, managers and others can not only record and describe financial transactions, but also aggregate, manipulate, extract, view and analyse relevant data. Yet, with the notable exception of Roberts, this subject is seriously neglected in the published literature, and is not always given the attention it deserves in organisations. Moreover, the potential contribution of information professionals to the design and development of such coding systems is rarely acknowledged: the parallels between accounts classification and coding schemes and library classification schemes, in terms of the knowledge and skills required should be obvious, but there is little evidence of information specialists being deliberately involved in this area, other than in their capacity as a manager or budget holder. (This situation may be changing with the convergence of library/information and computing/IT services – particularly where the IT function incorporates management information systems – and other boundary-spanning activities of information professionals in the context of broader interpretations of the information management function and growing interest in knowledge management.)

The parallels between accounts coding schemes and library classification schemes are further evidenced when one considers the main requirements for the *notation* for such systems. Account codes, through their notation, will ideally do the following:

- be easily learned and understood (for example, by using familiar signs or symbols)
- reveal the structure of the coding scheme (for example, by showing relationships between items)
- accommodate new categories and types of expenditure (for example, enabling new codes for electronic information resources)

- be easily memorised, written and spoken (for example, by using verbal extensions based on natural language).

In other words, an effective coding scheme will be *comprehensible, expressive, hospitable* and *mnemonic* in the same way that an effective (library) classification scheme is. Similarly, notations can be either *pure* or *mixed,* depending on whether they use numbers, letters or both – a combination is quite common. The notation of course only serves to *mechanise* the scheme, which first needs to be settled and written down, starting with the determination of the major categories of expenditure, before moving on to the more specific types of expense.

Expense categories
A good coding system will enable expenditure and income to be tracked, reported and analysed at various levels of detail and with different perspectives for the organisation as a whole or for individual departments, cost centres, etc. A fundamental requirement is that everyone in the organisation uses the same code for **primary expenses** (defined as a type of expenditure that cannot be divided further into two or more distinct types of expenditure) so that, for example, expenditure on wages and salaries, or on books and periodicals, can be aggregated across the whole organisation, as well as being reported for each department or other accounting unit involved.

Expenses can be categorised and classified in various ways; a fundamental categorisation is between *direct* and *indirect* expenses (reflecting the concepts of direct and indirect costs) but beyond that primary expenses can be listed according to what has been the nature or *subject* of the expenditure (such as salaries, materials, etc) or grouped according to the purpose or *object* for which the expenditure has been made (typically expressed in terms of organisational functions, business units, product lines, etc). Thus an accounting statement in *subjective form* lists expenditure in a way that gives totals for each kind of primary expense, while a statement in *objective form* groups expenditure to show how much has been spent on each department or area of activity – however that is defined. This gives us the two-dimensional classification of expenditure – first by type of expense, and secondly by type of activity – which forms the basis of most coding schemes.

Coding systems in practice vary considerably in the level of detail provided. Factors such as the size and type of organisation, its structure and culture, the scale and scope of operations, the formal accounting requirements and the strategic business objectives, will influence the choices made. Although in theory a simple one-dimensional scheme designed to provide a listing in subjective form which just shows expenditure totals for each kind of primary expense is an option, this approach is only likely to be adopted in very small organisations, as it offers very limited management information – people can see how much has been spent in each basic category, but not the purpose of the expenditure, and few organisations are truly single-function operations.

Many systems are designed around a minimum requirement of two coding elements to denote the expense category and the cost centre, with scope for further levels of analysis through the use of additional codes to identify more specific cost units or other perspectives on activities; departments/business units often have the freedom to decide their own levels of coding within an agreed overall organisational framework. By using several coding elements, managers can analyse the costs of their operations from different viewpoints. The initial division into cost centres often follows organisational lines (for example, functional departments, territorial divisions, etc) with additional codes used to supply other views (for example, a geographical focus if the main division is functional) or more detail (for example, identifying particular services, products, client groups, sub-groups, etc).

While information service managers generally have to work with the systems adopted by their parent organisations, there should be scope to specify codes reflecting their specialist activities within this overall framework (especially when the finance/accounting system is being upgraded or replaced). However, in some cases, the more detailed information will come not from third/fourth/fifth-level codes in the general accounting system, but from other systems that interface and/or feed in aggregated data. The most common example here is the library management system with an acquisitions module that records purchases item-by-item typically with subject/departmental fund codes. Libraries typically rely on their specialist systems to generate management reports at the required level of detail and upload automatically (or transfer manually) only the aggregate data to the general system.

Similar considerations arise with the use of project management software (or basic spreadsheets) to manage resources for projects, including externally-funded ventures whose reporting periods often do not coincide with the normal financial cycle. Even though there may be scope for tracking projects through the main finance system – some organisations designate cost centres specifically for this purpose – it is often simpler and more convenient to combine the recording of financial data with other aspects of project monitoring and planning. While there are valid arguments for maintaining separate systems in particular circumstances, the general aim should be to minimise overlap and avoid duplication of effort.

Control

As well as exercising budgetary and cost control, service managers are responsible for accounting and administrative control in line with organisational requirements and contractual obligations. Specific examples of such duties include procedures related to *assets registers* and *equipment inventories*. At a more general level, **internal control** can be described as a set of methods and measures to protect assets, check the accuracy and reliability of accounting, and ensure adherence to management policies and procedures. It is not just an accounting function, but is a system of both financial and non-financial practices, which involves all managers – and other staff – and many of its practical elements impact on day-to-day service operations and have implications for the way that work is organised, tasks are allocated and staff are managed. This whole area has become more important for library and information service managers, particularly managers who are responsible for large units, with not only substantial budgets, but also sizeable equipment inventories (as a result of developments in electronic information) and those whose staff routinely handle large amounts of cash (for example, from photocopiers and printers).

Formal requirements and arrangements for internal control vary from organisation to organisation, but will generally be determined by the parent body and managed through the finance and/or audit function. Departmental managers are responsible for compliance, maintenance and continuing vigilance in this context. One of the challenges here is to communicate to staff the need for such procedures without making them feel that they are not trusted or suspected of misconduct, particularly as the required procedures are often perceived as burdensome and inefficient (for example, involving two people in counting and recording cash receipts). Internal control procedures are typically based on the following **principles**, which can serve as a checklist for service managers:

- *reliable personnel* – careful selection (using a full job description and person specification) and effective training will improve the likelihood of trustworthy and competent staff, but sensible management will also minimise sources of temptation and in addition will be alert to any signs of unrest and changes in attitude or behaviour;
- *physical safeguards* – security tagging, intruder alarms and keycard/codenumber access to protect stock and equipment are now commonplace (supported by regular system tests and risk assessments) but the need for periodic reviews of the conduct, frequency and timing of cash transfers to banks is sometimes overlooked;
- *job segregation* – ideally ordering, receipting and paying for goods should be carried out by different people (similarly photocopy cash

collecting, meter reading and reconciliation) but if separation of duties is difficult on a day-to-day basis in small units it can often be managed intermittently through enforced vacations or job rotations;

- *formal procedures* – matters such as authorised signatories and their spending limits, cash-handling and record-keeping responsibilities, and key-holding arrangements, must be explicitly communicated, properly documented and kept up-to-date, ideally in a comprehensive policy and procedures manual, which details roles and responsibilities;
- *record-keeping* – accuracy, currency and completeness in the recording of financial transactions is the aim, which must include due attention to the transfer of data between systems and reconciliation of any apparent discrepancies in figures, and can also be assisted by use of pre-numbered forms for purchase orders and receipts;
- *independent checks* – organisations generally have continuous audit programmes, which entail periodic independent reviews of both individual departments and organisation-wide processes, checking compliance with established procedures (and also the continuing effectiveness of those procedures).

Information service managers have an additional challenge in attempting to safeguard the intellectual property in their care through compliance with copyright regulations and licensing agreements, which has become an even more difficult task in the electronic era.

Summary checklist

Are your finances under control?

Authority
Do you have the authority to vary expenditure between budget heads?
Do staff control the budgets related to the activities for which they are responsible?

Development
Have your staff received training in financial planning and management?
Are you actively seeking new income streams to fund service developments?

Costing
Is cost analysis an ongoing or regular activity?
Has organisational policy on overheads been established and explained to managers?

Budgets
Is your planning and budgeting integrated and co-ordinated with organisational processes?
Can your service/product costs be derived from your annual budget statements?

Accounts
Do your financial reports take account of depreciation and inflation?
Does your coding system relate expenditure to particular programmes or clients?

Control
Have principles and procedures for internal control been established and explained to staff?
Does your list of authorised signatories and spending limits reflect current responsibilities?

References

1. Roberts, S. A. *Financial and cost management for libraries and information services.* 2nd ed. London: Bowker Saur, 1998
2. Field, C. Building on shifting sands: information age organisations. *Ariadne: The Web Version,* (17) 1998 (available at: http://www.ariadne.ac.uk/issue17/main/)
3. Funding focus. *American Libraries,* **26** (9) 1995, 887
4. Trojahn, L. and Lewis, L. K. Of banks, books and balls: the Lobo Library credit card. *College & Research Libraries News,* **58** (1) 1997, pp. 10–11
5. British Library. *Strategic review: consultation paper.* July 1998 (p. 2)
6. Prentice, A. E. *Financial planning for libraries.* 2nd ed. Lanham, Md; London: Scarecrow Press, 1996
7. *e.g.* Annual periodical prices for 1998. *Library Association Record,* **100** (7) 1998, p. 363
8. *e.g.* Alexander, A. W. and Dingley, B. U.S. periodical prices – 1998. *American Libraries,* **29** (5) 1998, pp. 82–90
9. *see* archive at http://www.lib.unc.edu/prices
10. *e.g. Average prices of British academic books: January to June 1998.* Loughborough: Library and Information Statistics Unit, 1998
11. *e.g. Average prices of USA academic books: January to June 1998.* Loughborough: Library and Information Statistics Unit, 1998
12. *e.g. Public library materials fund and budget survey 1997–99.* Loughborough: Library and Information Statistics Unit, 1998
13. Warner, A. S. *Budgeting: a how-to-do-it manual for librarians.* New York: Neal-Schuman Publishers, 1998 (pp. 27–29)

14. Lancaster, F. W. *If you want to evaluate your library . . .* 2nd ed. London: Library Association Publishing, 1993
15. Enright, B. and others. *Selection for survival: a review of acquisition and retention policies.* London: British Library, 1989

Further reading

McKay, D. *Effective financial planning for library and information services.* London: Aslib, 1995 (Aslib Know How Guide)
   Concise practical guide (c.50pp) covering different methods of budgeting, costing and reporting/accounting. Includes chapter on software packages, examples showing use of spreadsheets for LIS budgeting, sample budget submission (for a special library) and concludes with lists of accountancy organisations and recommended reading material.

Coates, J., Rickwood, C., and Stacey, R. *Management accounting for strategic and operational control.* Oxford: Butterworth-Heinemann, 1996
   Comprehensive and extensively-referenced textbook (c.330pp) which includes separate chapters on strategic and budgetary planning, standard costing, activity based costing, management accounting in service industries, and budgeting and performance measurement in the public sector, as well as various aspects of control and performance assessment.

Prentice, A. E. *Financial planning for libraries.* 2nd ed. Lanham, Md; London: Scarecrow Press, 1996
   Wide-ranging text (c.195pp) with US and public-sector bias, but useful coverage of strategic issues and extensive bibliography. Covers the environmental context, the links between budgeting and planning, and special factors affecting information services. Describes data gathering, budgeting and accounting methods, and the use of reports as evaluative tools.

Roberts, S A. *Financial and cost management for libraries and information services.* 2nd ed. London: Bowker Saur, 1998
   Comprehensive textbook (c.400pp) which places detailed treatment of cost measurement in its strategic context. Discusses management information needs, explains accounting concepts and technical terminology, and provides checklists to determine costing methods. Also includes glossary, extensive lists of references and examples of data recording forms.

Funding

Wilkinson, J. Library fundraising techniques: a study based on a tour of North American libraries during July 1993. *British Journal of Academic Librarianship*, **8** (3) 1993, pp. 178–192
Discusses experience of academic and public libraries, covering organisational models, skills and staffing, techniques and tactics. Also comments on reasons for giving and programmes attracting support (such as naming opportunities) and suggests further reading.

Lomax, J., Palmer, S., Jefcoate, G and Kenna, S. *A guide to additional sources of funding and revenue for libraries and archives*. London: The British Library, 1997 (Library and Information Research Report 108)
Practical compendium (c.90p) of information and advice on a variety of sources and schemes. Includes guidance on project management, checklists for applicants and addresses of funding agencies, with 15 case studies from survey of 500 organisations. Covers appeals, friends and sponsorship, as well as charities, trusts and national funds.

Budgeting

Koenig, M. E. D. and Alperin, V. ZBB and PPBS: what's left now that the trendiness has gone? *Drexel Library Quarterly*, **21** (3) 1987, pp. 19–38
Explains distinctive features of Zero Base Budgeting and Planning Programming Budgeting Systems, noting a mismatch between published discussion and practical application in libraries. Argues that as technological change opens up more options for library managers, programme budgeting systems incorporating such features will deserve further consideration.

Foskett, D. J. and Brindley, L. Zero-base budgeting: the Aston experience. *Library Management*, **12** (4) 1991, pp. 25–33
Detailed account of ZBB exercise in a university library at a time of significant change, with examples of the forms used and information required. Compares process to planning a new university library and includes ranked list of 86 service increments. Highlights procedural difficulties and policy issues, but also points out the practical benefits and lessons learned.

Budd, J. M. Allocation formulas in the literature: a review. *Library Acquisitions: Practice & Theory*, **15** (1) 1991, pp. 95–107

Based on examination of more than 50 published articles and unpublished dissertations; discusses collection growth, the concept of allocation, the variable factors used in formulae, the specific means of formulation, and the political dimension, concluding that good decisions require a mix of exhaustive understanding, objective data and judgement.

Lowry, C. B. Reconciling pragmatism, equity, and need in the formula allocation of book and serial funds. *College & Research Libraries*, 53 (1) 1992, pp. 121–138
Explains the matrix formula developed co-operatively by academic libraries, which incorporates a book/serial dependency index and uses both linear and logarithmic bases to temper variables. Argues for more focus on institutional collection development policies in formulae, and on the selection of mathematical models (rather than the choice of variables).

Campbell, J. D. Getting comfortable with change: a new budget model for libraries in transition. *Library Trends*, 42 (3) 1994, pp. 448–459
Proposes budgetary changes for a Transitional Library Model to enable adaptability in the context of electronic services. Suggestions include specific allocations for staff education and training, investigation and experimentation, and user analysis, combined with fiscal empowerment of teams, use of quality management tools and new performance indicators. (Contribution to a thematic issue of 15 articles on library finance needs and models.)

Costing

Cooper, R. and Kaplan, R. S. Measure costs right: make the right decisions. *Harvard Business Review*, 66 (5) 1988, pp. 96–103
Argues that multiple product lines and rising overhead costs require sophisticated methods of apportionment. Explains process for designing and implementing activity-based costing system (with examples) and shows how to calculate and assign costs. Concludes that ABC offers better information on product profitability and also helps to identify strategic options.

Stephens, A. The application of life cycle costing in libraries. *British Journal of Academic Librarianship*, 3 (2) 1988, pp. 82–88
Presents a model developed for the British Library Review of Acquisition and Retention Policies, differentiating between monograph and serial acquisitions. Explains the eight cost components identified, comments on the apportionment of administrative,

accommodation and other overhead costs to each element, and discusses potential uses of the technique.

Kingma, B. R. *The economics of information: a guide to economic and cost-benefit analysis for information professionals.* Englewood, Co: Libraries Unlimited, 1996
Clearly presented and fully documented textbook (200pp) which introduces the basic economic concepts of demand, supply, benefits and costs, with examples and exercises taken from the information marketplace. Discusses resource-sharing, user fees, and the value of information, and explains the key steps and pitfalls of cost-benefit analysis.

Snyder, H. and Davenport, E. *Costing and pricing in the digital age: a practical guide for information services.* London: Library Association Publishing, 1997
Introductory text (166p) which explains concepts and techniques of accounting and costing in relation to operational decisions, investment appraisal, service pricing and internal control. Includes c.50 worked examples, ten exercises, references to accounting and library literature, and a glossary of technical terms. (Displays some bias towards US terminology.)

Broady, J. E. Costing of bibliographic services. *Journal of Librarianship and Information Science,* **29** (2) 1997, pp. 89–94
Introduces basic costing concepts and gives library-related examples of direct, indirect, fixed and variable costs. Uses the costs of book acquisition and processing to illustrate the difference between marginal and total absorption costing for budgetary control, and concludes with another example showing the calculation of unit costs for the same process.

Goddard, A. and Ooi, K. Activity-based costing and central overhead cost allocation in universities: a case study. *Public Money & Management,* **18** (3) 1998, pp. 31–8
Describes the application of ABC to library costs at the University of Southampton. Covers activity and cost analysis, identification of two stages of cost pools and cost drivers, and calculation of unit costs for seven 'user activities', but omits details of method for final allocation of costs to user groups. Indicates practical difficulties in service implementation.

Soete, G. *Measuring journal cost-effectiveness: ten years after Barschall.* University of Wisconsin-Madison, 1999. Available online at:

http://www.library.wisc.edu/projects/glsdo/Cost-Effectiveness.doc
*Reviews research at the University of Wisconsin into the economics
of journal provision, enabling comparison of costs for commercial
and not-for-profit publications, and describes method used to estimate impact and cost-per-use of titles as an aid to identifying cancella-
tions.*

Pricing

Winkler, J. *Pricing for results: how to set prices, how to present prices,
how to discount prices, how to negotiate prices.* Oxford: Heinemann
Professional Publishing on behalf of the Institute of Marketing, 1983
(1989)
*Aimed at both students and managers, as a practical guide (280pp)
to difficult pricing issues, such as handling price wars and morality
in pricing decisions. Covers cost-related, market-related and competitor-related systems, with numerous checklists, questionnaires, summaries and tips (including 140 ways to survive in bad times).*

Brindley, L. J. Information service and information product pricing.
Aslib Proceedings, **45** (11/12) 1993, pp. 297–305
*Discusses principles and practices of pricing and charging for
tradeable information, covering library-related services, the electronic information industry and government policy, with comments
on adding value, service levels and suggested further reading.*

Tilson, Y. Income generation and pricing in libraries. *Library Management,* **15** (2) 1994, pp. 5–17
*Based on questionnaire and interview survey of academic, public
and special libraries in London, and refers extensively to previous
published work on the subject. Discusses pricing techniques identified, attitudes towards cost recovery and policies determining which
services were free, regulated by charges, or priced to generate
income.*

Accounting

Carpenter, M. and Millican, R. The recognition of depreciation of library materials. *Library Administration & Management,* **5** (4) 1991,
pp. 222–229
*Explains the concept of depreciation and the cost basis for its calcu-
lation, with descriptions and comparisons of different methods used:
declining balance, half-life, replacement, retirement, straight line and
sum-of-the-years' digits (SYD). Concludes that SYD is the optimum*

method for modelling the decline in service potential of library materials.

Christianson, E. Depreciation of library collections: a matter of interpretation. *Library Administration & Management*, 6 (1) 1992, pp. 41–42
Explains concept of depreciation, arguing that if applied to library collections it should be based on the entire collection not on its individual parts, using a simple method requiring minimal record-keeping (such as straight-line depreciation). This article is followed by a rejoinder from Michael Carpenter, challenging Christianson's recommendations (p. 43).

Marmon, E. A method for establishing a depreciated monetary value for print collections. *Library Administration & Management*, 9 (2) 1995, pp. 94–98
Presents a case study of two public libraries moving from shared to separate collections, based on straight-line method but recognising varying 'life expectancies' of materials. Includes table of 'useful life in years' for main Dewey classes and different material types, and outlines five-step method, providing details of formula used with a worked example.

Control

Snyder, H. Protecting our assets: internal control principles in libraries. *Library Administration & Management*, 11 (1) 1997, pp. 42–46
Argues that established principles of internal control are central to effective library management and describes seven aspects: reliable personnel; physical safeguarding of assets; separation of duties; adequate documentation; independent checks; proper procedures and authorisation; and bonding, job rotation and enforced vacations.

Chapter 6

Achieving change

Implementing strategic decisions often proves more difficult and less successful than anticipated. All managers can point to examples of projects scaled down or abandoned, and planned improvements or initiatives that never happened. US consultant Richard Dougherty argues that librarians still have a lot to learn in this area, being "masters of 'talking the talk' of change, but ... less skilled at 'walking the walk'".[1] While every situation is different in some respects, there are certain similarities and common patterns that enable lessons to be learned about the problems and pitfalls of achieving strategic change. Drawing on published literature, personal interviews and a questionnaire survey of 93 organisations, Larry Alexander identified the ten most frequently occurring strategy implementation problems as follows:

- Implementation took more time than originally allocated
- Major problems surfaced that had not been identified beforehand
- Co-ordination of activities was not effective enough
- Competing activities and crises distracted attention
- Capabilities of staff involved were not sufficient
- Training/instruction given to support staff was not adequate
- Uncontrollable external factors had an adverse impact
- Leadership and direction provided by departmental managers were not adequate
- Key tasks and activities were not defined in enough detail
- Information systems used for monitoring were not adequate

Other problems often cited include vague goals, badly handled reviews and failure to modify objectives in response to changes.

Change management

The process of planning and implementing change deserves special attention as it remains a difficult issue for most organisations and it is easy to underestimate the time and effort required to manage change effectively. There is a huge volume of literature on the subject of change management, including a substantial amount devoted to change in library and information services, much of it based on lessons learned from practical experience. While managers will not find simple 'off-the-shelf' solutions to their problems in textbooks, reading about change can be a useful means of helping people to think before they act; published sets of precepts can have value as prompts, as long as they are not seen as the complete answer. Much of what is written on the subject is dismissed by cynics as amounting to no more than common sense, but it is surprising how often basic mistakes are made – hence the need to state the obvious.

The literature of change management offers various models to help managers prepare for change by adopting a coherent approach throughout the process, often culminating in a thorough assessment to identify adjustments required to ensure continuing success. Michael Armstrong summarises the different 'prescriptions' of eleven change gurus covering four decades from 1951 to 1992.[3] The classic example of this type of planned change is Kurt Lewin's three-step model of Unfreezing-Moving-Refreezing, which presents change as a process of moving from one fixed state to another. While a systematic approach has much to commend it, there are dangers in viewing change as a logical stream with an end-point and failing to recognise its cyclical nature, and the importance of treating it as an iterative and interactive process. Lewin's model seems somewhat unsuited to today's rapidly changing environment and participative management style, but his **force field analysis** technique, which involves identifying and quantifying *driving* and *restraining* forces as pressures for and against change is still widely used and is a valuable tool for thinking through change strategies.[4] (This is similar to the *equilibrium analysis* technique introduced in Chapter 2.)

Recent thinking, informed by chaos theory, prefers a 'radical/dynamic' view, as opposed to the 'mechanistic' model previously espoused. This interpretation rejects the notion of *managing* change as an incremental, evolutionary, linear and orderly process, and instead sees the process as one of *creating* change, viewing it as inherently transformational, revolutionary, circular/spiral, and essentially chaotic – but ultimately productive and beneficial. Moreover, it implies that the process is never-ending and that attempts to map the future beyond the initial direction will be futile, if not counter-productive. However, although instability and unpredictability are obviously recognisable features of the current information service environment, managers simply cannot afford to abandon attempts to plan and shape the future of their organisations; successful leadership of information services today requires commitment, imagination and energy, but above all the capacity to embrace change as a positive stimulus to organisational learning and development.

The key messages emerging from published comment emphasise the difference between various types of change, especially between incre-

Figure 6.1 Managing change – models and methods

TRADITIONAL-MECHANISTIC	RADICAL-DYNAMIC
Managing change	*Creating* change
• evolutionary	• revolutionary
• incremental	• transformational
• linear	• circular/spiral
SYSTEMATIC procedure	CHAOTIC process
• logical	• iterative
• orderly	• interactive
• end-point	• never-ending
TRAINING programme	DEVELOPMENT perspective
• current duties	• potential roles
• skills for services	• capacity for change
Change agent roles	Change agent roles
• expert	• facilitator
• auditor	• supporter
• telling/selling	• counselling/coaching
• recommended solutions	• problem-solving techniques

mental and discontinuous change; the significance of cultural or 'soft' issues, in particular the impact on service staff and customers; and the importance of effective communication throughout the process. Common themes which underpin current thinking on change include emphasis on the management of change as a *learning* process, more attention being given to *stakeholder* concerns, a move towards *bottom-up* and *open-ended* approaches, and stress on managing (and defining) the *transition* state, particularly in the context of large-scale long-term change. While there are differences in detail among the 'expert' views offered on the essential elements of successful change initiatives, four factors are common to most models:

• pressure for change, to ensure it is given high priority
• a clear shared vision, to sustain momentum over time
• actionable first steps, to prevent haphazard efforts or 'false starts'
• capacity for change, in terms of leadership and learning.

A strategic approach to **human resource development** is the essential component which is often neglected in change management. Education, training and development of staff needs to move beyond job-specific skills to building a more general capacity for quick flexible responses in as yet unspecified future roles. With technology and economics continuing as driving forces of change, technological awareness must be developed in all parts of the organisation (not confined to the 'systems' specialists) and likewise the sensitivity of service strategies to budget fluctuations must be part of everyone's thinking. The imperative to build skills, to 'overinvest in human capital', is a recurring theme of writers on change, exemplified by the following excerpt from the guiding principles of the Price Waterhouse Change Integration Team,

> "Build skills in your people at all levels. Broaden the technical, problem-solving, decision-making and leadership skills of those 'in the trenches'. Strengthen the facilitation, managerial, delegation, listening, communication and diversity skills of those at the top. Make skill building a key performance measure of all employees."[5]

At the practical (tactical) level, **communication** is generally acknowledged as the most critical aspect of the change process. This point was confirmed by the Institute of Management's Quality of Working Life survey of 5000 UK managers, which for the second year in succession identified the need to improve communication and consultation upwards and downwards as a priority action for directors and top management in the context of organisational change.[6] The timing, method and frequency of messages are as significant as their content. Various authors offer useful pointers and practical checklists to help ensure the important issues are addressed, and they stress that honesty is both the best policy and the most effective motivator, even when the message amounts to what is likely to be received as 'bad' news. The key questions are: why is change necessary? what will happen? who will be affected? how will it be accomplished? and when will it start? As is often the case, the challenge lies in striking the right balance between providing full and frank explanations and overwhelming people by giving them too much to absorb at once.

The first question is worth noting, as it is astonishing how often managers fail to explain the **real reasons** for change properly, with the result that staff often confuse *triggers* for change (like the arrival of a new boss or the recommendations of a service review) with the *root causes* – which are more likely to be related to environmental forces, such as financial pressures and technological developments. This frequently leads to further misunderstandings later in the process, thus underlining how communication is undoubtedly the key to success in managing change.

Resistance

Commentators stress that resistance to change is inevitable and managers have to allow for this, and appreciate that staff must not only understand the reasons for change but also feel the need themselves, so that they can become committed to it and contribute to planning the details. Some people welcome and relish change as stimulating and exciting, but most are worried or disconcerted by it, and many find it quite frightening. Reluctance to consider new ways of working is especially common among long-serving staff, who may feel threatened by proposed changes in their responsibilities and roles, but often resist change simply because of a generalised fear of the unknown.

Resistance to change is a natural phenomenon. People react to organisational change in a similar manner to personal loss, as they fear that changes in job content, staff structure, work location, etc., will mean loss of skills, status and social contacts, and possibly even redundancy. Research has shown that human beings confronted with major disruption in their lives go through a cycle of emotions which is largely predictable, although individuals will react with different intensity and therefore need varying periods of time to move through the cycle – hence the need for individual attention. Commentators typically identify a **transition curve of seven stages**, for example

- immobilisation
- denial
- anger
- bargaining
- depression
- testing
- acceptance

The labels given to the different stages of this curve or *coping cycle* vary, but the key point to note here is that line managers must be prepared for fluctuations in the moods and morale of their people – and corresponding variations in performance – and respond with sensitivity. Middle managers and supervisors have a key role in this process as potential blocks or levers. Communication, with full explanations of proposed changes and specific reassurances about particular issues, is the best way of dealing with this.

Consultants

Information service managers (or their bosses) sometimes bring in consultants for advice or assistance with major organisational change, and it can often help to buy in expertise not available locally or to obtain an objective view of the situation. However, the use of outsiders needs to be handled carefully. If their recommended actions are not accepted and 'owned' by the people who will have to put them into effect, the organisation may end up spending a great deal of time and money with little to show for it. For this reason, a more common approach now is for consultants to adopt more of a facilitating and coaching role, rather than that of expert adviser. Under this model, they can provide guidance and training for library staff to enable them to define problems and identify their own solutions. At a more specific level, an experienced counsellor can provide useful support for inexperienced managers or act as a confidential sounding-board for unsettled staff. Similarly, temporary staff can be recruited to ease the transition and provide extra cover for basic services to allow time for permanent staff to receive extensive training in new areas, but the risks of upsetting group dynamics by bringing in outsiders at a difficult time must not be overlooked.

Pitfalls

In a seminal article on why change efforts fail, Harvard Business School guru John Kotter identifies eight big mistakes which often undermine otherwise well conceived business changes:

1. Not establishing a great enough sense of urgency
2. Not creating a powerful enough guiding coalition
3. Lacking a vision
4. Undercommunicating the vision by a factor of ten
5. Not removing obstacles to the new vision
6. Not systematically planning for and creating short-term wins
7. Declaring victory too soon
8. Not anchoring changes in the corporation's culture.[7]

Process guidelines

- *Explain the real reason for change and ensure that everyone understands* – distinguish between the *triggers* (for example, arrival of a new boss, recommendations of a library review) and the *root causes* of change (reductions in funding, technological developments, etc.) and publicise these drivers of change.
- *Create a shared vision of the future and make it inviting to stakeholders* – engage people in discussion and present information and ideas in a user-friendly format, by developing *simplified descriptions* to convey *key messages* in a vivid narrative or graphical form.
- *Involve people at the planning stage and invite their proposals for action* – beware of *over-organising* and making too many plans at the outset; decide the destination at the start, but adopt *rolling-wave planning* and let the people concerned work out the details of the route stage by stage.
- *Promote holistic thinking and maintain awareness of external developments* – help everyone to see the *big picture* of the wider operating environment and the longer-term implications of current developments and to keep that firmly in mind, so that the changing environment is constantly evaluated.

- *Pay attention to individual concerns and respond to them properly and promptly* – tap the staff *rumour mill* by enlisting the help of spokespersons to find out how people really feel; give reassurances (for example, about training for new roles) but don't duck the difficult issues (such as job changes).
- *Acknowledge that change takes time and accept that there are costs involved* – think carefully about the timing and timescale for change and be prepared to invest time in preparation and planning, and to determine priorities between development projects and day-to-day tasks.
- *Communicate early and often, and be as candid and direct as practicable* – think about the timing and style of your messages as well as the content and method, and repeat messages as often as seems necessary, using different media, but without overwhelming people with information.
- *Provide the leadership to build a culture that accepts change as the norm* – build the top team but encourage leadership at all levels (particularly among middle managers and supervisors) and create a climate which assumes organisational development as a natural ongoing process.

Technological change

Information technology (IT) can be seen as both an *enabler* and a *driver* of change. It is also often promoted – by suppliers and paymasters – as a *solution* to problems such as expanding demand and reduced funding. The interaction of technological developments with other environmental forces (political, economic and especially legal) poses particular management challenges, and the pace of technological change is an added challenge. Changes involving IT are common in all types of organisation, and information service managers have arguably more experience and competence in this area than many others, but IT-related change deserves special attention in this context for several reasons:

- **mission critical** – for most information services, effective use of IT is fundamental to fulfilling their purpose and meeting service objectives;
- **multiple goals** – all too often, paymasters and service managers have different objectives, expectations and assumptions about the benefits of IT;
- **public access** – in many information services, IT-based systems are used directly by our customers, our 'public' users, who need training and support to do so;
- **ripple effects** – the organisational impact of IT developments is often

far more significant than first anticipated, in relation to human, physical and financial resources.

Library and information services have exploited IT to improve services, redesign processes and streamline administration. Examples range from self-service facilities and networked access, through electronic data interchange (EDI) with suppliers, to the use of standard business applications, such as e-mail, word-processing, spreadsheets, desktop publishing (DTP) and project management software. In addition, the *content* of libraries and information services continues to migrate to digital formats: reference works, such as abstracts and indexes, dictionaries and encyclopaedias, are now well-established in online and CD-ROM formats; electronic journals and newsletters are growing in number; and 'e-books' seem ready to be launched on the mass market, after a long gestation period – but with many unanswered questions about copyright control and technical standards.

Technological change projects can be large or small and can range from those where the technology is the prime focus (such as migration to a new library management system or the automation of a particular library function) to those where technology has more of a supporting role (for example, a quality improvement project which introduces IT just to manage a process more efficiently). 'Techno-change' has general characteristics in common with other types of organisational change, but as indicated above it also has particular problems: it tends to be on a larger scale, more complex and subject to confused objectives. It is also *stressful,* as the pace of developments often stretches management capacity, as well as upsetting users; and it is difficult to predict and control, especially in relation to timetables and costs. Both costs and benefits tend to be *open-ended,* as IT projects often bring benefits not actually envisaged, as well as falling short on expected deliverables. With techno-change projects, it is therefore particularly important to be clear about your *objectives,* realistic with everyone about *what* the technology is expected to deliver – and *when* – and generous in the amount of time allowed for introducing, instructing and supporting users (staff and 'public').

Objectives

IT can be introduced for all sorts of reasons, but usually it is to improve economy, efficiency or effectiveness. Business process *re-engineering* is a change concept particularly associated with the implementation of IT, and competitive *positioning* is a another significant factor influencing the adoption of new technology.

In information and library services IT rarely achieves substantial staff economies – contrary to top management hopes – generally because any staff time released by automation is redeployed to deal with new demands, but it has undoubtedly contributed to efficiency and effectiveness in speeding up transaction processing times, enabling more complex searches, and probably reducing error rates. (Library work covers a lot of repetitive tasks and machines do not get bored or tired, are less easily distracted, and generally more accurate than their human counterparts!) Tensions arise when information service managers see the introduction of new IT as a *value-adding* process, while their bosses see it more as a *cost-cutting* strategy and assume there will be compensatory staff savings – which underlines the need to be clear about the reasons for change and expected benefits. In practice, managers often have a list of both strategic and operational objectives in mind, covering areas such as adaptability, functionality, interoperability, productivity and reliability. It is quite legitimate for a project to have several objectives, but managers need to be aware of potential conflicts and be prepared to accept trade-offs in such circumstances. It is therefore essential to define project objectives, record them formally and communicate them effectively to all stakeholders.

A final point to note here is the importance of *strategic fit* and the *IT infrastructure*. Information service strategies cannot be developed in isolation, but need to be considered in the broader context of the overall information systems and management strategy of the organisation, and must also be consistent with (and reflected in) corporate plans and priorities for systems development. Electronic information service developments are dependent on having an effective IT infrastructure in place – locally, nationally and internationally. This embraces both technical aspects – ensuring systems connectivity and appropriate user interfaces – and service elements, such as operator support and help desk facilities, which ideally ought to be available to cover the whole 'working day' (however defined).

Timescales

Timing is another key aspect of planning system development or replacement projects. Large purchases usually necessitate formal tendering procedures, which may impose significant constraints on the timetable. The availability of key stakeholders also needs to be taken into account, and managers must also consider the impact of the project on day-to-day service operations. Academic libraries generally plan to change over to new systems during the long summer vacation to minimise disruption to users, and public libraries similarly often try to schedule the 'cut-over' during their quietest periods. Managers also need to consider exactly what form of change-over will best suit their situation – *pilot* installation, as a small-scale trial; *phased* introduction, by function or user group; *parallel* running of old and new systems; or *plunge* (direct cut-over or 'big bang'). Choice of implementation strategy will depend on both the particular type of system change and the relative priority of project goals. Ken Eason has identified five common goals for IT implementation projects and the table shows how the four strategies above match these goals.[8] Note that in some cases a *combination* of strategies may be required.

IT-related projects are particularly prone to unforeseen technical problems causing both slippages and overspends, so it is advisable to build in tolerance and contingencies to the timetable and budget. The impact on the **physical environment** is often under-estimated, in terms of the preparatory structural work required, special furniture (particularly in the context of health and safety regulations) and continuing operational effects, such as changes in temperature and noise levels. Items to consider here include air conditioning, alarm systems, cabling/ducting, chairs and tables, lighting and sound-proofing. These issues can take a long time to sort out and often have substantial cost implications.

Figure 6.2 Goals and strategies for technological change (adapted from Eason)

	Pilot	Phased	Parallel	Plunge
Achieving a worthwhile service for users			+	+
Minimising the risk to normal business		+	+	
Facilitating move to new organisation form	+	+		+
Pacing implementation to suit users	+	+		
Maximising the scope for local design	+			

Stakeholders

Early involvement of users in the definition and decision-making phases of the proposed change will help to gain their interest and commitment, and is in any case desirable to ensure that user needs are kept firmly in mind and that expectations are properly managed. Consultation methods must be chosen to suit the situation, and it will not always be practicable to involve large numbers in face-to-face discussions or hands-on evaluation, but giving people the opportunity to participate is important. Common approaches include setting up focus groups and/or electronic mail discussion lists. Existing channels of communication (such as newsletters, noticeboards, regular meetings) can also be used to announce the intention to change and ask users what they want from a new system.

Close co-operation with computing/IT specialists within the organisation is also essential from the outset, particularly in the context of networked services. The use of outside consultants is another option worth considering, often popular among smaller organisations without their own specialist staff. Such consultants can be engaged either to manage the whole project, or to assist with particular parts (feasibility study, operational requirement, contract preparation, acceptance tests, etc.).

The human aspects of information systems development are often overlooked or not given sufficient attention. The general human suspicion of change and fear of the unknown is exacerbated by the technology dimension, which can give rise to doubts about being able to use equipment competently and worries over role changes or redundancies. There are two common but quite different views of how computers affect jobs: the 'deskilling' camp sees machines taking work from people, downgrading their skills, structuring and pacing tasks, and controlling them in a way that causes social isolation; the 'enrichment' camp sees systems relieving people of drudgery, upgrading their status, supporting and prompting decisions, and helping them in a way that enhances social interaction. The situation is complicated by the fact that users of technology range widely from the very nervous to the over-confident, and the challenge lies in diagnosing and meeting the diverse needs of different groups and individuals; training will often require urgent action, but careful handling. People have traditionally had quite unrealistic expectations about IT, but this position has probably worsened in recent years (despite rises in IT literacy) with mass-market interest in the Internet and the Web reinforcing the myth that everyone can expect instant access to customised information at the touch of a button.

IT initiatives therefore have significant implications for staff development and training, and it is important to think through the strategic issues as well as addressing the immediate operational challenges. Advances in technology mean that information services staff at all levels need a wider skill set than before, which inevitably has an impact on training requirements. However, this impact is not confined to the implementation phase of particular initiatives, but is also leading to longer induction periods for new recruits; more updating/refresher sessions, to take account of software upgrades and system enhancements, or just remind less frequent users about features which they may have forgotten; and a need to balance demonstrations and instruction with opportunities for self-paced practice. Provision of both the time and physical facilities to enable training away from the public gaze needs to be considered. The proliferation of different systems installed in many information centres also raises policy questions about staff specialisation; this will reduce training effort, but must be weighed against reduced ability to help end-users properly as a result of concentrating expertise in particular systems among only a few staff.

Process guidelines

- *Involve operators / end-users extensively in identifying requirements and evaluating systems* – ask people what they see as the most important features of the new system and give them the chance to see (and try) prospective systems before taking the final decision to purchase.
- *Identify technical knowledge and skills required and ensure availability to project as needed* – decide whether you need to bring in additional expertise (from another department or outside the organisation) as a team member for the whole project or for particular stages.
- *State overall objectives and specific requirements clearly and communicate to key players* – ensure that people responsible for procurement and installation know the purpose of the change (to add value, cut costs, etc.) and that specification changes are formally documented.
- *Manage the wider organisational aspects of IT developments as part of the change project* – treat technical, organisational and people dimensions as inextricably linked factors and commit sufficient resources to cover 'invisible' costs (such as wiring, upgrades and training).
- *Plan carefully and take full account of the impact on key players and day-to-day operations* – consider the time needed and optimum timing for formulating operational requirements, conducting formal procurements, converting existing data and familiarising system users.
- *Clarify stakeholder expectations and strive for a realistic view of benefits and timescales* – avoid exaggeration, admit the downside (short-term disruption, loss of features, etc.) and the risks, and show that you have contingency plans if things do not work out as planned.
- *Organise systematic professional training and provide opportunities for hands-on practice* – aim to help people do more than 'get by' and make sure that instructions/manuals are in everyday language and organised around applications/functions, rather than system features.

Quality improvement

Information services and/or their parent organisations often identify the need for quality improvement in the course of a strategic review. Managers may decide that particular products, services or processes no longer fit users' needs, or they may decide to undertake a more general programme of quality improvement, and use the framework offered by a formal approach to quality management as a means of achieving wider organisational and cultural change. In the UK, various government initiatives over the past two decades have required or encouraged organisations in the public and private sectors to improve quality by paying more attention to customer needs, service standards and staff training – such as the promotion of ISO9000, the launch of the Citizen's Charter and the Investors in People (IiP) award.[9,10]

Irrespective of whether a formal programme is initiated, the principles and philosophy, and the tools and techniques of *quality management* can help to guide and focus service changes. Many of the practices and precepts associated with formal quality programmes are not new or radical in conception, prompting criticisms that quality management is no more than good management practice, and not worth the effort of special education and training programmes; quality management has actually been described in the literature as "applied common sense" and many of the methods employed (notably performance measurement and benchmarking) are familiar to information service managers. However, there is evidence that services which have adopted a more formal and rigorous approach to managing quality have experienced significant benefits. As well as genuine improvements to products and services *per se* managers have often seen important spin-offs from quality projects to 'business as usual'/day-to-day tasks – for example, staff who previously resisted performance measurement as something imposed from above recognising the need to monitor and measure operations, and others spotting the potential for applying tools introduced in quality projects to routine work (such as using control charts to monitor cataloguing throughput).

More generally, quality programmes can encourage customer focus, foster a participative management style and support cross-functional team-building, notably partnerships with suppliers and other service providers (internally and externally). Comprehensive models, such as Karl Albrecht's Total Quality Service (TQS) also offer a readymade framework for strategic management, as they place quality improvement goals in the broader context of business direction and strategy setting. Albrecht's planning hierarchy includes vision, mission and core values statements, business strategy, key result areas and business performance targets, as well as the 'customer value model' and 'customer value package'.[11] There is a growing volume of published literature reporting on the successful adoption of quality management in information services in the UK, North America and Australia.

Definitions and distinctions

'Quality' is another overused and poorly understood word in the vocabulary of management. It is a recurring theme in missions, goals and objectives, and often seems to add little of substance to such statements. However, while there is no single accepted definition of **quality** in the management literature, there is some general agreement about its meaning in this context, which is quite distinct from everyday usage (with its connotations of high class, luxury, premium grade, etc.). Most formal definitions centre on *fitness for purpose* and *conformance to requirements,* so at a practical level quality is about customer satisfaction or meeting agreed needs – every time. The distinction between 'quality' and 'grade' is critical, and it underpins this more precise use of the term. The key point is that the *grade* or **standard** of a product or service depends on its purpose, so our choice of grade may be high or low – but we always want perfect *quality* (to fit our purpose). To explain this in more concrete terms, to use the description 'quality press' as shorthand for broadsheet newspapers like *The Times* and *Daily Telegraph* is inappropriate, as customers may actually want a tabloid paper such as *The Sun* or *Daily Mirror.*

There are several different approaches to **quality management** which have evolved over many decades. These can be broadly categorised under three headings:

- *Quality Control* – the reactive detection of errors, through inspection after production (exemplified in a library by senior staff checking catalogue records created by others)
- *Quality Assurance* – proactive prevention of errors, through specification of procedures (for example, compiling a cataloguing manual to remove or reduce the scope for error)
- *Total Quality Management* – active improvement of the effectiveness and flexibility of the whole organisation, through both cultural change and standardised systems (for example, recognising that the effectiveness of a library catalogue depends not only on the accuracy and currency of the records, but also on the IT infrastructure and physical facilities, as well as the attitudes and competence of both library staff and library users).

There are other variants with different labels, for example *Total Quality Control, Process Quality Management,* and *Continuous Quality Improvement,* usefully summarised with a comparative table by Morris Foster and Susan Whittle in the *TQM Magazine.*[12] As indicated above, many organisations have made explicit commitments to one or more forms of quality management, which has generated debate about their relative merits. Advocates of Total Quality Management (TQM) often criticise the quality assurance approach, exemplified by ISO9000, for undue emphasis on means rather than ends. Some commentators have drawn quite definite distinctions between these two approaches, but in practice the situation is often not so clear-cut; organisations, including information services, often work towards ISO accreditation as part of a longer-term TQM programme.

Total Quality Management (TQM)

TQM is generally distinguished from other methodologies on the basis of its more strategic and holistic approach; while it is associated with particular technical tools, it is a management and organisational philosophy, rather than a system or set of techniques and procedures. John Oakland, one of the leading UK writers on quality, describes it thus,

> "TQM is an approach to improving the competitiveness, effectiveness and flexibility of a whole organization. It is essentially a way of planning, organizing and understanding each activity, and depends on each individual at each level. For an organization to be truly effective, each part of it must work properly together towards the same goals, recognizing that each person and each activity affects and in turn is affected by others."[13]

Commentators use different permutations of words and phrases to describe the core concepts, but the guiding principles can be summarised as follows.

TQM *core concepts*

- **Focus on the customer,** including the critical importance of supplier-customer relations (the 'quality chain') and the notion of 'internal' and 'external' customers often referred to as *'big C'* and *'little C'*
- **Process orientation** (rather than function) – with processes being likened to the streams of work that flow through or across an organisation, thus encouraging a *cross-functional approach*
- **Management by fact and data** (rather than taking decisions on the basis of hearsay or intuition) through the use of standard tools for *process analysis* and *performance measurement*
- **People-based management,** with the emphasis on involving everyone, facilitated by training and based on the view that people are needed to get results, and *the expert in a job is the person doing it*
- **Synergy through team-work,** based on the assumption that collective thinking about a problem produces more and better ideas than individual thought, with good *vertical and lateral communication*
- **Continuous quality improvement,** acknowledging that TQM must be an ongoing and total approach, covering all parts of the organisation and for all time – *not a 'one off' or quick fix*
- **Commitment at all levels,** but above all commitment from *top management* expressed through *leadership* and a shared *vision*.

Various American and Japanese quality gurus have set out their particular philosophies in the form of quality 'absolutes' or 'points' and many organisations have used these as a basis for drafting their own quality policy statements. Oakland has also produced a useful ten-point summary of these key messages in his widely-used textbook, which he condenses further into a single paragraph.

> "Total quality is the key to effective leadership through commitment to constant improvement, a right first time philosophy, training people to understand customer-supplier relationships, not buying on price alone, managing systems improvement, modern supervision and training, managing process through teamwork and improved communications, elimination of barriers and fear, constant education and 'expert' development, a systematic approach to TQM implementation."[13]

Additional tried and tested frameworks for designing and developing quality programmes can be found in the evaluation criteria for the various quality awards (such as the Deming Prize, Malcolm Baldrige National Quality Award, European and UK Quality Awards) which provide a rational basis for organisations to assess their progress towards quality. The British Quality Foundation has produced a guide showing how the Charter Mark, IiP and other quality-related initiatives link into the framework of the Business Excellence Model developed by the European Foundation for Quality Management and used for the European and UK awards.[14]

Tools and techniques

Many quality management tools and techniques are already familiar to information professionals; for example, the '7Q' key tools for quality control include flow charts and histograms, as well as the check sheets or tally charts that are often used to record enquiries in libraries. However, one of the distinguishing characteristics of many formal quality programmes is the use of such tools as part of a *structured approach* to problem-solving and process improvement. The basic tools for quality control and their uses are summarised below.

Seven tools for quality control (7Q)

- **Process flow charting** – *what is done*? A picture of what is actually done, which records the series of activities and events in a form that can be easily understood and communicated, using standard symbols for start and finish, activity, decision, delay, etc.
- **Check sheets or tally charts** – *how often is it done*? A simple method for collecting or ordering data, by recording tally marks against predetermined categories of items, usually grouped in multiples of five (also known as 'five-bar gates').
- **Histograms** – *what do overall variations look like*? A picture of the

variation or distribution of recorded values, in which data are grouped together and their frequencies represented as vertical bars (also known as 'vertical bar charts').

- **Pareto analysis** – *which are the big problems?* A Pareto chart is a special type of vertical bar graph which rank orders by frequency the 'vital few' important items or causes of a problem, in comparison with the less important or 'trivial many'.
- **Cause-and-effect analysis** – *what causes the problems?* Cause-and-effect or 'fishbone diagrams' provide a visual display of the possible causes of a problem in the form of a fishbone, with the ribs used to group major categories of causes (also known as 'Ishikawa diagrams' and as 'CEDAC' – Cause and Effect Diagrams with the Addition of Cards, when different coloured cards are used to distinguish the *facts* of problem causes from the *ideas* for solutions).
- **Scatter diagrams** – *what are the relationships between factors?* Scatter diagrams are pictures of possible relationships between factors, which help to determine the nature and strength of relationships between variables, and confirm or reject possible correlations.
- **Control charts** – *which variations to control and how?* A control chart is a special type of line graph or 'run chart' recording data in time sequence, with horizontal lines showing predetermined operating limits to help track performance (also known as 'Shewart charts').

Advocates have claimed that 90% of problems can be solved with these basic tools, which are explained in detail in many general TQM text-books, and also in Di Martin's Library and Information Briefing on the subject, which includes illustrations of the different tools with library-related examples.[15] Other tools commonly used in quality management, often in combination with the above, include:

- **Brainstorming** and its variant, *Nominal Group Technique* – one of the key methods of obtaining creative, imaginative input to complement the rational, logical approach represented by the 7Q;
- **Matrix diagrams** of various types, such as prioritisation/decision matrices, including those used in *Quality Function Deployment* to ensure that product/service design is based on customer demands and involves all supplier functions in the process;
- **Five-why analysis,** a systematic questioning approach that involves asking 'why' several times in succession to ensure the root cause of a problem is found – a simple but powerful tool in the continuous improvement kitbag;
- **Force field analysis,** which uses brainstorming to identify both favourable/positive/driving forces and unfavourable/negative/restraining forces, by asking – what will obstruct or help the change or solution?

Figure 6.3 Problem-solving methodology for process improvement

PHASES OR STAGES	STEPS	TOOLS AND TECHNIQUES
PLAN	*Deliberation* Identify and select the problems to solve –the processes in need of improvement	Brainstorming / Nominal group technique, SWOT analysis, Focus groups, Questionnaires, Interviews
DEFINE	*Definition* Establish the boundaries of the task and agree the project success criteria	Brainstorming / Nominal Group Technique, Flow charts, Voting, Prioritisation / decision matrix, Force field analysis
REVIEW	*Description* Collate relevant information available and specify additional data required	Performance indicators / management statistics, Check sheets Audit trails, Six-word diagrams (What? Why? How? etc)
INVESTIGATE	*Diagnosis* Collect and analyse specified data – find the root cause of the problem	Histograms / Pareto charts, Control charts, Scatter diagrams Brainstorming, Ishikawa / fishbone (cause-and-effect) diagrams
	Design Generate imaginative alternatives as potential solutions, evaluate options	Desk research (literature) Field research (site visits) Brainstorming, Mind-mapping, Reverse fishbone diagrams
VERIFY	*Decision* Decide the best option and test the preferred solution systematically	Voting, Prioritisation / decision matrix, Force field analysis Measurement tools used in previous steps, Gantt / bar charts
EXECUTE	*Approval* Gain acceptance for the proposal and obtain approval for the plan	Measurement tools used in previous steps, Gantt / bar charts
DO	*Action* Implement the change as planned, inform and train the stakeholders	Measurement tools used in previous steps
CHECK	*Appraisal* Audit the improved situation and decide on further action required	'Before and after' measurements (using the same tools) Focus groups / other forms of customer feedback
ACT	*Application* Recycle through process or move on – and act on the lessons learned	

Some people are sceptical about formal methods of solving problems on the basis that they inhibit creativity, but most of the quality methodologies encourage lateral as well as linear thinking. In the absence of a structured approach, people often 'jump to solutions' without defining the problem properly and then find that the problem recurs, because they have only dealt with the surface symptoms and not found the underlying 'root cause'. Two widely used frameworks for process improvement are the **PDCA cycle** – Plan, Do, Check, Act – also known as the Deming cycle (after its populariser) or Shewart cycle (after its originator) and the **DRIVE model** – Define, Review, Investigate, Verify, Execute – developed by John Oakland and his colleagues.[13] Another tried and tested step-by-step model for solving problems is shown in the composite figure here, which integrates the above two frameworks and also gives examples of relevant tools for use at various stages of the process.

Organising quality

A key point to note about quality management is that it is not a 'quick fix': it requires effort and a long-term commitment to get results. Even successful programmes tend to slow down after a while and may benefit from a change of tack to regain momentum. It makes sense to start with small-scale projects with potentially high impact in the hope of early visible results to encourage others. However, teams must have proper support and training to ensure that they tackle problems methodically and systematically, and that members do not become disheartened when things take a long time. Another demotivating factor is lack of resources to implement identified solutions, and it is therefore worth considering the creation of a quality improvements or projects fund for which teams can submit bids, preferably separate from the normal bidding process.

Business re-engineering

Managers seeking more rapid and striking results than the measured progress of quality improvement programmes have embarked on more ambitious and challenging methods to transform or 're-invent' their organisations. Michael Hammer and James Champy are generally credited with introducing the concept of *business re-engineering*, which they define as follows:

> "Re-engineering is the **fundamental** rethinking and **radical** redesign of business **processes** to achieve **dramatic** improvements in critical, contemporary measures of performance, such as cost, quality, service, and speed."[16]

In this context, a **business process** is "a collection of activities that takes one or more kinds of input and creates an output that is of value to the customer" – such as order fulfilment.[16] Alternatively, Thomas Davenport and James Short have defined a process as "a set of logically related tasks performed to achieve a defined business outcome"[17] and "the specific ordering of work activities across time and place, with a beginning, an end, and clearly defined inputs and outputs".[18]

Hammer and Champy identify the **driving forces** of re-engineering as individual customisation, intense global competition and accelerated constant change. They emphasise that Business Re-engineering is not another name for restructuring or downsizing, and is distinguished from other approaches to change by the strength of its process orientation, its ambition, rule-breaking, and creative use of information technology. Michael Earl has referred to it as "IT-enabled transformation along process lines" and "multi-dimensional change in business ... of a socio-technical nature".[19] IT is a key feature, and two recurrent themes are the use of telecommunications networks to co-ordinate, collocate and disseminate data and information (irrespective of time and space) and the use of shared databases/systems to automate, integrate and 'informate' functions. (IT automates a task or process when it *substitutes* for human effort; it informates a process when it *augments* human effort.) The existence of legacy systems and incompatible data often constrain re-engineering efforts. IT is also often used for process analysis and modelling as part of the re-engineering process.

The term 're-engineering' is somewhat unfortunate in that it does not adequately reflect the behavioural dimensions of this type of change process, which really needs to be seen as a *socio-technological* phenomenon – not merely a matter of technical reorganisation – requiring communication and interpersonal skills, as well as analytical and creative abilities. Hammer points up the risk involved in "an all-or-nothing proposition with an uncertain result" but argues that although it cannot be planned meticulously in small steps, Business Re-engineering does not have to be haphazard. He sets out seven **principles of re-engineering,** based on the work of early adopters:

- organise around outcomes, not tasks;
- have those who use the output of the process perform the process;
- subsume information-processing work into the real work that produces the information;
- treat geographically dispersed resources as though they were centralised;
- link parallel activities instead of integrating their results;
- put the decision point where the work is performed, and build control into the process;
- capture information once and at the source.[20]

Hammer and Champy describe the **characteristics of re-engineered processes** in the following terms: the steps in the process are performed in a natural order; checks and controls are reduced, reconciliation is minimised, and workers make decisions; as few people as possible are involved in the performance of a process, several jobs are combined into one, and a *case manager* provides a single point of contact; work is performed where it makes the most sense, processes have *multiple versions* and hybrid centralised/decentralised operations are prevalent. In the 'new world of work', operational units change from functional departments to process teams; jobs change from simple tasks to multidimensional work; people's roles change from controlled to empowered; the focus of performance measures and compensation shifts from activity to results; advancement criteria change from performance to ability; values change from protective to productive; managers change from supervisors to coaches; organisational structures change from hierarchical to flat; and executives change from scorekeepers to leaders.[16]

Thus while the focus of Business Re-engineering is on work processes, its potential impact on both organisation design and organisational behaviour is considerable, with significant implications for workforce skills, team structures, management styles, reward systems, etc. Words such as 'breakthrough', 'leapfrog', 'quantum leap' and 'turnaround' are commonly associated with the concept. Nick Obolensky offers a more extended definition of the transformation implied,

> "Business Re-engineering is what an organisation undertakes to change its internal processes and controls from a traditional vertical, functional hierarchy to a horizontal, cross-functional, team-based flat structure which focuses on the process of delighting customers... A Business Re-Engineering programme will typically move an organization from a 'chimney' to a 'grid', where newly established process teams cut across the functions, but the functions still exist, albeit in a thinned down way. The next evolution would be to move to 'bubbles' – teams of people who bring their specialisms and abilities to bear to focus on specific processes, change projects or technical support projects."[21]

Terminology and typologies

Business Process Re-engineering (BPR) is the phrase most commonly used as a generic label for change initiatives of this type, but there are many variants such as *Business Process Redesign, Business Process Regeneration, Business Process Restructuring, Business Process Simplification, Business Process Improvement* and *Process Innovation*. Some commentators use these phrases almost interchangeably, but others see them as representing different points along a spectrum, ranging, for example, from *correction* – returning a process to traditional levels of performance; through *simplification* – streamlining it by removing one or more steps; to *re-engineering* – rethinking the way a job is done. John Macdonald sees order of magnitude differences between process *improvement,* process *re-design* and process *re-engineering,* and presents a continuum differentiated by IT-based need, level of risk, scale of change, involvement of executives, time and cost, and expectation of results.[22]

Some see BPR as part of TQM, others see it as an extension or even a complete departure from it. As already indicated, there are both similarities and differences. They have in common a cross-functional and customer focus; both employ the operations management techniques of process analysis and performance measurement, and draw on the concepts and tools of systems analysis and the project life cycle. However, they often originate in different areas, and there are significant distinctions – largely arising from the *combination* of elements and *intensity* of application, rather than the elements themselves. In addition, BPR is more controversial than TQM, particularly because of its association with downsizing. The table summarises these differences in general terms.

BPR and TQM are best viewed as complementary approaches: organisations committed to continuous improvement may find they need to adopt a more innovative re-engineering approach where the performance level of a process is seen to be far behind their rivals, while organisations that have 're-invented' processes may need to make incremental changes to fine-tune and sustain the change. Davenport points out that quality gurus (such as Deming and Juran) actually advocated innovation and breakthroughs as part of quality improvement programmes.[24] Hammer and Champy see re-engineering as complementary to TQM, but draw a contrast between working with existing processes and replacing them with entirely new ones. There is also now a growing acknowledgement of the shortcomings of many early re-engineering efforts, particularly in respect of preparing and institutionalising the change. The recent trend is towards relating different improvement approaches and integrating radical regeneration projects and incremental improvement projects into a single coherent programme of operational change and process management – also known as *Business Process Management.*

Process selection

The selection of processes has emerged as a key issue for re-engineering efforts as failure to identify the most critical processes is widely cited as one of the reasons why many organisations have not seen performance improvements on the scale originally envisaged. Organisations typically

Figure 6.4 Distinctive features of Total Quality Management and Business Process Re-engineering

	TQM	BPR
Scale and style	Incremental improvement – slow, evolutionary *eg* ten per-cent change	Radical results – fast, revolutionary *eg* ten-fold gains
Starting point	'Brown field' / current state	'Green field' / clean slate
Cycle / timing	Ongoing – continuous	One-off – discontinuous
Process focus	Narrow, tactical – micro level	Broad, strategic – macro level
Participation	Middle-up-down – everyone involved – worker and management led	Top down – high-level involvement – often with consultants
Technical approach	Simplify – minimise variations – fragmented sequential tasks (statistical process control)	Multiply – optimise variations – integrated parallel processing (new information systems)
IT contribution	Incidental / 'automate'	Central / 'informate'
Individual impact	Activities and tasks	Jobs and roles
Organisational impact	Culture	Structure
Risks and rewards	Low to moderate	High

use three basic criteria to inform their choices: *dysfunction* or current level of performance; *importance* or relevance to business strategy; and *feasibility* or probability of successful change. Michael Loh provides a checklist of questions covering these points and some additional criteria:

- which processes are in the deepest trouble?
- which processes have the greatest impact on customers?
- which processes are at the moment most susceptible to successful redesign?
- which processes consume the largest amount of resources?
- which processes require the longest time?
- which processes have a high number of controls?
- which processes have a high number of manual functions?
- which processes have multiple data entries and pass-offs?
- which processes have a large amount of loop-back and rework?

- which processes have relatively high rates of error?[24]

Other commentators have referred to the significance of the *breadth* and *depth* of process redesign initiatives insofar as they cross organisational boundaries and penetrate fundamental issues, and have suggested various taxonomies and typologies of processes as a means of categorising and prioritising them for redesign.

Information service re-engineering

Most of the library and information service literature on BPR is speculative or prescriptive. There is not much published evidence of completed full-scale re-engineering initiatives, although there is an impressive account of a successful initiative at the AT&T Information Research Center, which involved five managers full-time over six months and then used an 'energised' form of TQM with a shorter improvement cycle – "Results Driven Quality" (RDQ) – to maintain the gains in a post-reengineered environment.[25] However, there is surely scope for re-engineering, or at least redesign, of processes in many information service units, and many process improvements have already taken place in the context of quality programmes. One obvious example is the reduction of end-to-end cycle times for acquisitions through online request facilities for customers at one end and electronic data interchange (EDI) with suppliers at the other end. Other areas where BPR principles have already been applied include the creation of FAQs databases to reduce professional time spent on routine enquiries, introduction of self-service facilities to 'disintermediate' routine transactions, and provision of direct links between library management systems and other organisational systems (such as Finance and Personnel).

Pitfalls

Hammer and Champy specify two key prerequisites for successful change – making the case for action, and articulating a vision statement – and identify seven common pitfalls in re-engineering efforts:

- trying to fix a process instead of changing it;
- neglecting people's values and beliefs;
- giving up too early and/or settling for minor results;
- placing prior constraints on definition and scope;
- dissipating energy across too many projects;
- dragging the effort out;
- trying to change things without making anybody unhappy.[16]

Project management

If we think of strategic planning as a coherent framework for a combination of projects directed towards a common purpose, then *project management* becomes a key competence for implementing our plans and achieving strategic change. Many information service managers have seen the benefits of using project management tools and techniques to plan and control large-scale projects, such as introducing a new computer system or moving a library collection. Some have also used similar methods on a smaller scale when a systematic approach to change was required, for example in launching a new product or service, especially IT-related initiatives, or developing/improving an existing service or process. Others, while not adopting formal project management practices, have recognised that a project-based mode of working has become the accepted way of handling operational changes. Irrespective of the size of information operation, the principles and precepts of project management offer ways to deal with change initiatives in an organised and structured manner, and to improve control over our most precious and pressurised resources – people and money.

There are many different ways of describing projects. David Cleland and William King define a project as ". . . a complex effort to achieve a specific objective, within a schedule and budget target, which typically cuts across organisational lines, is unique, and is usually not repetitive within the organisation".[26] Projects are thus distinguished by their impermanence, specificity and uniqueness: they have beginning and end-points, definable purposes and they involve some *novelty* – breaking new ground, or at least something out-of-the-ordinary for the organisation and/or individuals concerned, which brings with it *unpredictability,* including the likelihood of *knock-on effects.* Large projects are generally characterised by their complexity, interdependencies and risk: they are usually *cross-functional,* cutting across traditional organisational lines, and when combined with the unfamiliarity and uncertainty inherent in such undertakings this makes big projects more *risky* and means that the organisation invariably has something at stake. The work typically requires a team to be formed for this specific purpose, which is in effect *part-time* with people usually taking on project roles on top of their day-to-day responsibilities, thus giving rise to *conflicting pressures.* Projects often have many different *stakeholders* whose interests and involvements are hard to define, including people from other parts of the organisation and outside it.

It is beyond the scope of this book to cover project management in depth, but there are many guides and handbooks on the subject available, including publications specifically written for information professionals (*see* suggestions for further reading). This section introduces some core concepts and suggests a few tools and techniques judged most useful in the context of managing a portfolio or *programme* of projects to achieve strategic change.

Core concepts

Project management traditionally centres on three key parameters – *time, cost* and *quality* – which are often presented in the form of a **triangle**. Project control is all about tensions and trade-offs between objectives on these three dimensions. You can use the triangle to think about the *relative priorities* of project objectives in determining where you (and others) position a specific project. This exercise can be a helpful contribution to managing a programme of projects if carried out for a range of different undertakings, as in a simple visual display it can record agreed priorities and show where to concentrate monitoring and control activities at the programme level. (For example, time might be a critical issue in installing a new library accounting system, to ensure that it was operational for the start of the new financial year; but a less crucial aspect for creating a library marketing/contacts database, where its operation was not closely linked to the annual financial cycle.)

Three additional areas for attention that need to be added to the above parameters to complete the project management agenda are *scope, organisation* and *risk*. Organisation is a particularly important issue where people are having to combine project work with everyday tasks, and this issue is explored below and also later in this chapter. (Risk management is covered in the next chapter.) A fundamental concept is the dynamic **project life-cycle**, typically presented as a series of four phases, which can be equated with birth, growth, maturity and death, covering

- *conception* including proposal and initiation
- *planning* including definition and appraisal
- *implementation* including execution and control
- *completion* including termination and evaluation.

The literature of project management uses a variety of terms to describe and enumerate the key stages and steps; the phases and stages are not discrete and sequential, but dynamic and subject to review.

The term **programme management** refers to the co-ordinated management of a set of projects, which call upon shared resources to achieve related business objectives. Key aspects of programme management include approval of projects, prioritisation of work, allocation of resources, resolution of conflicts and monitoring of progress. Rodney Turner flags up its critical importance in strategy implementation, "Programmes of projects are the vehicles by which organizations implement their strategy, but many organizations fail to achieve their strategy because they fail to manage the selection process."[27]

Projects can be broadly classified into three types, in ascending order of risk:

- *runners* – 'bread-and-butter' undertakings, that occur quite frequently, and rarely present major challenges as the organisation is well set up to deal with them;
- *repeaters* – 'out-of-the ordinary' undertakings, that happen less often, and represent enough variation to require significantly more attention;
- *strangers* – 'one-off' undertakings, where the organisation has little/ no past experience, involving many interests and functions.[28]

Individual projects are often relatively low-risk undertakings in themselves, but interdependent objectives, shared resources and other demands on staff time increase the risks, making management of *project interfaces* a key issue. A prime reason for project failure is inadequate priority for resources alongside other projects and day-to-day operations. A useful concept here is **projectivity,** a term invented by Torbjorn Wenell, to bring together *projects, effectiveness* and *productivity,* which can be defined as an organisation's ability to achieve its development objectives through projects by managing the interface between operations and projects effectively.[29] The projectivity model assumes that operational staff are given time to work on projects, project plans are effectively communicated to line managers, and priorities are assigned to projects in the context of daily operations. For projectivity to work in practice, there must be:

- top management support, with each project having a senior manager as *sponsor*
- an overall programme manager, who assumes the role of *projectivity champion*
- a project management *methodology,* tailored to meet organisational needs
- staff awareness and acceptance that project work is a normal part of their job
- middle management commitment to balancing service development and delivery.

Tool and techniques

The challenge here is to formalise proceedings without introducing too much bureaucracy. Specialist texts on project management advocate an array of tools (including the use of specialist software packages) that are worth considering for large-scale projects, but for many information service projects a few basic tools will be sufficient, for example

- *proposal checklist* – some form of project initiation document is essential, but for small and medium-sized projects it is unrealistic (and unnecessary) to insist on the sort of project definition report specified in textbooks. A simple user-friendly checklist will suffice, along the lines shown, based on the familiar six-word diagram.
- *milestone plans* – at the project level, detailed activity planning and network analysis is not always necessary, but it is desirable for all projects to track and demonstrate progress. Simple milestone charts, presented in columns showing short verbal descriptions with planned and actual completion dates provide a useful summary. For multi-dimensional projects, milestones can be depicted as a network of 'result paths' showing dependencies.
- *programme schedule* – in a multi-project environment, it is vital to have an overview of the totality of work to be done and the relative timing of activities. Gantt charts (easy-to-read horizontal bar charts

Figure 6.5 Project proposal checklist (taken from Reading University Library)

WHY?	Overall aim (brief description, 25–30 words) Specified objectives (maximum of 5–8 points) Expected benefits
WHAT?	Scope/coverage (eg will include, will not include. . .) Proposed strategy/main tasks Deliverables (products/results)
WHO?	Project sponsor (senior manager) Project manager and team members Stakeholders/other contacts? (eg line-managers, advisers/ consultants)
WHEN?	Timescale (start and finish dates or estimated total duration) Milestones (project phases and deliverable dates) Critical timings (eg external deadlines)
HOW?	Procedures for monitoring (eg project log book) Methods of communication (eg e-mail list) Frequency of reports (weekly/monthly/quarterly)
COST?	Staff time (estimated total effort in person-days/hours for main players) Other costs (eg equipment, stationery, travel) Cost penalties (if any, direct or indirect, eg opportunity costs)
RISKS!	eg Interfaces with other projects and programmes

displaying task names and time periods for execution) can be used at the programme level as well as for individual projects.

- *responsibility charts* – as projects operate outside the usual organisational structures, there is often confusion over decision-making and communication. Matrix charts showing work elements as rows and human resources as columns can clarify the nature of the involvement of individuals and groups, using standard symbols or letters. (Codes commonly used are shown here and an example of a chart is given in the next chapter.)

Figure 6.6 Responsibility chart codes for programme and project management

X	Executes the work	T	Provides tuition on the job
D	Takes decisions solely or ultimately	C	Must be consulted
d	Takes decisions jointly or partly	I	Must be informed
		A	Available to advise
P	Manages work and controls progress		

A simpler version, known as a RACI matrix, can be used with just four codes: R – Responsibility; A – Accountability; C – Consultation; and I – Information.[28] Another four-code version used in change management interprets A as Approval, combines consultation and information under I and uses S to indicate Support, in the form of resources.[30]

Performance measurement

Performance measurement can serve many purposes. It is an essential element of strategic management, with a potential role at every stage of the planning cycle from situation analysis through strategy formation and implementation, to monitoring, evaluation and review. Gathering baseline data about your current situation is a necessary first step to establish your position, which can then be compared with the positions of your competitors or peers, and the expectations of your stakeholders (customers, funders, regulators, etc.). Data analysis should inform the objective-setting process and in turn support the monitoring and evaluation of the progress and success of the chosen strategy as and when it is implemented. Performance measurement also has a vital role in quality management and service level agreements. Andy Neely offers the following definition,

"... a performance measurement system enables informed decisions to be made and actions to be taken because it quantifies the efficiency and effectiveness of past actions through the acquisition, collation, sorting, analysis, interpretation and dissemination of appropriate data."[31]

Terminology

The term 'performance measurement' is commonly used to encompass a broad range of measurement and assessment activity, covering resource *inputs* process *throughputs,* product and service *outputs,* specific and general *outcomes,* and 'higher order' effects or *impacts.* A few authors regard the latter – outcome and impact measures – as distinct from *performance* measures, which they limit to input and output measures. Some organisations prefer the term *development* measures to emphasise their role in helping organisational development, rather than assessing individual performance. Other related terms which are often used almost interchangeably include *performance metrics, (key) performance indicators* and *critical success factors.* Some writers use the term *indicator* because they feel that *measure* suggests a degree of precision which is misleading; others use 'indicator' more specifically for indirect or *proxy* measures, which are derived from combinations or *ratios* of direct measures or *statistics.*

Further confusion surrounds the various types of measure or indicator, with the same terms used in different ways within the literatures of financial management, library management and quality management. For example, the terms 'efficiency' and 'effectiveness' are frequently defined in very simple terms as 'doing things right' and 'doing the right things' respectively, but in the literature of performance measurement they are often given more precise – and diverse – interpretations. Managers need to be alert to these variations and to be aware of the particular meanings given to such terms within their own organisations. The 'three Es' of Economy, Efficiency and Effectiveness feature in most taxonomies; other labels frequently used include Extensiveness, Outcome and Impact measures or indicators. At a general level these terms can be broadly grouped as concerned mainly with efficiency (including economy, productivity and unit costs) or effectiveness (including market penetration, quality and utility).

Traditional approaches to performance measurement have been criticised for their excessive focus on operational and financial data, their reflection of historical and internal concerns, and their failure to address current issues, strategic priorities and corporate goals. Organisations often measure too many things, persisting with measurements that are obsolete or of limited utility because they are easy to measure and/or their system does not integrate – or even relate – measurement and strategy. There is no doubt that things which are measured get attention, so the number and nature of measurements undertaken is important. Poor selection of measurements can result in short-termism and local or departmental optimisation to the detriment of the organisation or service as a whole. Measures which track performance on single isolated dimensions can be misleading as well as irrelevant, and measurement must include the customer perspective to be meaningful in a service environment.

Recent trends in performance measurement have broadened the framework and given equal or greater status to non-financial measures, including qualitative data, such as information gathered through customer, employee and supplier surveys. Market share, customer loyalty, service quality, employee commitment, product innovation and supplier relationships are among the areas often covered now, in addition to traditional measures such as productivity and profitability. Several factors have encouraged change here, notably global competition, quality initiatives, regulatory demands and technological advances. IT has radically increased the range of measurement options, while various management models such as the 7S framework (see Chapter 1) and the quality awards have made managers more aware of the impact of customer and employee satisfaction and other aspects of organisational performance on business results. Various new measurement systems have been proposed as alternatives to traditional accounting methods in an effort to look forwards (rather than backwards) and to look at intangible/intellectual assets, as well as physical/financial assets, and thus better reflect the true worth of an organisation, provide more useful information to stakeholders, and focus management attention more effectively.[32]

The best known and most widely used example of a system which takes account of non-financial measures is the **Balanced Scorecard** developed by Robert Kaplan and David Norton in the early 1990s, which provides a framework for a broader assessment of corporate health and reflects contemporary organisational imperatives and initiatives, such as cycle-time reductions, quality/process improvement and customer-supplier partnerships. As the name indicates, the Balanced Scorecard claims to give a *balanced presentation* of measures enabling managers to view the organisation from *several perspectives* simultaneously, to obtain a *fast* but *comprehensive* picture of the business. It combines financial measures of past performance with operational measures of current activities that determine future performance. This involves translating the organisation's strategic objectives (its mission and overall strategy) into a coherent set of measures (reflecting its specific goals and targets).

An effective transparent scorecard will enable an observer to deduce the organisation's *strategy* at a glance. Such systems require the involvement of senior managers generally – not only financial controllers – and can be replicated at different organisational levels to derive scorecards for business units and teams (or even individuals – some companies have developed pocket-sized personal scorecards). Kaplan and Norton recommend a limit of 16 to 20 'key measures' reflecting four perspectives –

customer, internal, innovation and learning, and financial. By identifying goals and measures under each heading, this model provides information from four different viewpoints and attempts to answer four basic questions:

- how do customers see us?
- what must we excel at?
- can we continue to improve and create value?
- how do we look to shareholders?[33]

Figure 6.7 Balanced business scorecard (adapted from Kaplan and Norton)

Shareholder/financial perspective *How do we look to our funders?*		Customer/service perspective *How do we look to our customers?*	
Goals	Measures	Goals	Measures
Solvency	Cashflow	Access	Hours open
Economy	Unit costs	Speed	Delivery times
Growth	Income generated	Quality	Satisfaction rating
Profitability	Return on sales	Loyalty	Member renewals

Internal/process perspective *What must we excel at?*		Innovation/learning perspective *Can we continue to improve?*	
Goals	Measures	Goals	Measures
Productivity	Unit costs	Creativity	Suggestions made
Zero defects	Items returned	Reskilling	People (re)trained
Streamlining	Throughput times	New lines	Products introduced
Reliable plant	Percentage downtime		

By bringing together seemingly disparate elements, the scorecard also guards against suboptimisation as managers can see when improvement in one area is being achieved at the expense of performance in another area. This model has been criticised for not explicitly including either an employee or supplier perspective; both these aspects are assumed to be part of the internal perspective, but some organisations have chosen to extend the basic model by adding their own perspectives to it.

Performance measurement criteria

For performance measures/indicators to be meaningful they must be:

- *recordable* – the activity must be observable or otherwise verifiable, and the data must be available, calculable or obtainable cost-effectively;

- *reliable* – the data must provide accurate, valid and timely feedback in order to help managers to track and manage performance change;
- *relevant* – the activity must be important to the organisation, its performance must be controllable by managers, and the information must be interpretable and actionable.

For a performance measurement system to be effective, it must be:

- *related* to other organisational systems and procedures – notably planning/budgeting and objective-setting, incentives and rewards;
- *reviewed* periodically and updated accordingly – seen as an ongoing evolving process.

There are some further checks that can be used to assess your approach. For the system to be effective and manageable at the individual level, managers should be able to recall their key diagnostic measures without recourse to a manual or other memory aid, otherwise people will be overwhelmed by having too many measures and they will be unsure about their accountabilities. (Seven is suggested as the absolute maximum number here.) To be motivating and mobilising, it should not focus primarily on negative measures (such as complaints, error rates, etc.) but include positive scores (for example, percentage of requests satisfied on time). In addition, an effective system will enable all staff to understand what is important, and frontline staff should be sufficiently aware of this to alert management to significant changes at the earliest opportunity.

As in other aspects of management, *communication* is a critical factor here, in explaining the purpose of performance measurement, in obtaining the co-operation and contributions of key people, and in disseminating and displaying the raw and interpreted data. Attractive graphic presentation and the use of dashboard-style figures (such as dials and gauges) is likely to be more effective than distributing information in tables or spreadsheets. The frequency of distribution and the specificity of information provided to different stakeholders also needs careful thought. The ultimate test of any measurement system is whether it actually results in action – as or when action is required.

Information services performance measurement

Performance measurement is an ongoing concern for information service managers with the continuing focus on accountability, quality and value for money in all sectors. There is a huge literature on the subject, predominantly concerned with academic and public libraries. The weaknesses in measurement systems used in business generally are equally evident in library and information services, namely concentration on operational and financial data, an internal and historical focus, and a tendency to 'measure the measurable' and devise over-elaborate systems. Many information service managers suffer from the DRIP phenomenon – they are Data-Rich, Information-Poor.

Academic library managers have been criticised for not being sufficiently strategic in their choice of measures and failing to relate library activities to organisational concerns through poor presentation of data.[34] Peter Hernon and Ellen Altman argue that a real concern for service quality means moving management attention and data collection from inputs and outputs to outcomes and impacts. They regard input and output measures as 'outdated' and advocate their replacement with more dynamic methods of quality assessment, such as measures specifically related to customer-oriented outcomes and evaluation concentrated on areas needing improvement. They criticise libraries for their focus on resource utilisation (money and staff used to purchase and process materials) and transaction totals (interactions recorded between library users and library materials, library materials and library staff, library staff and library users) and suggest a different set of measures to reflect the academic library's contributions towards teaching and research, for example

- the number of articles published using library resources;
- the number of books acknowledging the library and its staff;
- the number of courses using the library and for what purposes;
- the impact of the library on student retention, learning and research.[35]

Rebecca Linley and Bob Usherwood similarly argue that traditional supply (input) and output indicators for public libraries should be supplemented with qualitative data on intermediate and final outcomes of library use to reveal their social and economic impact and show how their value extends beyond their established functions (such as education, literacy, information, leisure and culture). On this basis, public library effectiveness would be related to the social objectives of the local authority and library contributions could be assessed on broader dimensions, for example personal development, social cohesion, community identity, business support and economic regeneration.[36]

Although the volume of literature is not so large, there are more published studies of the value and impact – or the *consequences* – of library and information services in the corporate and industrial sectors, including several publications by Jose-Marie Griffiths and Donald King. Having conducted more than 50 studies of special and public libraries, they have assembled evidence showing how library use contributes to organisational goals (including profitability, productivity and work quality) and to community goals (such as quality of life, lifelong learning and economic development). Griffiths and King have developed a generic framework for assessing information services setting out five kinds of specific measures and five further measures (or indicators) derived from relationships among the specific measures, related to four basic perspectives – library services, service users (actual and potential), organisation/community served, and the nation or society – thus offering a useful model from which a balanced scorecard might be developed for information services.[37]

Process guidelines

Decisions about what, how and when to measure require careful consideration of various stakeholder perspectives and different measurement functions. Information service managers need to distinguish between services/programmes/activities that need regular/continuous monitoring, those that need periodic checks and those that need special investigation. Customer surveys can help to assess current perceptions of both *per*

Figure 6.8 Importance / performance matrix indicating action required

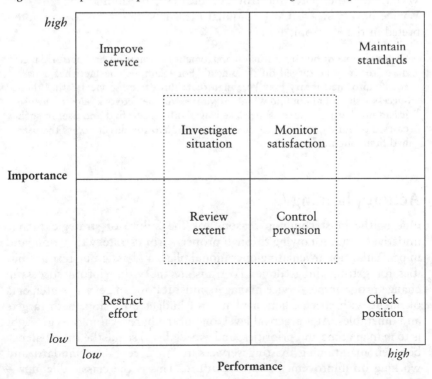

formance levels and *importance* rating, and thus identify what to monitor and measure.

Measures can be formulated and elaborated for both the library or information service as a whole and for its constituent parts (services, products, locations, facilities, activities, etc.) as well as being differentiated or categorised in relation to their management function (for example, operations management, service evaluation and strategic planning). Various models and frameworks can be found in the literature. In the example shown here, Christine Abbott groups different types of performance indicators in a hierarchy of three levels and identifies the fourteen 'essential indicators' which she considers to be the most important for library and information service managers.[38]

Electronic information service developments have complicated the task of performance measurement, with digital/networked resources on offer alongside or instead of traditional materials, and library/information services converging or merging with computing/IT services and other service units. There have been various efforts to develop measures for the new learning and research environment, notably the manual produced by Charles McClure and Cynthia Lopata for the (US) Coalition for Networked Information[39] and the report by Peter Brophy and Peter Wynne for the (UK) Electronic Libraries Programme. Brophy and Wynne have warned that traditional measures may need to be reinterpreted in the electronic library,

> 'Indeed, some of our traditional management information and performance measures may be turned on their head. For example, the fact that a user comes into the Library may be a sign of failure (poor service) rather than success – she could not find what she wanted via the network, either because it had not been provided or because it was difficult to find and use. In such cases the Library itself was a poor second-best to the direct access the user had first sought.'[40]

Action planning

One of the most common reasons for the failure of strategic change initiatives is not following through properly from strategy to action, and in particular not articulating **operational plans** and assigning responsibilities for getting things done. To translate the vision into a successful change programme, service managers must follow up general statements of intent with specific action plans and budget provision, with targets and timetables. At a practical level, one of the hardest things to get right is to manage time and priorities, and especially to strike the right balance between maintaining existing services to an acceptable standard and working on improvements for the future. This is the classic dilemma –

Figure 6.9 Generic performance indicators for information services (taken from Abbott)

Level	Attribute	Generic performance indicators
Macro	ECONOMY	1. Resources committed per 100 population / 100 users
		2. Proportion of budget committed
	MARKET PENETRATION	3. Registered users (of the library / specific service) as a proportion of population
		4. Correlation between registered users' profiles and population profile
		5. Take-up of specific services
Service	EFFICIENCY	6. Speed of supply, delivery, throughput
		7. Turnover rate
	EFFECTIVENESS	8. Timeliness of supply / product delivery
		9. Accuracy of supply / product delivery
		10. Failure rate / needs fill rate
	COST-EFFECTIVENESS	11. Cost per use / output / user of a given level of service
		12. Cost of service compared with degree of market penetration
Operational	COSTS	13. Unit cost per output
	PRODUCTIVITY	14. Outputs per relevant staff member

managing 'business-as-usual' alongside development and innovation – which is not easily resolved.

A prerequisite (as already suggested) is to agree strategic priorities with key stakeholders, as this then enables managers to identify the key result areas (KRAs), which must become a prominent element in tactical and operational planning. The difficulty of judging and achieving an appropriate balance between development work and day-to-day operations in terms of time management and staff deployment is a real challenge. If service developments take precedence over routine activities, standards may slip and service managers risk losing customer support when they most need it. But if managers let 'the urgent crowd out the important' and neglect development, their services will lag farther and farther behind competitors, which will also alienate customers – though the effects will take longer to show.

Developmental operations management

Sometimes, with major projects (such as installing a new computer system or moving into a new building), managers may be able to release staff from normal duties for fulltime project work. Several commentators on library management structures have argued that we should have staff *permanently* assigned to **development teams**, following the model of product development teams in industry, and some information services have actually done this – notably those operating converged library and IT services. For technically complex projects with critical deadlines it makes sense not to expose people to the frequent interruptions that occur in most service operations, but few managers of small and medium-sized services can afford the luxury of full-time project staff. Development teams then have to become part of a matrix management arrangement or *parallel organisation structure* which at least has the advantage of ensuring service developers keep in touch with day-to-day operations. Another cause of failure is to allow the desire for collective commitment and team ownership to confuse the issue of individual responsibility. It is essential to assign tasks and targets to named individuals and to spend time identifying enthusiasts for particular initiatives to drive the work forward and act as *product champions*.

Operational plans are the key to 'balancing the business' and *connecting the strategy* with everyday life by managing development while delivering current services to users. Effective operational planning enables managers to *integrate* strategic and operational objectives. The essentials are:

- *be realistic* about your objectives, basing them on an informed assessment of the time and other resources required;

- *break down* assignments into manageable components, providing intermediate objectives or milestones;
- establish a *review process* that enables you to monitor, evaluate and rethink plans and priorities in the light of experience and circumstance.

Managers seldom give enough thought to the frequency, level and timing of **progress reviews**: it is important for senior management to keep in touch with how things are going, but not to the extent that colleagues feel that they are not trusted to get on with their work. Monthly monitoring ought to be delegated to service managers/team leaders, with less frequent reports to the senior team concentrating on any problems identified, proposed rescheduling or other resource implications. A key point here is the creation of an *enabling climate* of trust and support, so that people are not afraid to admit difficulties or mistakes, and know they can get help if necessary.

The context for operational planning is this business of translating the top-level plan into an action programme, but there is also the issue of tracking back from tasks to strategy. The plans themselves need to serve as both practical *working tools* for daily use and a *quick reminder* of the organisation's strategic objectives. To fulfil this purpose, the **content** of operational plans must include items from the service's strategic plan (or representing the service's strategic initiatives) as well as significant regular or recurring activities, defined here as those where timing is critical and/or the time commitment is substantial (for example, in a university library, skills training for student groups). If you do not include both activities associated with the forward strategy and the major routine responsibilities of business-as-usual, you will probably have problems with time management.

Developmental operational plans – recommended core components

- *Mission statement* – purpose and functions for the service as a whole (why your service exists, what it does, whose needs it meets)
- *Specific objectives* for departments/teams/specialist units, and mission statement(s) if applicable – depending on service size, etc.
- *Development targets* for the current year, showing results required or main action steps towards strategic goals from service units
- *Key business tasks* – significant regular or recurring activities (where timing is critical and/or the time commitment is substantial)
- *Completion dates* for each item – at the level of specificity which helps management monitoring (typically monthly or quarterly)
- *Persons responsible* for ensuring that targets and tasks are achieved – either shown against each item or summarised in a matrix

Other elements sometimes included in operational plans (in the main text or as appendices) are an environmental commentary, to help set the strategic goals in context; a meetings/reports schedule, to remind people of the timetable for monitoring and review; other key dates, such as the cycle for planning and budgeting, and for staff appraisal; and the budget for the current year.

Production of such documents is much easier now with the widespread availability of suitable software, enabling networked access and frequent updating to record progress and incorporate additions and changes. Use of spreadsheet/database packages facilitates sorting by date, section, individuals, etc., and it is also becoming easier to combine this type of data with other management information (for example, output from library computer systems and budget reports). Many libraries – notably Cranfield University – now use Intranet technologies to disseminate planning information and supporting documentation to staff.[41] While electronic communication offers the desirable benefit of reducing the volume of paper in people's in-trays, do not overlook the motivational aspects of periodic distribution of hard-copy versions to individuals and prominent display on noticeboards of graphical output showing volume of day-to-day activities and progress towards key goals.

Summary checklist

Can you manage a strategic change programme?

Communication
Have you explained to people why change is necessary and what they can expect?
Have you listened to their comments and responded directly and honestly?

Involvement
Have you involved key stakeholders (eg staff, users) in planning and decisions?
Have you secured the timely input of any experts and specialists needed?

Training
Have you ensured that training will be timely and tailored to needs?
Have you also allowed time for general orientation and self-paced practice?

Projectivity
Have contributions of managers and others to project work been defined and communicated?
Do you have a system for initiating, prioritising and monitoring projects?

Indicators
Does your performance measurement system reflect identified stakeholder concerns?
Can your strategic objectives be deduced from your annual performance data?

Planning
Have you thought about significant recurring activities when scheduling development work?
Have you established the timing and type of progress reviews?

References

1 Dougherty, R. M. Getting a grip on change. *American Libraries,* 28 (7) 1997, p. 40.
2. Alexander, L. Successfully implementing strategic decisions. *Long Range Planning,* 18 (3) 1985, pp. 91–97.
3. Armstrong, M. *Human resource management: strategy and action.* London: Kogan Page, 1992 (pp. 86–93)
4. Lewin, K. *Field theory in social science.* New York: Harper & Row, 1951
5. Price Waterhouse Change Integration Team. *Better change: best practices for transforming your organization.* Chicago; London: Irwin, 1995 (p. 6)
6. Mann, S. Communication is vital in a changing world. *Professional Manager,* 7 (6) 1998, p. 3.
7. Kotter, J. P. Leading change: why transformation efforts fail. *Harvard Business Review,* 73 (2) 1995, pp. 59–67
8. Eason, K. *Information technology and organisational change.* London: Taylor & Francis, 1988 (pp. 158–65)
9. *BS5757/ISO9000/EN29000: 1987 – a positive contribution to better business.* London: Department of Trade and Industry, 1991 (Managing in the 90s series)
10. *Citizen's Charter.* London: HMSO, 1991 (Cm 1599)
11. Albrecht, K. *The only thing that matters: bringing the power of the customer into the center of your business.* New York: Harper Collins, 1992

12. Foster, M. and Whittle, S. The quality management maze. *TQM Magazine,* **1** (3) May 1989, pp. 143–148
13. Oakland, J. S. *Total quality management: the route to improving performance.* 2nd ed. Oxford: Butterworth Heinemann, 1993
14. *Links to the Business Excellence Model: Tomorrow's Company, QS 9000, IIP, Charter Mark, ISO 9000, ISO 14000, Management Standards.* London: British Quality Foundation, 1998
15. Martin, D. *Total quality management.* London: Library Information Technology Centre, 1993 (Library & Information Briefing 45)
16. Hammer, M. and Champy, J. *Reengineering the corporation: a manifesto for the business revolution.* London: Nicholas Brealey, 1995
17. Davenport, T. H. and Short, J. E. The new industrial engineering: information technology and business process redesign. *Sloan Management Review,* **31** (4) 1990, pp. 11–27 (p. 12)
18. Davenport, T. H. *Process innovation.* Boston: Harvard Business School Press, 1992
19. Earl, M. J. Business process re-engineering: a phenomenon of organization. In: Earl, M. J., ed. *Information management: the organizational dimension.* Oxford: Oxford University Press, 1996 (1998), pp. 53–76
20. Hammer, M. Reengineering work: don't automate, obliterate. *Harvard Business Review,* **68** (4) 1990, pp. 104–111
21. Obolensky, N. *Practical business re-engineering: tools and techniques for achieving effective change.* London: Kogan Page, 1994 (1996)
22. Macdonald, J. *Understanding business process re-engineering in a week.* London: Hodder & Stoughton, 1995
23. Davenport, T. H. Need radical innovation and continuous improvement? Integrate process reengineering and TQM. *Planning Review,* 21, May/June 1993, pp. 6–12
24. Loh, M. *Re-engineering at work.* 2nd ed. Aldershot: Gower, 1997 (p. 64–5)
25. Strub, M. Z. Quality at warp speed: reengineering at AT&T. *Bulletin of the American Society for Information Science,* **20** (4) 1994, pp. 17–19
26. Cleland, D. I. and King, W. R. *Systems analysis and project management.* 3rd ed. New York: McGraw-Hill, 1983
27. Turner, J. R. *Handbook of project-based management: improving the processes for achieving strategic objectives.* 2nd ed. Maidenhead: McGraw-Hill, 1999
28. Reiss, G. *Programme management demystified: managing multiple projects successfully.* London: E & FN Spon, 1996
29. Andersen, E. S., Grude, K. V. and Haug, T. *Goal directed project*

management: effective techniques and strategies. 2nd ed. London: Kogan Page, 1995

30. Beckhard, R. & Harris, R T. *Organizational transitions: managing complex change.* 2nd ed. Reading, Mass.; Wokingham: Addison-Wesley, 1987
31. Neely, A. *Measuring business performance.* London: The Economist/Profile Books, 1998 (pp. 5–6)
32. *e.g* Skyrme, D. Valuing knowledge: is it worth it? *Managing Information,* 5 (2) 1998, pp. 24–26.
33. Kaplan, R. S. and Norton, D. P. The balanced scorecard – measures that drive performance. *Harvard Business Review,* 70 (1) 1992, pp. 71–79.
34. Lindauer, B. G. Defining and measuring the library's impact on campuswide outcomes. *College & Research Libraries,* 59 (6) 1998, pp. 546–570 (pp. 546–547)
35. Hernon, P. and Altman, E. *Service quality in academic libraries.* Norwood, NJ: Ablex, 1996
36. Linley, R. and Usherwood, B. *New measures for the new library: a social audit of public libraries.* Sheffield: University of Sheffield, Department of Information Studies, Centre for the Public Library in the Information Society, 1998 (British Library Research & Innovation Centre Report 89)
37. Griffiths, J-M. and King, D. W. Libraries: the undiscovered national resource. In: Feeney, M. and Grieves, M, eds. *The value and impact of information.* London: Bowker-Saur, 1994, pp. 79–116 (British Library Information Policy Issues)
38. Abbott, C. *Performance measurement in library and information services.* London: Aslib, 1994 (p. 20)
39. McClure, C. R. and Lopata, C. L. *Assessing the academic networked environment strategies and options.* Washington, DC: Association of Research Libraries for the Coalition for Networked Information, 1996. (Available online at: http://istweb.syr.edu/~mcclure/network/)
40. Brophy, P. and Wynne, P. M. *Management information systems and performance measurement for the electronic library: eLib supporting study.* Preston: University of Central Lancashire, Centre for Research in Library & Information Management, 1997 (p. 81) (Available online at: http://www.ukoln.ac.uk/dlis/models/studies/mis)
41. Bevan, S. and Evans, J. Managing the Library Intranet at Cranfield University. *Managing Information,* 3, (9), 1996, pp. 38–40

Further reading

Change management

Beckhard, R and Harris, R T. *Organizational transitions: managing complex change.* 2nd ed. Reading, Mass.; Wokingham: Addison-Wesley, 1987
Slim volume (c. 120p.) distinctive for its emphasis on defining and managing the transition state, including suggestions for different transitional management structures. Also advocates development of midpoint scenarios and provides charts for mapping responsibility and commitment to change.

Plant, R. *Managing change and making it stick.* London: Fontana, 1987 (1991)
Short guide (150p.) which combines selected theory with practical advice and presents managing change as a five-stage process: recognising the need, mobilising commitment, building a vision, diagnosing current reality, and getting there. Includes two inventory tools for assessing individual role effectiveness and organisational development stages/cultural types.

Wilson, D. C. *A strategy of change.* London: Routledge, 1992
Concise wide-ranging survey (c. 150p.) which uses two-dimensional framework for comparative analysis of existing change theories and approaches. Considers different perspectives and issues (including gender) and criticises recipe-driven models, arguing for an integrated approach based on a broader and deeper understanding of the operating environment.

Eccles, T. *Succeeding with change: implementing action-driven strategies.* London: McGraw-Hill, 1994 (1996)
Concentrates on strategy implementation and the internal organisational factors that underpin successful change. Provides a framework of fourteen factors to analyse challenges facing organisations and their capacity to deal with them. Disputes current assumptions about the pace of change, role of empowerment and cultural issues. (c 270p.)

Information service change

Crook, A. Tough times and a large library: managing organisational change. *Australian Library Journal,* **39** (1) 1990, pp. 20–30.
Case study of the State Library of New South Wales, which

summarises environmental factors and organisational issues, and then outlines key features of the multi-faceted change programme implemented, including staff development, strategic planning, job redesign, technology awareness, service restructuring, team building and income generation.

Odini, C. The management of change in a library service. *Library Review,* **39** (4) 1990, pp. 8–20.
Examines factors to be considered by managers introducing change, especially psychological aspects. Provides checklists for effective communication and motivation, and comments on steps towards finding creative solutions to problems.

Whetherly, J. *Achieving change through training and development.* London: Library Association Publishing, 1998 (Library Training Guides)
Concise guide (c. 60p.) which introduces change theories and strategies, and discusses key aspects of change management with reference to development needs. Chapters cover individual and group needs, communication, involvement, resistance and the qualities of change agents. Concludes with samples of documents used by libraries in managing change.

Gallacher, C. *Managing change in libraries and information services.* London: Aslib, 1999 (Aslib Know How Series)
An accessible pocket-sized guide (c. 100p.) designed to help managers and supervisors understand, plan and manage change. Covers pressures for change, effects on people, the strategic context, structures and cultures, generating and selecting strategies, and planning and implementing projects. Also provides examples of a decision matrix, stakeholder map and communication chart, and concludes with summary of knowledge, skills and qualities needed.

Technological change

Beatty, C. A. and Lee, G. L. Leadership among middle managers: an exploration in the context of technological change. *Human Relations,* **45** (9) 1992, pp. 957–989
Draws on literature of leadership, technology and organisational change and develops a model of strategic direction and operational leadership for technological change. Concludes that a 'transformational' approach combining 'pathfinding' with people problem-solving and technical problem-solving skills is more effective than a 'transactional' approach.

Boddy, D. IT and organizational change. In: Earl, M. J., ed., *Information management: the organisational dimension.* Oxford: Oxford University Press, 1996 (1998), pp. 337–346.
Identifies characteristics of contemporary IT applications and argues that successful technological change depends on skilled project management, clear strategic objectives and appropriate organisational change. Concludes with nine guidelines for exploiting the innovative potential of new technologies under the headings Purpose, People and Process.

Sykes, P. Automation and non-professional staff: the neglected majority. *Serials,* 4 (3) 1991, pp. 33–43 (Originally published in *Library Management,* 12 (3) 1991)
Based on published literature and personal experience at a former polytechnic library, discusses typical reactions of library assistants to the introduction of new technology and suggests ways of managing change successfully, with particular emphasis on management style, sensitive communication, sensible training and proper involvement in the process.

Scott Cree, J. *Library systems migration: technical and management considerations.* London: Library Information Technology Centre, 1998 (LITC Report No 12)
In-depth examination (70pp.) of the management of systems migration projects in the libraries of ten UK government departments during the mid 1990s. Covers reasons for migration, use of consultants, specification and procurement, selection and evaluation, data conversion and testing, communication and training, with bibliography of 224 items.

Quality management

Oakland, J. S. *Total quality management: the route to improving performance.* 2nd ed. Oxford: Butterworth-Heinemann, 1993
Comprehensive textbook (c. 460pp.) aimed at both managers and students. Interprets the subject broadly and integrates the author's own model and theories with those of other experts. Covers basic ideas; quality standards and awards; use of tools and techniques; quality structures and approaches; leadership, teamwork, communication and training.

Kanji, G. K. and Asher, M. *100 methods for total quality management.* London: Sage Publications, 1996
A concise compendium (c 235pp.) of problem-solving tools and

techniques, prefaced by a short outline of TQM principles and arranged in four categories (management methods; analytical methods; idea generation; data collection, analysis and display) with notes on the purpose, application and benefits of each method, illustrated by a simple example.

Porter, L. J. and Tanner, S. J. *Assessing business excellence: a guide to self-assessment.* Oxford: Butterworth-Heinemann, 1996 (1998)
Explains how the different quality systems fit together, describes the background and criteria for the main quality awards (ISO9000, Deming, Baldrige, APQC and EFQM) and provides detailed comparison of Baldrige and EFQM. Sets out the key steps of self-assessment and the pros and cons of different approaches, concluding with case studies of award-winners.

Information service quality

Brophy, P. and Coulling, K. *Quality management for information and library managers.* Aldershot: Aslib Gower, 1996
Wide-ranging guide (c.200pp.) combining a general introduction to quality management concepts, theories and systems with discussion of their relevance and application to LIS. Includes chapters on the quality gurus, the customer perspective, TQM, service mission, effectiveness and performance measurement, criteria for four quality awards, and a bibliography of 12 pages.

O'Neill, R. M. *Total quality management in libraries: a sourcebook.* Englewood, Co: Libraries Unlimited, 1994
Reprints 13 review articles/case studies by various authors (including three on quality circles) and provides an annotated reading list of 140 items from library literature and 21 general management books; also includes 12-page glossary of quality terminology.

Milner, E., Kinnell, M. and Usherwood, B. Quality management: the public library debate. *Public Library Journal,* 9 (6) 1994, pp. 151–157
A wide-ranging review of the literature on quality management and related areas, which covers books, journal articles and reports relevant to information services in all sectors. Sections include: quality issues in the public sector; philosophers, gurus and evangelists; quality management; communications; strategic management; standards and benchmarking

Business re-engineering

Davenport, T. H. Need radical innovation and continuous improvement? Integrate process reengineering and TQM. *Planning Review*, 21, May/June 1993, pp. 6–12
Compares and contrasts BPR and TQM with alternatives (process value analysis and focussed operational restructuring) on basis of pace and degree of change (tactical/strategic). Argues the need to integrate different approaches and educate people about their relationship; offers four ways – by sequencing, categorising, limiting, or combining process change initiatives.

Obolensky, N. *Practical business re-engineering: tools and techniques for achieving effective change.* London: Kogan Page, 1994 (1996)
Explains in detail four iterative steps to achieving change (know what you want, make a plan, do it, monitor) and maintaining it; covers 'technical' and 'cultural' techniques, getting started and maintaining momentum. Part 2 includes eleven case studies, and Part 3 describes a selection of analytical and process tools, project planning techniques, and IT applications.

Thomas, M. What you need to know about: business process re-engineering. *Personnel Management*, 26 (1) 1994, pp. 28–31
Provides straightforward guide, explaining key concepts and assessing role of IT and claimed benefits, including links with empowerment. Notes prevalence of 'greenfield' operations among success stories and highlights human resource implications of BPR.

Information service re-engineering

Sweeney, R. T. Leadership in the post-hierarchical library. *Library Trends*, 43 (1) 1994 pp. 62–94
Describes the features of re-engineered library organisations based on a process orientation with adaptive structures and empowered networked cross-functional teams of flexible specialists. Explains why re-engineering is necessary and then details the characteristics and roles of leaders in this environment, and identifies ten critical library leadership strategies.

Anderson, G. Re-engineering the academic library: new services through institutional alignment and leadership. In: Helal, A. H. and Weiss, J. W., eds. *Towards a worldwide library: a ten year forecast.* Essen: Universitatsbibliothek Essen, 1997, pp. 115–135 (Publications of Essen University Library; vol. 21)
Explains the concepts of re-engineering in relation to the processes

of a research institution, offers three perspectives on how a process orientation can help a library to articulate its contribution to the parent organisation, and then suggests approaches to rethinking and redesigning library work, drawing on Davenport's taxonomy of knowledge work processes.

Wilson, T. D. Redesigning the university library in the digital age. *Journal of Documentation* **54** (1) 1998, pp. 15–27
Draws on BPR thinking and practice to consider how academic libraries could move from automating to 'informating' in response to environmental forces. Uses the insurance industry 'case officer' model to suggest how information services and systems could be integrated to provide interactive networked user support in place of current face-to-face frontline services.

Project management

Boddy, D. and Buchanan, D. *Take the lead: interpersonal skills for project managers.* New York; London: Prentice Hall, 1992
Takes broad strategic view of project management as the planning and management of change, concentrating on the interpersonal and political skills needed for novel and uncertain situations. Identifies danger signals of potential problems, and suggests skills and strategies for managing stakeholders, including the project team and other staff.

Turner, J. R. *The handbook of project-based management: improving the processes for achieving strategic objectives.* 2nd ed. Maidenhead: McGraw-Hill, 1999
Clear, comprehensive textbook (c.530p.) which draws on TQM as well as traditional project management tools and techniques, and considers projects in the context of strategic change. Presents a structured approach for managing project scope, organisation, quality, cost, time and risk, and explains the methods, tools and techniques in relation to the project life cycle. Includes numerous practical examples; also covers cultural issues of project-based working.

Information service projects

Black, K. *Project management for library and information service professionals.* London: Aslib, 1996 (An Aslib Know How Guide)
A short introduction (55pp.), which explains the basics, including scheduling methods (Gantt charts and network analysis) and how to cost labour, equipment and other resources. Also covers manage-

ment/reporting arrangements and the use of project management software. Draws particularly on experience of externally-funded projects.

MacLachlan, L. *Making project management work for you.* London: Library Association Publishing, 1996 (The Successful LIS Professional)
A concise guide (86pp.) suitable for all levels of staff; largely based on the PRINCE methodology and using library examples throughout. Covers formal project management techniques, including scheduling and also risk analysis. Appendices provide an annotated reading list and notes on popular software packages.

Lewis, A.C. The use of PRINCE project management methodology in choosing a new library system at the University of Wales Bangor. *Program,* **29** (3) July 1995, pp. 231–240
Shows how formal methodology and specialist software (Microsoft Project) can monitor and control progress. Includes examples of charts and reports produced using software, as well as comments on benefits of thorough documentation and other lessons learned.

Performance measurement

Neely, A. *Measuring business performance.* London, The Economist/ Profile Books, 1998
Clear compact guide (c.200pp.) to performance measurement, which explains why and how managers are moving beyond traditional financial ratios to more comprehensive and strategic measures. Covers purposes, roles and benefits of measurement at strategic and operational levels, supported with numerous checklists, models, tables and references.

Harvard Business Review on measuring corporate performance. Boston, MA: Harvard Business School Press, 1998
Reproduces eight articles from the 1990s by leading academics and consultants, including a classic contribution from Peter Drucker and three from Kaplan and Norton on the 'balanced scorecard'. Also covers measures for cross-functional teams and contains a 13-page index.

Lancaster, F. W. *If you want to evaluate your library ...* 2nd. ed. London: Library Association, 1993
Comprehensive guide (c. 350p.) to the selection of methods for

evaluating services provided by libraries and information centres, illustrated with examples of questionnaires and forms used in US libraries. Covers evaluation of collections, database searching, answering reference questions and bibliographic instruction, as well as considering cost-effectiveness, cost/benefit studies and continuous quality control.

Abbott, C. *Performance measurement in library and information services.* London: Aslib, 1994 (The Aslib Know How Series)
A wide-ranging practical guide (c.60pp.), which explains the purposes and benefits of performance measurement, clarifies terminology, and advises how to develop performance indicators and organise data collection. Provides a typology of indicators and also a comprehensive listing of illustrative examples for 13 typical information service functions

Russell, C. Using performance measurement to evaluate teams and organizational effectiveness *Library Administration & Management,* 12 (3) 1998, pp. 159–165.
Discusses the replacement of a traditional staff appraisal system at the University of Arizona Library with a new Performance Effectiveness Management System (PEMS) relating individual work and learning goals to team objectives, quality standards and performance measures, aiming for a balanced assessment of their mission-critical activities.

Operational planning

Tuck, J. Operational planning and performance measurement in the John Rylands University Library of Manchester. *The New Review of Academic Librarianship,* 1, 1995, pp. 15–31.
Discusses use of surveys and evaluation as means of implementing and monitoring the Library's strategic plan, concentrating on four key areas and concluding with proposals for adoption of operational planning and performance indicators throughout the Library.

Chapter 7

Securing capability

In order to maintain and sustain a programme of strategic change, managers need to consider several infrastructure issues and other continuing concerns. This chapter is inevitably selective in the topics covered and depth of treatment, but the subjects chosen reflect those things often cited as making a significant difference to the quality of information service delivery – the things managers must get right to enable their service to survive and thrive through a programme of continuous development. Most of the topics covered here have been mentioned earlier (for example in the Seven S Framework in Chapter 4) but not given as much attention as their significance warrants. The need for effective management and development of important resources is a recurring theme of this chapter, especially the development and training of information service staff.

Customer focus

Focus on the customer was mentioned in the last chapter as a core concept of quality management, but the imperative to relate service strategies to customer needs has been a recurring theme of the whole book, from stakeholder relations and customer surveys in the second chapter to the physical environment and organisational structures in the present one. Quality consultant Karl Albrecht defines *customer-centred organisations* as follows, "They see the customer as the starting point, listening post, and ultimate arbiter for everything they do. They start with the customer's needs and expectations – the attributes that are desired. Then they develop and evolve products or services to satisfy them." Albrecht depicts the customer-centred organisation's relationship to its customers as a **service triangle**, showing how *strategy, people* and *systems* need to be aligned to deliver value to the customer at the centre.[1]

Information service managers have responded to the customer service imperative in various ways, for example

- interpersonal and assertiveness skills training for frontline staff
- formal complaints procedures and suggestions schemes (for both staff and customers)
- customer surveys, focus groups and user panels to identify needs and priorities

- planned public relations programmes, including 'friends' organisations
- customer charters and service codes, definitions, standards or targets

In practice, many 'customer care' programmes have not delivered their expected benefits because they have been too narrowly conceived, concentrating on communication skills training for frontline staff rather than pursuing customer focus at the strategic level as an integral part of the overall service strategy. Real customer care requires a *comprehensive view* of service delivery, starting with the needs and expectations of customers, embracing everything and everybody involved in the service (including the physical environment and senior management) and pursuing customer focus as a long-term strategy. It is thus not just about training, although the education, training and *professional development* of staff at all levels is the key to success, but this must inculcate a genuine customer orientation and be more than the empty 'have-a-nice-day' patter. Tailoring services to needs requires *effective communication,* liaison and teamwork, not only communication with service users, but communication among service staff – upwards, downwards and sideways – indicating that true customer care depends on *staff care* in every sense of that term.

A simple five-step model for a customer focus programme with a strategic perspective is given below. This model is based on the plan set out by John Pluse in his seminal article on customer focus, which explains the holistic approach required.[2] The model takes the most relevant steps from a typical strategic review, and shows how the development of a stronger customer focus involves more than training targeted at the front line but needs to cover a wider interpretation of the customer interface.

- Survey current perceptions (via questionnaires, interviews, discussions, complaints, etc.)
- Determine the scope, formulate a strategy and set standards for the service
- Educate, train and develop staff – this must be a consistent ongoing effort
- Appoint a leader and team to act as staff champions and a clearinghouse for ideas
- Communicate and consolidate – inform, listen, respond, monitor, evaluate and review

Service level agreements

Service standards or targets are often recorded in more comprehensive documents as service level agreements (SLAs). In common with other service managers, many information service managers are now required to draw up and implement detailed formal agreements with customers or client departments about the services which they will provide. SLAs were introduced in the IT services sector as a means of dealing with concerns about the performance and cost of central computing/IT departments. They have subsequently spread to other service areas, and are particularly associated with organisations committed to formal quality systems and those operating an *internal market* for services with systems for *cross-charging* users of centrally provided services or facilities (see Chapter 5). SLAs are now widely used for a range of inter-departmental services in business and industry, in local and central government, and in the academic and health sectors. They are frequently implemented to manage *partnership* or *outsourcing* arrangements (see Chapter 4) as well as for more conventional customer-supplier relationships. In the UK information services community, examples exist in all sectors, and also cross-sectorally – notably between universities and National Health Service clients, booksellers/library suppliers and individual libraries, and subscription agents and library consortia.

As the words suggest, SLAs can be described as *agreements* between the provider and client, which define not only the *service* to be provided but also its *level,* normally expressed in quantifiable terms representing a minimum acceptable standard (with estimated costs). Andrew Hiles defines a Service Level Agreement as "an agreement between the provider of a service and its customers which quantifies the minimum quality of service which meets the business need". Hiles also uses the phrase "quantified availability, serviceability and reliability" but acknowledges that both public bodies and commercial organisations often find it difficult to specify precise business targets.[3] In addition to service targets, SLAs generally specify client obligations, reporting procedures and negotiating mechanisms. SLAs have been described as 'proxy contracts' in the sense of being formal agreements entered in good faith but not having the full status of a formal legal obligation. Other names used by information and library services for similar documents include *service codes* and *service definitions,* as well as *service standards* and *service targets.* Service specifications in general are viewed as a means of improving both the quality of service delivery and the accountability of the provider to the customer. Among the benefits cited are the prevention of overprovision, by identifying actual needs and priorities – the real current service requirement – and imposing discipline, on both the provider and the customer.

SLAs are typically (re)negotiated annually to fit in with organisational reporting and budgeting cycles, which can result in excessive focus on unit costs and other quantifiable aspects of service at the expense of a longer-term strategic perspective. In organisations where strategic management is absent or weak, service managers need to make a particular effort to place SLAs in a business context beyond day-to-day operational transactions, which means having a strategic plan or framework to inform negotiations. One possible approach is to present service costings for three to five years ahead which make explicit provision for *strategic initiatives* throughout the period, while accepting that only the first year's funding may be formally agreed. An alternative strategy is to take account of planned strategic developments in estimating annual costs and try to incorporate them in the budget. Creative thinking is required here as funders tend to be reluctant to approve budget lines labelled as 'unallocated' or 'contingencies'.

Cost, time and *quality* are thus key parameters for SLAs, and the relative importance given to each dimension will vary according to circumstances. Some of the terminological variants of SLAs (for example, 'service definitions', 'service standards') are especially concerned with quality and specify performance targets for different service components, but do not break down service costs to the same level. Other approaches require cost data for each component service, which often necessitates a shift from functional-based to service-based budgeting – a major task to undertake in addition to other work involved in the introduction of SLAs. One feature of SLAs that often appeals to service managers is having the chance in turn to specify the responsibilities of their customers. For example, university libraries can require academic staff to liaise with them over proposals for new programmes, to provide reading lists by a specified period in advance of the start of a course, and to notify them before recommending a text as essential to their students.

Although the decision to introduce SLAs is more often taken by organisational top management than by information service management, many service managers have found the process beneficial in aligning service provision to organisational priorities and strengthening links with clients. In this sense, they can be viewed as marketing and communication tools that can help to improve service quality and customer satisfaction, as well as demonstrating value for money. Developing a dialogue with users enables better management of their expectations and provides the opportunity to agree both the level or standard of service required and the criteria for measurement of performance. The potential **benefits** of introducing SLAs can be summarised thus:

- establishes the actual needs and priorities for information service provision
- imposes discipline on both parties and draws attention to the obligations of customers
- enables better integration of service planning with plans of other units/ the parent body
- provides a framework for service review and a meaningful context for PIs

- improves liaison with customers through regular monitoring meetings
- builds mutual understanding and respect among service staff and customers
- raises awareness of the resource implications of changing the existing service mix
- clarifies the different cost components of services, including variable and fixed costs
- demonstrates accountability, justifies funding levels and facilitates cost attribution
- reduces unpredictability of demand and introduces some measure of control.

However, it is often hard to predict the level and nature of demand, especially for services based on developing technologies. Monitoring can also be problematic: continuous monitoring is very expensive for some types of service, but periodic sampling or 'snapshot' monitoring does not necessarily provide a true picture of service performance (see Chapter 6). The **pitfalls** to consider are:

- documentation and negotiation can take up a huge amount of time and effort
- over-specified agreements may restrict what information service staff can do and how
- introduction of agreements may be interpreted as a defensive move
- service descriptions may appear to trivialise some information service activities
- the process of negotiation can be divisive and undermine good relations.

SLAs vary significantly in their content, format and length. In some organisations, managers are expected to draft SLAs in a prescribed format; in other cases, they have more flexibility and freedom to determine the size and style of the document, and the headings used. It is worth remembering that even if you are working within an established formal system, you are probably the only person (or one among a small group) charged with documenting information services, which puts you in a strong position to influence how the SLA process is adopted – and adapted – in your particular service area. In addition, even where content is tightly defined, there will usually be scope for including other information as annexes or appendices to the specified documentation.

Among the issues to consider are whether to negotiate separate agreements with different client groups or opt for a blanket agreement for all customers, and how many service elements or increments to document as discrete entities. One approach, used at Aston University, is to divide services into 'standard' ones, offered to all users on the same basis (for example, online catalogue, general reference collection, photocopying facilities) and 'tailored' ones, designed to meet specific needs of particular groups (such as current awareness or information skills programmes) and then to negotiate a single agreement on standard services with representatives of the whole community, and a series of agreements on tailored services with different client groups.[4] Much of the documentation can be re-used (which reduces the intellectual effort) but holding separate meetings with each group acknowledges their differing needs and priorities, allows the discussion to focus on their concerns, and conveys positive signals about customer-orientation.

Other factors influencing the choice of services and customers to be covered by an agreement, include potential for outsourcing and relative cost of services. (For example, university libraries often exclude services to administrative departments from the SLA process, as they account for a small fraction of the total service cost in comparison with the costs of serving their principal users – the students and staff of academic departments.)

The information and data required to document services effectively in this context falls naturally into three categories relating to the concepts implied by the three words of the title 'Service Level Agreement'. Some of this information is of a general nature and can usefully be separated out from the more specific details related to each particular service component; this general information can be further sub-divided into *background information* about the information/library service, and what amounts to the standard terms and conditions or *contractual information* of the agreement. The core part of the documentation will be the *detailed specification* and any supporting data showing the level of provision for each service component or category. A checklist of services and items to consider for each part of the documentation is given in Appendix 4.

Tips for successful implementation

- Promote the wider benefits of SLAs not just being about cost control
- Start with a small pilot and consider selective or simplified use of SLAs
- Make some provisions for inflation, especially on acquisition costs
- Build in scope for service development or opportunistic activity
- Aim to negotiate one-year agreements within at least a three-year planning horizon
- Ensure that staff training and representational work are properly acknowledged
- Use plain English and explain any service jargon or ambiguous terms
- Include a contents list and/or executive summary if your document is lengthy

- Use appendices/separate schedules for information liable to change (eg charges)
- State job titles rather than personal names when specifying responsibilities.

Space matters

As indicated in Chapter 4 under Supporting Strategies, the operational facilities and physical setting of information and library services have a significant effect on the quality of service delivery, and this also represents an important part of the resource management responsibilities of service managers, who must consider the need to remodel, adapt or otherwise improve their existing accommodation to match changing demands. In order to inform both long-term and short-term decisions on space matters, managers need to form a view of the library or information centre as a physical place. There has been much discussion about the 'digital library', the 'electronic library', the 'logical library', the 'networked library' and the 'virtual library' in recent decades, and different opinions expressed on how library and information services will be affected by information and communication technologies, and whether they will continue to exist as physical entities in anything resembling their current form. In his seminal article published in 1986, John Sack offered a radical view,

> "the library might disappear simply because it blended so successfully into the background of a scholar's activity that the scholar never needed to regard it explicitly as a place to go. . . Thus, libraries disappear because they become invisible and because their location is wherever you are: 'without walls'. . . More than a physical location, the library becomes a medium or ubiquitous utility, a service always ready at hand."[5]

Information professionals and policy makers continue to debate and speculate about the long term. F W Lancaster lists a range of views on the future of the library, along a kind of continuum:

1. Libraries will not be needed at all.
2. Libraries will become nothing more than switching centres.
3. Libraries will be switching centres but will build indexes and other tools to facilitate access to network resources.
4. Libraries will take on important new roles in building databases, creating new information composites, and possibly in some electronic publishing activities.
5. Libraries will remain important as *places* that people visit, at least in the foreseeable future.[6]

There is currently considerable support for the view that 'the library will have walls' at least for the foreseeable future. Despite predictions to the contrary, information technology has actually increased space requirements and building costs for libraries.[7] The term 'hybrid library' is now gaining currency as a way of conveying the message that new modes of service delivery will co-exist with traditional print-based collections, a credo expressed as 'And, Not Or' by Walt Crawford of the Research Libraries Group, who believes in

> "a future of inclusion, not exclusion. A future of both print and electronic communication; both linear text and hypertext; both mediation and direct access; both physical collections and electronic access. . . . future libraries that are both edifice and interface: that serve 'beyond the walls' but that are also distinctive places with distinctive place-based services".[8]

Planning space

Many professionals thus believe that library buildings will retain their importance in the electronic environment, with continuing and expanded functions as places for instruction and interaction, reflection and refreshment. Assumptions that are being made about libraries in the academic sector are increasingly applicable to both public and special libraries with the current convergence of interests around the theme of community learning, whether expressed in terms of lifelong learning for individuals or organisational learning for companies. Many corporate information centres and industrial library services are being reinvented as *learning centres* or *knowledge centres,* as organisations introduce formal skills development and knowledge management programmes. In the UK, the role of public libraries in supporting part-time, independent and distance learners is set to expand and develop over the next decade with growth in access to networked resources and provision of electronic content as learning materials. Common to all sectors is the trend towards combining libraries with other specialist and more general facilities (for example, IT resources, media services, print units, retail outlets, seminar rooms, training suites).

Information service managers also need to consider general trends in working practices and office design, such as the development of 'tele-working', 'virtual offices' and 'anytime, anywhere' work environments. In *virtual offices,* staff are not based at a fixed work location, but work in any place where they can get work done – at home, on trains, or with clients (for example, an information specialist based in a client department). In order to optimise use of space and equipment, some organisations have introduced 'non–territorial offices' and 'hot desking', so that staff do not have their own permanent desks but move around available accommodation to occupy vacant cubicles or workstations. Advocates claim that mixing people up in this way fosters creativity, but others are concerned about the reductions in regular social interaction, the impact on job satisfaction and the effect on team spirit. Managers

Figure 7.1 Common assumptions about future learning environments

Planning assumptions	Design implications
Learning is more collaborative	Need for "collaboratories" – group study tables / carrels / rooms with shared access to technology and presentation facilities
Learners have different preferences	Need variety and 'zoning' – quiet private areas and busy social areas, with low-level seating / tables and refreshment facilities
Technology is developing rapidly	Need facilities for continual training and retraining of users and staff – in large classes, small groups and as individuals
Access to network resources is universal	Need cable management for wired-up study places (workstations and plug-in points) with adjustable seating
Demand for multimedia resources is high	Need equipment to enable images to be incorporated into text documents – colour copiers, printers, scanners, etc
Self-service issue / return predominates	Central service counters are smaller, supplemented by multiple service points distributed throughout the building
Inter-disciplinary studies are the norm	Less use for separate departmental/subject-based collections, but more demand for local access to information specialists

need to balance potential gains in space utilisation against personal preferences to have a fixed physical base for individuals and teams, but some types of information work are less place-dependent (for example, abstracting and indexing).

Service managers also need to bear in mind that provision of *quiet space* is another key factor for service staff, as well as for service users: a report on workplace design from PA Consulting Group, *Balancing the bargain,* identified this as a priority issue for the future, pointing out that the important thing is to provide a variety of spaces where different types of activity can be carried out.[9] Francis Duffy, regarded as the guru of modern office design, has codified office environments into four types:

- *hive* – open plan and at worst inhumanely regimented;
- *cell* – private, study-like;
- *club* – informal and communal, in the manner of 18th century coffee houses;
- *den* – easily confused with club, but a bit more hive-like.[10]

Managing space

Space management is a relatively neglected area of professional education and practice. It is all too common to find roles and responsibilities in relation to space matters not properly assigned – either not made explicit or not covering all the necessary areas and tasks. This is somewhat at odds with the perceived importance of 'the library as a place' and represents a significant shortcoming in resource management, as noted by Andrew McDonald,

> "Space is a precious and expensive resource that should be planned and managed within a strategic framework for the development of the service as a whole, but it has sometimes received less professional attention than the other resources the librarian manages."[11]

Operational management responsibilities for safety and security, portering, cleaning, etc., are the most likely areas to be formally assigned. Strategic management responsibilities for space are often assumed to rest with the service head, but some services – usually larger libraries – have explicitly assigned this role to a member of the senior management team, on the basis that this will help to focus attention, establish a continuing interest and encourage a proactive approach. Every space-related decision should be seen as an opportunity to adapt to new conditions and to create a better environment, thus representing short-term incremental steps towards longer-term change.

In many libraries, space management is largely a reactive process, characterised by solving problems – rather than anticipating them – and putting things right only when a customer comments or complains. Regular tours of inspection tend to be associated with health and safety obligations, taking place at best every three or four months. In order to create and manage a customer-oriented environment, all staff – from the front line to senior management – need to accept a continuing responsibility for maintaining and improving the physical environment, and an individual or group should be given a specific remit to monitor the situation actively and initiate any changes desired.

Disaster management

Disaster management is a convenient term used to describe a set of activities or measures intended to enable organisations to cope with unforeseen disasters. Other terms often used for this concept include *disaster preparedness, disaster control planning* or *emergency planning,* and the less negative *contingency planning* or *business continuity planning.* Disaster preparedness has been acknowledged as a management concern in libraries ever since the damage caused in Florence by the flooding of the River Arno in 1966. Over the last two decades, the British Library has sponsored various initiatives in this area, including publication of an outline disaster control plan in 1987.[12] In the UK, recent widely publicised disasters – the IRA bomb which hit the Commercial Union Library in the City of London,[13] the fire at Norwich Central Library,[14] and the flood at the Fawcett Library of London Guildhall University[15] – have raised professional awareness of the risks, yet many information services are still inadequately prepared.

The most common examples of disasters in the library and information services context are floods and fires, but the term covers a range of natural and man-made phenomena, including storms, earthquakes, pests, explosions, asbestos, bombs, thefts and civil disorder. People tend to think of disasters as events of catastrophic proportions, but small incidents (such as a burst pipe, a leaking window, missing tiles or poor wiring) can cause large amounts of damage, especially if they happen at the 'wrong' time. Library dependence on computer-based systems for record-keeping and service delivery has complicated matters: electronic systems may be easier to back-up than manual files, but managers often have to rely on others (for example, IT departments, system suppliers) for system/software back-ups.

Disaster management is generally seen as having **four key elements:**

- *Prevention* – reducing the likelihood of a disaster occurring. This is generally pursued through a programme of risk assessment, remedial action and regular inspection, drawing on expert advice from within and outside the organisation. Effective prevention requires continuing attention to operating procedures and constant vigilance by service staff; proper systems for reporting problems and recording actions taken are vital.
- *Preparation* – enabling an effective response when a disaster occurs. This is typically achieved through a combination of documented plans, emergency supplies and staff training, supported by internal and external contact arrangements. Plans need to be simple and flexible, using checklists and flowcharts for ease of use; names and addresses of contacts must be kept up-to-date, and similarly with refresher training for staff.

- *Reaction* – includes raising the alarm, evacuating the building and organising initial and immediate actions to protect undamaged materials, to salvage damaged materials and to stabilise the environment. As well as contacting emergency services and staff 'on call' this may involve contacting advisers and insurers (for damage assessment) and communicating with service users, other stakeholders and the local media.
- *Recovery* – includes resuming service provision, restoring damaged resources and reviewing management procedures, which can extend over a long period if a major programme of conservation and/or refurbishment is required. Maintaining service continuity can be particularly challenging (especially if this has to be done from an alternative operating site) and can add to the physical and mental stress for service staff.

The award-winning web site of the M25 (London) Consortium of Higher Education Libraries offers a planning template covering the above components.[16] Many of the published guides to disaster planning include detailed advice on identifying and assembling resources for emergency use; Susan George lists useful items (with quantities) for both a small basic 'disaster kit' and a larger central 'disaster closet'.[17] *Staff training* is a critical component of disaster planning and can take a variety of forms including awareness talks, briefing sessions, hands-on practice, simulation exercises and video presentations. Information service managers often involve local fire officers and other experts to reinforce and supplement input from service staff with designated responsibilities for emergencies. Joint training events with neighbouring library and information services on a one-off or annual basis can be a useful means of sharing expertise and a lead-in to pooling resources and considering back-up arrangements.

Technology infrastructure

Information services are now critically dependent on information technology. Whereas twenty years ago library housekeeping, online searching and office applications were separate systems with their own specialist users, today everyone is involved in using a much wider range of integrated systems, with electronic linkages to internal and external partners, end-user searching of standalone and networked databases and an IT infrastructure supporting communications, 'knowledge bases' (of frequently asked questions, service procedures, etc.) and workgroup computing. This greater degree of technology dependence means more attention needs to be given to the prevention of operational disasters arising from breakdowns, hackers, viruses, etc. Management of the technology infrastructure is now a strategic issue requiring senior management attention within the information service, not something that can be left to the 'systems librarian', 'online services librarian' and other IT enthusiasts to sort out between them. Information service managers need to attend to the following issues, which are generally acknowledged as the issue set for the strategic management of IT:

- how to get strategic advantage from the technology;
- how to align the technology/systems strategy with the service/business strategy;
- how to organise the systems function;
- how to manage the changing boundaries between users and specialists;
- how to plan, build and manage the technology infrastructure;
- how to cope with the latest technologies.[18]

Many libraries and information services have established planning and budgeting processes, but few have developed formal information technology or information systems strategies to underpin their service development plans at the level of detail necessary to support the financial planning of ongoing investment in the IT infrastructure. The replacement cycle for equipment has shortened considerably in recent years, so most services need to plan for a rolling programme of replacement and upgrading of PCs, printers and the like, as well as budgeting for regular commitments (such as software licences, maintenance contracts and computer consumables). They may also need to make provision for larger capital purchases, such as a new automated system or a CD-ROM network. Developing the systems/technology strategy needs to be seen as a general management task, rather than a specialist responsibility of systems people, though the latter should obviously be expected to make a substantial input.

Alignment of systems and business strategies involves more than developing an IT strategy to support service thrusts. Alignment needs to be two-way, with technical experts helping to shape the vision, by identifying the business opportunities (and threats) posed by IT, thus acknowledging that technology can be the *driver* as well as the *enabler* of strategy. This sort of debate requires systems people who have a good general knowledge of the business and service managers who understand the technology and are prepared to take an organisation-wide view. Holistic cross-functional thinking is needed to generate imaginative proposals for new systems to support service operations; to facilitate communication and exchange of data with service partners; or to support, augment or restructure the work of managers and specialists (see the section on business re-engineering in Chapter 6).

IT strategies for information services need to be aligned with both the overall library/information service strategy and the organisational/ corporate IT strategy. Peter Weill and Marianne Broadbent advocate articulation of 'IT maxims' at the corporate level to express succinctly the strategic intent for information technology and identify the ways in which the organisation needs to

1. Lead or follow in the deployment of IT in its industry/sector
2. Electronically process transactions
3. Connect and share data sources across different parts of the organisation
4. Connect and share data sources and systems across the extended enterprise (customers, suppliers, etc.)
5. Maintain common IT architectures across the organisation, including policies and standards
6. Access, use and standardise different types of data (financial, product, customer)
7. Identify appropriate measures for assessing the business value of IT.[19]

The networked environment is forcing organisations (including information service units) to rethink the roles and responsibilities of both line managers and IT specialists in relation to information systems development and management. Restructuring the library and IT unit into one 'converged' organisation is an example of this trend, but that is only part of the story. Many large libraries have now recognised the need to have a senior manager heading up a specialist systems team – often including both information ('content') and IT ('conduit') specialists – replacing the traditional practice of locating the systems responsibility in a 'bibliographic' or 'technical services' unit.[20] This strategic role is significantly different to the operational responsibility of systems librarians of previous eras. Ideally the postholder will have a high degree of technical capability, good cross-functional expertise and sound ability to manage change, acting as a *technology champion* for the service.

The new-style systems teams increasingly include a range of specialists, responsible for library management systems, multimedia services, web sites, etc.[21] The current generation of library systems assume a continuous development path, which makes it desirable to have dedicated in-house development capability. In most services, the core systems team is extended to include functional managers who have some responsibilities for the systems supporting their particular operational areas. Some services have taken this distributed model further and have designated staff members in each functional, geographical or client team who provide basic IT support for their colleagues as part of their jobs. If the core team does not include any IT (conduit) specialists, partnerships are often formed with the organisation's IT department to ensure that relevant specialist expertise is available when needed. This relationship can be managed via a Service Level Agreement or less formally through inter-departmental task forces and project teams. IT specialists need to become proactive in systems development, making suggestions for improving or transforming processes without waiting for requests (or complaints).

In this distributed computing environment there is a blurring of roles between specialists, managers and other IT users, so that organisations need to consider and clarify the responsibilities of different parties in planning, developing and managing information systems. A responsibility chart of the type often used in project management (see previous chapter) can be a useful aid in establishing the various contributions of information service staff and others in this area. The example here lists a range of possible activities and potential actors.

The complexity and ubiquity of IT-based systems places new demands on information service managers in respect of their own *continuing professional development* as well as the development of their staff, as both managers and specialists need a broader and deeper understanding of the technology to plan, develop and deliver services effectively. More effort needs to be put into keeping up with leading-edge developments in the field and also into educating the community of stakeholders about options and constraints, including issues such as intellectual property and rights management. In the context of "this rapid and uncertain period of technological and institutional change", Stephen Griffin (Program Manager, Digital Libraries Initiative, National Science Foundation) has provided a short list of suggestions which constitute useful tips for information service managers grappling with such issues,

- learn new vocabularies in order to understand technology and techno-logists more fully;
- encourage interaction among technical and non-technical staff to build a collaborative work environment in which these groups under-stand each other;
- carefully match technologies, users and use;
- reach out to and educate users;
- prepare for loss of control, or at least a sense of control, because much use of a library's resources will be unmediated;
- connect and communicate by participating actively in local, national and international professional organisations, events and work-groups.[22]

Management structures

The formal structure adopted can significantly affect an organisation's business and financial performance because of its impact on efficiency

Figure 7.2 Responsibilities for planning and managing information systems

	Outside specialists	Internal specialists	Senior managers	Functional managers	Operating staff	Service customers
Tracking developments						
Planning systems						
Allocating resources						
Establishing standards						
Prioritising projects						
Acquiring systems						
Maintaining inventory						
Managing licences						
Developing systems						
Running systems						
Maintaining systems						
Supporting systems						
Training end-users						
Managing suppliers						

Key:
X Executes the work; **D** Takes decisions solely/ultimately; **d** Takes decisions jointly/partly; **P** Controls progress; **C** Must be consulted; **I** Must be informed; **A** Available to advise

and effectiveness, in particular on the quality of decision-making, ability to respond to changing circumstances, and the morale and motivation of individuals. Service expansion places demands on management structures and often strains reporting relationships, so it makes sense to rethink structure and reporting periodically, especially in the context of strategic change. Restructuring can also be an effective way to encourage a *change in culture,* particularly if it involves altering the physical layout or moving whole departments, as giving people new roles, responsibilities and relationships often forces new behaviour and fosters different attitudes.

Organisational structure determines issues such as allocation of responsibilities, assignment of tasks, communication of information, co-ordination of operations and the grouping of individuals in units, sections, etc. Structures must be designed to suit particular enterprises or institutions – there are no standard 'textbook' solutions, but published work offers useful guidance on factors to take into account as well as examples from real-life experience. It is important to note that the issues surrounding organisational design are not just technical questions: they have behavioural and political dimensions, as they relate to questions about power and control; and they will be subject to various cultural influences, depending on the business and professional context, and also on the social/national setting.

Structural deficiencies are often manifest in problems of co-ordination and integration. Danger signals include complaints from customers, contractors or external partners; overloading of top management or support staff; proliferation of committees or preponderance of procedures; and persistent conflict between departments. Another sign of the need to consider regrouping is when the actual informal patterns of communication and interaction differ significantly from those implied or intended. Fitting the design to the organisation's situation requires consideration of the external environment as well as internal issues. The following factors are relevant:

- *age and size* – older and larger organisations tend to be more formalised;
- *technology* – automation and networking can humanise and reduce bureaucracy;
- *stability* – dynamic, unpredictable conditions require flexible, informal co-ordination;
- *complexity* – sophisticated technical systems encourage selective decentralisation;
- *stakeholders* – strong external control encourages a centralised formalised structure;
- *market diversity* – broad range of clients/services encourages market-based units;
- *hostile environment* – an extreme situation drives towards (temporary) centralisation;
- *management fashions* – many organisations are seduced by 'the structure of the day'.

The shift from *tall* to *flat* structures and consequent reduction in *management layers* is one of the most widely-discussed changes in organisational design. Negative aspects of traditional **hierarchical pyramids** have been frequently and extensively enumerated, for example: communication is cumbersome, slow and distorted; senior management control and influence is diluted; responsibilities at different levels are hard to clarify; supervisors and subordinates are often bypassed; individual initiative and discretion is limited; rigid departmentalism prevents effective co-operation; status, rank and grade are unduly emphasised; and administrative overheads are costly. **Flat structures** require acceptance of individual responsibility and accountability, shedding of the 'dependence mentality' and mutual trust among all categories of staff. There are numerous ways of shaping the *superstructure* by grouping activities to form teams, sections, departments, etc. – for example, by work process or function; by the knowledge/skills or other categorisation of workers; by product or service output; by customer/client group; or by geographical region or service outlet. These can be broadly summarised as organising on a *functional* or *market* basis, the former reflecting a focus on means, the latter on ends.

Functional groupings emphasise different specialisms, they are inherently more efficient, and they offer economies of scale and lower training costs; but they lack a built-in mechanism for co-ordinating the work flow and tend to be rather bureaucratic, and also to focus on unit/section goals, with a short-term outlook – and they are not suited to turbulent times. **Market groupings** acknowledge the need to integrate specialist contributions in a complete work cycle, they offer different perspectives on problem-solving, they can do more tasks and can change tasks more easily, and people become more involved in their work and hence more productive; but they are less able to do specialised or repetitive tasks, and can be wasteful of resources.

Structures are rarely a pure type, but more often combine both function and market features. A **mixed structure** uses different principles of division in different parts or levels of the organisation – for example, organising finance and personnel specialists on a functional basis, but structuring other departments along service or geographical lines; grouping technical services on a functional basis, sub-dividing reference services by both subject and material, with branch libraries representing a geographical focus; or having market-based responsibilities at a senior level, with functional units at the operational level. A **matrix structure** – also known as a *grid* or *multiple command* structure – is multidimensional and combines a functional focus with a product or market focus, so that individuals have two roles and two bosses. Henry Mintzberg describes the matrix structure as 'the ultimate liaison device', while noting that it sacrifices the classic principle of unity of command.

Mintzberg distinguishes two types of matrix, a permanent form or *true matrix*, where interdependencies remain fairly stable, and likewise the units and people in them; and a temporary arrangement or *shifting matrix*, which uses task forces or project teams to bring different functional specialists together on a short-term basis for specific purposes.[23] In the former, there is theoretically an equal balance between functional and cross-functional roles and responsibilities; in practice, organisations often designate one boss as the primary manager, while requiring full attention to both roles, and input from the second manager to the appraisal process. The latter model is more common in organisations generally, but the former has often been adopted by information services – though not always explicitly acknowledged as a matrix structure.

The case for matrix arrangements is based on the desire to optimise two potentially conflicting benefits – retaining the economic operation and technical efficiency of functional grouping, while effectively co-ordinating and applying those resources to different organisational outputs. It is variously seen as a response to **environmental complexity**, a means of achieving differentiation without decentralisation, and an attempt to balance the needs of uniformity/consistency and diversity. It is result-oriented and information-related, and it can combine a focus on *customer care* (client needs and priorities) with the development of *specialist skills*. Matrix structures are particularly suited to situations where there is a high degree of interdependency, a frequency of non-routine tasks and/or a need to develop new activities with scope for devolved responsibility. Commentators argue that matrix structures work well when functional resources are in short supply, or an organisation wishes to place less emphasis on that aspect. Andrew Kakabadse presents the matrix as a strategy for changing the market ethos of an organisation, which captures much of the thinking underlying restructuring plans in many information service organisations,

> "Matrix structure management is needed when an organisation has developed a somewhat unresponsive and inflexible culture, . . . [it] is a way of generating greater flexibility over task activity and more market responsive attitudes amongst managers and specialists in the organisation."[24]

Such structures have both benefits and pitfalls.

Advantages of matrix structures

- *communication* – information flow is enhanced vertically (from the flatter structure) and especially laterally;
- *competency* – multi-tasking enables staff to develop and apply knowledge and skills in a wider context;
- *efficiency* – specialist (functional) expertise can be shared across service projects and customer groups;

- *flexibility* – frequent contact between people with different skills enables more adaptive responses;
- *integration* – clear and workable mechanisms exist for co-ordinating work across functional lines;
- *projectivity* – capabilities required for project work are developed through cross-functional working;
- *quality* – tailored co-ordination of expert output (through customer focus) results in better end-product.

Disadvantages of matrix structures

- *administration* – management overheads can easily increase with additional effort put into co-ordination;
- *confusion* – dual reporting relationships create uncertainties about personal authority and accountability;
- *conflict* – divided commitments and competition for scarce (staff) resources can result in power struggles;
- *delay* – extensive consultation and consensus decision-making can result in undesirably slow reaction time – but this problem has been lessened by electronic communication
- *demands* – co-operative attitudes and high levels of interpersonal skills are a necessity for a matrix to work well.

Flexibility and adaptability are key features required in information service structures as it is obvious that IT-related change will be a continuing issue, and it is likely that services will wish to create new specialist roles to cope with emerging technologies. Despite the many *interdependencies* in libraries, some are characterised by *compartmentalisation* with staff often unaware of developments in other sections. Matrix arrangements improve the flow of information among teams and enable cross-fertilisation of ideas; they also help to institutionalise *cross-functional teamworking* and to prepare staff for involvement in service-wide development projects. This structure requires a tolerance of ambiguity, but a matrix situation often already exists in all but name, and formally acknowledging it may actually reduce stress. Confusion with a new structure can be a significant issue initially, but can be addressed by various communication strategies, including open forum meetings and discussions with individuals to resolve specific problems. The matrix looks a good choice for the foreseeable future as information services staff continue to adapt to the networked world.

Process guidelines

Published literature suggests the following factors contribute to successful restructuring:

Figure 7.3 Design objectives, service characteristics and structural features

Common design objectives and organisational characteristics	Typical structural features
Control and inspection High-risk, highly-specified or cost-conscious operations	• rules and procedures • detailed job descriptions • narrow spans of control • long chains of command
Connections and interactions Customer focus, service ethos and long-term relationships with suppliers	• quality circles • empowerment • strategic alliances • market / product divisions
Creativity and innovation Risk-taking, open communication, networking, learning, individuality	• flat structures • small groups / venture units • close interaction of functions • innovation champion at senior level
Commitment and involvement Low control, high trust, shared values demonstrated by senior management	• motivating jobs • cohesive work groups • rewards and incentives • involvement in decision-making
Co-ordination and integration High interdependence – shared resources, reciprocal activities, sequential operations	• liaison officers • co-ordinating roles • matrix management • cross-functional teams

- *communication and consultation* – even if the decision to restructure is irreversible, it is important to explain things properly and invite views on the details;
- *physical proximity* – it is much easier to get people working together effectively if they are based in the same place;
- *real plans* – a shared vision and a framework for implementation will help to motivate people, preferably a major unifying project with acknowledged benefits.

If the reorganisation involves merging or converging previously separate operations, extra care is required and more resources (time and money) can make a significant difference:

- *evolutionary development* – it helps to bring people together first for one-off projects, then involve them in ongoing planning, and finally in operational processes;
- *pump-priming funds* – additional earmarked investment for joint projects in the early stages will create a 'win-win' budget situation (rather than a 'zero-sum game')

Organisation culture

Culture is frequently mentioned in the context of strategy and change, but its coverage in the library literature is rather patchy in view of its importance and relevance to promoting a service ethos and managing strategic change. Culture underlies much human activity in organisational life, and it pervades decision-making and problem-solving. Lack of cultural awareness can result in decisions with unanticipated and undesirable consequences; cultural understanding and insight enables managers to assess such situations more effectively.

The influence of culture on *strategy* is considerable, for example culture determines scanning behaviour, and the perception and interpretation of environmental events; and also determines organisational mission, and the values and assumptions underlying planning. The strategy or plan is itself a cultural artefact, but may not be entirely consonant with prevailing culture. If the service thrusts identified as strategically important are *culturally incompatible* – "we don't do things like that around here" – managers need to consider various **options**, such as

- managing around the culture by changing implementation plans;
- modifying the culture to fit the strategy, which is likely to be a slow process;
- adapting the strategy to fit the culture.

Organisation culture is a nebulous concept. There are numerous **definitions**, ranging from the rather abstract, "all the shared, taken-for-granted assumptions that a group has learned throughout its history"[25] to the more colloquial "the way things get done around here".[26] Peter Antony points out that "It is in the nature of a culture to be unperceived by those who share it and difficult to penetrate by those who do not".[27] Most commentators agree that culture is about the views, values, symbols, stories, routines, rituals, beliefs, behaviours, attitudes and assumptions held in common by a group or community – explicitly or tacitly. A few separate the *empirical* (the way people *do* things) from the *cognitive* (the way people *think* about things). Some refer to the *personality* or *character* of an organisation, others have equated culture with organisational *ideology* or *anthropology*. Edgar Schein sets out a three-level model, moving from the visible *artefacts,* which are observable, though not usually decipherable; through espoused *values,* which may be just rationalisations or aspirations; to invisible *assumptions,* which are the ultimate sources of values and actions.[25]

At a more practical level, Charles Handy clarifies what is meant in this context by a 'way of life' or 'set of norms' with a series of **questions** to explore deep-set beliefs about the way work should be organised, the way authority should be exercised, how people are rewarded, and how they are controlled:

- what are the degrees of formalisation required?
- how much planning and how far ahead?
- what combination of obedience and initiative is looked for in subordinates?
- do work hours matter, or dress, or personal eccentricities?
- what about expense accounts, and secretaries, stock options and incentives?
- do committees control, or individuals?
- are there rules and procedures or only results?"[28]

It is generally agreed that the main influences on culture are the founder's or leader's personality, the organisational/business context and the society/regional/national culture. The *strength* of a culture is measured by the extent to which individuals have internalised the values of a group or organisation; groups with stable membership and organisations with low staff turnover are likely to develop strong cultures. The *espoused* culture of managers often differs from the culture in practice; some commentators reserve the term **corporate culture** for the proposed or promoted view, and use **organisational culture** for the 'real' version. Culture is also rarely unitary or homogeneous: most organisations contain identifiable *sub-cultures,* which have formed around different functions, levels or sites (for example, head office, frontline staff, dispersed branches). Sub-cultures can help to create a common sense of purpose, but they can make co-ordination difficult and cause internal conflict. There can be related, overlapping or competing **sub-cultures:**

- *enhancing subcultures,* where the sub-group adheres to the principal beliefs and values more strongly than the rest of the organisation (for example, a group of long-serving staff)
- *orthogonal subcultures,* where the sub-group subscribes to the core values and simultaneously to separate but unconflicting values (for example, a specialist group with strong professional values)
- *counter cultures,* where the sub-group subscribes to values that are in direct conflict with those of the dominant culture (for example, trade union groups or staff in organisations that have been merged or taken-over).

Cultural analysis

Various typologies or classifications of types of organisational cultures have been developed as a means of helping people to understand how organisations work – or don't work. The models differ widely in their sophistication, range of variables considered and applicability. One of the best known and most influential is Roger Harrison's four-fold model developed in the 1970s, which was modified and popularised by Charles Handy:

- the *Power* culture largely depends on charismatic personal leadership – typically that of the owner or founding group of a successful business;
- the *Role* culture is governed by rules and committees, and rewards are associated with consistency and protocol – exemplified by the civil service;
- the *Achievement* or *Task* culture assumes people enjoy working towards common goals, allowing neither rules and regulations, nor personal or social needs to get in the way – typified by consultancy firms and research teams;
- the *Support* or *Person* culture is more oriented towards individual needs, primarily those of its members but also empathising with its clients or customers – exemplified by co-operative organisations and voluntary bodies.

The main features of these cultural types are summarised in the comparative table.

Figure 7.4 Typical features of organisation cultures (based on Harrison and Handy)

	Power	Role	Achievement	Support
Values	Control Loyalty Strength Decisiveness	Order Stability Procedures Responsibility	Creativity Distinction Competition Independence	Sharing Friendship Involvement Relationships
Power-base	Resources	Legitimacy	Expertise	Contacts
Leadership style	Tell	Tell and sell	Consult	Involve
Decision-making	Political Top-down	Formal Analytical	Intuitive Conceptual	Consensus Behavioural
Design basis	Productivity	Efficiency	Flexibility	Autonomy
Structural types	Centralised Web/wheel Flat pyramid	Hierarchy Bureaucracy Tall pyramid	Hybrid Net/matrix Decentralised	Cluster Collegial Self-managed
Principles of job design	Control the workforce	Create a rational system	Optimise skills for results	Quality of working life
Model for skills development	Understudy	Formal training	Action learning	Personal growth

Handy notes that role organisations will be found where economies of scale and depth of specialisation are more important than innovation and adaptability. They are associated with stable controllable markets but are ill-equipped for turbulent environments and the era of customer choice. The achievement culture thrives where speed of reaction and breadth of integration are significant issues; it works less well when resources are tight, but it is the culture most in tune with modern organisation themes of teamworking, empowerment and change management.[28] Harrison argues that culture is the key to understanding **service quality** and that each cultural orientation has a typical attitude and characteristic style of customer service which is a reflection of the organisation's values:

- *role* organisations are characterised by high-volume fast efficient delivery of *standard* products;
- *achievement* organisations are characterised by high-technology professional expert delivery of *innovative* products and services;
- *support* organisations are characterised by highly-interactive personal caring development of *responsive* services.[29]

In an article specifically concerned with culture in libraries, James Nichol argues that while the achievement culture is probably the information professional's instinctive *modus vivendi* it is not necessarily the best basis for meeting customer needs, asserting that "When the achievers can't promote their services successfully, they interpret it as the client's failure to comprehend the benefits being offered".[30]

More recently, Rob Goffee and Gareth Jones have analysed social relationships or the **social architecture** in organisations along two dimensions: *sociability* – affective, non-instrumental relations between individuals; and *solidarity* – task-centred, instrumental co-operation between unlike individuals and groups. Their model shows four cultural types which each have a negative 'twin', representing their darker side. Goffee and Jones point out that there is no 'one best model' as any of these cultural types can be successful, as long as the culture fits the business environment and is built around critical processes.[26]

All cultural models of this sort are inevitably characterised by their generality and simplicity, but they are useful tools to aid thinking and identification of significant organisational factors. The methods generally used to discover and examine culture are direct observation, questionnaire surveys and facilitated workshops. Goffee and Jones also use observational checklists (covering physical space, interpersonal communication, time management and personal identity) and critical incident analysis, with ten scenarios for each cultural type.[26] The most widely used **questionnaire** is the instrument originally designed by Harrison and subsequently promulgated by Handy, which has been reproduced in

Figure 7.5 Organisation cultures based on social architectures (from Goffee and Jones)

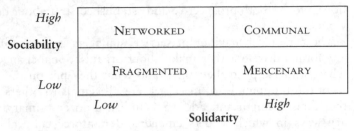

several textbooks. Schein argues that such surveys do not have sufficient breadth or depth, and the questions are open to several interpretations. He favours a structured process based on one or more **workshops** with the following steps,

1. *Define the business problem* – identify a strategic or tactical goal (something you want to change or improve) to provide a context for your discussion;
2. *Clarify the culture concept* – ensure group members understand the three-level model of artefacts, espoused values and shared tacit assumptions;
3. *Identify the visible artefacts* – write down on flip chart paper all the things that visibly characterise what it is like to work in your organisation;
4. *Identify the espoused values* – repeat the above process, including values mentioned in relation to artefacts and those captured in your vision;
5. *Compare values with artefacts* – look for inconsistencies and then identify the deeper tacit assumptions that represent the embedded culture.[25]

Cultural change

Changing the culture of an organisation is best seen as an **incremental process** as the notion of instant replacement of longstanding values is unrealistic. It is more sensible to think in terms of *encouraging* rather than *controlling* cultural change, and worth noting that it is more likely to happen if an organisation is outward-facing and forward-looking. Many commentators advocate using structure and systems to change the culture and climate. Restructuring a library into client-oriented teams as the main organisational unit sends a clear message to both staff and users about the importance of customer focus. Introducing cross-functional task forces or project teams while retaining the basic management structure can be a useful preliminary step. Stressing attributes such as creativity and flexibility in job advertisements and person specifications informs both prospective and established staff about desired behaviours.

The personal behaviour of **service managers** is just as important as any formal decisions they make about organisational changes: how and where leaders spend their time, and what they put on the agenda and record in the minutes of meetings, are all signals to others about what they think is important. Edgar Schein lists a dozen primary and secondary ways in which leaders embed and reinforce cultural elements in organisations:

Primary embedding mechanisms

- What leaders pay attention to, measure, and control
- How leaders react to critical incidents and organizational crises
- Observed criteria by which leaders allocate scarce resources
- Deliberate role modelling, teaching, and coaching
- Observed criteria by which leaders allocate rewards and status
- Observed criteria by which leaders recruit, select, promote, retire, and excommunicate organisational members

Secondary articulation and reinforcement mechanisms

- Organisation design and structure
- Organisational systems and procedures
- Organisational rites and rituals
- Design of physical space, facades, and buildings
- Stories, legends, and myths about people and events
- Formal statements of organizational philosophy, values, and creed.[25]

In his earlier seminal work on organisational culture and leadership, Schein concludes with a message for managers, "Give culture its due" and provides five **tips** for approaching culture change:

1. Do not oversimplify and do not confuse culture with other useful concepts, such as 'climate', 'values', or 'corporate philosophy' – culture operates at one level below these others and largely *determines* them.
2. Do not assume that culture applies only to the human side of an organisation's functioning – culture also determines the organisation's most basic sense of mission and goals.
3. Do not assume that culture can be manipulated like other matters under the control of managers – culture controls the manager more than the manager controls culture.
4. Do not assume that there is a 'correct' or 'better' culture, and do

not assume that 'strong' cultures are better than weak cultures – effectiveness depends on the match between cultural assumptions and environmental realities.

5. Do not assume that all aspects of the culture are relevant to the effectiveness of the organisation.[31]

Professional development

The education, training and development of staff is a key area for information services, with the pace of technological change and the range of services and systems typically used in day-to-day operations. Few information service managers can hire and fire at will, thus putting further pressure on the development process to acquire the new capabilities needed for new or improved services. Information service staff today need an extended skillset covering business, management and technical abilities, as well as information, organisational and personal skills. In the UK the government-initiated **Investors in People** (IiP) programme has had a significant impact on organisational commitment to training and development. Launched in 1991 by the Employment Department and delivered through a national network of Training and Enterprise Councils, this national standard has raised awareness of good practice as encapsulated in its **four basic principles**:

- a public *commitment* to develop all employees to achieve business objectives;
- regular *review* of the training and development needs of all employees;
- *action* to train and develop individuals at recruitment and throughout employment;
- *evaluation* of the investment in training and development to assess achievement and improve future effectiveness.[32]

In particular, the IiP standard makes an explicit link between staff development and business goals and requires the resources for training and developing staff to be identified in the business plan. Many library and information services have achieved IiP accreditation as part of organisation-wide initiatives, some have done so on their own account, and others have used the assessment indicators and related documentation as policy guidelines.[33] Following on from the above, in view of the critical importance of staff development for information services, as a minimum requirement all services should have:

- a formal *policy statement* for staff development;
- a designated *senior manager* as development co-ordinator;
- an annual *resource allocation* for development activities.

Staff development **policy statements** vary significantly in content and length. Typical headings included in such documents are shown in the box. (Opportunities here can make explicit reference to on-the-job development, as well as more formal options.) In addition, it makes sense to show how the policy links with the information service strategy, as well as with related processes (for example, staff appraisal).

Figure 7.6 Outline contents for staff development policies

Main headings for policy statements	
o Objectives	o Opportunities
o Priorities	o Programmes
o Responsibilities	o Record-keeping
o Entitlements	o Evaluation

Larger information service units often set up an *advisory group* with members representing the different categories of staff to assist the co-ordinator with planning and evaluation of programmes. Various guidelines have been suggested for resource allocation, for both development budgets and staff time (for example, 1% of total spend or 2% of payroll costs). In 1993, the Fielden report on human resource management in academic libraries recommended that UK higher education institutions should allocate a minimum of 5% of library and information service staff time to training and development.[34] More recently, the SCONUL Newsletter reported that at the University of Lincolnshire and Humberside all full-time staff have an entitlement and a requirement of four hours staff development a week.[35] Such figures can be a useful starting point, but they need to be seen as only part of the picture, as they do not adequately reflect the fact that a large proportion of development activity takes place on or around the job, rather than through formal planned events. Another trend evident in information services is the use of a *weekly training hour* to provide a guaranteed miminum time allocation for all staff to update knowledge and skills (following the model adopted by many banks and shops). Some organisations are also experimenting with individual *personal development budgets*.

Development options and opportunities

Opportunities for learning and development arise both on and off the job, and can be formal or informal, planned or *ad hoc*, at work or elsewhere. Over the last two decades, the focus has shifted away from formal courses towards various forms of action learning and self-development, with more acknowledgement of the potential contribution of project work and task force membership and other day-to-day activities to learning and development.

Figure 7.7 Selected examples of staff development options

In-the-job	Changes to jobs	Off-the-job
o Complaints	o Attachments	o Courses
o Delegation	o Challenging assignments	o Diagnostic instruments
o Feedback	o Exchanges	o Further study
o Instruction	o Job rotations	o Guided reading
o Observation	o Lateral transfers	o Interactive media
o Problem-solving	o New responsibilities	o Lectures / talks
o Mistakes	o Projects	o Open learning
o Trouble-shooting	o Restructuring	o Self-paced training
o Unfamiliar tasks	o Secondments	o Visits to other services
o Working groups	o Temporary promotion	o Workshops

Development roles and responsibilities

Development should be seen as a shared responsibility, requiring active collaboration among several players working as a *development partnership* with a common purpose. The key roles are as follows:

- The *employer* or *organisation* has prime responsibility for formulating policies and plans, and allocating resources and time, to ensure that all employees are properly trained to carry out their assigned tasks. This responsibility is normally discharged through departmental or service heads, and in larger organizations is usually delegated to a senior person acting as the staff development or training officer for the business unit. The responsibility also extends to ensuring opportunities for professional development, providing information and advice to those involved, and giving support and guidance to line managers.

- The *line-manager* or *supervisor* has particular responsibility for identifying, acting on and monitoring the training and development needs of his or her team, both as individuals and as a group. This includes agreeing development objectives and plans, finding opportunities for both training and practice, offering encouragement and help, and giving clear and timely feedback (for example, not leaving this until an annual appraisal discussion). Where people are involved in a range of activities supervised by different managers, some of these responsibilities will have to be shared, but the line-manager should assume a co-ordinating role.

- The *individual* as an *employee* has personal responsibility for being an active (rather than a passive) participant in this process and for approaching his or her own development in a collaborative spirit. This includes assessing and communicating his or her needs, making good use of opportunities offered, evaluating events and activities, applying learning to day-to-day tasks, and sharing experience with colleagues.

The individual may also have formal responsibilities for others as described above, as none of the roles set out here are mutually exclusive.

- Other *helpers* and *mentors* have casual or formal roles and responsibilities in providing personal support for individuals, within and outside the workplace, for general or specific purposes (such as induction or special projects). This includes acting as role models, facilitating access to expertise and resources, interpreting organisational culture and politics, offering a sounding board for ideas, and providing constructive criticism. David Clutterbuck has identified four broad mentoring roles and fifteen different types of mentoring behaviour, reflecting active and passive styles for emotional and intellectual support.[36]

Development needs analysis

Staff development needs can arise from environmental developments, strategic initiatives (which should be reflected as task objectives in individual forward plans agreed at appraisals) and individual objectives (represented as learning objectives in personal development plans). Some categories of staff at particular stages of development may require structured programmes or special attention, for example newly-qualified professionals working towards chartership of the Library Association; newly-promoted people becoming line managers for the first time; and longstanding 'plateaued' performers needing reinvigoration to prevent stagnation. (Induction/orientation programmes for newly-appointed staff are more sensibly seen as part of the *recruitment* process, rather than a *development* process.)

Formal analysis of development needs should bring together top-down and bottom-up inputs. Service heads need to look into the future when formulating staff development strategies. Pamela Jajko (Manager, Corporate Library and Information Center, Syntex Inc) has identified six **questions** to be considered here,

- will the focus shift from the virtual library to the virtual librarian?
- what is the new work in a virtual library and who will do it?
- what new skills are needed to get the work done and how will the staff either be recruited or trained?
- what are the new client/staff relationships and how can they be encouraged and supported?
- what is the balance in the librarian's roles of information manager, information navigator, educator, researcher, designer, finder, subject specialist, warehouser and applier?

- what is the optimal organisational structure to facilitate the virtual librarian's changing roles?[37]

Many organisations use standard checklists of skills or sets of competencies to assist this process. Such lists can be a useful prompt for individuals, but should not be used as a substitute for the regular self-audit which ought to be part of every professional's continuing development programme. Diagnostic instruments, such as questionnaires that give feedback on management styles, team roles, etc., can be valuable here. Individuals often find it helpful to work through a structured series of questions as a preliminary to setting individual learning objectives. A simple checklist is shown below, together with a suggested format for **personal development plans** (overleaf).

Personal development planning checklist

- Knowledge, skills and insights acquired to date
- Achievements in previous/present job(s)
- Preferred activities and personal strengths
- Performance problems or prime issues
- Career ambitions and anticipated future roles
- Competency developments/improvements needed
- Development methods successfully used in past
- Preferred types and styles of learning
- Sources of personal help available
- Other resources potentially available

It is sensible to warn people here to beware of the temptation to collect too many objectives. Managers should be encouraged to consider the scale of importance of the various needs, and to ask themselves, are they

- desirable? or crucial?
- interesting? or usable?
- generally valuable? or specifically relevant?
- wanted by one individual? essential for all managers?
- important for the current job? or significant for a future role?

Evaluation

Evaluation of training and development activity is a traditionally weak area, not least because effects are quite likely to take some time to be realised and it is hard to prove a direct link between attendance at an event and improved performance. Nevertheless, efforts should be made to evaluate specific development events in order to inform future investments, and also to encourage participants to reflect on their experiences and share their learning with colleagues. However, it is important to

Figure 7.8 Sample format for personal development plans

Objective *What competency do you want to develop?*	Purpose *Why do you want to develop in this area? (e.g. current job, probable future role, eventual career move)*	Methods *How do you plan to learn and develop?*	Timescale *When do you plan to begin / complete this?*	Responsibility *Who else will you involve, if anyone?*	Resources *What financial/ other resources are needed?*

keep evaluation methods simple as people may be reluctant to attend events if they have to write a long report afterwards. One option is to use a simple form or a short checklist of questions, which prompts people for the basic information required and provides scope for more extended comments if people wish. Some suggestions for headings and questions are given below.

Development event evaluation checklist
- *Novelty* – what did you learn as a result of attending this event – new information or ideas? examples of innovation or good practice?
- *Speakers* – how effective were the presenters/group leaders? are there any names we should deliberately seek out or avoid in future?
- *Contacts* – did you make any new contacts at the event or renew existing ones?
- *Handouts* – do you have any notes, papers or additional information that could be made available for circulation or consultation?
- *Recommendations* – have you any suggestions for specific action to be taken as a result of attending this event? do you think we should send staff to similar events in the future?
- *General* – any other things worth noting (for example, accommodation, catering arrangements, equipment, facilities)

Individuals can also be asked to keep their own personal records of training and other development activities, and some may choose to use a diary or learning log for this purpose. At a more general level, Sheila Creth (University Librarian at the University of Iowa) has compiled two brief checklists – for the service as an organisation and for the individual as a manager – to help evaluate overall performance in staff development.[38] These lists are reproduced in Appendix 5.

Risk management

The need for risk assessment has been mentioned in several contexts, notably in relation to strategy evaluation, project management and disaster prevention. Projects are inherently risky because they involve doing new things (or doing things in new ways) and risk management ought to be a continuous process throughout any major project undertaken. Risks in this context include anything preventing the project going according to plan, such as machines not working, people not being available or outputs not meeting quality standards. Day-to-day operations are also prone to problems of this type as well as being exposed to the risks of the sort of disasters considered earlier (fires, storms, thefts, etc.). Adopting a formal structured approach to risk analysis and management should enable information services to deal more efficiently and effectively with all these sources of risk.

The **key steps** involved in risk management are *identifying* the risk drivers; *estimating* both the *likelihood* of occurrence and the *level* of impact or consequence on performance; and then *deciding* on *responses* in the form of plans and/or actions to contain the problem.

Identifying risks

There are two basic ways to approach *risk identification*, which are often used in combination – standard *checklists* and organised *pondering*. The *checklist* is a popular approach, seen as a convenient and simple method, based on past experience and the fact that many things that go wrong in projects and services are caused by generic problems (such as an inexperienced manager, a new system, a tight timetable or an untried supplier). However, it is risky to rely solely on checklists because they have limitations in identifying complexities, interdependencies and multiplicities of risks arising from single drivers; they are best seen as prompts or starting points, rather than as definitive statements.

Pondering involves the manager (and other stakeholders) pooling experience and thinking about what might happen, analytically and intuitively, frequently in a brainstorming exercise and often using some form of prompt. One approach is to use an Ishikawa or fishbone (cause-and-effect) diagram, taking the three key areas of risk – cost, time and quality – and speculating likely causes for each effect (overspend, overrun, etc.) and then breaking these down into more specific issues. Another approach is to use a variant of the six-word diagram (who, why, what, etc.) and consider risks associated with different stakeholders and their objectives, in relation to various aspects of the undertaking.

In the context of project management, Chris Chapman and Stephen Ward propose a more elaborate framework, suggesting that the roots of project uncertainty are associated with six basic questions – 'the six Ws' – that need to be addressed:

1. *who* – who are the parties ultimately involved? (initiators, later players, other parties)
2. *why* – what do the parties want to achieve? (profit, other motives)
3. *what* – what is it the parties are interested in? (design)
4. *whichway* – how is it to be done? (activities)
5. *wherewithal* – what resources are required (resources)
6. *when* – when does it have to be done? (timetable)

In the project context, risk needs to be assessed in relation to all the phases or stages of the project life cycle, and this process can be assisted by considering the six Ws in this way. Chapman and Ward prefer an eight-stage model (rather than the traditional four phases) because of the different tasks involved in different aspects of planning and completion.[39]

Figure 7.9 Sources of risk in the project life cycle

Phases	Stages	Parties	Motives	Design	Activities	Resources	Timetable
Conceive	Define						
Plan	Design						
	Plan						
	Allocate						
Implement	Execute						
Complete	Deliver						
	Review						
	Support						

Assessing risks

The next step is to assess the probability and potential impact of the risk, either by assigning a numerical weighting to each on a five- or ten-point scale, and then multiplying the figures together to arrive at a *hazard rating*, or by categorising them broadly as 'high', 'medium' and 'low'. The results of this analysis can be summarised diagramatically on a simple **risk map** using a nine-box matrix to identify major and minor risks, as shown in the example overleaf, which is based on CCTA guidance on the management of project risk.[40]

In the CCTA model, boxes 1–3 represent *minor* risks, boxes 4–6 represent *intermediate* risks and boxes 4–6 represent *major* risks. The map can be extended to a four- or five-point scale for complex projects.

Deciding responses

There are several generic responses to risk, which can be broadly categorised as **containment** or **contingent** strategies. Containment involves action *in advance* to lessen the likelihood of the risk or its consequences occurring. The contingent approach involves action *after the event* to minimise or mitigate consequences. (Both types of response can be pursued for serious risks.) Responses can be further classified as *avoidance, reduction, allowance* and *absorption,* as shown in the table, which is based on Chapman and Ward's classification.[39] In addition, managers can consider the scope for *deflection* – transferring or sharing the risk

Figure 7.10 Map showing areas of major, intermediate and minor risk

Consequence on performance

		Low	Medium	High
Likelihood of occurrence	High	4	7	9
	Medium	2	5	8
	Low	1	3	6

Key	Likelihood	Consequence
Low	but not impossible (0–20% probability)	small schedule slip (0–10%) small increase in cost (0–10%) a few shortfalls in secondary parameters
Medium	fairly likely to occur (20–50% probability)	significant slip in schedule (10–30%) significant increase in cost (10–30%) minor shortfalls in one or more key parameters
High	more likely than not (>50% probability)	large delay (>30%) large increase in cost (>30%) major shortfalls in one or more key parameters

with another party via financial instruments (such as insurance or guarantees) or other contractual arrangements. (Such responses might be classified as avoidance, but are more likely to be prevention or mitigation.) As well as analysing risks individually, we need to determine and respond to the cumulative effects arising from *interdependencies* or *combinations* of events and their consequences.

Having identified and analysed the risks and planned your responses, it is good practice to record decisions and actions in a **risk register**, covering the following points for each risk:

• title and description;
• probability/impact rating and ranking;
• response, with the name of the person responsible;
• interdependencies and related actions required.

It is essential to agree with everyone involved the frequency for reviewing

Figure 7.11 Generic responses to risk (adapted from Chapman and Ward)

Containment	
	Modify objectives Change (reduce or raise) performance targets
Avoidance	
	Avoid Eliminate the identified source of uncertainty
	Prevent Reduce likelihood of occurrence
Reduction	
	Mitigate Modify impact of risk
Contingent	
	Develop contingency plans Set aside resources to provide reactive ability
Allowance	
	Keep options open Delay choices and commitment, select versatile options
	Monitor Collect/update data about probabilities, impacts and other risks
Absorption	
	Accept Accept risk exposure as it is, but do nothing about it

identified risks. The risk register then becomes a working tool to be reconsidered and updated as events take place. As indicated above, this process can be used to manage risk in relation to a specific project, a programme of projects or more generally in the context of day-to-day service operations.

Summary checklist

Can you sustain continuous service development?

Staff
Have responsibilities for developing their skills and knowledge been defined and communicated to staff?
Do managers actively seek out opportunities for individual and team development?

Service
Have the types, levels and prices of services offered been defined and communicated to staff and customers?

Is performance against standards/targets regularly reviewed and reported?

Space
Have responsibilities for maintaining and improving the physical environment been defined and communicated?
Are staff prepared and trained to deal with disasters and emergencies?

Technology
Have roles of managers, specialists and operators in systems management and development been defined and communicated?
Do service managers and systems experts collaborate over technology planning?

Structure
Does the formal management structure reflect practical working relationships?
Does the management structure reinforce service values and priorities?

Culture
Does the perceived organisational culture support identified strategic thrusts?
Are there any competing sub-cultures in direct conflict with strategic objectives?

References

1. Albrecht, K. *The only thing that matters: bringing the power of the customer into the center of your business*. New York: HarperCollins, 1992
2. Pluse, J. Customer focus: the salvation of service organizations. *Public Library Journal*, 6 (1) 1991, pp. 1–5.
3. Hiles, A. N. Service level agreements: panacea or pain. *The TQM Magazine*, 6 (2) 1994, pp. 14–16
4. Corrall, S. M. The access model: managing the transformation at Aston University. *Interlending & Document Supply*, 21 (4) 1993, pp. 13–23
5. Sack, J. R. Open systems for open minds: building the library without walls. *College & Research Libraries*, 47 (6), 1986, p. 535
6. Lancaster, F. W. and Sandore, B. *Technology and management in library and information services*. London: Library Association Publishing, 1997 (p. 239)
7. *Space requirements for academic libraries and learning resource centres* prepared by Andrew McDonald on behalf of the SCONUL

Advisory Committee on Buildings. London: Standing Conference of National and University Libraries, 1996 (p. 2)

8. The danger of the digital library. [Interview with Walt Crawford.] *The Electronic Library*, 16 (1) 1998, pp. 28–30

9. Trapp, R. Pushing back the frontiers of space. *The Independent*, 23 April 1998

10. North, R. D. Flights of future fancy. *The Daily Telegraph*, 22 October 1998

11. McDonald, A. Space planning and management. In: Baker, D., ed. *Resource management in academic libraries*. London: Library Association Publishing, 1997, pp. 189–206

12. Tregarthen Jenkin, I. *Disaster planning and preparedness: an outline disaster control plan*. London: British Library, 1987 (British Library Information Guide 5)

13. Saunders, M. How a library picked up the pieces after IRA blast. *Library Association Record*, 95 (2) 1993, pp. 100–101

14. Fire rekindles debate. *Library Association Record*, 96 (9) 1994, p. 69

15. Wise, C. The flood and afterwards: a new beginning for the Fawcett Library. *Library Conservation News*, 48, 1995, pp. 1–2

16. Available at: http://www.M25lib.ac.uk/M25dcp

17. George, S. C. Library disasters: are you prepared? *College & Research Libraries News*, 56 (2) 1995, pp. 80–84

18. Earl, M. J. Integrating IS and the organization: a framework of organizational fit. In: Earl, M. J., ed., *Information management: the organizational dimension*. Oxford: Oxford University Press, 1996, pp. 485–502

19. Weill, P. and Broadbent, M. *Leveraging the new infrastructure: how market leaders capitalize on information technology*. Boston, Ma: Harvard Business School Press, 1998 (pp. 143–4)

20. Lavagnino, M. B. Networking and the role of the academic systems librarian: an evolutionary perspective. *College & Research Libraries*, 58 (3) 1997, pp. 217–231

21. van der Wait, Pieter W. and van Brakel. Pieter A. The Webmaster: a new player in the information centre's online team. *The Electronic Library*, 15 (6) 1997, pp. 447–454

22. Taking the initiative for digital libraries. [Interview with Stephen M Griffin.] *The Electronic Library*, 16 (1) 1998, pp. 24–27

23. Mintzberg, H. *Structure in fives: designing effective organisations*. Englewood Cliffs, NJ: Prentice Hall International, 1983 (p. 86)

24. Kakabadse, A., Ludlow, R. and Vinnicombe, S. *Working in organisations*. London: Penguin, 1988 (p. 333)

25. Schein, E. H. *The corporate culture survival guide: sense and nonsense about culture change*. San Fancisco, Ca: Jossey Bass, 1999

26. Goffee, R. and Jones, G. *The character of a corporation: how your company's culture can make or break your business.* New York: HarperCollins, 1998
27. Antony, P. *Managing culture.* Buckingham: Open University Press, 1994
28. Handy, C. *Understanding organizations.* 3rd ed. London: Penguin, 1985
29. Harrison, R. Organization culture and quality of service. In: Harrison, R. *The collected papers of Roger Harrison.* Maidenhead: McGraw-Hill, 1995, pp. 183–210
30. Nichol, J. Zen and the art of user friendly service: 1 – organisational culture. *State Librarian,* **35** (3) 1987, pp. 35–37, 39
31. Schein, E. H. *Organizational culture and leadership: a dynamic view.* San Francisco, Ca; Oxford: Jossey Bass, 1985 (pp. 314–15)
32. Investors in People UK. Web site: http://www.iipuk.co.uk
33. Tucker, M. Investor in people: the Gloucestershire experience. *Public Library Journal,* **10** (5) 1995, pp. 127–128
34. John Fielden Consultancy. *Supporting expansion: a report on human resource management in academic libraries for the Joint Funding Councils' Libraries Review Group.* Bristol: The Councils, 1993
35. Sparks, M. Skills for a digital future: report on 'Training Together 6', Sheffield, 3rd March 1998. *SCONUL Newsletter,* **(13)** 1998, pp. 34–35
36. Clutterbuck, D. *Learning alliances: tapping into talent.* London: Institute of Personnel and Development, 1998. (Developing Practice)
37. Jajko, P. Planning the virtual library. *Medical Reference Services Quarterly,* **12** (4) 1993, pp. 51–67
38. Creth, S. D. Staff development: where do we go from here? *Library Administration & Management,* **4** (3) 1990, pp. 131–132
39. Chapman, C. and Ward, S. *Project risk management: processes, techniques and insights.* Chichester: John Wiley, 1997
40. CCTA. *Management of project risk.* London: HMSO, 1995

Further reading

Customer focus

Pluse, J. Customer focus: the salvation of service organizations. *Public Library Journal,* 6 (1) 1991, pp. 1–5.
   Criticises superficiality of 'customer care' initiatives and explains in detail issues that must be addressed to achieve genuinely customer-oriented service. Includes pertinent comment on mission statements

and service strategy, managerial example and support for front-line staff, 'motivational' and 'formative' feedback, organisational structures, and a five-step action plan.

Pfeiffer, S. and Algermissen, V. A unique heavy users forum: a program to involve a library's most frequent users. *Medical Reference Services Quarterly*, **11** (3) 1992, pp. 17–27.
Describes initiative to set up a new style of 'personal communication forum' for customers of the University of Alabama Health Sciences Library. Reports how the Heavy Users Group (HUG) programme generated 35 specific suggestions for service improvements, two-thirds of which have been implemented with the rest at an advanced planning stage.

Bessler, J. M. *Putting service into library staff training: a patron-centered guide.* Chicago; London: American Library Association, 1994 (Library Administration and Management Association Occasional Papers Series)
Concise guide (c.70pp.) which draws on customer service research in various sectors. Combines a strategic approach with practical advice on topics such as building service into recruitment, training resistant staff, avoiding 'super-service backlash', defining levels of empowerment, dealing with difficult staff and users, and measuring service.

Arthur, G. Customer-service training in academic libraries. *Journal of Academic Librarianship*, **20** (4) 1994, pp. 219–222
Compares and contrasts different approaches and methods adopted by US academic libraries, ranging from frontline skills training to top-down management workshops. Discusses key issues and success factors, including follow-up and evaluation methods.

Freemantle, D. *What customers like about you: adding emotional value for service excellence and competitive advantage.* London: Nicholas Brealey, 1998
Argues that successful customer service is about adding emotional value to relationships and interactions, which requires connectivity, integrity and creativity. Offers practical guidance based on extensive research, covering both operational and strategic issues; includes chapters on likeable behaviours, likeable organisations, likeable leaders, and recruiting likeable staff.

Service level agreements

Ford, G. Service level agreements. *The New Review of Academic Librarianship*, **2**, 1996, pp. 49–58

Explains various reasons for introducing Service Level Agreements, and discusses their format and content, including related background material. Provides examples of specific services covered and gives sample targets for a few key activities. Outlines the benefits and risks, and offers some solutions to the problem of multiple constituencies.

Payne, P. User empowerment: striking back for the customers of academic libraries. In: Pinder, C. and Melling, M., eds. *Providing customer-oriented services in academic libraries.* London: Library Association Publishing, 1996, pp. 59–86
Devotes a substantial section to SLAs, covering questions such as: whether you need one; who should be in control of the process; what mechanisms to use for negotiation; how to involve staff; how service standards should be set and monitored; how SLAs should be disseminated; what happens if standards are not met; and how frequently to renegotiate.

Pantry, S. and Griffiths, P. *The complete guide to preparing and implementing service level agreements.* London: Library Association Publishing, 1997
A compact introduction (c.130p.) to service level agreements for library and information services written by experienced senior managers from the government/health information service sector. Provides definitions, outlines contents, and suggests wording for service descriptions, their availability and turnaround times; also covers monitoring, charges, communication, and SLAs between LIS and their internal and external suppliers.

Space matters

Michalak, S. Planning academic library facilities: the library will have walls. *Journal of Library Administration,* 20 (2) 1994, pp. 93–113
Identifies environmental and service trends affecting building layout and space utilisation; anticipates shorter change cycles in future, suggests different approaches to reallocating space, and argues for preparation of a long-range facilities master plan and consideration of wider campus changes to inform strategic short-term moves in library facilities planning.

Barnatt, C. Office space, cyberspace and virtual organization. *Journal of General Management,* 20 (4) 1995, pp. 78–91
Traces development of organizational forms from the classical hierarchies of mass production to dynamic networks for flexible special-

*isation; outlines new work practices associated with virtual organis-
ations (such as hotelling and touch-down facilities) suggesting that
such concepts will be commonplace by 2005.*

Disaster management

Kahn, M. Fires, earthquakes and floods: how to prepare your library
and staff. *Online*, May 1994, pp. 18–24
*Reports how various information centres and special libraries set up
emergency services in response to disasters and identifies key planning issues as authority; money and insurance; information
resources, including computers; alternative locations and forms of
communication; and testing. Emphasises importance of backing-up
data files and essential documentation.*

Ashman, J. *Disaster planning for library and information services.*
London: Aslib, 1995 (An Aslib Know How Guide)
*Concise guide, written by a conservation specialist, arranged in four
main sections covering disaster prevention; disaster preparedness;
salvaging water-damaged materials; and conservation. Includes diagrams showing options for salvaging books and non-book media,
an example of a damage list form and an annotated list of suggested
further reading.*

Matthews, G. and Eden, P. *Disaster management in British libraries:
project report with guidelines for library managers.* London: British
Library, 1996 (Library and Information Research Report 109)
*Based on a comprehensive study of disaster management experience
and practice in British libraries, archives and museum services,
which drew on published literature, on-site interviews and management documents. Reports findings and provides detailed guidelines,
supported by a list of emergency supplies and a bibliography
arranged by topic.*

Technology infrastructure

Gallimore, A. *Developing an IT strategy for your library.* London: Library Association Publishing, 1997
*Clear and comprehensive guide (c.190pp.) which explains the needs
and benefits of an IT strategy and elaborates the components of the
process from objectives to implementation. Covers internal audit,
external context, physical infrastructure, policy issues, management
aspects, strategy evaluation, implementation planning, monitoring
progress and updating.*

Gallimore, A. A public library IT strategy for the millennium. *Journal of Librarianship and Information Science*, **28** (3) 1996, pp. 149–157
Case study of a large public library, which sets out the main elements of an IT strategy and relates it to key corporate policies, other external influences and user expectations. Includes checklist of elements for IT audit and issues for future strategy development, such as network development, public access, staff skills, management efficiency and partnerships.

Bevan, N. and Dolphin, P. Preparing an IT strategy. *SCONUL Newsletter*, (**12**) 1997, pp. 16–21
Case study of a small academic library, which discusses the participative developmental process used to develop an IT strategy for incorporation into the library's strategic plan, involving nine groups over six months. Outlines the aspects of IT covered, the methods of research used, and the set of issues addressed in presentations and reports of each group.

Raitt, D. Factors and issues in creating an Internet strategy. *The Electronic Library*, **16** (3) 1998, pp. 155–159
Outlines Internet general capabilities and typical applications, identifies basic categories of information/services available via the Web, and raises issues organisations need to address to achieve a coherent strategy, including communications objectives, corporate identity, redundancy/duplication, publishing authority, updating/maintenance, and access control.

Management structures

Sadler, P. *Designing organizations: the foundation for excellence.* 2nd ed. London: Kogan Page, 1994
Introductory guide (c.200pp.) which considers organisational design in relation to five objectives: control, connections, creativity, commitment and co-ordination. The final chapter anticipates the impact of environmental forces on future structures, systems and procedures, and cultures/values.

Cho, N. How Samsung organized for innovation. *Long Range Planning*, **29** (6) 1996, pp. 783–796
Uses the case study of a Korean company to discuss three typical interrelated responses to environmental forces: cross-functional teams, flatter structures and network organisations. Introduces con-

cept of the 'clustered web' and points out key issues arising, such as rewards and career prospects for former middle/senior managers.

Information service structures

Lewis, D. W. An organizational paradigm for effective academic libraries. *College & Research Libraries,* **47** (4) 1986, pp. 337–353
Relates organisation theories of Mintzberg and other management gurus to the library environment and advocates a modified "professional bureaucracy" (flat structure, delegated decisions and multi-tasked groups) with flexible resource allocation, effective management information, reduced production functions and shared philosophy.

Line, M. B. Library management styles and structures: a need to rethink. *Journal of Librarianship and Information Science,* **23** (2) 1991, pp. 97–104
Discusses management problems in libraries with particular reference to hierarchical structures, their focus on line management and unsuitability for handling change and complexity. Predicts future developments and requirements, including flatter structures, greater delegation, more awareness of management trends and workforce planning.

Gerryts, E. D. Organisational transformation. *IATUL Proceedings,* **14,** 1995, pp. 57–72
Charts the rebirth of the University of Pretoria library service as an 'integrator of systems', with a new matrix structure replacing subject librarians with a marketing group, roles instead of jobs, multi-skilling and 'broad banding', salaries based on relevant expertise, and a strategic framework covering both tangibles and intangibles.

Stanley, N. M. and Branche-Brown, L. Reorganizing acquisitions at the Pennsylvania State University Libraries: from work units to teams. *Library Acquisitions: Practice & Theory,* **19** (4) 1995, pp. 417–425
Describes radical restructuring and cultural change, removing three management layers with use of quality techniques and self-directed teams. Key features include a phased approach, ownership of the whole process and back-up support through cross-training.

Euster, J. R., Paquette, J., Kaufman, J. and Soete, G. Reorganizing for a changing world. *Library Administration and Management,* **11** (2) 1997, pp. 103–114
Four related articles about an organisation review and design project

*at the University of California, Irvine, over more than three years,
covering origins and outcomes; the design process, using the new
ARL model with library staff; implementation, including reassign-
ment of staff; and the contribution of a resident consultant to team
development.*

Organisation culture

Harrison, R. Understanding your organization's character. *Harvard
Business Review*, 50 (3) 1972, pp. 119–128
*Introduces his theory of organisational culture as four distinct and
competing 'ideologies' (representing power, role, task and person
orientations) and discusses their strengths and weaknesses in relation to external and internal pressures. Includes table showing how
well each type serves six key organisational and individual interests.*

Handy, C. *Understanding organizations.* 3rd ed. London: Penguin, 1985
*Substantial but accessible text (c.490p.) arranged to suit practising
manager. Introduces core concepts under seven headings, and then
discusses their application to key organisational issues. Includes
chapters on organisation cultures (reproducing Harrison's diagnostic questionnaire) and structures, job design and management
of diversity. Relegates discussion of theories and documentary
sources to separate section.*

Pheysey, D. C. *Organizational cultures: types and transformations.*
London: Routledge, 1993.
*Discusses the Harrison/Handy four-fold cultural model with refer-
ence to various aspects of organisational behaviour, such as organisational structure, job design, motivation, decision-making and leadership styles. Contains 23 short case studies/exercises (mainly public
sector) and an extensive bibliography, including 'culture sort'
checklist based on Business Organization Climate Index.*

Brown, A. D. *Organisational culture.* London: Pitman, 1995.
*Textbook (270pp.) providing comprehensive survey of theories and
frameworks, with numerous case studies and bibliographic references. Covers definitions, components, sources and functions of culture; typologies and models for cultural change; and relationship of
culture, strategy and performance. (Reproduces Harrison's diagnostic questionnaire.)*

Information service culture

Malinconico, S. M. Managing organizational culture. *Library Journal*,
    109 (7) 1984, pp. 791–793
    *Summarises key messages about culture with reference to general
    management articles and books, emphasising mutual trust, manager-
    ial consistency and staff training as fundamental requirements for
    cultural change. Uses examples of catalogue computerisation to
    demonstrate benefits of involving staff in communicating change.*

Shaughnessy, T. W. Organizational culture in libraries: some manage-
    ment perspectives. *Journal of Library Administration*, **9** (3) 1988,
    pp. 5–10
    *Draws particularly on the writings of Edgar Schein, contrasting ana-
    lytical and 'managerial' approaches to cultural change, and arguing
    that understanding your library culture (and sub-cultures) will help
    to anticipate problems and improve performance.*

Davies, A., Kirkpatrick, I. and Oliver, N. The organisational culture of
    an academic library: implications for library strategy. *British Journal
    of Academic Librarianship*, **7** (2) 1992, pp. 69–89
    *Describes mapping the culture of a multi-site university library by
    identifying and investigating staff views of management philosophy,
    and formal and informal rules of behaviour. Justifies time required
    by pointing to insights gained into mismatches between management
    and staff preferences and interpretations of service strategies.*

Professional development

Mumford, A. *How managers can develop managers.* Aldershot: Gower,
    1993
    *A practical guide (c.220pp.) geared to the unplanned reality of
    managerial work, which explains how individual and group devel-
    opment can be built into the job with benefits to all concerned.
    Covers informal and formal processes, and offers help on clarifying
    roles, identifying needs, producing plans, using opportunities and
    developing yourself.*

Cannell, M. Practice makes perfect. *People Management*, **3** (5) 1997,
    pp. 26–33
    *Discusses current approaches to on-the-job training(OJT) including
    formal involvement of peer colleagues as volunteer trainers. Uses
    examples of good practice to show benefits of a more structured
    approach, and includes checklist of OJT training tips.*

Information service staff

DeLon, B. A. Keeping plateaued performers motivated. *Library Administration & Management*, 7 (1) 1993, pp. 13–16
Suggests various strategies for stagnating staff, such as giving accurate feedback to minimise unrealistic expectations, and using special projects, cross-functional task forces, job rotations and lateral transfers to bring sense of accomplishment and broaden skill bases.

Trotta, M. *Successful staff development: a how-to-do-it manual.* New York; London: Neal Schuman Publishers, 1995.
Practical primer (110p.) which concentrates on in-house staff training linked to service development, providing guidance and checklists with sample training programmes and handouts for orientation, communication, teamwork, time management and customer service training. Also covers mentoring, performance evaluation, reward and recognition.

Grealy, D., Jones, L., Messas, K., Zipp, K. and Catalucci, L. Staff development and training in college and university libraries: the Penrose perspective. *Library Administration & Management*, 10 (4) 1996, pp. 204–209
Describes development of wide-ranging staff development programme at Denver University arising from campus network developments, covering professional and personal development as well as software training. Discusses strategic planning, needs assessment, formal evaluation, programme outcomes, future plans and success factors.

Whetherly, J. *Management of training and staff development.* London: Library Association Publishing, 1997 (Library Training Guides)
Provides an overview of factors relevant to planning and organising training and development programmes, including practical guidance on formulating policy, identifying needs, selecting methods, assessing outcomes and clarifying responsibilities. Appendix reproduces examples of library policies and programmes.

Stenson, A., Raddon, R. and Abell, A. *Skills and competencies in the corporate sector.* London: British Library Research and Innovation Centre, 1999 (British Library Research and Innovation Report 162)
Based on desk research and company interviews in the UK banking, pharmaceutical and information provision sectors, provides competency grids, radar models and additional lists specifying key attrib-

utes required by information professionals for first- and second-level jobs.

Risk management

Heemstra, F. J. and Kusters, R. J. Dealing with risk: a practical approach. *Journal of Information Technology*, 11 (4) 1996, pp. 333–346

Discusses basic definitions and concepts of risk management, and then describes a formal method for managing risk in IT projects, using a structured checklist of 36 risk factors under nine headings: sponsor; users; user management; the system; specifications; project planning; developers; means; and systems management. (The list is reproduced as an appendix). [Contribution to a special issue containing nine articles on risk management in IT projects.]

Chapter 8

Managing flexibility

Strategic management is about deciding and refining organisational objectives and working persistently and consistently to translate them into actions and results. Strategy provides boundaries, direction and guidance for operational management, but success in the contemporary environment also requires flexibility. Strategic planning can be further defined as the continuous development of objectives and strategies through an interactive and self-renewing process that ensures the flexibility and capability to change in time. People are often reluctant to spend time thinking and planning, but decisions and actions at every level benefit from upfront mental investment, a culture that encourages reflection and questions, and a structure that enables cross-fertilisation of ideas. Having a plan makes it easier to focus activity, monitor developments and modify or change the strategy as necessary. This chapter offers further perspectives on the planning process including comments on operational aspects and then concludes by suggesting a few 'content' and 'process' issues for future attention.

Process perspectives

In Chapter 1, planning processes were broadly categorised into formal planning models, which separated the 'thinking' and 'doing' parts of strategy, and the incremental/learning view, which rejected that model. Before considering the process of strategy formation in more detail, it is pertinent here to distinguish between the 'official line' typically expressed in a plan or formal statement of strategic objectives and often referred to as *intended strategy* and the direction actually taken in practice – the *realised strategy* – as the two frequently differ, and sometimes by a great deal. This **strategy gap** between intent and reality can happen when the intended strategy is simply unrealistic, but is more likely to arise from competing organisational influences. At the top level, there may be conflicting views about the desired direction held by, for example, top management on the one hand and the heads of business units on the other; alternatively, at a more basic level, operational strategies may not have been properly developed to deliver the corporate-level and business-level strategies. There are also often other forces that affect the development and delivery of strategy.

Johnson and Scholes present a spectrum of views of how organisational strategy comes about, ranging from the **formal/rational** explanation, where managers' decisions direct the future of the business, to the
natural/ecological interpretation, where organisational success and survival depends on the extent to which its way of doing things coincides
with the operating environment, and the influence of managers is not so
significant. Between these two extremes of proactive choice-and-control
and inactive conditions-and-coincidence are three other (reactive) views:
logical incrementalism suggests that strategies develop less formally than
through a formal planning system, but are determined or crafted by
managers' actions, based on their experience and learning; **chaos theory**
suggests that strategies evolve through managers' sensitive and largely
intuitive responses to the complexity of their environment, and so their
capacity for intuition becomes a determinant factor; and **cultural/institu-
tional** theorists suggest that strategies are significantly constrained by
managers' institutionalised or culturally determined responses, which
limit their ability to depart from accepted practices.[1] This influence of
established routines, systems, etc. can be referred to as *automatic strategy*. In his latest book, Mintzberg identifies ten different perspectives on
the strategy-formation process, which he subdivides into three *prescriptive* schools (design, planning and positioning) concerned with how strategies *should* be formulated; six *descriptive* schools (entrepreneurial, cognitive, learning, power, cultural and environmental) concerned with how
they *do* form in practice; and an *integrative* school (configuration) which
combines the others and is concerned with *change*.[2]

Published case studies provide echoes of the above views on what
drives business direction. The chairman of Unilever emphasises the role
of experience and intuition in strategic decisions (as well as thorough
analysis) and also points to "concern that strategic direction had
developed informally through a process dependent on coincidence".[3] At
GEC, where there is no formal planning procedure, Lord Weinstock
mentions flair – "The best plan is the best thought of the best
people. . ."[4] The planning manager at ICI, which has a 'tightly knit'
formal process, nevertheless stresses that analytical techniques should
not substitute for experience and judgement.[5] At Shell, the head of planning, cites managers' ability to absorb what is going on in the business
environment and act on that information as the critical factor – "planning as learning".[6] Until the mid 1980s, Barclays's plans were based on
economic factors – inflation rates, interest rates, demand for advances –
but now its strategy is driven more by technological and social trends.[7]
These large multinational corporations also point to a mix of 'top-down'
and 'bottom-up' elements in the relative influence of the centre and
operational units in determining both corporate/group and business unit
strategies.

Most organisations exhibit a mixture of such influences, which in effect together drive the business, but the strength of each influence depends on organisational type, size, etc. While public sector and voluntary organisations have more in common with the private industrial and commercial sector than many people realise, they also have some distinctive features that affect their strategy-making. The notion of an *imposed strategy* is especially relevant here, exemplified by government policy – though government actions can also have a significant impact on the private sector (for example, through legislation and taxation). Stakeholder values and expectations are particularly significant in the not-for-profit sector; such organisations are increasingly operating with multiple sources of funding, which means having to serve and satisfy multiple constituencies. Overall, public-sector bodies generally have less flexibility than their private-sector counterparts as a result of in-built systems and procedures – in addition to 'cultural' tendencies in that direction – and thus struggle to adapt to a changing environment.

Planning timeframes

Both *planning horizons* (the timespan covered by the plan) and *planning timetables* (the time taken for the process) have shortened significantly in recent years.

In past decades, long-range plans covered five, ten or even twenty years, but organisations today typically opt for three, five or seven years, with five years being the most common. Irrespective of the period covered, strategic plans are usually reviewed annually (to inform annual plans and budgets) and often 'rolled forward' by dropping the first year and adding another at the end. This practice might work for a year or two, but managers may fall into the trap of simply edging forward incrementally from the existing plan, instead of projecting further into the future and then working back to check whether action steps previously specified are still valid. It is therefore advisable periodically to conduct a more fundamental review and produce a completely new plan every three or four years, limiting the roll-forward exercise to no more than two or three iterations.

In a provocative critique of current strategic planning practices, Dan Simpson actually advises against *annual* reviews of strategy on the basis that it takes a lot of work if properly done and fundamental strategies should be resilient for more than twelve months. He recommends a fundamental review every three years, with a more frequent review only if circumstances require it, for example

- the *performance* of a unit is significantly different to expectation, higher or lower by an order of magnitude;

- the *assumptions* underpinning the strategy have changed, requiring re-examination of the foundation to adjust it;
- the *management* of a unit has undergone major changes, so the strategy is no longer owned by those in charge.[8]

Other triggers for strategic reviews include financial or operational problems, actions by competitors or suppliers, or significant changes in the customer base or wider marketplace. Planning cycles are also affected by production lead-times and product life-cycles, which are often sector-specific.

The amount of effort and length of time spent on planning exercises has also been reduced in most organisations. In the 1980s, when many libraries and information units embarked on strategic planning for the first time, it was quite common for the process to be conducted over a period of twelve months or longer, with some services taking up to eighteen months to complete such exercises. Today the period of any formally defined process is more likely to be no more than three to six months, as the pace of change is such that an extended gestation period makes no sense. Shorter, tighter timescales for formulating plans may also be imposed in particular circumstances, notably in the context of business restructuring, or mergers and acquisitions. Newly appointed information service heads are often expected to articulate their vision and plans for the future in some form within a few months of taking up their posts. This compression of the formal strategic planning process into only a few months or weeks makes the requirement for managers to engage continuously in less formal strategic thinking about the issues and questions raised in earlier chapters even more important than before.

Operational models

In Chapter 1, strategic management was conceptualised as 'a series of fundamental questions' and 'a set of interlocking components'. The elements of the strategy process were outlined under the headings of *environmental appraisal, strategic profiling, strategy development* and *programme management,* noting various alternative groupings and terms used by different writers. Models for operationalising the strategic planning process are similarly varied and need to be considered in relation to the size and type of organisation and the scope and purpose of the plan. Traditional strategic planning exercises were dominated by top management, driven by a central team of planners, and documented in considerable detail. Formal systems of this type originated when market conditions were quite different to the contemporary operating environment, so it is hardly surprising that they do not suit the turbulence and uncertainty which characterises the world today. In the last decade or so there has been a definite trend away from the 'annual planning ritual' to a continuous process of 'real-time strategy' owned and led by line managers rather than central planners, with significantly more involvement of staff and other stakeholders. This shift is less noticeable in the information services sector as few services had dedicated *planning teams* of the kind found in large companies and staff designated as *planning officers* typically operated in co-ordinating and facilitating roles, providing information and support rather than determining or dictating strategy and plans.

As indicated above, large-scale lengthy planning exercises are unlikely to be a practical proposition in the contemporary environment, so strategic management and planning have been effectively redefined to scale down the *planning* element and place more of the process firmly in the domain of ongoing *management* responsibilities. The process is generally described as comprising the same tasks or steps as before, but the assumption is that as environmental scanning and strategic debates are ongoing activities, the formal or organised planning process is more concerned with capturing and documenting insights and information than undertaking a comprehensive analysis or formulating elaborate strategic objectives. Nevertheless, it is worthwhile periodically to consider conducting a more fundamental review for the reasons outlined in the previous section. The sequencing of tasks is essentially a matter of personal (or organisational) choice, except for the important preliminary step of defining the overall task or *planning to plan*. John Bryson and Farnum Alston offer a useful checklist of questions to clarify the scope of the project and the people involved, which forms the basis of the **planning profile** given in Appendix 6.[9]

The **key tasks** involved in a practical planning exercise can be summarised thus:

- define the project
- audit the situation
- set strategic objectives
- identify strategies
- evaluate alternatives
- formulate the plan
- construct budgets
- initiate action programme
- monitor performance
- modify projects

Each of these tasks can be interpreted at various levels, as shown by the detailed treatment of the above topics in Chapters 2 to 6. For example, 'set strategic objectives' could include a thorough review of organisational values, purpose and functions, and the development of a vision statement in several versions, or it might be confined to determining new directions and priorities in the form of strategic thrusts and goals for the next three years. Similarly, 'identify strategies' could involve elaboration of many alternatives to meet half a dozen or more goals, or it might be limited to selection of a few generic strategies to focus resources more effectively. The last three tasks move beyond planning to implementation and also point up the fact that this list should not be seen as a linear sequence as often information obtained and insights gained at the later stages mean that earlier ideas need rethinking and previous steps have to be repeated. It is also worth noting that many different sequences have been suggested in published guides to strategic planning, for example some commentators advise starting with the vision (before environmental appraisal) whereas Simpson advocates working on mission, vision and values at the very end of strategy development work.[8]

There are also many different ways to approach the tasks in question. The models, techniques, etc. referred to in earlier chapters are offered as aids to thinking and decision-making, but individuals must choose and use those that seem most useful in their particular situations.

Strategic feedback

Monitoring and control procedures are often not given proper attention in strategic change programmes. This whole area becomes more import ant as strategy creation becomes an ongoing process in the context of a rapidly changing environment. It is significant that Peter Drucker stressed the importance of **systematic feedback** in his early tripartite definition of strategic planning thus,

> "[Strategic planning] is the continuous process of making present risk-taking *decisions* systematically and with the greatest knowledge of their futurity; organizing systematically the *efforts* needed to carry out these decisions; and measuring the results of these decisions against the expectations through organized, *systematic feedback*."[10]

Strategic control is not just about checking expenditure against financial projections and monitoring progress on implementing plans, it means evaluating success in achieving objectives and tracking changes in the operating environment, in order to see whether there is a need to revise strategies, modify goals or reconsider the vision. As indicated in the Balanced Scorecard model (*see* Chapter 6) strategic control systems need to provide information on *financial performance, customer satisfaction, process management* and *organisational development,* as well as on the wider environment.

It is important to check progress *regularly* and to review/amend plans in the light of early results and changing circumstances. The monitoring process is crucial at all levels; if neglected, plans cease to function as working tools. As suggested earlier, responsibility for monthly monitoring of *operational plans* is most sensibly devolved to service managers, with progress reports to senior management at appropriate intervals, highlighting any problems identified and/or budget revisions proposed. Monitoring of *environmental trends* also needs to be built into the system, preferably by designating key individuals to track developments in particular areas and alert colleagues to any changes or unpredicted events affecting planning assumptions. Scheduling quarterly, half-yearly or annual reviews of environmental trends helps to ensure that such responsibilities are taken seriously.

Tips

- Concentrate on your strategic priorities – don't monitor everything.
- Relate information to management need – don't give everyone the same type of report.
- Make use of qualitative indicators – don't rely solely on quantitative data.
- Take action as the situation requires it – don't forget to follow things through.

Planning pitfalls

Formal research and practical experience have shown how planning can go badly wrong if mismanaged or misunderstood by those involved. George Steiner lists 50 pitfalls confirmed by his survey of more than 200 American organisations. Steiner's respondents were asked to rank these mistakes in order of importance, for which he then derived a list of the "most critical pitfalls" as follows:

1. Top management's assumption that it can delegate the planning function to a planner.
2. Top management becomes so engrossed in current problems that it spends insufficient time on long-range planning, and the process becomes discredited among other managers and staff.
3. Failure to develop organisational goals suitable as a basis for formulating long-range plans.
4. Failure to assume the necessary involvement in the planning process of major line personnel.
5. Failure to use plans as standards for measuring managerial performance.
6. Failure to create a climate in the company which is congenial and not resistant to planning.

7. Assuming that corporate comprehensive planning is something separate from the entire management process.
8. Injecting so much formality into the system that it lacks flexibility, looseness and simplicity, and restrains creativity.
9. Failure of top management to review with departmental and divisional heads the long-range plans which they have developed.
10. Top management's consistently rejecting the formal planning mechanism by making intuitive decisions which conflict with formal plans.[11]

In his textbook on strategic management, the British writer David Hussey also devotes a whole chapter to the reasons why planning sometimes fail. He also stresses the importance of management commitment and involvement, the need to co-ordinate and connect planning with day to day activities, and the dangers of oversophisticated systems. In addition, Hussey warns against three other pitfalls, namely

- allowing some managers to opt out
- planning through a committee
- confusion of strategic and operational planning.[12]

The above lists highlight common problems identified in a wide variety of organisations, many of which are relevant to **information services**. Organisational politics and the corporate culture can also help or hinder the process. In addition, there are other problems that seem particularly prevalent in the library and information services sector, some of which are related to the position of the library or information unit in the organisational structure and the role of the service head in the resource allocation process. It is vital to assess the *resource implications* of strategic plans at an early stage and to take steps to secure the capital and recurrent funding required; all too often one sees service plans with no proper financial projections, and hence no basis for making a case for additional budget provision. Secondly, bearing in mind the need for information services to obtain broad support for their plans, it makes sense not only to identify the key issues and priorities that will give the plan the desired focus, but also to deal with any other *stakeholder concerns* whose neglect might undermine the chances of success.

Finally, it is essential to take a *long-term holistic view* of your service when reviewing and determining objectives, even if the horizon set for the particular planning exercise is relatively short, and there must be a *top-down strategic input* to plans to ensure that they are more than a consolidation of individual submissions. It is surprisingly common to find service plans with lengthy 'shopping lists' under standard headings with no obvious strategic thrusts signalling the major directions for change and acting as unifying themes for the goals and tasks itemised.

Strategic issues

The previous chapters have pointed up numerous questions and suggestions about the purposes and functions of information services both now
and in the future. In this concluding chapter three particular areas are
identified for the attention of information service managers in the context of planning for the longer term with some comments (and further
readings) offered to stimulate thought.

Adding value

The need to add or create *value* and deliver it to stakeholders has been
a recurring theme of this book. For example, adding value was mentioned as a fundamental requirement of strategy in Chapter 1, and also
in Chapter 2 in relation to auditing and demonstrating value-for-money,
in Chapter 3 in the context of information service missions and core
competencies, and again in Chapter 6 in relation to performance measurement.

The concept of **added value** (or 'value added' – the terms are used
interchangeably) acquired particular significance in the information services sector in the 1980s as information gained more importance as a
tradeable commodity with the opportunities for service development and
improvement offered by advances in information technology. People
often associate 'value-added services' with fee-based information provision, but the concept is more generally applicable to information and
library services, although it is especially useful when considering charging and pricing policies. (In the discipline of economics, 'value added'
has a specific meaning in the context of *wealth creation,* but in other
contexts it is used variously to denote the characteristics or attributes
added during a process; the *'exchange value'* or *'apparent value'*
attached to the process or its end-product by the recipient; or the *benefit*
which ultimately accrues to the recipient as a result.)

The most thorough treatment of the subject is Robert Taylor's classic
study of 1986, *Value-added processes in information systems,* which
identifies four general processes (from initial data gathering, through
various transforming operations, to final use) and provides some
examples of **value-adding activities** associated with each part of the spectrum. The figure here is based on Taylor's model but includes some more
specific examples of process outputs.

Taylor argues that document-based systems, such as abstracting and
indexing services and libraries, are **value-adding entities** operating prin-
cipally at the *organising* level, whereas data analysis centres and research
services operate at the *analysing* and *judgemental* levels. He goes on to

Figure 8.1 Value-adding activities and processes (adapted from Taylor)

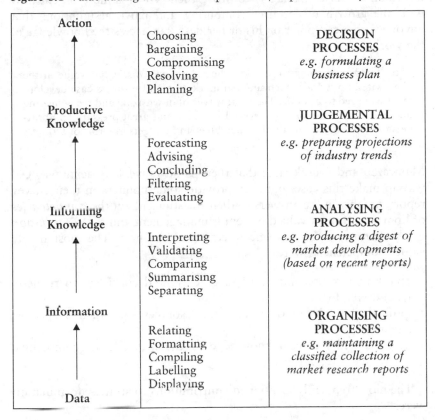

Action	Choosing Bargaining Compromising Resolving Planning	**DECISION PROCESSES** *e.g. formulating a business plan*
Productive Knowledge	Forecasting Advising Concluding Filtering Evaluating	**JUDGEMENTAL PROCESSES** *e.g. preparing projections of industry trends*
Informing Knowledge	Interpreting Validating Comparing Summarising Separating	**ANALYSING PROCESSES** *e.g. producing a digest of market developments (based on recent reports)*
Information	Relating Formatting Compiling Labelling Displaying	**ORGANISING PROCESSES** *e.g. maintaining a classified collection of market research reports*
Data		

develop his basic analysis into a more complex model, which translates these simple value-adding activities into 23 **values**, which he relates to six user *criteria of choice* – ease of use, noise reduction, quality, adaptability, time-saving and cost-saving. He points out that the values added may be either external or internal to the information content – or both – and may be *tangible* signals (such as a descriptor) or an *intangible* value (such as validity of data). Although dated in some respects, Taylor's work offers a conceptual framework that enables information service managers to consider the different ways in which particular services currently add value or could do so in the future. As such, it can be used to inform decisions on charging and pricing, as well as underpinning discussions about service levels and organisational benefits. A modified version of his table with additional examples showing typical library and information services or processes is given in Appendix 7.[13]

In the context of a survey of senior management's perceived value of libraries, James Matarazzo and Laurence Prusak argue that the need for information service managers to prove their worth is more urgent now with the growth in end-user computing and naive assumptions that anyone with a computer on his or her desk can access the knowledge of the world.

> "For librarians hoping to preserve their function's *distinctive* value in the new, wired-up world, much internal marketing and business case development will need to be done. The great waves of downsizing and reengineering undergone by many of our surveyed firms has put great pressure on librarians continuously to justify their activities and budgets in terms of *business value*."

Matarazzo and Prusak state that there is no universally acknowledged way to make this case, but they provide some pointers in their survey report, notably in the answers to their questions about the *competencies* of library staff most valued by senior management and the *contribution* of the library to the strategic direction of the firm. The most highly valued **competencies** were:

- ability to interpret and respond quickly (and concisely) to requests from users (36%)
- in-depth knowledge of information sources and their respective strengths (28%)
- business and technical knowledge of the firm and its competitive environment (25%)

The most frequently mentioned **contributions** to strategy formulation were:

- providing the information base used by management to make strategic decisions (32%)
- keeping current on the latest research and technology that might bear on the strategy (31%)
- conducting confidential research on new products, new services and new ventures (11%)

Like many other commentators, Matarazzo and Prusak advocate a shift in perspective to reorientate information services to the current business preoccupation with organisational **knowledge**, moving beyond internal documents to internal *expertise*. They warn information professionals that reluctance to move in this direction is likely to have serious consequences, ". . . those librarians who continue to focus primarily on acquisition and distribution of information, in paper or online form, will likely be absorbed into other functions (perhaps MIS), or be increasingly relegated to the sidelines of an exciting business environment."[14]

Knowledge management

There has been much discussion in the professional press about current and future opportunities for information service managers to 'reinvent' themselves as knowledge centre managers or even 'chief knowledge officers'. Some information professionals have successfully repositioned themselves and their services and taken on prominent roles in corporate knowledge initiatives, notably in the big consultancy firms. Others have not been extensively involved in the early stages of knowledge initiatives, but have been brought in later when the ongoing management of content emerged as a significant technical challenge. The need to structure and codify information, to have a common language for retrieval, and to manage selective dissemination of information has highlighted information specialists' skills in indexing systems, thesaurus construction and user profiling for customer alerting.

However, their future is by no means assured as there is no shortage of other people ready to take on these tasks, regardless of whether they have the competence to do so. In addition librarians' perceived reluctance to move beyond the information *container* towards analysis and interpretation of its *contents* has resulted in organisations overlooking their potential contribution, even in areas where their competence should be obvious. Research undertaken by TFPL on behalf of the (UK) Library and Information Commission confirmed views expressed by other commentators, revealing that library and information service professionals are often seen as primarily concerned with the acquisition and distribution of external information and also, more damagingly, as not fully engaged with 'the business' (because of their strong professional identity). Various surveys have shown that despite cynics' dismissal of knowledge management as just the latest management fad, most organisations regard knowledge management as an imperative, close behind globalisation on their list of priorities. Irrespective of whether the label 'knowledge management' continues to be used, it is clear that as a *business concept* it is here to stay.[15]

In practice, most so-called knowledge initiatives have concentrated on 'explicit' (formalised, systematic) knowledge initially, simply aiming to make what is known in the organisation more visible and usable, by creating knowledge repositories and directories, and thus do not involve a lot more than the **information management** systems and processes already established in many companies. (This makes the lack of involvement of information specialists an even more significant factor.) Making 'tacit' (informal, private) knowledge more public and useful is altogether more challenging, because of the need not only to *capture* what is known, but also to have a *culture* that encourages learning and sharing.

The competencies needed to manage knowledge successfully are therefore a mix of technical, organisational and interpersonal skills, and are best represented as a set of roles, showing how abilities in handling and understanding information and IT are necessary but not sufficient to the task. The emerging consensus is that **knowledge professionals** need to be able to perform effectively in the following roles:

- *business professional* – well-informed about the core processes, products, services and performance of the organisation and the broader industries and economies in which it competes;
- *technology manager* – familiar with current and emerging information and communication technologies, and a confident user of generic and specialist tools (such as databases, intranets and groupware)
- *content organiser* – expert in selecting, sourcing, structuring and synthesising data, information and knowledge (requiring skills in metadata management, thesaurus construction, etc.)
- *communicator* – effective in capturing and articulating information and ideas, verbally and graphically;
- *change agent* – able to make a substantial contribution to organisational development as coach, facilitator, negotiator and project manager;
- *entrepreneur* – flexible and innovative in exploiting opportunities to use information and knowledge creatively for organisational benefit;
- *team player* – active in building multidisciplinary communities and promoting cross-functional working.

The above list is not significantly different from the competencies that most information professionals claim they already possess, but the point to note is that many senior managers in organisations apparently do not share this view. Information service managers therefore need to clarify their ambitions in this area and determine strategies for achieving their aims.

Service convergence

Convergence is the term generally used to describe the coming together, merging or blending of related technologies, services, roles and operations – typified in business and industry by bringing telecoms and IT specialists into a 'supertechnology department', where the most common pattern is for the telecoms manager to become part of the IT department, as the larger of the two operations (Shell and Zeneca being two notable examples here). Jonathan Moules identifies some of the potential benefits of such structural change – user convenience, operating economies and pooled expertise,

"To most people, convergence means e-mailing from a mobile phone, surfing the Internet on a television set or capitalising on low cost 'web phone' calls. To hard-nosed board members, convergence is more likely to mean an opportunity to cut operating costs by restructuring two expensive departments. But it also presents an ideal opportunity to liberate internal information by fusing the networking knowledge of telecoms managers with the computer skills of the IT department."[16]

In the further and higher education sectors, convergence more often refers to the confluence not just of *computing* and *networking* technologies, but of information *conduit* and *content* into an enlarged information organisation, a trend which dates back to the mid 1980s in the US and slightly later in the UK. In the corporate sector, the bringing together of IT and information specialists has more recently been associated with **knowledge management** initiatives. Both the structure and scope of converged information services varies considerably. In the higher education sector, the range of services with which libraries have been combined includes:

- academic computing (especially user support services)
- administrative data processing or management information systems
- audiovisual provision, including television production units
- careers information and advisory services
- computer-based learning and educational technology
- language laboratories and lecture theatres
- photography, printing and publishing
- telephones

The management arrangements are equally varied. At one end of the spectrum is the **merged service**, *integrated* at all levels, and *unified* under a single executive director, and at the other is **collaborative provision** based on *informal* co-operation of *separate* services. Between these two extremes there are several other common models, such as

- *formal co-operation,* based on a service level agreement;
- *peer co-ordination,* with one service head acting/rotating as lead partner for strategic planning and budget bids;
- *administrative unification,* with common reporting lines via a senior administrative (or academic) officer and/or an information strategy committee.

The Fielden report usefully distinguishes two main types of convergence, *organisational* and *operational,* the former referring to formal structures and the latter to service delivery, noting that the two types can exist either separately or together.[17] Commentators cite various reasons for pursuing convergence, which can be summarised as follows:

- *customer need / service imperative* – the progressive shift to electronic provision and desktop delivery means that information users expect 'one-stop-shopping' and do not want to have to work out whether problems encountered are related to content or conduit;

- *organisational need / economic imperative* – continuing financial constraints mean that institutions are eager to find ways of achieving scale economies and resource synergies by bringing related operations together and optimising scarce technical knowledge and skills;
- *technological need / strategic imperative* – library dependence on the IT infrastructure combined with a general shift to electronic communication and the need to manage information corporately and ensure interoperability among all organisational systems makes holistic planning essential.

In the UK, the Follett report urged higher education institutions to consider convergence, and this message was strengthened by its advocacy of **integrated information strategies** and the suggestion that organisational convergence was the way to develop such strategies.[18] There are also more *ad hoc* or expedient causes of restructuring, such as the opportunity to save the large salary of a departing service head, the perceived weakness of an existing service head, or simply the desire to follow the crowd.

Convergence at the **operational** level facilitates delivery of seamless services to users and is exemplified by shared or co-ordinated help/ enquiry and joint induction/training sessions. This sort of team-working at the point of delivery is possible without organisational convergence but depends on good working relationships between staff on the frontline and their supervisors/managers. However problems can arise when service developments or improvements are identified, as these types of collaborative projects often require financial as well as human resources, thus depending not only on the willingness of frontline staff to work together but the ability of their managers to commit funds from separate service budgets and agree their respective contributions to the project. Convergence at the **organisational** level sometimes does not extend below the top level so that jobs below senior management do not change significantly and the impact on service users is minimal; budgets are often consolidated for the sole purpose of submitting bids, but not informed by holistic planning for information service as a whole, so expected efficiency gains and strategic initiatives do not happen. Other factors that determine the extent and effectiveness of convergence include the *managerial style* of the institution and individuals, the *physical dispersion* of sites and services, and the *technical complexity* of the organisation and its operations. Organisational politics, individual personalities, service cultures and staff competencies are also important driving and restraining forces here.

The potential **benefits** of various forms of convergence have already been indicated from the customer and organisational perspectives. In addition to the service changes outlined above, a potential benefit of formal convergence is the rationalisation of client liaison responsibilities by allocating one person to act as the primary contact for both information and IT needs; this can spread staff effort more effectively and save time spent in meetings but it requires significant changes to individual roles. There are also potential gains for service staff: library staff can have quicker access to a wider range of IT expertise, and staff from both backgrounds can play to their strengths and also gain from different perspectives and knowledge bases applied to problem-solving, as well as having opportunities for information sharing and skills development (which should improve their employability). A larger service unit should also have more influence within the organisation and a combined budget can enable more cost-effectiveness and **flexibility** in resource allocation.

There are also potential **pitfalls**. Cultural divergence is the issue most frequently mentioned, but these differences are not just about a service/people orientation versus a technology/task orientation: there are often significant disparities in salaries, qualifications and education which cause resentment and can make informal convergence a more attractive option. It can be argued that multi-tasking dilutes specialist expertise and results in the loss of professional identities, but sensible distribution of responsibilities with retention of specialist roles where it makes sense to do so will minimise this. (Library systems specialists caught between two cultures may feel particularly threatened by convergence.) In any case the extent and *limits* of overlap need to be clearly defined if role confusion – for both staff and customers – is to be avoided. Instead of increasing its influence, a larger unit may provoke hostility and charges of 'empire-building' within the organisations. A combined service is also vulnerable to bias reflecting the background of the service head: while it is dangerous to generalise, most library/information specialists probably see the need to invest significant sums in the 'conduit', but many computer/IT specialists possibly do not have the same appreciation of 'content' needs.

Information service managers are not always directly involved in decisions to restructure their services, but there have been examples where they have taken the initiative to do so, in collaboration with other service heads. Recent evidence suggests a definite trend in this direction, so it is worth thinking about the options available, in terms of both *strategic partners* and *structural arrangements*. Convergence with IT services is only one of several options; others include research and development, marketing and corporate planning.

Strategy imperatives

This concluding section returns to some more general themes of strategic management, which have been highlighted by strategy gurus as critical success factors and also deserve attention from information services managers.

Involvement

In recent years, many commentators have highlighted the crucial role of **middle managers** in the strategy process. (The term 'middle managers' should be broadly interpreted here to include all people in the middle of organisations, such as team leaders, supervisors, etc.) Steven Floyd and Bill Wooldridge point out that these people have traditionally been seen as primarily involved in the 'doing' part of strategy – the implementation and control system – in defining tactics, monitoring performance and taking corrective action. However, they really need also to be involved in the 'thinking' part – the planning system – in screening and championing proposals from colleagues, interpreting and synthesising information, and adapting strategy to facilitate change. Floyd and Wooldridge argue that it is people in *boundary-spanning* roles, that interact with customers, suppliers and technologies, who can make the most significant strategic contribution.[19]

Jane Dutton and colleagues similarly see middle managers as key players in setting an organisation's strategic agenda, arguing that in complex dynamic environments they are often better placed than top management to detect, interpret and handle environmental challenges. Being closer to customers and other stakeholders and also being more in touch with internal concerns, they know what strategic issues require attention, and can have a significant impact by choosing when, where and how to 'sell' issues to top management. Middle managers' engagement or avoidance will therefore determine the issues addressed and decisions taken. Dutton identifies the following key factors encouraging issue-selling by middle managers:

- top management willingness to listen
- supportiveness of the culture
- competitive and economic pressures
- ongoing change in the organisation.[20]

Gary Hamel argues that in times of rapid change the strategy-making process needs to be freed from the 'tyranny of experience' and become more democratic by involving not only the "much maligned middle managers" but also **new voices** thus supplementing the *hierarchy of experi-*

ence with a *hierarchy of imagination.* He identifies three particular groups usually under-represented in the strategy process:

- people with a youthful perspective
- people at the geographical periphery of an organisation
- people who are new recruits to the organisation and free of industry dogma.

However, he also stresses that the process must involve a **diagonal slice** of the organisation to bring top and bottom together, rather than replace top-down planning with bottom-up strategy,

> "To achieve diversity of perspective and unity of purpose, the strategy-making process must involve a deep diagonal slice of the organization. A top-down process often achieves unity of purpose: the few who are involved come to share a conviction about the appropriate course of action and can secure some degree of compliance from those below. A bottom-up process can achieve diversity of perspective: many voices are heard and many options are explored. But unity without diversity leads to dogma, and diversity without unity results in competing strategy agendas and the fragmentation of resources. Only a strategy-making process that is deep and wide can achieve both diversity and unity."[21]

Dan Simpson supports Hamel's views on 'new voices' and also advocates involvement of business partners and others who are not members of the organisation, pointing out that in the "emerging world of networked organizations" boundaries between employees, suppliers and customers are blurring.[8]

Insight

Both Hamel and Michael Porter identify insight as another key ingredient. Hamel predicts that *knowledge* (like information before it) will provide a commercial return for a while, but it will in due course turn into a commodity, so organisations need to think not only about managing knowledge but also about *creating insight,*

> "In a world where you will constantly have to create innovation and change the rules, the thing that is not going to be a commodity is the ability to constantly generate genuinely new insights".[22]

He suggests two **questions** in this context:

- are you learning as fast as the world is changing?
- what proportion of your learning over the past year has come from outside your industry boundaries?

In one of his most recent articles, Porter similarly identifies **fast learning** and insight as critical to success,

"The companies that are going to become successful, or remain successful, will be the ones that can learn fast, can assimilate this learning and can develop new insights".[23]

Integration

Porter also emphasises the "capacity to link and integrate activities" as a critical factor in sustainable advantage and goes so far as to assert that "the essence of strategy is cross-functional, cross-activity integration".[23] Irrespective of how their services are configured (or converged) information service managers need to pursue integration at several levels, both *horizontally* and *vertically* – within their service units, with other support services or business units, and with selected suppliers and business partners – to achieve **complementarities** across diverse operations. The means to achieve this will increasingly include organisation-wide IT-based systems for processing transactions, supplying information, promoting communication and supporting decisions, but success will undoubtedly require more than *systems* integration, notably a *climate* of collaboration, commitment and trust. Service managers in addition need to integrate *operations* and strategy, so that on the one hand incidents and insights at the customer interface inform longer-term planning, and on the other shared values and strategic objectives inform frontline actions.

David Hussey cites five essentials or critical elements that an organisation must have if it is to achieve lasting strategic success. Three of these (analysis, creative strategic thinking and strategy implementation) have been covered extensively in earlier chapters, but the others are worth noting here:

- a strategic decision process
- the capabilities of decision leaders.[24]

It is perhaps stating the obvious to point out that the quality of any strategy depends on the **capabilities** of the people who create it, but it is remarkable that many managers are expected to think and act strategically without being given much guidance or advice in this area. John van Maurik has tried to remedy this situation in his book on skills for strategists, which he concludes with ten 'vital tips' to help people develop judgement and the effective ability to implement their strategies:

1. Be focused in your aims. Use searching questions to analyse the situation and illuminate direction. Vigorous use of a strategic process model will ensure discipline of approach and control of outcomes.
2. Be creative and foster breakout thinking in other people. Think

objectively about the power of the mind and the different forms creativity can take.

3. Value the power of the team – teams usually outperform the individual when it comes to creating new ideas and deciding how to implement them.

4. Be a change agent, develop a love of change without losing your perspective.

5. Appreciate that strategies must be led; so be a leader.

6. Value models of strategic analysis for the help they can give and the commercial perspective they add.

7. Embrace innovation as the key to progress and seek to develop organisational structures that encourage it.

8. Be persuasive, politically adept and streetwise in your dealings with others.

9. Be confident in yourself and in the value of the strategies you are seeking to implement – demonstrate that confidence in what you say and do.

10. Find a successful strategist as a tough role model – look to see what makes that person so good. Can you distil and bottle those talents for future use?[25]

Summary checklist

Do you have a flexible framework for strategic change?

Linkage
Is your strategy-making process integrated with organisational strategy processes?
Are the themes and concerns of other organisational plans reflected in your plans?

Novelty
Does your strategy process involve people at the periphery and on the front line?
Does the process foster new perspectives and force consideration of options?

Focus
Have you selected the 'vital few' projects from the many desirable possibilities?
Have you agreed who will be accountable and responsible for each project?

Clarity
Does the strategy provide guidance for people in their day-to-day decisions?
Does it create discretion and room for manoeuvre at the sharp end?

Feedback
Do you actively track what is happening internally and externally?
Are your assumptions, strategies and plans refined as the situation changes?

Change
Do people accept and expect continuous change?
Do they anticipate and initiate developments and improvements?

References

1. Johnson, G. and Scholes, K. *Exploring corporate strategy*. 5th ed. London: Prentice Hall, 1999
2. Mintzberg, H., Ahlstrand, B. and Lampel, J. *Strategy safari: a guided tour through the wilds of strategic management*. London: Prentice Hall, 1998
3. Maljers, F. A. Strategic planning and intuition in Unilever. *Long Range Planning*, 23 (2) 1990, pp. 63–68
4. Turner, G. GEC's pragmatic planners. *Long Range Planning*, 18 (1) 1985, pp. 12–18
5. Pink, A. I. H. Strategic leadership through corporate planning at ICI. *Long Range Planning*, 21 (1) 1988, pp. 18–25
6. de Geus, A. P. Planning as learning. *Harvard Business Review*, 66 (2) 1988, pp. 70–74
7. Turner, G. A new strategy at Barclays. *Long Range Planning*, 18 (3) 1985, pp. 12–16
8. Simpson, D. G. Why most strategic planning is a waste of time and what you can do about it. *Long Range Planning*, 31 (3) 1998, pp. 476–480 and [Part II] 31 (4) 1998, pp. 623–627
9. Bryson, J. M. and Alston, F. K. *Creating and implementing your strategic plan: a workbook for public and nonprofit organizations*. San Francisco, Ca: Jossey-Bass, 1996
10. Drucker, P. F. *Management*: an abridged and revised version of *Management: tasks, responsibilities and practices*. Oxford: Butterworth-Heinemann, 1974 (1988)
11. Steiner, G. A. *Strategic planning: what every manager* must *know*. New York; London: Free Press, 1997

12. Hussey, D. *Strategic management: from theory to implementation.* 4th ed. Oxford: Butterworth-Heinemann, 1998
13. Taylor, R. S. *Value-added processes in information systems.* Norwood, NJ: Ablex, 1986
14. Matarazzo, J. M. and Prusak, L. *The value of corporate libraries: findings from a survey of senior management.* Washington, DC: Special Libraries Association, 1995
15. *Skills for knowledge management – building a knowledge economy: a report.* London: TFPL, 1999. *See also* Skills for knowledge management: a briefing paper. London: TFPL, 1999. Available at: http://www.lic.gov.uk/publications/executivesummaries/kmskills.html
16. Moules, J. Converge and rule. *Information Strategy,* 2 (9) 1997, pp. 44–47.
17. John Fielden Consultancy. *Supporting expansion: a report on human resource management in academic libraries for the Joint Funding Councils' Libraries Review Group.* Bristol: The Councils, 1993
18. Joint Funding Councils' Libraries Review Group. *Report.* Bristol: The Councils, 1993 (Chairman: Professor Sir Brian Follett)
19. Floyd, S. W. and Wooldridge, B. Dinosaurs or dynamos? Recognizing middle management's strategic role. *Academy of Management Executive,* 8 (4) 1994, pp. 47–57
20. Dutton, J. E. and others. Reading the wind: how middle managers assess the context for selling issues to top managers. *Strategic Management Journal,* 18 (5) 1997, pp. 407–425
21. Hamel, G. Strategy as revolution. *Harvard Business Review,* 74 (4) 1996, pp. 69–82
22. Hamel, G. Killing convention. *Information Strategy,* 3 (7) 1998, pp. 44–46
23. Porter, M. Creating tomorrow's advantages. *Strategy,* March 1999, pp. 7–8
24. Hussey, D. *Strategy and planning: a manager's guide.* Chichester: John Wiley, 1999
25. van Maurik, J. *The effective strategist: key skills for all managers.* Aldershot: Gower, 1999 (p. 150)

Further reading

Bryson, J. M. *Strategic planning for public and nonprofit organizations: a guide to strengthening and sustaining organizational achievement.* San Fransisco, Ca: Jossey-Bass, 1988
A comprehensive guide (c.300p.) which relates lessons learned in

business and industry to public-sector organisations. Notable for its emphasis on stakeholder concerns and organisational mandates. The main chapters include process guidelines as well as summaries; Resource Section contains sample worksheets and additional comment on 'advanced concepts'.

Napuk, K. *The strategy-led business: step-by-step strategic planning for small and medium sized companies.* rev ed. London: McGraw-Hill, 1996 (orig. pub. 1993)
A practical guide (c.230p.) offering a simple planning model based on experience in SMEs and non-profit organisations, covering the formulation of a vision, objectives, goals and strategies, as well as implementation issues. Contains lots of checklists and end-of-chapter summaries. A separate chapter summarises models and views of other writers.

Mintzberg, H. The fall and rise of strategic planning. *Harvard Business Review,* 72 (1) 1994, pp. 107–114
Seminal article, based on the author's book on this topic, which reinforces his earlier messages about crafting strategy and suggests how planners and managers can work together to use both hard data and soft insights in creating, developing and programming strategies.

Colenso, M. *Strategic skills for line managers.* Oxford: Butterworth-Heinemann, 1998
Guidebook (c.200p.) designed to help mid-level managers and team leaders contribute to corporate strategy and manage their own units strategically. Introduces and interprets strategy concepts at both corporate and departmental level, and provides step-by-step model for developing and agreeing strategic purpose, intent, vision, values, critical success factors, core competencies and performance measures, using numerous activities, questions and examples.

Information services

Jacob, M. E. L. *Strategic planning: a how-to-do-it manual for librarians.* New York; London: Neal Schuman, 1990
A step-by-step guide (c.120 pp.) which contains practical advice and information, with checklists, worksheets and examples taken from US library practice; features include sample scenarios (Information Industry Association and OCLC) and models of value-added services.

Asantewa, D. *Strategic planning basics for special libraries.* Washington, DC: Special Libraries Association, 1992
A detailed practical guide (c.60p.) on how to organise, develop and manage a strategic plan, covering the composition and responsibilities of the planning team; situation analysis and survey methods; formulation of mission, goals/objectives, policies, rules and procedures; and use of the budget as a planning tool, concluding with a worked example for a mythical library.

Birdsall, D. G. and Hensley, O. D. A new strategic planning model for academic libraries. *College & Research Libraries,* 55 (2) 1994, pp. 149–159
Describes a six-phase model which differs from other approaches in its emphasis on involving representatives from impact areas in the planning team, ensuring acceptance of the agenda by partners and constituencies, and systematically securing adoption of the plan over five stages.

Himmel, E. and Wilson, W. J. *Planning for results: a public library transformation process: the guidebook.* Chicago; London: American Library Association, 1998
Sets out a planning process of 23 tasks organised as six steps – prepare, envision, design, build, implement and communicate. Part 2 sets out 13 specific roles or 'service responses', with guidance on service components, target audiences, resource issues and performance measures for each role..

Weingand, D. E. *Future-drive library marketing.* Chicago: London, American Library Association, 1998
Practical guide (c.200p.) which shows how conventional marketing/ planning tools and techniques can be combined with futuring methods to develop a more future-oriented approach to strategy and planning. Covers the planning process, mission and vision, environmental analysis, market research, the Delphi method, scenarios, trend extrapolation, cost-benefit and cross-impact analysis, decision trees, technological forecasting and simulation gaming.

Case studies

Ensor, P. et al. Strategic planning in an academic library. *Library Administration & Management,* 2 (3) 1988, pp. 145–150
Details the data gathering and writing components of the strategic planning process followed at Indiana State University Libraries, and subsequent consideration of the document at a library retreat; repro-

duces the full questionnaire used for interviews with teaching staff as an appendix.

Allen, L. Strategic planning for libraries: a convergence of library management theory and research. *International Journal of Information and Library Research*, 1 (3) 1989, pp. 197–212
Discusses the use of Soft Systems Methodology as a framework for strategic planning in the Library and Information Service of Western Australia – a state/public library service – advocated as a means of forcing 'blue-sky' thinking and avoiding a 'recipe book' approach; follows the process through from mission statement, corporate objectives and strategies to programme definition and evaluation, reproducing examples of forms used to document the process.

Gratch, B. and Wood, E. Strategic planning: implementation and first-year appraisal. *Journal of Academic Librarianship*, 17 (1) 1991, pp. 10–15
Describes the strategic planning process adopted at Bowling Green State University Libraries, Ohio, including a full account of events following completion of the document and advice on ensuring that the plan becomes an effective working tool.

Barrish, A. and Carrigan, D. Strategic planning and the small public library: a case study. *Public Libraries*, 30 (5) 1991, pp. 283–287
Discusses experience of the Crawford Memorial Library in Monticello (New York) of using the ALA Public Library Association manuals on role-setting and output measures, and relates this to strategy concepts in the corporate world, referring to Andrews, Ansoff and Porter.

Donlon, P. and Line, M. Strategic planning in national libraries. *Alexandria*, 4 (2) 1992, pp. 83–94
Identifies distinctive aspects of planning for national libraries, including government influences, international responsibilities and diverse audiences; discusses published examples, with particular reference to the National Library of Ireland.

Adding value

Koenig, M. The importance of information services for productivity: "under-recognized" and under-invested. *Special Libraries*, 83 (4) 1992, pp. 192–210
Reports on research into the relationship between the provision of information services and the productivity of organisations, noting

the relative paucity but remarkable uniformity of the literature in confirming the cost-effectiveness of investing in information services. Also identifies characteristics of productive information environments and information workers.

Keyes, A. M. The value of the special library: review and analysis. *Special Libraries,* **86** (3) 1995, pp. 172–187
Surveys published literature on establishing a monetary value for special libraries and discusses methods based on time savings, productivity gains, and cost-benefit analysis (drawing on work by King Research). Suggests a four-step approach to cost-benefit ratios, and concludes with extensively annotated bibliography of 24 articles and reports.

Knowledge management

Klobas, J. E. Information services for new millennium organizations: librarians and knowledge management. In: Raitt, D., ed., *Libraries for the new millennium: implications for managers.* London: Library Association Publishing, 1997, pp. 39–64
Discusses opportunities and threats facing librarians as other professional groups develop knowledge management skills. Argues the need for librarians to improve their analytical skills, business focus and understanding of information technology and systems, and suggests 'information science' may be a more helpful label than 'librarianship' for roles in the new era.

Stear, E. B. and Wecksell, J., Information Resource Center Management (IRCM). *Bulletin of the American Society for Information Science,* **23** (4) 1997, pp. 15–17.
Traces IRC development from information repository through centre for distributed interactive information to new role with enterprise knowledge management systems, noting organizational and technological imperatives, and predicting high failure rates.

Broadbent, M., The phenomenon of knowledge management: what does it mean to the information profession? *Information Outlook,* **2** (5), 1998, pp. 23–36.
Explains the concept of knowledge management, drawing on examples of good practice and published literature. Emphasises the significance of organizational learning and information politics, stressing the need for an holistic and multi-disciplinary approach, and considers the potential role of librarians and their capacity for knowledge work.

Service convergence

Lovecy, I. *Convergence of libraries and computing services.* London: Library Information Technology Centre, 1994 (Library & Information Briefings no 54).
Ten-page overview of trend towards convergence in the UK, covering pressures and issues, managerial justification, practical arrangements and perceived problems. Refers to two dozen American and British publications and an informal UK e-mail survey.

Schwartz, C. A., ed. *Restructuring academic libraries: organizational development in the wake of technological change.* Chicago: Association of College and Research Libraries, 1997 (ACRL Publications in Librarianship no 49)
Contains 19 contributions covering different aspects of boundary-spanning developments in US libraries, ranging from convergence of public and technical services, through collaborative realignment of libraries and computer centres, to wider institutional and inter-institutional arrangements. Includes six case studies and one chapter specifically on strategic planning.

Pugh, L. *Convergence in academic support services.* London: British Library Research and Innovation Centre, 1997. (British Library Research and Innovation Report 54)
Based on survey of 114 UK higher education institutions, includes literature review, summary of results from questionnaire and five in-depth case studies, covering process and strategy; structures; organisation culture; teams; leadership; and organisational learning. Concludes convergence is primarily about organisational development and learning to live with ambiguity, requiring unifying structures, team building and participative management.
For a shorter account of this research, *see* Pugh, L. Some theoretical bases of convergence. *The New Review of Academic Librarianship,* 3, 1997, pp. 49–66

Field, C., Building on shifting sands: information age organisations, *Ariadne,* (17) 1998, pp. 6–7. Full version with references available online at: http://www.ariadne.ac.uk/issue18/main/
Based on experience of large-scale convergence at the University of Birmingham, covering libraries, IT, computer-based learning, teaching space and language laboratories; considers environmental imperatives of new structures and prerequisites for successful change, with particular emphasis on the flexible deployment of financial, spatial, and human resources.

Appendix 1

Survey questionnaire

Adapted version of the SERVQUAL instrument

(See section on Surveys in Chapter 2)

Note: *The ratings on questions E/P10, 11, 12, 13, 18, 19, 20, 21 and 22 need to be reverse-scored prior to data analysis. Survey users are recommended to present the questions in random order rather than following the sequence given here.*

Directions (Part 1)

This survey deals with your opinions about information services. Please show the extent to which you think organisations offering such services should possess the features described by each statement. Do this by picking one of the seven numbers next to each statement. If you strongly agree that these service providers should possess a feature, circle the number 7. If you strongly disagree that these service providers should possess a feature, circle 1. If your feelings are not strong, circle one of the numbers in the middle. There are no right or wrong answers – all we are interested in is a number that best shows your **expectations** about organisations offering information services.

"Strongly Disagree" 1 2 3 4 5 6 7 "Strongly Agree"

E1	The service should have up-to-date equipment.	1 2 3 4 5 6 7
E2	Its physical facilities should be visually appealing.	1 2 3 4 5 6 7
E3	The service staff should be well presented.	1 2 3 4 5 6 7
E4	The appearance of the physical facilities should be in keeping with the type of services provided.	1 2 3 4 5 6 7
E5	When the service providers promise to do something by a certain time, they should do so.	1 2 3 4 5 6 7
E6	When customers have problems, the service providers should be sympathetic and reassuring.	1 2 3 4 5 6 7

[1] Parasuraman, A, Zeithaml, V A and Berry, L L. SERVQUAL: a multiple-item scale for measuring consumer perceptions of service quality. *Journal of Retailing,* 64 (1) 1988, pp. 38–40

E7	The service providers should be dependable.	1 2 3 4 5 6 7
E8	They should provide their services at the time they promise to do so.	1 2 3 4 5 6 7
E9	They should keep their records accurately.	1 2 3 4 5 6 7
E10	They should not be expected to tell customers exactly when services will be performed.	1 2 3 4 5 6 7
E11	It is not realistic for customers to expect prompt service from staff of these organisations.	1 2 3 4 5 6 7
E12	Their staff do not always have to be willing to help customers.	1 2 3 4 5 6 7
E13	It is acceptable if they are too busy to respond to customer requests promptly.	1 2 3 4 5 6 7
E14	Customers should be able to trust service staff.	1 2 3 4 5 6 7
E15	Customers should be able to feel safe in their transactions with these service staff.	1 2 3 4 5 6 7
E16	The service staff should be polite.	1 2 3 4 5 6 7
E17	The staff should get adequate support from the organisation to do their jobs well.	1 2 3 4 5 6 7
E18	These service providers should not be expected to give customers individual attention.	1 2 3 4 5 6 7
E19	Staff of these services cannot be expected to give customers personal attention.	1 2 3 4 5 6 7
E20	It is unrealistic to expect staff to know what the needs of their customers are.	1 2 3 4 5 6 7
E21	It is unrealistic to expect these service providers to have the best interests of their customers at heart.	1 2 3 4 5 6 7
E22	They should not be expected to have service hours convenient to all their customers.	1 2 3 4 5 6 7

Directions (Part 2)

The following set of statements relate to your feelings about XYZ information service. For each statement, please show the extent to which you believe XYZ has the feature described by the statement. Once again, circling a 7 means that you strongly agree that XYZ has that feature, and circling a 1 means that you strongly disagree. You may circle any of the numbers in the middle that show how strong your feelings are. There are no right or wrong answers – all we are interested in is a number that best shows your **perceptions** about XYZ.

"Strongly Disagree"   1 2 3 4 5 6 7   "Strongly Agree"

P1	XYZ has up-to-date equipment.	1 2 3 4 5 6 7
P2	XYZ's physical facilities are visually appealing.	1 2 3 4 5 6 7
P3	XYZ's staff are well presented.	1 2 3 4 5 6 7
P4	The appearance of the physical facilities of XYZ is in keeping with the type of services provided.	1 2 3 4 5 6 7
P5	When XYZ promises to do something by a certain time, it does so.	1 2 3 4 5 6 7
P6	When you have problems, XYZ is sympathetic and reassuring.	1 2 3 4 5 6 7
P7	XYZ is dependable.	1 2 3 4 5 6 7
P8	XYZ provides its services at the time it promises to do so.	1 2 3 4 5 6 7
P9	XYZ keeps its records accurately.	1 2 3 4 5 6 7
P10	XYZ does not tell customers exactly when services will be performed.	1 2 3 4 5 6 7
P11	You do not receive prompt service from XYZ's staff.	1 2 3 4 5 6 7
P12	Staff of XYZ are not always willing to help customers.	1 2 3 4 5 6 7
P13	Staff of XYZ are too busy to respond to customer requests promptly.	1 2 3 4 5 6 7
P14	You can trust staff of XYZ.	1 2 3 4 5 6 7
P15	You feel safe in your transactions with XYZ's staff.	1 2 3 4 5 6 7
P16	Staff of XYZ are polite.	1 2 3 4 5 6 7
P17	Staff get adequate support from XYZ to do their jobs well.	1 2 3 4 5 6 7
P18	XYZ does not give you individual attention.	1 2 3 4 5 6 7
P19	Staff of XYZ do not give you personal attention.	1 2 3 4 5 6 7
P20	Staff of XYZ do not know what your needs are.	1 2 3 4 5 6 7
P21	XYZ does not have your best interests at heart.	1 2 3 4 5 6 7
P22	XYZ does not have service hours convenient to all their customers.	1 2 3 4 5 6 7

Appendix 2

Plan contents

List of chapters and sections for annual public library plans[1]

(See section on Formal Plans in Chapter 4)

Part A (triennial)

Mission statement

- a short-form mission statement
- an extended statement/subsidiary aims

Background

- profile of local authority characteristics
- corporate objectives
- linkage to corporate or other plans
- organisational relationship with other council services and departments
- the scope of the library service
- the impact of national standards and policies

Service delivery

- lending services for adults
- services for children
- reference, information service and specialist collections
- IT as a service
- services for minority groups
- agency services
- other council services
- services to business

---

[1] Guidelines issued by the Department for Culture Media and Sport, 1998. *See also* Institute of Public Finance. *Appraisal of annual library plans 1998: final report.* Croydon: IPF, 1999

- wider community use

Resources

- finance
- books and materials
- buildings
- IT systems
- mobile libraries
- co-operation with other library providers
- staff
- use of volunteers

Customer response and quality assessment

- user surveys
- public consultation exercises
- market research
- complaints and commendations
- quality assessment

Performance appraisal

- trend data for the local authority
- similar group comparisons
- national/local authority sector analysis

Strengths and weaknesses

- service levels
- resource levels
- efficiency and effectiveness

Medium term strategy

- IT strategy
- service improvements and variations
- managing and utilising resources
- medium term action plan

Part B (annual)

Review of last year

- achievement of last annual plan
- performance appraisal

New initiatives

- responding to national initiatives
- local developments

The way ahead

- action plan – current year and next
- performance targets – update

Appendix 3

Cost concepts

Glossary of common terms

(See section on Costing in Chapter 5)

Costs can be classed in two main categories:

- **Direct costs**, those which can be directly identified with a particular job, product or process (e.g. productive labour, or materials which form part of a product – such as the binding of a publication). *Direct* costs are also known as **prime costs.**
- **Indirect costs**, those costs of the business which cannot be identified with specific outputs (e.g. executive staff, or services/utilities which support production – such as heating and lighting). *Indirect* costs are also known as **overhead costs**, although the term 'overheads' is sometimes used specifically to denote the *aggregated* indirect costs.

There is another fundamental categorisation:

- **Variable costs**, those which vary *directly* with changes in the level of an activity (e.g. materials consumed in delivering a service – such as paper in photocopying – but not necessarily the associated labour costs, see below). *Variable* costs are sometimes known as **operating costs.**
- **Fixed costs**, those costs which are not directly affected by changes in volume but are incurred irrespective of activity level – at least in the short term (e.g. salaried operators, rent and rates). *Fixed* costs all become *variable* costs in the long term; also fixed costs for a narrow range of output – referred to as the *relevant range* – may vary over a wider range.

Costs do not conform neatly to this pattern:

- **Mixed costs** are those where there is a fixed amount of cost and also an element which varies with output (for example, for a telephone, the line rental is a fixed amount but the call charges are variable). *Mixed* costs are alternatively known as **semi-fixed** or **semi-variable costs.**
- **Stepped costs** are a category of fixed costs which vary with the level of output, but in large steps or jumps, rather than gradually and pro-

portionately to output (for example, when demand for photocopying requires an additional machine, but machine costs then stay fixed until demand grows significantly again).

In addition to these basic categories, there are numerous other terms used to explain the behaviour and functions of different types of cost data. The following list is a quick reference guide to terminology and concepts in common use.

- **Discretionary costs** are expenditures based on managerial judgement rather than analysis, and as such are both **controllable** costs and relatively easy to change.
- **Full costs** are figures representing a combination of the *allocated* direct costs and *apportioned* indirect costs of a product, service, task or other unit. These can alternatively be presented as a combination of all the variable costs and an appropriate share or proportion of the fixed costs. Full costs are also known as **total costs.**
- **Historical costs** are figures representing the cost of an item in service at the time of its purchase for use, based on the price originally paid for the asset and recorded at the time of its acquisition. These can be contrasted with **current costs**, based on the price that would have to be paid for an asset at the present time.
- **Incremental costs** are increases or decreases in total costs that result from any variation in operations. These are also known as **differential costs**. Incremental costs can be either short-run or long-run; *marginal* costs are a specific type of incremental costs, which are essentially a short-run concept (see below).
- **Life cycle costs** are the total costs associated with an asset over its entire life, covering not only its initial acquisition (from development and decision to purchase and installation, including training and promotion) but also the annual operating and maintenance costs (such as consumables, operators and utilities).
- **Marginal costs** are a specific type of *incremental* costs, representing the change in total costs that results when output is varied by one unit – that is, the additional cost of the next unit, based on the costs of variable inputs which must be employed to produce an additional unit of output.
- **Opportunity costs** represent the highest value of the alternative opportunities foregone by consuming a good or service, based on not only the money spent purchasing a good, but also the value of the time spent and opportunities lost when the good or service was consumed. (This is an economic, rather than an accounting term.)
- **Standard costs** are notional costs – predetermined figures representing what it should cost to produce a unit of a given product or service, based either on a detailed analysis or an informed estimate. They are

used as criteria or benchmarks for measuring performance, and may be either *ideal cost standards*, those that can only be met under optimum conditions, or *practical cost standards,* those that can reasonably be met by an efficient and motivated worker.

- **Sunk costs** are costs for which an outlay has already been made, and therefore cannot be affected by current decisions (for example, the non-refundable purchase of a computer).
- **Unit costs** are the monetary measure of the amount of resources used to produce one unit for a particular purpose – that is, the costs of providing a specified product or service unit, based on the total cost divided by the total output over a given period of time (and usually including the costs of fixed inputs or overheads). They are typically used to compare performance from year to year, from team to team, or from library to library. These also known as **average costs.**

Appendix 4

Service level agreements

Checklist of items for documentation

(See section on Customer Focus in Chapter 7)

The Agreement – contractual information

- *definitions* of terms, such as 'the customer', 'the provider', 'the supplier', etc.
- *purpose* and *scope* of the agreement (and the documentation)
- *benefits* expected for both parties – an important selling point
- *duration* of the agreement and timetable for its (re)negotiation or termination
- *negotiation* and review mechanisms, specifying contacts for both parties
- *responsibilities* of both parties (referring to more specific duties as necessary)
- *monitoring* and *liaison* arrangements, including frequency of reports and meetings
- *costs* and *charges* (if applicable) with allocation and billing/payment methods
- *resolution* of disputes and procedure for complaints (with penalties/remedies)
- *variation* of requirements (of customer) and/or variance of costs (of provider)
- *dependencies* on third parties (e.g. external suppliers, internal support services)
- *contingencies* or *caveats* – 'escape clauses' to cope with unpredictable events.

The Service – background information

- *strategic perspective* – edited and condensed extracts from existing strategy documents, covering mission and objectives, environmental commentary, and development targets or paths envisaged for the next three to five years (an absolute maximum of two pages)
- *planning assumptions* – critical points underpinning the service

strategy and the agreement document, covering issues such as organisational commitment to central support services, information service policy on access and holdings, inflation estimates for acquisitions

- *quality assurance* – statement of policy and practice on inviting user feedback, and assessing customer satisfaction (for example, customer comments forms, consumer councils/liaison committees, focus groups, user surveys)
- *organisation structure* – copies of organisation charts/line management diagrams, enabling customer departments to understand reporting lines and to see where their contacts fit into the overall service structure
- *service schedule* – a summary statement of all the services covered by the agreement (maybe grouped into various categories) with short scope notes explaining what each service is and who uses it.

The Level – core specification

- *service definition,* scope and objective – describing the service and its extent (e.g. hours of availability) and explaining its purpose, in no more than two to three sentences
- *customer entitlement,* obligations and communication – setting out both the rights and the responsibilities of customers, and proposed liaison arrangements
- *quality standards,* performance indicators and targets – both quantitative and qualitative (e.g. turnaround times, percentage take-up, satisfaction ratings)
- *costing method,* cost elements and estimated service costs;
- *charges,* charging basis and chargeable service increments (e.g. subscription or transaction-based; additional charges for 'urgent action' requests or lengthy enquiries).

The above points need to be considered in relation to each discrete service component or category, depending on the complexity of the service and the amount of detail required. Terms such as 'availability' and 'downtime' need to be carefully and unambiguously defined at the outset to guard against later disputes over what is meant. If a detailed approach is used, with separate sections for discrete services, it is helpful to include in the definition statement a reference to *related services* where applicable.

Checklist of services for inclusion

- online catalogue
- quick reference enquiries

- bibliographical checking
- photocopying
- general reference collections
- specialised research collections
- loans from stock
- inter-library loans / remote document supply
- standalone and networked databases
- user documentation
- online searches
- induction tours
- information skills training
- journal and report circulation
- purchasing of publications
- binding of materials
- current awareness
- selective dissemination of information
- research assistance
- specialist advisory services

Basic self-service facilities must not be overlooked, including those housed in the library but managed/maintained by internal or external third parties: for example, audio-visual, multimedia and personal computing workstations; printing and photocopying; individual, group and private study facilities; catering and other vending machines. It is also important not to overlook the backroom/maintenance tasks that support the frontline services, and to include such costs with the relevant services (for example, processing of stock, reshelving of loans, withdrawal of material).

Appendix 5

Staff development

Checklists for organisational and individual evaluation[1]

(See section on Professional Development in Chapter 7)

Staff development evaluation for the organisation

- Policy on staff development exists and is distributed to all staff.
- Training plans for new employees are required and used, and on-the-job training is evaluated regularly.
- Information on local, regional, and national conferences and workshops is routinely communicated to staff.
- Release time is provided to attend training and developmental programmes/conferences outside of the library.
- A needs assessment has been conducted to solicit the views of staff regarding their learning needs.
- An individual is assigned specific responsibility for co-ordinating staff development functions.
- Centralised and well-organised training has been established for preparing staff for the online system and other aspects of automation.
- Supervisors are evaluated in relation to their priority and success with staff development activities.
- Staff development is considered as part of the library planning process.
- Funds are identified to support the staff development programme and staff are clear on what activities will receive financial support.

Staff development evaluation for the manager / supervisor

- You prepare training plans for all new staff no matter what the person's experience or background, and for staff with new assignments.

[1] Creth, S. D. Staff development: where do we go from here? *Library Administration & Management*, 4 (3) 1990, pp. 131–132

- You consider your success and that of your department to rely on the success of your staff.
- You are clear in articulating performance expectations to each staff member as well as improvements you wish to have occur.
- You act as a mentor with staff as they examine job growth and career opportunities.
- You meet with staff no less than annually to acknowledge contributions and to indicate ways in which you feel the person should improve, and you encourage them to express their ideas for improvement in the department.
- Your consider staff development as one of the highest priorities you have as a manager/supervisor and allocate time on a regular basis to this function.

Appendix 6

Planning profile

Checklist for planning to plan[1]

(See section on Operational Models in Chapter 8)

1. What is the scope of the plan?
   e.g. the whole organisation
   the whole organisation and separate plans for divisions, units, etc
   a division, unit, programme or other part of the organisation
   another entity, such as a community network partnership
2. What is the period to be covered?
   e.g. one year
   three years
   five years
   seven years
3. Have any planning guidelines been laid down by a higher-level body?
4. Are there any particular concerns, specific problems or strategic issues that the plan must address?
5. What other internal or external plans are related or relevant?
6. What information and expertise is needed and available?
7. Who is sponsoring the process?
   e.g. outside body
   senior management
   middle managers
   others
8. Who is championing the process?
9. Who will form the project team?
   (Consider what kind and size of team works best in your organisation)
10. How will the team work?
11. Who will manage the project?
12. Who should be involved in developing the plan?

[1] Adapted from Bryson, J. M. and Alston, F. K. *Creating and implementing your strategic plan: a workbook for public and nonprofit organizations*. San Francisco, Ca: Jossey-Bass, 1996

13. Who should be involved in deciding the plan?
14. Who should be involved in reviewing the plan
15. Who should be involved in receiving the plan?
16. Will you use outside consultants or other experts?
17. What type or length of written plan is envisaged or required?
    e.g. short executive summary
    summary with action plan and financial projection
    full document with appendices
18. What is the timescale for completing the plan?
19. What steps/tasks will be included in the planning process?
20. What resources will be required for the planning effort?

Appendix 7

Adding value

Examples of values added by common information service processes[1]

(See section on Strategic Issues in Chapter 8)

USER CRITERIA	INTERFACE *Values added*	SERVICE EXAMPLES Value-added processes
Ease of use	*Browsing*	Displays of new acquisitions
		Open access stacks
	Formatting	Standardised catalogue entries
		Tailored database print-outs
	Mediation	Reference interviews, online searches
		Serviced (staff-operated) photocopying
	Orientation	User induction and instruction
		System documentation
	Ordering	Alphabetical/classified arrangement
		Segregation of special collections
	Physical accessibility	Personal delivery of items to offices
		Facilities for wheelchair users
Noise reduction	*Item identification*	Descriptive cataloguing
		Spine labels
	Subject description	Classification schemes
		Subject headings
	Subject summary	Abstracts
		Contents lists
	Linkage	Referral to other information centres
		Guides to library/network resources
	Precision	Analytical catalogue entries
		Ranked output from database searches
	Selectivity	SDI profiles
		Stock editing/weeding

[1] Adapted from Taylor, R. S. *Value-added processes in information systems*. Norwood, NJ: Ablex, 1986

USER CRITERIA	INTERFACE *Values added*	SERVICE EXAMPLES Value-added processes
Quality	*Accuracy*	Database editing
		Proof-reading
	Comprehensiveness	Blanket ordering
		Inter-library lending
	Currency	Automated claims for journal issues
		Standing orders for immediate supply
	Reliability	Quality assurance systems
		Staff training
	Validity	Analytic notes
		Indicators of bias
Adaptability	*Closeness to problem*	Client liaison committees
		Subject specialist staff
	Flexibility	Customisation facilities
		Database search options
	Simplicity	Jargon-free guides
		Intuitive interfaces
	Stimulatory	Meeting room space
		Scholarly seminars/publications
Time-saving	*Response speed*	'Urgent action' document supply
		Computerised search systems
Cost-saving	*Cost-saving*	Institutional/block purchases of
		discounted database searches

AUTHOR INDEX

Index of authors cited in the text

SUBJECT INDEX